Global Backlash

NEW MILLENNIUM BOOKS
IN INTERNATIONAL STUDIES
Deborah J. Gerner, Series Editor

NEW MILLENNIUM BOOKS issue out of the unique position of the global system at the end of the Cold War, the end of the twentieth century, and the beginning of a new millennium in which our understandings about war, peace, identity, sovereignty, security, and sustainability—whether economic, environmental, or ethical—are likely to be challenged. In the new millennium of international relations, new theories, new actors, and new policies and processes are all bound to be engaged. Books in the series will be of three types: compact core texts, supplementary texts, and readers.

Titles in the Series

Forthcoming in the Series

Globalization and Belonging: The Politics of Identity in a Changing World
By Sheila Croucher

The Global New Deal: Economic and Social Human Rights in World Politics
By William F. Felice

Liberals and Criminals: IPE in the New Millennium
By H. Richard Friman

International Law in the 21ˢᵗ Century
By Christopher C. Joyner

Global Politics As If People Mattered: World Political Economy from the Ground Up
By Ronnie D. Lipschutz and Mary Ann Tetreault

The Peace Puzzle: Ending Violent Conflict in the 21ˢᵗ Century
By George A. Lopez

The New Foreign Policy
By Laura Neack

Political Violence
By Philip A. Schrodt

Global Backlash

*Citizen Initiatives for a
Just World Economy*

Edited by
Robin Broad

ROWMAN & LITTLEFIELD PUBLISHERS, INC.
Lanham • Boulder • New York • Oxford

ROWMAN & LITTLEFIELD PUBLISHERS, INC.

Published in the United States of America
by Rowman & Littlefield Publishers, Inc.
An Imprint of the Rowman & Littlefield Publishing Group
4720 Boston Way, Lanham, Maryland 20706
www.rowmanlittlefield.com

12 Hid's Copse Road, Cumnor Hill, Oxford OX2 9JJ, England

British Library Cataloguing in Publication Information Available

Library of Congress Cataloging-in-Publication Data

Global backlash : citizen initiatives for a just world economy / edited by Robin Broad.
    p. cm. — (New millennium books in international studies)
  Includes bibliographical references and index.
  ISBN 0-7425-1033-6 (cloth : alk. paper) — ISBN 0-7425-1034-4 (paper : alk. paper)
    1. International economic relations. 2. Globalization—Economic aspects. 3. Globalization—Social aspects. 4. Globalization—Environmental aspects. 5. International business enterprises—Management—Citizen participation. 6. Economic policy—Citizen participation. 7. Sustainable development—Citizen participation. I. Broad, Robin. II. Series.

HF1359 .G566 2002
337—dc21
                                           2001058717

Printed in the United States of America

∞™ The paper used in this publication meets the minimum requirements of American National Standard for Information Sciences—Permanence of Paper for Printed Library Materials, ANSI/NISO Z39.48–1992.

To the memory of
Abraham "BamBam" dela Cerna

and to
Romulo "Billy" J. de la Rosa,

who each, gently and patiently, began my education on
"corporate-led globalization" in the Philippines in 1977 and 1978.

I am forever grateful.

Brief Contents

Detailed Contents

Part II: The Historical Context

Part III: Realigning Trade Rules

Acknowledgments

First and foremost, I want to thank those who authored the readings—the books, articles, internal documents, discussion papers, conference decrees, and so on—that form the core "voices" in this book. Do be sure to turn to the "credits" pages for the appropriate acknowledgments.

Next in line for thanks are my students in the International Development Program at the School of International Service, American University in Washington, D.C. In fact, this book grew from a graduate seminar on economic integration and development that I have been teaching for more than a decade. Over the years, my students' feedback—their energy, excitement, queries, and insights—helped shape the foundation analysis upon which my introductions to the readings are based. Their reactions also helped me realize that reading the array of proposals coming from the global backlash was not only educational, it was empowering. I have been especially fortunate to have been blessed with some wonderful research assistants: Dekila Chungyalpa, Erica Dholoo, Jay Gutzwiller, Zahara Heckscher, Maureen Meyer, and Sharmi Sobhan collectively saw this project from conception to conclusion.

Also high on my list for thanks is the Ford Foundation, which provided funding for this book project through a grant to the Center of Concern in Washington, D.C. I have learned a great deal from Center of Concern's director, Jim Hug, research associate Maria Riley, and the International Gender and Trade Network. I would also like to thank the John D. and Catherine T. MacArthur Foundation under whose grant for research and writing I began assessing backlash proposals and initiatives.

As for publishers, I cannot sing Rowman & Littlefield's praises loudly enough. I was impressed with Jennifer Knerr, executive editor at Rowman & Littlefield, from the very first time we spoke and she has never disappointed me. She embraced this book project with insight and fervor. In addition to Jennifer, Rowman & Littlefield provided the most capable of hands: project editor

Jehanne Schweitzer and editorial assistant Renée Legatt carried on with the skill and just plain niceness that Jennifer led me to expect of Rowman & Littlefield. I would also like to thank proofreader Barbara Negley and indexer Jennifer Rushing-Schurr for excellent work. I am honored to have this book be a part of the press's New Millennium Books in International Studies series, and for that I thank series editor Deborah Gerner and the series editorial board.

I was very fortunate to receive feedback on my manuscript from various individuals whose expertise and work I admire: Lance Compa reviewed all my introductions with great care, as did my research assistants Sharmi Sobhan and Zahara Heckscher as well as Ph.D. candidate Rebecca de Winter. John Cavanagh read the whole manuscript more times than he probably wants to remember. Economists Robert Blecker, Maria Floro, and John Willoughby each commented in wise detail on specific parts of the book—without complaining about the ridiculously short turnaround time I gave them. Vicki Golich and Tim Shaw reviewed pieces of the book and provided perceptive feedback. Collectively these reviewers educated me while keeping me from some potentially embarrassing mistakes. I extend sincere thanks. Needless to say, any remaining mistakes are my own.

Sarah Anderson, Medea Benjamin, Ken Conca, Michael Conroy, Jonathan Fox, Audie Klotz, George Lopez, Manuel Montes, and Dave Ranney were kind enough to contribute thoughtful input at various stages of this project. Lisa Adams of the Garamond Agency also provided extremely useful counsel at the outset.

I am not sure how to begin thanking those who fielded my and my research assistants' questions. We were pests. We hounded historians, asked editors and staff at backlash journals to go through past issues (from pre-Internet days), sought advice from numerous activists and scholars as to what were seminal or insightful readings that should be a part of this book, and sent my paragraphs across the globe for fact-checking. The result has been almost magical interchanges that have not only improved this book but also enlarged my community; at the other end of cyberspace, I have discovered dear friends from long ago as well as others who have become new friends. People were wonderful—I cannot think of one instance where my requests and subsequent nagging were ignored. To you all, I give collective thanks. As they say in the Philippines, I have *utang na loob*—I owe you one.

In truth, my greatest fear in writing these acknowledgments and in sending my manuscript off to be published is this: that I will unwittingly insult some group or some individual by overlooking them—either in the acknowledgments or in the book itself. Reader, beware: it is a huge movement out there and the whole global citizen backlash to economic globalization cannot possibly be made to fit into these few hundred pages.

Among my friends, two very special ones kept me going through this project: Annalee Saxenian and Catherine Varchaver. And I am especially fortunate to have a support community that includes Walden Bello, Susan Davis, Richard Falk, Chip Fay, Harold Goodman, Jane Grissmer, Debbie Katz, Erik Leaver, Thea Lee, Nonette Royo, Mark Simon, Harold Wain, and my family.

My husband John is, fortunately, a patient person, a good listener, and a glorious optimist. He not only truly receives great pleasure from his work, he also sincerely believes that individuals and the organizations they create have the power to make the world a better place. What better sort of person with whom to share one's life? He is the solid foundation upon which I stand. To say that I would have never finished this project without him is, in this case, even truer than in my other writing. I bestow upon him infinite thanks and apologies for all the demands that my writing of this book put on him.

I also want to thank my now four-year-old son Jesse for "letting Mama write"—for the days he spent at day-care so that I could work on this project. (And let me also extend my deepest gratitude to the gifted child-care providers—from Marilyn Dookharan, to Soraia Leventhal, to Francie Gallishaw and the teachers at Takoma Children's School—under whose loving care he has thrived.) I do hope that one day Jesse will pick up this book with curiosity if not eagerness. After all, it was he who once complimented me on a skirt I was wearing. "It is from Indonesia," I replied—talking to a toddler who had traveled with his parents to Southeast Asia on his first "field research trip" before the age of two. "No," my child of perhaps three replied, "but what's the name of the woman who made it?" Out of the mouths of babes. If I do not know the names of the spinners, weavers, and sewers of the skirt, then at least I should know that the conditions under which they worked were good for them and for the earth.

Acronyms

AFL-CIO	American Federation of Labor and Congress of Industrial Organizations
AIP	Apparel Industry Partnership
ATO	Alternative Trade Organization
ATTAC	Association for the Taxation of Financial Transactions for the Aid of Citizens
CERES	Coalition for Environmentally Responsible Economics
COVERCO	Commission for the Verification of Codes of Conduct
FLA	Fair Labor Association
FSC	Forest Stewardship Council
FTAA	Free Trade Area of the Americas
GATT	General Agreement on Tariffs and Trade
ICFTU	International Confederation of Free Trade Unions
IFG	International Forum on Globalization
ILO	International Labor Organization
ILRF	International Labor Rights Fund
IMF	International Monetary Fund
ITT	International Telephone and Telegraph
ITO	International Trade Organization
LDC	Less Developed Country
MAI	Multilateral Agreement on Investment
NAAEC	North American Agreement on Environmental Cooperation
NAALC	North American Agreement on Labor Cooperation
NAFTA	North American Free Trade Agreement
NGO	Nongovernmental Organization
NIEO	New International Economic Order
OECD	Organization for Economic Cooperation and Development

OPEC	Organization of Petroleum Exporting Countries
OPIC	Overseas Private Investment Corporation
PPM	Production Process Method
TNC	Transnational Corporation
TRIPs	Trade-Related Intellectual Property Rights
UN	United Nations
UNCTAD	United Nations Conference on Trade and Development
UNCTC	United Nations Commission on Transnational Corporations
USAS	United Students Against Sweatshops
WRC	Worker Rights Consortium
WTO	World Trade Organization

Introduction

Of Magenta Hair,
Nose Rings, and Naïveté

Why should you read this book? And why did I write it amidst the avalanche of books for and against globalization?

The idea for this book grew in part from my frustration over the simplistic way in which opponents to current forms of economic globalization were being portrayed in the mainstream media. Pick a protest—Genoa in summer 2001, Quebec City in spring 2001, Prague in fall 2000, or Seattle in fall 1999. The same images are projected over and over again in the press: rowdy students, black-masked anarchists—desperately in need of a shower—smashing a window or burning a car. Too many journalists write as if this movement were a composite of a caricature: an idealistic, privileged student with magenta hair and a nose ring who will one day grow up and understand the way things really are.

In fact, typically, both sides of the debate are portrayed in simplistic terms. On one side, the protesters are portrayed as ignorant, or at least naïve, and as opposed to globalization—the "anti-globalists." On the other side are the law-abiding, well-groomed, and mature people who are rational enough to understand that globalization is inevitable and good. As a result, most of the media suggest only two choices: you are either for economic globalization or you are against it. And, if you are in the latter group, you *probably* know what you are against, but you have no real concrete proposals for what you want. Or what you are calling for is presented as a return to the past; your vision is that of a modern Luddite who wants to take away the benefits of civilization and take us back to the stone age.

My vantage point is different. As an academic, I have taught about these issues for more than a decade. As a researcher, I first encountered the impact of trade, investment, and aid in 1977 when I lived with a community of indigenous subsistence peasants in the southern Philippines near the pineapple plantations of Del Monte. As a "public scholar" over the course of my adult life, I have tried to put my knowledge to use in the service of social movements. I know parts of this

1

movement and individuals within it, but I often hardly recognize them from most of their portrayals in the media.

I am not the only one to notice this deficiency in the mainstream media. Author and environmentalist Paul Hawken, writing of his experiences in Seattle during the 1999 demonstrations, has a telling vignette:

> [O]ne of the two *Newsweek* reporters in Seattle, called me from her hotel room at the Four Seasons and wanted to know if this was the '60s redux.
> No, I told her. The '60s were primarily an American event; the protests against the WTO are international.
> Who are the leaders? she wanted to know.
> There are no leaders in the traditional sense. But there are thought leaders, I said.
> Who are they? she asked.
> I began to name some. . . .

Hawken goes on to mention at least a dozen and a half individuals and their institutions. His story continues:

> Stop, stop, she said. I can't use these names in my article. Why not? Because Americans have never heard of them. Instead, *Newsweek* editors put the picture of the Unabomber, Theodore Kaczynksi, in the article because he had, at one time, purchased some of [anarchist leader] John Zerzan's writings.[1]

The protests and the property damage caused by a decided minority of protesters make global headlines and television news. But little is written about the tens of thousands who attend teach-ins and conferences or about what those giving talks and leading workshops at such events, even at the demonstrations themselves, actually have to say. Unreported in most coverage of the Seattle protests in 1999, for instance, was the fact that a half block outside the area for which the Seattle government declared a curfew, in the Seattle Town Hall, the International Forum on Globalization hosted a very civilized debate covering all sides and it proceeded without incident.[2] And shockingly unreported in most media accounts is the organizational diversity of this "global backlash," now spanning tens of millions of trade unionists and environmentalists, and millions more from organizations of farmers, students, religious activists, women, and indigenous peoples across the globe.

Indeed, the mainstream media seem rather content to keep the image of the protesters simplistic. Perhaps this sells more newspapers and advertisements. Perhaps it is just easier. Or perhaps it is, in some unconscious or conscious way, an attempt to make the protesters less legitimate and therefore less powerful.

But What Do They Want?

Among various media reports, it was an interview I heard on the radio that convinced me of the need for this book. The reporter was interviewing Juliette Beck, a young organizer with the San Francisco–based Global Exchange on the streets of

Washington, D.C., at the April 2000 protests against the World Bank. The coverage began with the usual terrain, with the reporter presenting Beck and her compatriots as against globalization and the institutions that pushed globalization. But then it got better: what exactly, the reporter asked, were they for? As I recall it, Beck gave an answer along the lines of: "Look, I'm an organizer. I can answer that question but you really shouldn't ask me about that. Behind us organizers are lots of brilliant people who have detailed ideas of what should be done. You should talk to them." And she mentioned some specific names—with overlaps to Hawken's list. Just blocks away was another "teach-in" at which those very "idea" people were providing details to an enraptured audience of thousands, but the reporter did not pursue the lead.[3]

What *do* these "idea" people have to say about what the "global backlash" is for? What *is* the backlash for? My students want to know and so do my mother and my mother-in-law. Indeed, my conversations ever since Seattle convince me that a wide swath of people, whether or not they are sympathetic to the backlash, want to know more about the protesters. Recently I attended a dinner party with a rather eclectic mix of people. When asked what I did, I began to describe this book. "But what do they want?" a businessman asked. As someone who made a living consulting for global corporations, he really wanted to know concrete proposals. He continued (now I am paraphrasing): "I keep reading the newspaper articles to find out what they want, but I never can find it." Another guest happened to be a retired editor from one of the United States' top newspapers; he did not disagree. Even the man who is fixing my chimney was curious to discover that the "Seattle protesters" actually had proposals. And others not only want to know, they need to know: As South Africa's finance minister Trevor Manuel—who was chairing an official session of the 2000 meetings of the World Bank and International Monetary Fund in Prague while "protesters paralyze[d]" the Czech capital—told a journalist: "I know what they're against but have no sense of what they're for."[4]

Many in the mainstream media also portray the fact that the backlash has so many parts as one of its key disadvantages—i.e., the protesters talk of too many things to have cohesion or a concrete vision. The Vietnam-era activists were against the Vietnam War. But the current protests bring up a smorgasbord of issues—from the World Bank and the World Trade Organization, to exploited labor, to environmental degradation, to gender inequality, to indigenous peoples' rights.

There is, however, an overarching umbrella uniting the backlash: opposition to corporate control of the global economy. "What was that all about?" asked a headline in the *Washington Post* the Sunday after Seattle. Under that headline, Tom Hayden, a leader of the student protests in the 1960s, wrote with palpable admiration, awe, and excitement as he tried to explain the complexity of the issues articulated by the protesters:

> I have to say I am glad to have lived long enough to see a new generation of rebels accomplish something *bigger* here in 1999 than we accomplished in Chicago in 1968 with our disruptive protests at the Democratic National Convention.
>   . . . .

Seattle will have greater consequences. In Chicago, we were dealing with a single issue: the Vietnam War. The Seattle activists were confronting the very nature of the way economics, environmentalism, and human rights are going to be shaped for the rest of our lives. The so-called new world order has to do with everything: exports, prevailing wages, sweatshops, sea turtles, the price and quality of food. The Vietnam War was going to end eventually, but the new world order will not. You will either be part of it or you'll be frozen out.[5]

These are complex issues. They cannot possibly have one simple solution.

A "Swarm" of "Anti-Globals"?[6]

As Global Exchange organizer Juliette Beck tried to explain, behind the protests are numerous, very sophisticated organizers and idea people (and some wearing both hats) who have visions of different ways for the global economy to work. They come from richer and poorer countries. Their skin comes in all shades. They are women, men, old, young, poor, rich, and in-between. They meet in person and they interact in cyberspace.

They inevitably spend time and energy on a defensive agenda—trying to defeat pro-globalization initiatives such as the Multilateral Agreement on Investment or a new "round" of global trade negotiations (the goal of Seattle), both of which would have strengthened corporate rights. But they also have an offensive, proactive agenda. They have proposals for what to do, many of which are actually on-the-ground initiatives and innovations. Not only do they hold every conceivable form of educational forum, but some lobby governments to have their proposals enacted. Others "lobby" corporations. Still others simply start initiatives on their own. They have had notable success in all three.

And, within the backlash, although they share many values and visions, they also debate ideas—often hotly. Indeed, although one can hardly decipher this from most mainstream media coverage, the "citizen backlash to economic globalization" is not a monolith that can be summed up as "anti-globalization." There are differences within and between groups, as should be expected given the size of the movement and of its undertaking, as Hayden explained.

Given the divide between media portrayal and backlash reality, the purpose of this book is to get inside the backlash to some of its visions, proposals, and debates. The book will introduce you to different parts of the movement—not so much by listing who's who but by presenting what they are trying to do to change the way the world economy works. I will share and explore key proposals emanating from different parts of the movement. The book not only will focus on basic proposals for change, but will highlight the innovative parts of the various proposals and ongoing initiatives.

My purpose is not to offer a book explicating the broader debate between the proponents and so-called opponents of globalization (although that is the subject of one part of my book). Similarly, my aim is not to view the resistance through a more theoretical microscope. Both are valid aims (although I often find the duality between pro- and anti-globalization to be artificial, as argued above). But both have been the subject of enough books.[7]

In part my intention is to provide a framework for thinking about the various responses of the "citizen" or "global" backlash and for understanding the basis of some of the debates. As the reader will discover, parts of the backlash are trying to rewrite the rules of the global economy to strengthen protections for workers and the environment. Others are trying to "stop" or "roll back" aspects of economic globalization, such as the global trade in water or the transboundary flow of speculative investment. As I will argue, that divide—between those who see the goal to be "reshaping" economic globalization or those who strive to "roll back"—is a key analytical distinction in the backlash. But within these two broad backlash groupings there are also debates that I will highlight.

Looking in the Mirror

All of this—the visions, the proposals, the debates—is exciting material. So part of why I decided to edit this book is to uncover what the backlash is and what it wants. I also decided to write this book because, as a result of my dealings with various parts of the backlash, I came to believe that, in order to understand itself better as a movement, the citizen backlash needed to examine closely its various parts.

Take, for instance, the dynamic anti-sweatshop student movement. Since 1998, college campuses in the United States and Canada have witnessed an upsurge in student activism. It all began when some U.S. students traveled to Central America to investigate the conditions under which the T-shirts, hats, and other items sold in their campus stores were produced. They discovered exploited, college-aged (and younger) workers stitching apparel with college logos, and they returned from this firsthand education in the workings of the global economy to spread the word. Their tales were strengthened by those of a nineteen-year-old former collegiate-apparel stitcher from the Dominican Republic who toured U.S. campuses to tell of inadequate wages and abusive treatment.[8] Since then hundreds of campuses have been abuzz with anti-sweatshop advocacy and action to try to ensure that collegiate apparel becomes "sweat-free."

For me, it is a welcome change in the academic environment. Many students' grasp of the global economy grows alongside their organizational efforts. The 1998 establishment of the United Students Against Sweatshops (USAS), with chapters across the United States and Canada, turned into rallies and sit-ins at Duke, Notre Dame, Brown, Georgetown, and elsewhere. Students demanded that college administrators do something to ensure "sweat-free" merchandise. Soon their demand became more specific: join a new organization called the Worker Rights Consortium. And then they merged their global concerns with local realities: In 2001, students took over the administrative offices at Harvard and refused to vacate until that well-endowed university agreed to study paying workers a "living wage." A new generation of student activists, in joining the quest to change the way the global economy works, have become a vigorous and potent component of the citizen backlash.[9]

But, as USAS student leaders themselves admitted before their annual meeting in 1999, they are experts on one aspect of the work to change economic globalization.[10] By and large, however, they are not experts on other arenas of related backlash initiatives such as attempts to change the way the World Trade Organization works. And the parts of the backlash that work on the World Trade Organization, by and large, are not experts on alternative trade organizations (ATOs) such as Equal Exchange, which markets its environmentally and socially responsible "fair trade" coffee outside the dominant corporate-controlled trade routes. And those who are involved in making ATOs viable may have few free moments to follow backlash attempts to press apparel corporations like Guess or Liz Claiborne to voluntarily enforce "codes of conduct." And those who innovate ways to enforce and monitor such corporate codes may not be aware of the movement to stop the privatization of municipal water systems. And, whatever they work on, unless they are old enough to have been active in the 1970s, the majority of backlash members are unaware of the fact that their work in the twenty-first century builds on a foundation of related work on corporations and aid institutions in the 1970s, never mind that there is a history of resistance to economic integration going back hundreds of years.

Overview of This Book

Given that the purpose of this book is to insert the reader inside the citizen backlash, only Part I is devoted to presenting the broader spectrum of views on economic globalization. While that broader debate is the focus of much of the literature that exists on globalization, this first part presents some nuances in the "pro" and the "anti" positions. There are, I argue using the readings as evidence, not simply two views on the subject.

The rest of the book concentrates on the backlash itself. I chose to center this book on what I see as key backlash proposals to change global economic integration, by which I mean changing the way in which corporate-controlled trade, investment, and financial flows are pulling parts of the world together and in which the global (multilateral) institutions that manage the world economy are finessing an increase in corporate control.

Part II reminds the reader that economic integration through trade, investment, and financial flows is not something that started in the 1990s with the growing popularity of the term "globalization." Nor did resistance to this integration erupt only recently. These twenty-first century visions and proposals have important historical roots and precedents—some as far back as over 500 years ago and some from the 1970s—many of which are little known today. As someone very involved in the 1970s efforts to use the United Nations to curb abuses of transnational corporations once remarked to me, the current resistance is "a movement that does not for some reason recognize its own history."[11]

Moving from the full spectrum of views (Part I) and the historical context (Part II), the next two parts of the book zero in on proposals to "change the rules" of the world economy—that is, backlash responses that attempt not so much to fight globalization but rather to reshape the rules under which its corporate actors operate so as to reduce its environmental and social costs. Part III begins with readings investigating the "social clauses" on labor and environment that the governments of Canada, Mexico, and the United States eventually agreed to attach to the North American Free Trade Agreement (NAFTA). It then moves to a key debate within the backlash at Seattle and elsewhere, with backlash proponents debating the pros and cons of creating binding labor and environmental protections in the World Trade Organization and other subsequent trade and investment agreements. In that section, I try to dispel the myth that "Northerners" have one view on this subject and "Southerners" another. Once again, the reality proves to be far more complex—and interesting.

In a second "changing the rules" section (Part IV), we move from the regulatory world of trade agreements to proposals that rely on "voluntary" corporate initiatives—notably codes of conduct for corporations and certification schemes. This section explores how the backlash has prodded corporations such as the Gap to set up their own voluntary environmental and social rules and then to "monitor" those codes through various mechanisms. The section also looks in more detail at Rugmark, an anti–child labor labeling initiative that came out of South Asia, and the Forest Stewardship Council, an environmental certification scheme for wood based in Mexico. Here is where the book will cover the debate over how best to make the global apparel sector, including collegiate apparel, sweatshop-free.

Parts of the backlash argue that economic globalization is not inevitable and that aspects of it should—and can—be stopped or rolled back. This is the subject of Part V. As will be seen, some of the backlash "stop" campaigns focus on what is sometimes called the "global commons"—goods such as water, virgin forests, endangered species, seeds, and other life forms. The case studies presented in Part V focus on backlash proposals to localize food systems, to give peasants (and not foreign corporations) the intellectual property rights to their rice seeds, and to stop the control of water by transnational corporations. As will be highlighted, other parts of the "rollback" movement focus on stopping the global flow of pernicious or immoral goods and services such as the debt repayments that are hemorrhaging out of poorer countries and the speculative short-term capital that is wreaking havoc on vulnerable economies.

Caveats

I am currently based in the United States, and that influences my analysis. I have, however, spent many years of my life overseas, notably in the Philippines, where I have lived and researched off and on since 1977. I have worked hard to project varied voices in the excerpts reprinted in this book. More often than not, the backlash speaks eloquently for itself. My role, therefore, is to provide the overview chapters that stitch the excerpted material together. But as much as possible, you will read original documents, assessments by participants, and proposals by participants. I have tried to choose readings that are "seminal" in some way or that do an excellent job of explaining complex realities and proposals.

Each of the book's five sections begins with an introductory essay by me. These introductions are meant to provide a foundation—facts, chronologies, concepts, and analysis—to explain why I have selected each reading and how the individual readings fit together. You can read my introductions and not the excerpts, but you will miss the real voices.

Semantics around globalization are important. I have chosen to follow *Business Week,* UN Secretary-General Kofi Annan, and C. Fred Bergsten (former U.S. assistant secretary of the treasury for international affairs, now director of the Institute for International Economics) and use the term "backlash." Some in the backlash may not be happy with that term, as it connotes a defensive posture of being in response to something. But I do think that is the reality—the citizen backlash grew to its current stature because of the adverse ramifications of the current stage of global economic integration, which has come to be known as economic globalization. (For those who prefer a more positive image, I encourage you mentally to replace my "backlash" with Princeton professor and international law expert Richard Falk's "globalization from below.")[12]

On another question of semantics, when I write of the citizen backlash, I am referring to civil society. "Nongovernmental organizations" (NGOs) is an umbrella term for the organized part of civil society—encompassing the range of citizen groups from grassroots "popular organizations" to membership groups like unions to more amorphous groupings of citizens.[13]

By and large, I have tried not to take a position among various parts of the backlash. This is not difficult for me as I truly do not believe that one part of the backlash or another has all the answers. Where there are debates or differences, my goal is to present and analyze these disagreements, not to insert myself.

There exist no terms with which I am comfortable to label the "richer" countries of the world or the "poorer" countries of the world. At times, I use these inadequate terms. Likewise, at times, I fall back on other easy but unsatisfactory terms: "North" versus "South" albeit a geographical misnomer, and "developed" versus "less developed countries" or "developing countries" even though they may in fact not be "developing" economically or socially. Poorer, South, Third World, less developed, developing—these are all short cuts for what should read "countries of Africa, Asia and the Pacific, Latin American and the Caribbean, and the Middle East," but that is a wordy mouthful.

A note on the editing of the readings: In order to keep this book to a manageable length (and a reasonable price), I have had to cut back the length of the original readings in many cases. My cuts are indicated by three different possible markings: (1) three periods (". . .") if the deletion is within one sentence; (2) four periods (". . . .") if the deletion includes the period at the end of one sentence; and (3) three periods within brackets ("[. . .]") if more than one sentence is deleted. Ellipses indicating deleted material at the beginning and ending of articles have been omitted. I have striven to find readings that maintain their integrity even when only a portion is reprinted. And, as much as possible, I have opted to reprint whole sections and minimize the number of deletions.

Where the original excerpts included notes, these have also been reprinted. So as not to confuse the reader who might want to find the longer original document from which an excerpt has been culled, I have maintained the original numbering of those notes even when I deleted text accompanied by notes. In a few cases in which the original text is available in full online but has extensive notations or citations, I have deleted notes that are either explanatory or give information of the "for further information" variety. This I have done rarely and only due to the exigencies of space and book price. Anyone who wants the full text or the complete set of notes for these readings can consult the original sources using the information provided in the citation at the bottom of the first page of each excerpt.

In Brief

The backlash to economic globalization may not be powerful enough yet to win all the time or to become the prevailing view. But, as a collectivity, its members are certainly too powerful simply to be relegated to the current media caricature. Nor is the backlash going to disappear in the wake of the terrorism of 11 September 2001, as some pundits have suggested. The citizen backlash is no longer simply a "fringe" movement that governments, international institutions, and private corporations can ignore. It has provided the pressure to achieve some debt cancellation and has defeated certain trade agreements. It has the World Bank, the International Monetary Fund, and the World Trade Organization on the defensive; so too with pharmaceutical, apparel, biotech, and other transnational firms. Take it from a vice president of Business for Social Responsibility, a U.S.-based group with more than 1,400 corporate members or affiliates ranging from Stonyfield Farm Yogurt to L.L.Bean, Wal-Mart, and General Motors: "The protests in the streets of Seattle were both an illustration of current opinion and a harbinger of things to come. The protesters, though derided by many in the U.S. media, got the clear attention of major U.S. corporations. There may be some immediate impact as well as long-term changes."[14]

So: who are they and what in fact do they *really* want?

Notes

1. Paul Hawken, "N30 [November 30] WTO Showdown," *Yes! A Journal of Positive Futures* (Spring 2000): 51.

The specific names mentioned by Hawken include "Martin Khor and Vandana Shiva of the Third World Network in Asia, Walden Bello of Focus on the Global South, Maude Barlow of the Council of Canadians, Tony Clarke of Polaris Institute, Jerry Mander of the International Forum on Globalization, Susan George of the Transnational Institute, David Korten of the People-Centered Development Forum, John Cavanagh of the Institute for Policy Studies, Lori Wallach of Public Citizen, Mark

Ritchie of the Institute for Agriculture and Trade Policy, Anuradha Mittal of the Institute for Food & Development Policy, Helena Norberg-Hodge of the International Society for Ecology and Culture, Owens Wiwa of the Movement for the Survival of the Ogoni People, Chakravarthi Raghavan of the Third World Network in Geneva, Debra Harry of the Indigenous Peoples Coalition Against Biopiracy, José Bové of the Confédération Paysanne Européenne, Tetteh Hormoku of the Third World Network in Africa, Randy Hayes of the Rainforest Network."

2. Moderated by *Business Week*'s Paul Magnuson, the six-person debate included Ralph Nader, and, for the globalists, Columbia University professor Jagdish Bhagwati. A video tape of the debate can be ordered through the IFG (see web site bibliography).

3. For a more detailed story on Beck, see William Finnegan, "After Seattle: Anarchists Get Organized," *The New Yorker*, 17 April 2000, 40–51.

4. Trevor Manuel's quote is from William Drozdiak and Steven Pearlstein, "Protesters Paralyze Prague" *Washington Post*, 27 September 2000, A16, as is the phrase on events in Prague.

5. Tom Hayden, "The Battle in Seattle: What Was That All About?" *Washington Post*, Outlook section (5 December 1999), B1, B5.

6. The term "anti-globals" is from Sarah Delaney, "A Tense Silence Blankets Genoa," *Washington Post*, 20 June 2001, A22. "Swarm" is from "NGO Swarm" which was coined by David Ronfeldt and John Arquilla in a study they wrote for RAND. See www.rand.org/publications for their work. For a quick summary of their work, see "The Non-Governmental Order," *The Economist*, 11 December 1999, 21.

7. See the "For Further Reading" section of Part I for more specific references.

8. See Bob Herbert, "Sweatshop U.," *New York Times*, 12 April 1998. Herbert's piece, on the *Times*' Sunday op-ed page, certainly helped spread the word.

9. See Part IV for more details on this.

10. Various formal and informal comments by students attending the United Students Against Sweatshops (USAS), in "Leveraging Student Power in Anti-Sweatshop Organizing," 1999 pre-conference to annual USAS conference, Washington, D.C., 7–8 July 1999.

11. Harris Gleckman, personal communication to author, July 1999. Gleckman was chief of the Environmental Unit at the late UN Center on Transnational Corporations. (The UNCTC is discussed in Part II.)

12. "BACKLASH: Behind the Anxiety over Globalization" announced the cover of *Business Week* regarding its 24 April 2000 cover story by Aaron Bernstein (pp. 38–48). See also Kofi Annan (Reading 1.2); and C. Fred Bergsten, "The Backlash against Globalization," speech delivered at Trilateral Commission Meeting, Tokyo, 9 May 2000, reprinted in Trilateral Commission, "Tokyo 2000," *Trialogue* 54 (2000): 48–53.

For Richard Falk's early use of the term "globalization from below" (which was then picked up by author Jeremy Brecher and others), see Richard Falk, "The Making of Global Citizenship," in *Global Visions: Beyond the New World Order*, ed. Jeremy Brecher, John Brown Childs, and Jill Cutler (Boston: South End Press, 1993). See also Falk's "Resisting 'Globalisation-from-above' through 'Globalisation-from-below,'" *New Political Economy* 2 (1997): 17–24.

13. For more on NGOs and the flowering of civil society, see Jessica T. Mathews, "Power Shift," *Foreign Affairs* 76, no. 1 (January/February 1997): 50–66; and Alan Durning, "Mobilizing at the Grassroots," in *State of the World 1989*, ed. Lester R. Brown et al. (New York: W. W. Norton, 1989): 154–73. David Korten's *Getting to the 21st Century: Voluntary Action and the Global Agenda* (Hartford, Conn.: Kumarian Press, 1990), 91–132, provides a useful typology of NGOs.

14. Aron Cramer, "Ethical Sourcing: The Indicators of Serious Intent," in *Visions of Ethical Sourcing*, ed. Raj Thamotheram (London: Financial Times Prentice Hall for Shared View Social Responsibility Ltd., with financial support from Société Générale de Surveillance [SGS], 2000), 26. For more on BSR, see "Frequently Asked Questions," www.bsr.org/faq/index.asp, pp.1–3, accessed 15 February 2000.

Part I

THE CLASH OF VISIONS

Part I

The Clash of Visions

Just as the Cold War defined the half century after World War II, "economic globalization" is emerging as a defining framework of the first part of the new millennium. But debates rage over even what the term means. And, more to the point, there are vastly different interpretations of the benefits and costs, the winners and losers, and prescriptions for the path forward. Public opinion polls around the world suggest that much of the public is confused about economic globalization. Some believe that more trade and investment flows across borders are beneficial, but others fear that workers, communities, and the environment often suffer.

A Road Map

In the midst of these raging debates and the intense volleys of assertions and counter-assertions, this first section is intended to provide a "road map" to the overarching debate over economic globalization. As noted in the general introduction, this book is primarily not about this larger debate, but about the "global citizen backlash" to economic globalization, and the proposals, innovations, and debates emanating from different parts of that backlash. In Parts III through V of the book, I will focus on three sets of proposals and debates: voluntary initiatives through codes of conduct for corporations, "regulatory" proposals to mandate reforms through so-called social clauses, and proposals to exclude certain items from globalization altogether. It makes sense, however, to begin the book by situating the backlash—and its proposals, initiatives, and debates—within the broader spectrum of contemporary views on economic globalization.[1] This is the task of Part I, while Part II frames the backlash and its proposals in a historical context.

What are the main assertions about economic globalization made by the principals in this current debate, and what are their visions of a better way forward?

At the ends of the spectrum of views regarding economic globalization stand a "protectionist" school and a "free-market" school (often simply called a "free trade" school). Free-market advocates assert that open borders encourage more trade and cross-border investment which, in turn, bring growth, prosperity, and even peace and democracy. On the other hand, protectionists argue that it is necessary to erect some barriers to trade and investment in order to foster vibrant industries, protect family farmers and industrial workers, and promote stable communities. The debate between proponents of these two positions is long-standing. For two and a quarter centuries, for instance, this debate has raged in the United States—going back to the clashing visions of free-trader Thomas Jefferson and protectionist Alexander Hamilton. For the historical record, Hamilton's side won the first round and the United States began with a clearly protectionist policy agenda in the 1790s (which continued up to the 1920s).

While relatively protectionist development strategies swept Latin America and other parts of the Third World in the 1950s and 1960s, the 1980s and 1990s were the heyday of the "free traders" with the emergence of British Prime Minister Margaret Thatcher, U.S. President Ronald Reagan, and German Chancellor Helmut Kohl in the early 1980s. With strong corporate support, these governments championed free trade, free investment, deregulation, and privatization as the best route to growth. In 1990, economist John Williamson (then of the Washington, D.C.–based Institute for International Economics and later of the World Bank) summed up what was then a growing consensus in ten areas of economic reform that reflected free-market strategies to achieve export-led growth—with specific policies ranging from trade liberalization to cutting government budget deficits to privatization of state-owned enterprises. This "Washington Consensus," he argued, was shared by "both the political Washington of Congress and senior members of the administration, and the technocratic Washington of the international financial institutions, the economic agencies of the U.S. government, the Federal Reserve Board, and the think tanks."[2] While (as I will detail below) some interesting disagreements have emerged among free-market advocates in recent decades, these two major schools—free market and protectionism—remain strong today in many parts of the world.

What is new in the past two decades is the emergence of a third major school in the economic globalization debates, a worldview that is usually defined by the media in terms of what it is against: the *anti*-globalization movement or the backlash *against* globalization. This school—growing from movements of workers, environmentalists, farmers, religious activists, women, consumer advocates, indigenous peoples, human rights activists, and youth, North and South—has challenged both major paradigms, free market and protectionism. "Backlash" supporters have argued that free-market approaches are harmful to the majority, and thus often have been incorrectly accused of being protectionists. Rather, the backlash offers alternatives to both traditional free-market and traditional protectionist policies: proposals to stop certain aspects of globalization, slow down others, and reshape the rules and institutions that govern economic globalization. While some attempt to label their movements as being for "fair trade" or "responsible trade" or "ethical trading" or "living democracy," it is perhaps most accurate at this moment in history to refer to them overall as the "global citizen backlash."

Free Markets versus Protectionism

Hence, the key to understanding the new economic globalization debates is getting a handle on the main actors, arguments, assertions, and visions of these three schools of thought: the free-market school, the protectionists, and the citizen backlash. However, this section offers nine readings instead of three to capture subtle but critical gradations within schools.

Let us start with the free-market school. Here, I offer three readings instead of one. Free-market advocates tend to articulate one of two sets of arguments when they argue for freer trade and investment. First, proponents in the United States and other richer countries focus on the benefits of freer markets for two sets of actors within their countries: consumers and workers. In terms of consumers, their argument is that freer trade and investment flows offer cheaper goods in greater variety to more consumers—cantaloupes and strawberries in the winter, for example. And, workers in export-oriented jobs, they claim, tend to get higher wages. These are the arguments that dominate newspaper editorial pages in richer countries as well as the speeches of most political and business leaders. To kick off this section, an excerpt from a widely circulated book with the catchy title of *Globaphobia*, published by three prominent pro-free-trade think tanks, nicely lays out this set of arguments (Reading 1.1).

Second, free-market proponents in the poorer countries, or those in richer countries who concentrate on the impact of globalization on the poorer countries, argue that such freer trade and investment flows generate growth in these countries and hence alleviate poverty and social unrest. Yes, people may lose jobs or parts of the environment may be despoiled in the process, but these can be taken care of by government programs with the proceeds from that economic growth.[3] This second claim is now at the center of the intellectual thrust of the World Bank, the dominant international development institution.[4] The argument is captured well in the second reading of the section, a speech—or more accurately a press release containing the text of a speech—by United Nations Secretary-General Kofi Annan warning of the *potential* power of the backlash to win Southern government support and derail advances in the pro–economic globalization agenda. In a somewhat ironic twist of fate, the speech was never delivered precisely because of the *actual* potency of the backlash. The speech was to have been delivered on the opening day of the Seattle ministerial meeting of the World Trade Organization in November 1999, on the very day that thousands of protesters closed down the meetings. Annan offers a more nuanced view than *Globaphobia*, admitting that free trade and investment policies need to be tempered with some protections for the vulnerable, but the thrust of the free-market argument is well articulated. (During the heyday of the Washington Consensus in the 1980s and 1990s, such subtlety or concern for equity, environmental, or social ramifications was rare.[5])

I offer a third free-market reading (Reading 1.3) to illuminate a significant division that was emerging in free-market ranks as early as the Reagan presidency, but which, it may be argued, by 2000 was creating cracks in the free-trade consensus. Some who view themselves as staunch defenders of pure free markets unfettered by government interference began criticizing the major intergovernmental institutions set up after World War II to set rules and promote freer trade, investment, and financial flows: the World Bank, the International Monetary Fund, and the General Agreement on Tariffs and Trade (supplanted by the World Trade Organization in 1995; see Part II on these institutions). These institutions, in the view of such prominent "ultra free-market" proponents as former Citibank chairman Walter Wriston and U.S. President Nixon's Secretary of State Henry Kissinger, often interfered in the efficient functioning of markets by guaranteeing that loans, even bad loans, would get repaid. These elite and well-known individuals from both the private and public sectors were backed up by such influential conservative think tanks as the Heritage Foundation, the American Enterprise Institute, and the Cato Institute in the United States. Among their key arguments was that, for instance, when the International Monetary Fund "bailed out" Russia in 1998 with emergency loans, it rewarded private banks for bad loans. Furthermore, they continued, this created what is called a "moral hazard" because such actions encouraged more bad loans since private bankers again would expect to get bailed out.

In 2000, the most influential articulation of these "ultra free-market" views in recent years was in the deliberations of what is known as the Meltzer Commission in the United States—more formally the International Financial Institution Advisory Council. A group of experts chosen and mandated by the U.S. Congress and chaired by Carnegie Mellon University professor Allan Meltzer, the commission examined the institutions that govern the world economy. Its report, excerpted in Reading 1.3, may sound tame on first reading, but the commission's demands imply at a minimum a radical restructuring of these institutions. As a dissenting member of the commission later said publicly, the majority view should be understood as "serious proposals in the United States from a Congressional commission . . . which essentially wants to abolish the International Monetary Fund and the World Bank."[6]

Thus, the free-market camp today comprises traditional free-market proponents, proponents of a somewhat gentler free-market approach such as Annan, and the ultra free-market advocates. As the "ultra" free-market school renegades exemplified by the Meltzer Commission try to pull the Washington Consensus in one direction, another break-off group led by former World Bank chief economist Joseph Stiglitz is tugging in another direction. I will return to these "cracks" in Reading 1.9, which will expand on the views of 2001 Nobel laureate Stiglitz.

Moving next to the modern-day protectionists, I include in the readings a speech by tireless U.S. presidential contender Pat Buchanan, who has counterparts in many other rich nations, such as Jean-Marie Le Pen in France, Jörg Haider in Austria, Gerhard Frey in Germany, and Gianfranco Fini in Italy. The core allure of the protectionists is their appeal to economic nationalism and the concept of sovereignty. Countries should not, they argue, cede political authority to multilateral bodies that can undermine national law. Countries should be able to discriminate in favor of local firms and local workers. And countries should seal off borders to immigrant flows.[7] Some "protectionists" are more pragmatic and less xenophobic than Buchanan and his conservative colleagues and counterparts in other countries, and the line between free traders and protectionists is often fuzzy. Some members of the U.S. Congress, for example, see themselves as free-market advocates, but they also support protectionism for industries in their own districts. Although a distinct minority in the globalization debates, protectionist movements are strong enough in almost every rich country to elect representatives to legislative bodies where they represent the protectionist interests of small firms being undermined by global corporations and globalizing rules. Hence, they become a component of the forces slowing down the momentum of free traders.

The Global Backlash

Finally, I move to the citizen backlash "school" for the next four readings. While it is important to exercise caution in making generalizations about an emerging paradigm that is emanating from so many different social critics and social movements, there is a rather clear, unifying critique of the free-market school reflected in most writings of the backlash: corporate-driven economic globalization in both the North and South hurts workers, the environment, small farmers, the poor, indigenous peoples, consumer safety, women, and so on.

Indeed, as parts of the backlash argue, one even has to be wary of the fallacy of the terms used by the so-called free-market school: trade and investment flows currently are not *free* but are *managed* through intellectual property rights and other institutions, and much of trade occurs between units of the same corporations. The political agenda advanced in the late twentieth and early twenty-first centuries by these so-called free traders is a different animal from pure, theoretical free trade (i.e., open markets); rather, the political agenda calls for more rules and agreements to expand investors' rights and protect corporate interests. Likewise, the political agenda has moved so-called free-market advocates into new terrain—pushing for prohibitions on capital controls and for condemning domestic social and environmental regulations as illegal trade barriers.

Citizen movements of various stripes across the globe began registering strong disapproval of the reigning Washington Consensus school as early as 1980, but the backlash hit the radar screen of the wider public only after large street demonstrations beginning in Seattle in 1999. The fifth reading, by economist Mark Weisbrot, codirector of the Washington, D.C.–based Center for Economic and Policy Research, and a backlash scholar who is an expert on the World Bank and IMF, sums up the main elements of the critique.

Different aspects of this critique have been elaborated on in a flurry of books critical of globalization and, more crucially, on the ground in numerous documents drafted at global meetings that have brought together representatives of different facets of the citizen backlash. In Lusaka, Zambia, African members of Jubilee South wrote a "Lusaka Declaration," noting that their "objectives were . . . to establish a new 'African Consensus' on sustainable development (to replace the bankrupt 'Washington Consensus'); to identify demands, strategies, and enhanced roles for . . . civil society more broadly; and to define and undertake a plan of action leading to debt cancellation and genuine development, based on freedom, justice, and equality for all genders and all communities."[8] And, at a meeting in Grenada in December 1999, forty-eight participants from Africa, Asia, the Caribbean, Europe, Latin America, North America, and the Pacific met and established the International Gender and Trade Network composed of seven regional networks of women doing research, advocacy, and economic literacy work on trade and development, with a secretariat at the Washington, D.C.–based Center of Concern.[9]

The discussions at such meetings and the documents that result not only share similar critiques of economic globalization (as articulated by Weisbrot in Reading 1.5), but also offer similar alternative principles that should undergird economic activity, centered on democracy, sustainability, equity, and respect for core human rights and for diversity. Yet, as the various components of the citizen backlash begin to focus on their vision of alternatives to what they call "corporate-driven globalization," I find an important divergence that I mentioned briefly in this book's introduction. I will use three readings in the current section to illustrate this divergence, but it will be examined in depth in the core of this book (Parts III through V).

A first subsector of the backlash—often rooted in an environmental critique—is intent on stopping certain aspects of globalization (for example, halting the export of water in bulk or the patenting of indigenous rice seeds) and slowing down other aspects (for example, reducing the flow of short-term and volatile speculative financial flows). Its constructive agenda gives priority to invigorating local economies.

This view is captured in the sixth reading, a program of alternatives by the International Forum on Globalization (IFG). Starting in 1994, the IFG has pulled together dozens of leaders of the citizen backlash from North and South to form a global network of globalization researchers and activists. In addition to providing a forum for these leaders to discuss and debate among themselves, the IFG has held massive educational "teach-ins" (reminiscent of the anti–Vietnam War teach-ins) to coincide with the events and meetings advancing the pro-globalization agenda. Its Seattle teach-in, for instance, drew a crowd of 2,500 (limited by room size). The IFG's alternative program, excerpted in Reading 1.6, was drafted over a two-year period by a team of twenty-four IFG members—including Vandana Shiva from India, Martin Khor from Malaysia, Walden Bello from the Philippines, Sara Larrain from Chile, Tony Clarke from Canada, and Jerry Mander, Lori Wallach, David Korten, and John Cavanagh from the United States. Like many backlash documents, it is not a final document but a "living document" in that it will be revised and built on in regional workshops around the world during 2002 and 2003.

A second subsector of the backlash—with strong roots in trade unions and women's organizations in both North and South—is less intent on stopping economic globalization. Instead, its alternatives focus more on "reshaping" the current rules and institutions of economic globalization so that globalization's burden does not fall on workers, communities, the environment, women, and other more marginalized sectors of society while global corporations receive the lion's share of the benefits. (This portion of the citizen backlash, focused on reshaping the rules, has important differences within its ranks, as we will see in Parts III and IV when we turn to the debate over social clauses and corporate codes of conduct.)

This "reshape" approach is captured in an April 1998 speech (Reading 1.7) by John Sweeney, the president of the U.S. labor federation, the AFL-CIO, which represents 13 million U.S. workers. Sweeney was elected president of the AFL-CIO in the mid-1990s, after an upsurge in labor activism against the North American Free Trade Agreement. In his speech, Sweeney expounds on the "new internationalism" that he sees replacing the more traditional protectionist sentiments that once characterized the AFL-CIO. Sweeney outlines the principles of this "new internationalism" which would reshape the rules and institutions of the global economy to benefit workers, communities, and the environment in the United States and abroad. In the eighteen months after this speech, Sweeney and the AFL-CIO put his words into action, rallying tens of thousands of workers to Seattle for the massive protests against the WTO, and earning the labor federation a leading role in the global backlash.

A document from the Hemispheric Social Alliance (Reading 1.8) provides another look at the "reshape" portion of the backlash. The Alliance is a network of leading trade unions, environmental groups, and women's, farm, and other social movements from around the Western Hemisphere with its secretariat in Mexico; its members collectively represent approximately 50 million people. Coming together starting in the late 1990s to oppose the expansion of the North American Free Trade Agreement via the creation of an intergovernmental, pro-globalization Western Hemispheric "Free Trade Area of the Americas," the Alliance quickly moved on to deliberate and delineate an alternative vision shared by its members. The resulting document, "Alternatives for the Americas" (released in Quebec City in April 2001), is notable for its content, which details a counterproposal to the intergovernmental Free Trade Area of the Americas, as well as for the cross-border participatory process by which it was drafted.

The excerpt I chose from that Hemispheric Social Alliance document outlines general principles and then emphasizes an important analytical point made by many within the citizen backlash, be they proponents of rollback or reshape: economic globalization has a deleterious impact not only on workers and the environment, but also on the more marginalized and disempowered sectors of society such as women and indigenous communities. Focusing on gender ramifications, Reading 1.8 argues that women are affected by economic globalization in ways that are different and more detrimental than for men. Once again revealing the North–South collaboration behind many backlash initiatives, the "gender" part of the document was collaboratively drafted by Marceline White of Women's Edge in the United States and Patricia Roman of Alianza Chilena por un Comercio Justo y Responsable of Chile, with input from other Alliance members.

As can be seen in comparing Readings 1.6–1.8, across the global backlash spectrum from reshape to rollback, the global backlash shares broad principles. Backlash goals are not more trade and more investment, but more equity, more social, community, and democratic control over economic life, more empowerment for the marginalized, and so on. There are differences in the tactics chosen to reach these goals, and also in the emphasis put on various principles. John Sweeney of the AFL-CIO or the Hemispheric Social Alliance—the two reshape examples in the excerpts in Part I—would put less emphasis than the IFG on subsidiarity. But, as we will see when we look at proposals by rollback proponents in Part V, this difference of emphasis is unlikely to flare into a big controversy. Rollback and reshape advocates, for the most part, see themselves as allies. Indeed, the line between the two can at times be blurry, even for some individuals who may prescribe rollback solutions to certain problems and reshape solutions to others.

Momentum

During the late 1990s, the schools of dissent were strong enough to break the momentum of the pro-globalization free-market forces. In 1997 and again in 1998, citizen backlash and protectionist forces in the United States blocked President Bill Clinton's request for authority to negotiate free-trade and investment agreements that could not be amended by Congress—so-called fast track authority (now termed "trade promotion authority"). Globally, citizen backlash coalitions in 1998 stalled a significant initiative offered by proponents of increased economic integration through trade and investment flows: the Multilateral Agreement on Investment (MAI)—at the Paris-based Organization for Economic Cooperation and Development—which was to have greatly expanded the rights of and protections for transnational corporations in host countries and at one point was considered a relatively easy sell. With such public pronouncements as that of the Meltzer Commission (Reading 1.3), ultra free-market critiques of the IMF and World Bank added momentum to citizen-backlash street protests against the institutions that manage the global economy. Citizen coalitions intersected with a number of increasingly bold Third World government representatives who (while not necessarily agreeing with the protesters) began to stand up more forcefully to the richer-country members within the WTO. Actions by both blocked an attempt to strengthen the World Trade Organization at the Seattle ministerial meeting in late 1999. And, in an unprecedented move, the World Bank canceled its annual conference on development economics, which was to have been held in Barcelona, Spain, in June 2001, rather than deal with the backlash protesters.[10]

What is the relative power of these different schools in the early years of the twenty-first century? The free-market school is on the defensive against the multi-sided attacks from the global citizen backlash, the ultra free-market advocates, and the protectionists like Buchanan. Combined with what became known as the Asian financial crisis, which boomeranged from East Asia around the globe in 1997 and 1998, these growing attacks signal a crisis of legitimacy for the free-market

Washington Consensus, which had reigned supreme in the 1980s and 1990s. A final reading (Reading 1.9), by John Cavanagh (director of the Institute for Policy Studies in Washington, D.C.) and myself, analyzes the extent to which these and other events are leading to the "death" of the prevailing free-trade Washington Consensus. Cavanagh and I describe the defection of those in the Meltzer Commission camp and the defection of others such as Nobel prize–winner and former World Bank chief economist Joseph Stiglitz to suggest that the cracks in the pro-globalization consensus are not yet fatal but could be so.

To get a sense of the momentum of the citizen backlash at the onset of the new century, ponder the words of an article in the pro-free-trade *Economist* magazine a week after the Seattle protests:

> The non-governmental organizations (NGOs) that descended upon Seattle were a model of everything the [government] trade negotiators were not. They were well organized. They built unusual coalitions (environmentalists and labour groups, for instance, bridged old gulfs to jeer the WTO together). They had a clear agenda—to derail the talks. And they were masterly users of the media.[11]

Today, the debate over economic globalization is rich—and loud and heated. No one school or view reigns supreme. As the globalization debates rage on, the ability of forces aligned against the "Washington Consensus" to "derail" (to use the *Economist*'s words) new economic globalization initiatives raises the profile of alternative proposals and initiatives by the citizen backlash to stop, slow down, and reshape economic globalization.

Notes

1. I will use the words "views" and "schools of thought" interchangeably to mean "worldview" or "paradigm."

2. John Williamson, *The Progress of Policy Reform in Latin America*, Policy Analyses in International Economics, no. 28 (Washington, D.C.: Institute for International Economics, January 1990), 9–33. Quote is from p. 9. For a complete list of the ten policies that Williamson termed the "Washington Consensus," see note 1 in Reading 1.9.

3. See Gene M. Grossman and Alan B. Krueger, "Economic Growth and the Environment," *Quarterly Journal of Economics* CX, no. 2 (May 1995): 353–77.

4. See, for instance, World Bank, *World Development Report 2000/2001: Attacking Poverty* (New York: Oxford University Press, 2001).

5. See Williamson, *Progress of Policy Reform in Latin America*, 83; and John Williamson, "Democracy and the 'Washington Consensus,'" *World Development* 21, no. 8 (1993), 1329.

6. C. Fred Bergsten, "The Backlash against Globalization," speech delivered at Trilateral Commission Meeting, Tokyo, 9 May 2000, reprinted in Trilateral Commission, "Tokyo 2000," *Trialogue* 54 (2000): 49.

7. In discussing illegal immigration from Mexico: "I will build a security fence. We will seal the borders of this country cold. We will stop illegal immigration in its tracks if I am elected. You have my word on it. I will do it." Patrick J. Buchanan, "Preparing America for the 21st Century," address to the United We Stand America Conference, Dallas, 12 August 1995.

8. "The Lusaka Declaration and Areas of Action," document affirmed by African organizations of civil society working on debt from Burkina Faso, Lesotho, Kenya, Malawi, Mozambique, Nigeria,

Cameroon, Swaziland, Tanzania, Togo, Uganda, South Africa, Zambia, and Zimbabwe, 19–21 May 1999, Lusaka, Zambia. See also Reading 5.6.

9. See Jeanette Bell, "Women's Strategic Planning Seminar on Gender and Trade," organized by the Center of Concern and DAWN Caribbean, Grenada, West Indies, 8–11 December 1999.

10. John Vidal and Charlotte Denny, "Cyber War Declared on World Bank," *Guardian* [UK], 20 June 2001, www.guardianunlimited.co.uk/globalisation/story/0,7369,509697,00.html.

11. "Citizens' Groups: The Non-Governmental Order," *The Economist,* 11 December 1999, 20. See also Curtis Runyan, "Action on the Front Lines—The Third Force: NGOs," *World Watch Magazine* 12, no. 6 (November/December 1999): 12–21.

1.1

Globaphobia:
Confronting Fears about Open Trade

Gary Burtless, Robert Z. Lawrence,
Robert E. Litan, and Robert J. Shapiro

We have written this book to demonstrate that the fear of globalization—or "globaphobia"—rests on very weak foundations [. . .]

First, the United States globalized rapidly during the golden years before 1973, when productivity and wages were growing briskly and inequality was shrinking, demonstrating that living standards can advance at a healthy rate while the United States increases its links with the rest of the world. In any event, it is useful to keep in mind that the U.S. economy is no more globalized today—measured by the share of trade in its total output—than it was *before World War I.*

Second, even though globalization harms some American workers, the protectionist remedies suggested by some trade critics are, at best, short-term palliatives and, at worst, harmful to the interests of the broad class of workers that they are designed to help. Sheltering U.S. firms from imports may grant some workers a short reprieve from wage cuts or downsizing. But protection dulls the incentives of workers and firms to innovate and stay abreast of market developments. As a result, its benefits for individual workers and firms are often temporary. Indeed,

protection invites foreign exporters to leap trade barriers by building plants in this country—as foreign manufacturers of automobiles, automobile parts, film, and other products have done. We are not criticizing this result: the United States has a strong national interest in attracting foreign investors, who typically bring technologies and management practices that ultimately yield higher wages and living standards for U.S. workers. But the movement to the United States of foreign companies and their plants simply underscores how erecting barriers to imports is often fools' gold for those who believe that protection will permanently shelter jobs or the profits of employers.

Third, erecting new barriers to imports also has an unseen boomerang effect in depressing exports. This is one of the most important, but least understood, propositions that we discuss in this book. While higher barriers to imports can temporarily improve the trade balance, this improvement would cause the value of the dollar on world exchange markets to rise, undercutting the competitive position of U.S. exports and curtailing job opportunities for Americans in export industries. Moreover, by increasing the costs of input (whether imported or domestic) that producers use to generate goods and services, protection further damages the competitive position of U.S. exporters. This is especially true in high-tech industries, where many American firms rely on foreign-made parts or capital equipment. The dangers of protection are further compounded

Gary Burtless, Robert Z. Lawrence, Robert E. Litan, and Robert J. Shapiro, excerpt from *Globaphobia: Confronting Fears about Open Trade* (Washington, D.C.: Brookings Institution, Progressive Policy Institute, and Twentieth Century Fund, 1998), 6–11.

to the extent it provokes retaliation by other countries. In that event, some Americans who work in exporting industries would lose their jobs, both directly and because higher barriers abroad would induce some of our exporting firms to move their plants (and jobs) overseas. In short, protection is not a zero-sum policy for the United States: it is a *negative sum* policy.

Fourth, globaphobia distracts policymakers and voters from implementing policies that would directly address the major causes of the stagnation or deterioration in the wages of less-skilled Americans. *The most significant problem faced by underpaid workers in the United States is not foreign competition. It is the mismatch between the skills that employers increasingly demand and the skills that many young adults bring to the labor market.* For the next generation of workers, the problem can be addressed by improvements in schooling and public and private training. The more difficult challenge is faced by today's unskilled adults, who find themselves unable to respond to the help wanted ads in daily newspapers, which often call for highly technical skills. It is easy to blame foreign imports for low wages, but doing so will not equip these workers with the new skills that employers need. The role of government is to help those who want to help themselves; most important, by maintaining a high-pressure economy that continues to generate new jobs, and secondarily, by facilitating training and providing effective inducements to displaced workers to find new jobs as rapidly as possible.

Fifth, Americans in fact have a vested interest in negotiating additional reductions of overseas barriers that limit the market for U.S. goods and services. These barriers typically harm the very industries in which America leads the world, including agriculture, financial services, pharmaceuticals, aircraft, and telecommunications. The failure of Congress to grant the president fast-track negotiating authority sends an odd and perverse message to the rest of the world. The United States, which once led the crusade for trade liberalization, now seems to have lost faith in the benefits of trade. Over time, this loss of faith may give ammunition to opponents of free trade in other countries, not only in resisting further trade liberalization but in imposing new barriers.

Sixth, it cannot be stressed too heavily that open trade benefits consumers. Each barrier to trade raises prices not only on the affected imports but also on the domestically produced goods or services with which they compete. Those who would nonetheless have the United States erect barriers to foreign goods—whether in the name of "fair trade," "national security," or some other claimed objective—must face the fact that they are asking the government to tax consumers in order to achieve these goals. And Americans must decide how willing they are to pay that tax. By contrast, lowering barriers to foreign goods delivers the equivalent of a tax cut to American consumers, while encouraging U.S. firms to innovate. The net result is higher living standards for Americans at home.

Finally, to ensure support for free trade, political leaders must abandon the argument traditionally used to advance the cause of trade liberalization: that it will generate *more* jobs. Proponents of freer trade should instead stick with the truth. Total employment depends on the overall macroeconomic environment (the willingness and capacity of Americans to buy goods and services) not on the trade balance (which depends on the difference between the amounts that Americans save and invest). We trade with foreigners for the same reasons that we trade among ourselves: to get better deals. Lower trade barriers in other countries mean *better* jobs for Americans. Firms in industries that are major exporters pay anywhere from 5 to 15 percent more than the average national wage. The "price" for gaining those trade opportunities—reducing our own trade barriers—is one that Americans should be glad to pay.

In spite of the enormous benefits of openness to trade and capital flows from the rest of the world and notwithstanding the additional benefits that Americans would derive from further liberalization, it is important to recognize that open borders create losers as well as winners. Openness exposes workers and company owners to the risk of major losses when new foreign competitors enter the U.S. market. Workers can lose their jobs. This has certainly occurred in a wide range of industries exposed to intense foreign competition—autos, steel, textiles, apparel, and footwear. Indeed, the whole point of engaging in trade is to shift resources—capital and labor—toward their most productive uses, a process that inevitably causes pain to those required to shift. In some cases, workers are forced to accept permanent reductions in pay, either in the jobs they continue to hold in a trade-affected industry or in new jobs they must take after suffering displacement. Other workers, including mainly the unskilled and semiskilled, may be forced to accept small pay reductions as an indirect effect of liberalization. Indeed, the job losses of thousands of similar workers in traded goods industries may tend to push down the wages of *all* workers—even those in the service sector—in a particular skill category.

We acknowledge that these losses occur, though their size is vastly exaggerated in media accounts and the popular imagination. Nonetheless, we believe the nation has both a political and a moral responsibility to offer better compensation to the workers who suffer sizable losses as a result of trade liberalization. . . . Decent compensation for the workers who suffer losses is easily affordable in view of the substantial benefits the country enjoys as a result of open trade. Liberal trade, like technological progress, mainly creates winners, not losers. Among the big winners are the stockholders, executives, and workers of exporting firms such as Boeing, Microsoft, and General Electric, as well as Hollywood (whose movies and television shows are seen around the world). There are many millions of more modest winners as well, including the workers, re-tirees, and nonworking poor, who benefit from lower prices and a far wider and better selection of products.

One problem in making the case for open borders is that few of the winners recognize the extent of the gains they enjoy as a result of free trade. The losses suffered by displaced workers in the auto, apparel, or shoemaking industries are vividly portrayed on the nightly news, but few Americans realize that cars, clothes, and shoes are cheaper, better made, or more varied as a result of their country's openness to the rest of the world. Workers who make products sold outside the United States often fail to recognize how much their jobs and wages depend on America's willingness to import as well as its capacity to export. People contributing to a pension fund seldom realize that their returns (and future pensions) are boosted by the fund's ability to invest overseas, and almost no borrower understands that the cost of a mortgage or car loan is lower because of America's attractiveness to foreigners as a place to invest their money. All of these benefits help improve the standard of living of typical Americans, and they can be directly or indirectly traced to our openness. They are nearly invisible to most citizens, however; certainly far less visible than the painful losses suffered by workers who lose their jobs when a factory is shut down.

1.2

Address to
WTO Ministerial Meeting

Kofi Annan

Because of the events yesterday, 30 November, in Seattle, Secretary-General Kofi Annan was unable to deliver his address to the Third Ministerial Meeting of the World Trade Organization. Following is the text of the address as distributed to representatives of the media:

Let me begin by thanking the city government and people of Seattle for hosting this very important, but evidently very controversial, conference. I wonder if they realized what they were letting themselves in for!

Personally, I am delighted to be here, and deeply honoured to be invited to address this gathering, which is indeed very important. I hope and believe it will be remembered as the Conference which launched the "development round", and laid the foundations of a world trade system which will be fair as well as free.

In the past, developing countries have been told time and again that they stand to benefit from trade liberalization, and that they must open up their economies.

They have done so, often at great cost. For the poorest countries the cost of implementing trade commitments can be more than a whole year's budget.

But, time and again, they have found the results disappointing—not because free trade is bad for them, but because they are still not getting enough of it.

In the last great round of liberalization—the Uruguay Round—the developing countries cut their tariffs, as they were told to do. But in absolute terms many of them still maintain high tariff barriers, thereby not only restricting competition but denying crucial imports to their own producers, and thus slowing down economic growth.

Even so, they found that rich countries had cut their tariffs less than poor ones. Not surprisingly, many of them feel they were taken for a ride.

Industrialized countries, it seems, are happy enough to export manufactured goods to each other, but from developing countries they still want only raw materials, not finished products. As a result, their average tariffs on the manufactured products they import from developing countries are now four times higher than the ones they impose on products that come mainly from other industrialized countries.

Ever more elaborate ways have been found to exclude third world imports; and these protectionist measures bite deepest in areas where developing countries are most competitive, such as textiles, footwear and agriculture.

In some industrialized countries, it seems almost as though emerging economies are assumed to be incapable of competing honestly, so

Kofi Annan, "In Address to WTO Ministerial Meeting, Secretary-General Says 'Economic Rights and Social Responsibilities Are Two Sides of the Same Coin,'" United Nations press release SG/SM/7237/Rev.1, (New York, 26 November 1999).

that whenever they do produce something at a competitive price they are accused of dumping—and subjected to anti-dumping duties.

In reality, it is the industrialized countries who are dumping their surplus food on world markets—a surplus generated by subsidies worth $250 billion every year—and thereby threatening the livelihood of millions of poor farmers in the developing world, who cannot compete with subsidized imports.

So it is hardly surprising if developing countries suspect that arguments for using trade policy to advance various good causes are really yet another form of disguised protectionism.

I am sure that in most cases that is not the intention: those who advance such arguments are usually voicing genuine fears and anxieties about the effects of globalization, which do need to be answered.

They are right to be concerned—about jobs, about human rights, about child labour, about the environment, about the commercialization of scientific and medical research. They are right, above all, to be concerned about the desperate poverty in which so many people in developing countries are condemned to live.

But globalization must not be used as a scapegoat for domestic policy failures. The industrialized world must not try to solve its own problems at the expense of the poor. It seldom makes sense to use trade restrictions to tackle problems whose origins lie not in trade but in other areas of national and international policy. By aggravating poverty and obstructing development, such restrictions often make the problems they are trying to solve even worse.

Practical experience has shown that trade and investment not only bring economic development, but often bring higher standards of human rights and environmental protection as well. All these things come together when countries adopt appropriate policies and institutions. Indeed, a developing civil society will generally insist on higher standards, as soon as it is given the chance to do so.

What is needed is not new shackles for world trade, but greater determination by governments to tackle social and political issues directly—and to give the institutions that exist for that purpose the funds and the authority they need. The United Nations and its specialized agencies are charged with advancing the causes of development, the environment, human rights, and labour. We can be part of the solution.

So too can the private sector. Transnational companies, which are the prime beneficiaries of economic liberalization, must share some of the responsibility for dealing with its social and environmental consequences.

Economic rights and social responsibilities are two sides of the same coin. This is why, earlier this year, I proposed a Global Compact between business and the United Nations, under which we will help the private sector to act in accordance with internationally accepted principles in the areas of human rights, labour standards and the environment. The response so far has been encouraging, and I believe we can achieve a great deal by working together more closely.

But this meeting, and this Organization, must not be distracted from their vital task—which is to make sure that this time a new round of trade negotiations really does extend the benefits of free trade to the developing world. Unless we convince developing countries that globalization really does benefit them, the backlash against it will become irresistible. That would be a tragedy for the developing world, and indeed for the world as a whole.

Trade is better than aid. If industrialized countries do more to open their markets, developing countries can increase their exports by many billions of dollars per year—far more than they now receive in aid. For millions and millions of poor people this could make the difference between their present misery and a decent life. And yet the cost for the rich countries would be minuscule.

In fact, industrialized countries might even be doing themselves a favour. The European Union, for instance, is currently spending between 6 and 7 percent of its gross domestic product on various kinds of trade protection measures, according to one recent study. No doubt some groups of Europeans are benefiting from this, but surely there must be a cheaper and less harmful way for their fellow citizens to help them!

This time, tariffs and other restrictions on developing countries' exports must be substantially reduced. For those of the least developed countries, I suggest, duties and quotas should be scrapped altogether.

And developing countries should receive technical assistance, both in the negotiations themselves and in implementing and benefiting from the agreements once reached. At present, some of them do not even have missions in Geneva. But the United Nations Conference on Trade and Development (UNCTAD) is there to help, if given the resources to do so.

In exactly one month we shall leave the twentieth century behind. The first half of it saw the world almost destroyed by war, partly as a result of its division into rival trade blocs.

The second half, by contrast, has seen an unprecedented expansion of global trade, which has also brought unprecedented economic growth and development, even if as yet very unequally distributed.

That expansion did not happen by accident. After the carnage and devastation of the Second World War, far-sighted statesmen deliberately constructed a post-war economic and political order governed by rules which would make free trade possible and thereby, they believed, make future wars less likely. Broadly speaking, they were right.

Several factors combined, at that time, to make such a liberal world order possible. One of them was a broad consensus on the role of the State in ensuring full employment, price stability and social safety nets. Another was that most big firms were still organized within a single country—so that international economic relations could be negotiated between States, each of which corresponded to a distinct national economy, and could be controlled by raising or lowering barriers at national frontiers.

And that in turn made it relatively easy to put in place a set of international organizations which were based on, and in their turn supported, the economic order: the World Bank, the International Monetary Fund, the General Agreement on Tariffs and Trade and the United Nations.

Today's world is very different. Today, networks of production and finance have broken free from national borders, and become truly global. But they have left the rest of the system far behind.

Nation States, and the institutions in which they are represented, can set the rules within which international exchanges take place, but they can no longer dictate the terms of such exchanges exclusively among themselves. Economic life is no longer embedded in a broad framework of shared values and institutionalized practices.

The result is that, on top of the gross imbalance of power and wealth between industrialized countries and developing ones, there is now a second imbalance: the gap between the integration of the world economy and the continued parochialism of political and social institutions. While economics is global, politics remains obstinately local. It is for this reason, I believe, that so many people, even in the industrialized world, feel vulnerable and helpless.

And that, Excellencies, is why this is such a historic moment.

It will depend on what we decide here, and in a few other crucial meetings over the next few years, whether the twenty-first century will be like the first half of the twentieth, only worse—or like the second half, only better.

Let's not take the onward march of free trade and the rule of law for granted. Instead, let us resolve to underpin the free global market with genuinely global values, and secure it with effective institutions. Let us show the same firm leadership in defence of human rights, labour standards and the environment as we already do in defence of intellectual property.

In short, let us emulate the wisdom, and the will-power, of those who laid the foundations of the liberal world order after the Second World War. They made change work for the people—and we must do the same.

1.3

Report of the International Financial Institution Advisory Commission

Allan H. Meltzer

In the last two decades, large crises in Latin America, Mexico, Asia, and Russia heightened interest in the structure and functioning of international financial institutions. Calls for additional capital for the International Monetary Fund to respond to these crises raise questions about how the Fund uses resources, whether its advice increases or reduces the severity of crises and its effect on living standards.

Growth in private lending and capital investment, and the expanding objectives of the international development banks, raise questions about the adequacy and effectiveness of these institutions. Repeated commitments to reduce poverty in the poorest nations have not succeeded. A large gap remains between promise and achievement.

[. . .]

In November 1998, as part of the legislation authorizing approximately $18 billion of additional funding by the United States for the International Monetary Fund, Congress established the International Financial Institution Advisory Commission to consider the future roles of seven international financial institutions: the International Monetary Fund, the World Bank Group, the Inter-American Development Bank, the Asian Development Bank, the African Develop-

ment Bank, the World Trade Organization, and the Bank for International Settlements.

The Commission was given a six-months life. It held meetings on twelve days and public hearings on three additional days.

[. . .]

The Commission's report recommends many far-reaching changes to improve the effectiveness, accountability, and transparency of the financial institutions and to eliminate overlapping responsibilities.

[. . .]

The postwar financial institutions established at Bretton Woods in 1944 are unique in many ways. The mission of the Bretton Woods institutions was to promote monetary and financial stability, to reconstruct countries devastated by war, and to expand the reach of the market system by offering open trade and market access to all countries. Never before have the victors in war established a framework to promote growth, development, and global prosperity.

These institutions and the U.S. commitment to maintain peace and stability, have had remarkable results. In more than fifty postwar years, more people in more countries have experienced greater improvements in living standards than at any previous time. With the help of our allies, we have avoided global war. Our former adversaries are now part of the expanding global market system. They seek to achieve the benefits of freer trade and exchange in a system based on

Excerpt from *Report of the International Financial Institution Advisory Commission*, by Allan H. Meltzer, chair (Washington, D.C.: Government Printing Office, 2000), 1–3 and 15–22, USGPO #048-000-00531-4.

growth of personal liberty and increased ownership of private property.

The postwar economic order permitted countries to adopt a strategy of export-led growth. This policy required imports of technology, services, and raw materials that spread prosperity to other countries. The international framework provided a sufficient degree of financial stability to absorb costly oil shocks, regional wars, and occasional financial disturbances.

Expansion of trade, capital flows, and economic activity permitted improvements in health care, longevity, education, and other social indicators. Growth provided resources to solve old environmental problems and address new ones. Peace, economic and social progress, and stability contributed to the spread of democratic government and the rule of law to many countries.

The Congress, successive administrations, and the American public can be proud of these achievements. The United States has been the leader in maintaining peace and stability, promoting democracy and the rule of law, reducing trade barriers, and establishing a transnational financial system. Americans and their allies have willingly provided the manpower and money to make many of these achievements possible. The benefits have been widely shared by the citizens of developed and developing countries.

The dynamic American economy benefited along with the rest of the world. Growth of trade spread benefits widely. Per capita consumption in the United States tripled. As in other countries, higher educational attainment, improved health services, increased longevity, effective environmental programs, and other social benefits accompanied or followed economic gains.

Serious challenges remain. The beneficiaries of globalization must include the poorest members of the world economy. Instability of the world economy must be mitigated.

The Institutions

The principal Bretton Woods Institutions are the International Monetary Fund (IMF) and the World Bank Group (Bank). The initial role of the IMF was to smooth balance-of-payments adjustment in a system of fixed but adjustable exchange rates. The Bank's original charge was to foster postwar reconstruction in war-devastated regions and to encourage economic develop-

ment by lending to developing countries. Initially, neither institution had the resources or the experience to make major contributions. The Marshall Plan and other assistance from the United States, and the prodigious efforts of people in the war-devastated countries, achieved postwar reconstruction.

Beginning in the 1960s, countries created regional development banks to supplement the Bank's work. The Inter-American Development Bank (IDB, 1959), the African Development Bank (AfDB, 1964) and the Asian Development Bank (ADB, 1966) provide loans and grants for development in their respective regions.

The General Agreement on Tariffs and Trade (GATT) joined the IMF and the Bank in 1948. Through successive rounds of multilateral negotiation, GATT reduced most tariff barriers to negligible values. Nontariff barriers remained. In 1995, GATT ended, replaced by the World Trade Organization (WTO) with broader powers and expanded responsibilities to settle trade disputes. The U.S. economy continued to benefit greatly from the expansion of world trade and participation in the WTO.

New Conditions, New Challenges

The economic environment in which the founders expected the IMF and the Bank to function no longer exists. The pegged exchange-rate system, which gave purpose to the IMF, ended between 1971 and 1973, after President Nixon halted U.S. gold sales. Instead of providing short-term resources to finance balance-of-payment deficits under pegged exchange rates, the IMF now functions in an expanded role as a manager of financial crises in emerging markets, as a long-term lender to developing economies and former Communist countries, as a source of advice and counsel to many nations, and collector of economic data on its 182 member countries.

Building on their experience in the 1930s, the founders of the Bank believed that the private sector would not furnish an adequate supply of capital to developing countries. The Bank, joined by the regional development banks, intended to make up for the shortfall in resource flows. With the development and expansion of global financial markets, capital provided by the private sector now dwarfs any volume of lending the development banks have done or are likely to do in the future. And, contrary to the initial presumption, most crises in the past quarter-century involved not too little but too much lending, particularly short-term lending that proved to be highly volatile.

Beginning with the Latin American debt problems of the 1980s, followed by Mexico's crisis in 1994–95, and the Asian financial and economic problems of 1997–98, parts of the world economy have experienced the largest financial traumas and recessions of the post-war years. Liabilities of bank failures in crisis countries often reached 20% of annual income, a far greater financial collapse than occurred in any developed country, including the United States, during the depression of the 1930s or the banking and U.S. savings-and-loan failures in the 1980s.

The crises in developing countries destroyed large parts of the wealth of their citizens. In an interrelated global economy, financial flows and trade declined, particularly U.S. and European exports and inter-regional exports and imports. The effects spread to other developing and developed countries. The frequency and violence of these crises, and the weakness of many emerging countries' financial systems show the need for a new framework and new policies to restore and strengthen economic stability, growth and development.

The Commission recognizes that financial crises have occurred throughout history and cannot be eliminated entirely. However, the frequency and severity of recent crises raise doubts about the system of crisis management now in place and the incentives for private actions that it encourages and sustains. The IMF has given too little attention to improving financial structures in developing countries and too much to expensive rescue operations. Its system of short-term crisis management is too costly, its responses too slow, its advice often incorrect, and its efforts to influence policy and practice too intrusive.

High cost and low effectiveness characterize many development bank operations also. The World Bank's evaluation of its own performance in Africa found a 73% failure rate.[1] Only one of four programs, on average, achieved satisfactory, sustainable results.

In reducing poverty and promoting the creation and development of markets and institu-tional structures that facilitate growth, the record of the World Bank and the regional development banks leaves much room for improvement. Six principal reasons for the development banks' poor record in poverty reduction and institutional reform are:

1. by far the largest share of the Banks' resources flows to a few countries with access to private capital;
2. the amount of funds provided by development banks to their largest borrowers is small compared to the private-sector resources received;
3. the host government guarantee, required by all Bank lending, eliminates any link between project failure and the Bank's risk of loss;
4. money is fungible so that any linkage between development bank resources and specific projects or policy changes is difficult to trace and often nonexistent;
5. countries do not implement reforms unless they choose to do so, and they rarely sustain reforms imposed by outsiders; and
6. development projects typically succeed only if the recipient country has a significant interest in the project and directs its efforts to achieve success.

IMF and Bank Assistance

In the past, the Fund has worked to achieve growth and economic stability by making loans conditional on changes in monetary, fiscal, exchange rate, trade or labor-market policies. The World Bank has added other conditions. Countries often face a long list of conditions that, if followed, would restrict the role of national political institutions and the development of responsible, democratic institutions.

While it is always difficult to know what would have happened in the absence of the IMF's or Bank's conditions, their research, as well as considerable research by outsiders, finds no evidence of systematic, predictable effects from most of the conditions.[2] A recent summary of conditional lending concludes:

"[I]t is now well-accepted that Fund-supported programs improve the current account balance and the overall balance of payments. The results for inflation are less clear. . . . In the case of growth, the consensus seems to be that output will be depressed in the short-run as the demand reducing elements of the policy package dominate."[3]

A main reason for the IMF's modest success is that countries come to the IMF mainly when they have serious problems, often when they are in crisis. The IMF's relatively standard advice includes reducing domestic spending and permitting the country's currency to depreciate. Reducing spending lowers incomes. Reduced spending and a depreciated currency typically improve the current account and may reduce inflation.

If the IMF did not exist, the market would force a country in crisis to follow similar policies. Perhaps the IMF's assistance cushions the decline in income and living standards. Neither the IMF, nor others, has produced much evidence that its policies and actions have this beneficial effect. One reason may be that IMF loans permit some private lenders to be repaid on more favorable terms, so the benefits have gone mainly to those lenders. Or, the IMF's loans may permit governments to maintain spending that remains politically attractive despite its low social value.

The last possibility receives support in recent work at the World Bank. *Assessing Aid* summarizes the results of experience and research:

"Foreign aid has at times been a spectacular success . . .

"On the flip-side, foreign aid has also been, at times, an unmitigated failure . . .

"Financial aid works in a good policy environment . . .

"Improvements in economic institutions and policies in the developing world are the key to a quantum leap in poverty reduction . . .

"Aid can nurture reform even in the most distorted environment—but it requires patience and a focus on ideas, not money."[4]

The Commission believes that the effectiveness of foreign aid and progress against poverty would increase and financial crises would be reduced in number, frequency and severity, if current programs of the IMF and the development banks change to focus atten-

tion on institutional reform, incentives for improved domestic arrangements and policies, greater transparency and accountability, reduced opportunities for corruption in developing and restructuring countries, and the provision of global public goods. These improvements will yield maximum benefit only if governments continue to foster open markets and further reduce barriers to trade in goods, services, and long-term capital.

The Role of the Commission

[. . .]

At its start, the Commission agreed unanimously to consider the roles and tasks that should be assigned to these institutions if they were created anew in the year 2000. The members recognized that the new or changed roles and assignments might require changes in the institutions' charters, their size and the scope and directions of their activities. It agreed that the economic environment had changed greatly in the more than fifty years since the principal institutions began operations and that the institutions had grown and changed in response to crises and changes in the world economy. Many of these changes were unplanned or opportunistic. Some of the institutions, particularly the World Bank, have become so large and have taken on so many different tasks that effectiveness has been sacrificed. Frequent reorganization and changes of mission have reduced efficiency and wasted resources. Programs that overlap with IMF or regional bank activities have led to conflict and failure to achieve agreed-upon goals.

The Commission believes that to encourage development, countries should open markets to trade, and encourage private ownership, the rule of law, political democracy and individual freedom. Market economies work best when they operate in an environment where national governments and international institutions follow predictable policies that maintain economic stability, protect political freedom and private property, and sustain incentives for efficient, purposeful behavior leading to wealth creation that benefits all members of the society.

The principal role of public-sector institutions is to provide global public goods, create and maintain the framework and rules that permit the private sector to function productively, generating wealth to reduce poverty and pay for social improvements. Effective international financial institutions can contribute importantly to this process.

Notes

1. Underlying data are from the World Bank's web site.

2. See *Assessing Aid*, Oxford University Press for the World Bank, 1998 and, at the IMF, the many papers by Mohsin Khan and his associates, most recently N. Ul Haque and M.S. Khan, "Do IMF-Supported Programs Work? A Survey of Cross-Country Empirical Evidence." IMF Working Paper, November 15, 1999 (unpublished).

3. Ul Haque and Khan, *op. cit.*, pp. 16–17. Comments made by Graham Bird, when the paper was presented, suggest that the conclusion is supported in several previous studies.

4. *Assessing Aid, op. cit.*, pp. 1–4. Much additional work at the Bank by David Dollar and his collaborators provides evidence for these conclusions.

1.4

Free Trade Is Not Free

Patrick J. Buchanan

This is a prestigious forum; and I appreciate the opportunity to address it. As my subject, I have chosen what I believe is the coming and irrepressible conflict between the claims of a new American nationalism and the commands of the Global Economy.

As you may have heard in my last campaign, I am called by many names. "Protectionist" is one of the nicer ones; but it is inexact. I am an economic nationalist. To me, the country comes before the economy; and the economy exists for the people. I believe in free markets, but I do not worship them. In the proper hierarchy of things, it is the market that must be harnessed to work for man—and not the other way around.

As for the Global Economy, like the unicorn, it is a mythical beast that exists only in the imagination. In the real world, there are only national economies. . . .

In these unique national economies, critical decisions are based on what is best for the nation. Only in America do leaders sacrifice the interests of their own country on the altar of that golden calf, the Global Economy.

What is Economic Nationalism? Is it some right-wing or radical idea? By no means. Economic nationalism was the idea and cause that brought Washington, Hamilton and Madison to

Philadelphia. These men dreamed of creating here in America the greatest free market on earth, by elimination [of] all internal barriers to trade among the 13 states, and taxing imports to finance the turnpikes and canals of the new nation and end America's dependence on Europe. It was called the American System.

The ideology of free trade is the alien import, an invention of European academics and scribblers, not one of whom ever built a great nation, and all of whom were repudiated by America's greatest statesmen, including all four presidents on Mount Rushmore.

The second bill that Washington signed into law was the Tariff Act of 1789. Madison saved the nation's infant industries from being buried by the dumping of British manufactures, with the first truly protective tariff, the Tariff Act of 1816. "Give me a tariff and I will give you the greatest nation on earth," said Lincoln. "I thank God I am not a free trader," Theodore Roosevelt wrote to Henry Cabot Lodge.

Under economic nationalism, there was no income tax in the United States, except during the Civil War and Reconstruction. Tariffs produced fifty to ninety percent of federal revenue. And how did America prosper? From 1865 to 1913, U.S. growth averaged 4% a year. We began the era with half Britain's production, but ended with twice Britain's production.

Yet, this era is now disparaged in history books and public schools as the time of the Robber Barons, a Gilded Age best forgotten.

Patrick J. Buchanan, excerpt from "Free Trade Is Not Free," address to the Chicago Council on Foreign Relations, 18 November 1998, 1–7.

Not only did America rise to greatness through the economic nationalism, so did every other first-rank power in history—from Britain in the 18th century, to Bismark's Germany in the 19th, to post-war Japan. Economic nationalism has been the policy of rising nations, free trade the practice of nations that have commenced their historic decline. Today, this idea may be mocked by the talking heads, but it is going to prevail again in America, for it alone comports with the national interests of the United States. And this is the subject of my remarks.

[. . .]

The great free-market economist Milton Friedman, is credited with the line, "there is no free lunch." Let me amend to Friedman's Law with Buchanan's Corollary: Free trade is no free lunch.

And it is time its costs were calculated.

Back in 1848, another economist wrote that if free trade were ever adopted, societies would be torn apart. His name was Karl Marx, and he wrote: ". . . the Free Trade system works destructively. It breaks up old nationalities and carries antagonism of proletariat and bourgeoisie to the uttermost point . . . the Free trade system hastens the Social Revolution. In this revolutionary sense alone . . . I am in favor of Free Trade."

Marx was right. Here, then, is the first cost of open-borders free trade. It exacerbates the divisions between capital and labor. It separates societies into contending classes, and deepens the division between rich and poor. Under free trade, economic and social elites, whose jobs and incomes are not adversely impacted by imports or immigration, do well. For them, these have been the best of times. Since 1990, the stock market has tripled in value; corporate profits have doubled since 1992; there has been a population explosion among millionaires. America's richest one percent controlled 21 percent of the national wealth in 1949; in 1997 it was 40 percent. Top CEO salaries were 44 times the average wage of their workers in 1965; by 1996 they were 212 times an average worker's pay.

How has Middle America fared? Between 1972 and 1994, the real wages of working Americans fell 19 percent. In 1970, the price of a new house was twice a young couple's income; it is now four times. In 1960, 18 percent of women with children under six were in the work force; by 1995 it had risen 63 percent. The U.S. has a larger percentage of women in its work force than any industrial nation, yet median family income fell 6 percent in the first six years of the 1990s.

Something is wrong when wage earners work harder and longer just to stay in the same place. Under the free trade regime, economic insecurity has become a preexisting condition of life.

A second cost of global free trade is a loss of independence and national sovereignty. America was once a self-reliant nation; trade amounted to only 10 percent of GNP; imports only 4 percent. Now, trade is equal to 25% of GNP; and the trade surpluses we ran every year from 1900–1970 have turned into trade deficits for all of the last 27 years.

Since 1980 our total merchandise trade deficit adds up to $2 trillion. This year's trade deficit is approaching $300 billion. Year in and year out, we consume more than we produce. This cannot last.

Look at what this is doing to an industrial plant that once produced 40 percent of all that the world produced. In 1965, 31 percent of the U.S. labor force had manufacturing equivalent jobs. By 1997, it was down to 15 percent, smallest share in 100 years.

More Americans now work in government than in manufacturing. We Americans no longer make our own cameras, shoes, radios, TV's, toys. A fourth of our steel, a third of our autos, half our machine tools, two-thirds of our textiles are foreign made. We used to be the world's greatest creditor nation; now, we are its greatest debtor.

Friends, this is the read-out of the electrocardiogram of a nation in decline. Writes author-economist Pat Choate, "a peek behind the glitter of record stock prices and high corporate profits reveals a deepening economic dry rot—a nation that is eating its seed corn and squandering its economic leadership position, here and abroad."

And American sovereignty is being eroded. In 1994, for the first time, the U.S. joined a global institution, the World Trade Organization, where America has no veto power and the one-nation, one-vote rule applies. Where are we headed? Look at the nations of Europe that are today surrendering control of their money, their immigration policy, their environmental policy, even defense policy—to a giant socialist superstate called the EU.

For America to continue down this road of global interdependence is a betrayal of our history and our heritage of liberty. What does it profit a man if he gain the whole world, and suffer the loss of his own country?

A third cost of the Global Economy is America's vulnerability to a financial collapse caused by events beyond our control. Never has this country been so exposed. When Mexico, with an economy no larger than Illinois', threatened a default in 1994, the U.S. cobbled together a $50 billion bailout, lest Mexico's default bring on what Michel Camdessus of the IMF called "global financial catastrophe."

When tiny Asian dominoes began to fall last year, the IMF had to put together $117 billion in bailouts of Thailand, Indonesia, South Korea, lest the Asian crisis bring down all of Latin America and the rest of the world with it.

In the Global Economy, the world is always just one default away from disaster. What in heaven's name does the vaunted Global Economy give us—besides all that made-in-China junk down at the mall—to justify having the U.S. financial system at permanent risk of collapse—if some incompetent foreign regime decides to walk on its debts?

A fourth cost of this Global Economy is the deindustrialization of America and the de-Americanization of our industries. Many of our Fortune 500 corporations have already shed their American identity.

[. . .]

Many companies still carry fine old American names, but their work forces are becoming less and less American. In 1985, GE employed 243,000 Americans; ten years later, it was down to 150,000. IBM has lopped off half of its U.S. workers in the past decade. Here is author William Greider:

> "By 1995, Big Blue had become a truly global firm—with more employees abroad than at home . . . Intel . . . shrank U.S. employment last year from 22,000 to 17,000. Motorola's . . . work force is now only 56 percent American. . . . Ma Bell once made all its home telephones in the U.S. and now makes none here."

Boeing's Philip Condit says he would be happy if, twenty years from now, no one thought of Boeing as an American company.

Here is Carl A. Gerstacker of Dow Chemical: "I have long dreamed of buying an island owned by no nation and of establishing the World Headquarters of the Dow Company on the truly neutral ground of such an island, beholden to no nation or society." A Union Carbide

spokesman agreed: "It is not proper for an international corporation to put the welfare of any country in which it does business above that of any other."

To this new corporate elite, putting America first betrays a lack of loyalty to the company. Some among our political elite share this view. Here is Strobe Talbott, Clinton's roommate at Oxford and architect of his Russian policy: "All countries," said Talbott in 1991, "are basically social arrangements . . . No matter how permanent and even sacred they may seem at any one time, in fact they are all artificial and temporary . . . within the next hundred years . . . nationhood as we know it will be obsolete; all states will recognize a single, global authority."

This is the transnational elite, our new Masters of the Universe.

The Cold War has been succeeded by a new struggle. "The real divisions of our time," writes scholar Christisan Kopff, "are not between left and right, but between nations and the globalist delusion." That struggle will shape the politics of the new century; and a familiar question is being asked again across America: When the commands of the Global Economy conflict with call of patriotism, whose side are you on?

If you would see the consequences of free trade ideology, go to Detroit. In the 1950s this was the forge and furnace of the Arsenal of Democracy, with 2 million of the most productive people on earth. Compare Detroit then to Detroit now. Free trade is not free.

Forty years ago, Japan exported 6000 cars. Today, Japan has as large a share of the U.S. auto and truck market as GM.

[. . .]

Remember NAFTA. This treaty was going to open Mexico to U.S. auto exports. Well, in 1996, we shipped 46,000 cars to Mexico; and Mexico sent 550,000 cars back to us. Where did Mexico get its booming auto industry? From Michigan, Ohio, and Missouri.

In the 1950s, "Engine Charlie" Wilson immortalized himself with the remark, "What's good for America is good for General Motors, and vice versa." What Engine Charlie said was true, when he said it. We see that now as we watch GM closing factories here and opening up abroad. GM's four newest plants are going up in Argentina, Poland, China, and Thailand. "GM's days of building new plants in North America may be over," says the Wall Street Journal.

GM used to be the largest employer in the United States; today, it is the largest employer in Mexico where it has built 50 plants in 20 years. In Juarez alone, there are 18 plants of Delphi Automotive, a GM subsidiary. Across from Juarez, El Paso is becoming a glorified truck stop, as Texans watch their manufacturing jobs go south.

Volkswagen has closed its U.S. plant in the Mon Valley and moved production of its new Beetle into Mexico, where it will produce 450,000 vehicles this year. Wages at Volkswagen's plant in Puebla average $1.69 an hour, one-third of the U.S. minimum wage.

Let me make a simple point here. If you remove all trade barriers between a Third World economy like Mexico and a First World country like the United States, First World manufacturers will head south, to the advantage of the lower wages, and the Third World workers will head north, to the advantage of the higher wages. Economics 101.

Since the free-trade era began, 4000 new factories have been built in northern Mexico, and 35 million immigrants, most of them poor, have come into the United States—among them five million illegal aliens, mostly from Mexico. Free trade is not free.

But the free traders respond: Who cares who makes what, where? What's important is that consumers get the best buy at the cheapest price. But this is Grasshopper Economics. Americans are not only consumers; we are producers and citizens. We have obligations to one another and to our country; and one of those obligations is not to behave like wastrel children squandering a family estate built up over generations. A family estate is something you can sell off—only once.

What is the wealth of nations? Is it stocks, bonds, derivatives—the pieces of paper traded on Wall Street that can be gone with the wind? No, the true wealth of a nation lies in its factories, farms, fisheries, and mines, in the genius and capacities of its people. Industrial power is at the heart of economic power, and economic power is at the heart of strategic power. America won two world wars and the Cold War because our industrial power and technology proved beyond the ability of our enemies to match.

[. . .]

The day is not too distant when economic nationalism will triumph [. . .]

America First, and not only first, but second and third as well.

1.5

Globalism on the Ropes

Mark Weisbrot

Let us begin with the simplest, most commonly accepted definition of globalization: an increase in international trade and investment. Is this necessarily beneficial for everyone involved? Or even for the majority of people in any given country? In the United States, trade is now almost twice as large, as a percentage of GDP, as it was in 1973. Foreign investment, both outward and inward, has also risen sharply. At the same time, the median real wage in the United States has been stagnant over the past twenty-six years. This one statistic tells a very big story. "Median" refers to the fiftieth percentile, which means that half of the entire labor force is at or below that wage. This group includes office workers, supervisors, everyone working for a wage or salary—not just textile workers or people in industries that are hard hit by import competition. Real wages, by the way, are adjusted for inflation and quality changes. Thus, it is not acceptable to argue, as is often done, that the typical household now has a microwave and a VCR. That has already been taken into account in calculating the real wage. This means that over the last twenty-six years, the typical wage- or salary-earner has not shared in the gains from economic growth. Now compare this result with the previous twenty-seven years (1946–73), when foreign trade and investment formed a much smaller part of the U.S. economy and were more restricted. During this time, the typical wage increased by about 80 percent.

These statistics are not in dispute among economists; their validity is also verified by the experience of most people who are old enough to have lived through the first half of the post–World War II era. In the Sixties and Seventies, it was not uncommon for an average wage-earner to buy a home, support a family, and even put his children through college with one income. This is no longer true. There are differences among economists as to how much of the typical employee's misfortune has been due to globalization, but few would deny that it is a significant factor. Even William Cline, a staunchly pro-globalization expert in this area, has estimated that 39 percent of the increase in wage inequality from 1973 to 1993 has resulted from increased trade.

In conventional economic theory, the gains from increased trade arise on the import side of the ledger. These gains result from importing goods that are more efficiently produced elsewhere. When economists measure these gains for the United States, they turn out to be very small. For example, the best estimate for the Uruguay Round of the General Agreement on Tariffs and Trade—the last round of negotia-

Mark Weisbrot, excerpt from "Globalism on the Ropes," rev. (Washington, D.C.: Center for Economic and Policy Research, 2001).

tions, which culminated in the creation of the WTO in 1994—would put the direct benefits of tariff reduction to the U.S. economy at about $700 million per year. Even if we were to triple this figure for the effect of non-tariff barrier reduction, we are still talking about less than three hundredths of one percent of GDP.

The conventional theory also predicts that "low-skilled" workers will be harmed by increased international trade. Economists commonly define "low-skilled" workers as including about 70 percent of the labor force. In other words, the overwhelming weight of the empirical evidence, and even economic theory, indicates that the typical American has little to gain from the present course of globalization and in fact has already lost quite a bit from the process.

This should not be surprising, given the form and substance of the institutional changes that we have witnessed over the past three decades. Our political leaders have chosen to negotiate a series of trade and commercial agreements that throw American workers into increasing competition with their much-lower-paid counterparts throughout the world. One does not need a Ph.D. in economics to guess the likely results of such measures. Although manufacturing workers have been most directly affected, the lowering of their wages and the general weakening of labor's bargaining power reduce compensation throughout most of the labor force.

It must be emphasized, because the contrary is so commonly believed, that this process is not driven by technology. Rather it is the result of quite deliberate political decisions. Our leaders could do the same thing to the salaries of doctors. We could, for example, initiate and monitor licensing and training procedures in foreign medical schools, which would make it easier for foreign doctors to practice here and would thereby increase the supply of doctors. With a fraction of the effort and resources that it has taken to raise foreign trade and investment to current levels, and without sacrificing the quality of health care, doctors' salaries would fall. The potential savings to consumers are quite large—$70 billion per year could be saved just by lowering doctors' salaries to European levels. This would be a hundred times larger than the direct gains from tariff reduction in the Uruguay Round of the GATT. But it is not likely to happen anytime soon, because doctors have enough political clout to prevent such an assault on their

living standard. The same cannot be said for most of the labor force.

Lacking economic arguments on the domestic front, many proponents of globalization have presented it as a helping hand to the poorer countries of the world. This statement by Treasury Secretary Larry Summers, quoted without correction in the *New York Times*, is typical: "When history books are written 200 years from now about the last two decades of the 20th century, I am convinced that the end of the cold war will be the second story. The first story will be about the appearance of emerging markets—about the fact that developing countries where more than three billion people live have moved toward the market and seen rapid growth in incomes." This is not likely, unless the historians of the future are innumerate. In Latin America, for example, income per person has hardly grown at all over the last two decades: about 6 percent total for 1980–98. If we compare this with the previous two decades, before the "Washington Consensus" of liberalized trade and investment was adopted, the contrast is striking: from 1960 to 1980, income per person grew by 75 percent. Summers seems to be excluding Africa, where per capita income grew by 36 percent from 1960 to 1980 but has since fallen by about 15 percent. Some of the "emerging markets" of Asia (China, Indonesia, South Korea) have in fact grown rapidly over the last twenty years, but they also grew rapidly in the previous decades. And even these countries are mainly the exceptions that prove the rule: the "crony capitalists" who have largely disregarded Washington's advice; and China, a country that does not have convertible currency, maintains state control of its banking system, and allows little foreign ownership in equity markets.

All this simply evaluates the globalization effort on the terms of its proponents: the growth of per capita income. But that is merely the most basic measure of economic progress; it says nothing about the distribution of income, which has also worsened both within and between countries as globalization has proceeded, or environmental destruction, the loss of biodiversity, labor or human rights, or any of the other issues raised by the protesters in Seattle.

For most commentators, however, these questions do not arise, because the entire process is seen through a prism of technological and market determinism. Their narrative is a simple one: the poorer countries are passing through stages that we completed in the last century. Child labor, poverty-level wages, intolerable levels of pollution—these are things that will recede with development, helped along by trade and inflows of foreign investment. But in fact no nation has ever pulled itself out of poverty under the conditions that Washington currently imposes on underdeveloped countries. Economists have long known that markets by themselves—whether international or domestic—would not accomplish the task of economic development. Although there have been many paths to development, virtually all have required a host of interventions by the state deliberately designed to alter the comparative advantage of the national economy. The protection of northern manufacturing was a major cause of our own civil war, with the southern slaveholders unsuccessfully trying to raise the banner of free trade. And the few countries that have successfully industrialized after Europe and America—such as Japan, South Korea, Taiwan—have, as latecomers, needed much higher levels of protection, planning, industrial policy, and other measures. Such policies are now increasingly prohibited.

This raises another crucial question: even if our political leaders were right, and the current miseries of globalization were but a temporary hurdle on the road to economic progress, how should this process be directed? The WTO, the IMF, and the World Bank—the three most important international economic institutions—are often described as "institutions of global governance." But in practice they are much more of a global anti-government, unaccountable to any electorate. Indeed one does not need a conspiracy theory to notice the progressive transfer of economic decision-making from governments to unelected bureaucrats.

Ironically, the WTO is the least controlling of the three institutions; the IMF and the World Bank, still flying mostly below radar, are invested with vastly greater and more autocratic powers. The Fund, which has 182 member nations but is basically run by the U.S. Treasury Department, makes the major economic decisions for more than fifty countries. To get a feel for what it is like to be one of the IMF's clients, imagine that London or Paris had to approve Alan Greenspan's latest term as chairman of the Federal Reserve, the Fed's decisions every six weeks on interest-rate policy, the director of the Office of Management and Budget, and the major legislation considered by the House and Senate finance committees. This makes the Fund one of the most powerful institutions, of any kind, in the whole world. And most of the time the Fund exercises this power without having to lend very much money; IMF approval is a prerequisite for other sources of multilateral credit and for most private credit as well.

Washington is very attached to this arrangement. To take just one example: in the summer of 1997, when the Thai currency began to fall and the Asian financial crisis was just beginning, the Japanese government offered to set up a fund that would provide the necessary guarantees to stem the hemorrhaging of capital. As the major foreign banks were well aware, this was exactly what was needed; a panic was setting in, foreign currency reserves were dangerously low throughout the region, and investors were selling local currencies just to get out before they fell further. China, Taiwan, Hong Kong, Singapore, and other countries offered support for a $100 billion fund to stabilize these currencies. But the idea did not sit well with Treasury, and Larry Summers (then deputy secretary) was quickly dispatched to Asia to kill it. The orders from Washington were clear: any bailout would have to go through the IMF, with results that turned out to be an economic and human disaster.

For now, Washington's globalist agenda has been stopped dead in its tracks. Not coincidentally, ever since NAFTA created the first public debate on U.S. foreign economic policy, every major administration initiative to extend its principles has failed, including fast-track authority for the president to negotiate new trade and commercial agreements, the Free Trade Area of the Americas, and the Multilateral Agreement on Investment. Then there was the collapse of the Millennium Round of the WTO in Seattle. [. . .]

The world's financial and corporate elite have reason to be concerned. But their warnings of worldwide economic malaise brought on by a backlash against globalization, their visions of a world on the brink of slipping into protectionist, isolationist chaos—as if no one would engage in trade or foreign investment unless they were bound by Washington's rules—are self-serving and overblown. Here is a more likely scenario: The collapse of the globalist agenda will be followed by a more honest and inclusive debate over international economic integration. As the iron grip of insti-tutions such as the IMF and the World Bank is loosened, much of humanity will be freed to pursue new experiments; some of the many possible paths to social and economic develop-ment that have been blocked for so long will open up. The demise of the Washington con-sensus will give rise to new hopes and oppor-tunities for a better world.

1.6

Alternatives to
Economic Globalization

International Forum on Globalization

Society is at a crucial crossroads. A peaceful, equitable and sustainable future depends on the outcome of escalating conflicts between two competing visions: one corporate, one democratic.

[. . .]

[W]e have seen tens of thousands and, in some cases in Asia, millions of people marching in protest, or attempting to block the meetings and plans for accelerated economic globalization. In the past two years, giant protests have taken place in the United States, Canada, Mexico, Brazil, Argentina, Venezuela, France, Germany, Italy, England, India, the Philippines, New Zealand, Australia, Kenya, South Africa, Thailand, Malaysia, and Indonesia, with many smaller events in other countries. The protests typically include huge numbers of environmentalists, labor activists, small farmers and peasants, religious organizations of many stripes, consumer groups, women's organizations, human rights activists, AIDS and other health activists, indigenous people, small businesses and artisanal producers, opponents of military globalization and corporate control of space, prison reform groups, and a smattering of anarchists.

These are joined by countless individuals deeply concerned about livelihoods, their communities, and the erosion of democratic institutions. In fact, it is one of the more remarkable characteristics of the anti-globalization movement that it has so many streams of engagement, reflecting different interests and regions, that nonetheless align and converge into a much broader and more powerful force.

All of these groups and individuals argue that global economic elites have appropriated from citizens and local and national governments the rights to determine their own economic options, and to nurture them. They charge they have been excluded from any meaningful democratic participation in this new model, imposed from the top down.

They assert that the model is marginalizing millions of people; increasing poverty rather than decreasing it; harming the global South, not helping it; and bringing a host of new health and disease crises combined with world-wide environmental problems that threaten the balance of nature. They see many of these problems as intrinsic to the global economic design, requiring drastic revision or abandonment.

Despite repeated entreaties from political and corporate leaders, opposition groups and millions of people clearly do *not* trust the global elite decision-making process as being legitimate, and view it as mainly in the service of cor-

International Forum on Globalization, Alternatives Task Force, excerpt from *Alternatives to Economic Globalization*, Interim Report (San Francisco, July 2001), 1–2, 6–10, www.ifg.org.

porate power. The opposition is demanding not only a place at the table, but a new table with new rules, and new processes that feature entirely different hierarchies of values, goals, plans and structures of governance. These opponents of globalization do not view their opposition as utopian; they view the present model as a utopia for global corporations and for no-one else, and that it has failed to live up to its advertising.

[. . .]

. . . [B]eyond specific achievements, the movement has catalyzed a new larger "democracy movement" that is growing both within countries, as well as among citizen organizations globally. In India it is being called a "living democracy" movement that views democracy through the prism of local empowerment and community control of resources. In Canada, hundreds of organizations have articulated a new "Citizens' Agenda" that has attempted to wrest control of governmental institutions back away from corporations. In Chile, coalitions of environmental groups have created a powerful Sustainable Chile movement that seeks to reverse Chile's drift toward neoliberalism and reassert control of national priorities and resources. Similar movements have blossomed in Brazil, focused especially on the rights of the poor and landless; in Bolivia, where a mass peasant movement has blocked the privatization of water; in Mexico, where Mayans have reignited the spirit of Zapata as they seek confirmation of indigenous rights to land and resources; in France, where farmers have risen up in revolt against the rules of trade that threaten to destroy small scale farming; in England, where construction of new highways through the rural landscape have brought hundreds of thousands of people out to march, blaming globalization and its need for high speed transport as the cause of this unnecessary invasion.

Other such movements have been springing up across the planet—some are local in nature; others are national; others are international—but they link together in the common assertion of the illegitimacy and the false promise of corporate-led globalization, and the need to drastically diminish the powers of its dominant corporate-run institutions, while revitalizing democracy at the national, regional and local levels.

[. . .]

Eight Principles
for an Alternative Agenda

The current organizing principles of the governing institutions of the global economy are narrow and serve the few at the expense of the many and the environment. Economic growth has been the central goal of the International Monetary Fund (IMF), the World Bank, and the General Agreement on Tariffs and Trade (GATT), as well as its successor, the WTO. The expansion of international trade and investment flows has been viewed as an end in itself.

The governing formula of the past half century has been: unfettered trade and investment will bring prosperity, which will bring democracy. This formula has guided the declarations of U.S. presidents from Truman to Bush as well as the policy pronouncements of most leaders the world over, particularly since the early 1980s. The persistent mantra of corporate and government leaders alike has been that the necessity of remaining competitive in a global economy requires governments to cut regulations and to encourage the most favorable climate for foreign investment, often at the cost of worker rights and environmental integrity. In the words of Council of Canadians chair Maude Barlow: "Stateless corporations have given rise to corporate states."

Healthy societies are rooted in certain core principles. The following eight core principles have been put forward in various citizen programs that are emerging around the world. Economic policies, rules, and institutions should seek to further these principles:

A. New Democracy/Popular Sovereignty

The rallying cry of the amazing diversity of civil society that converged in Seattle in late 1999 was the simple word "democracy." Democracy flourishes when people organize to protect their communities and rights and hold their elected officials accountable. For the past two decades, governments have transferred much of their sovereignty to the hands of global corporations. We advocate a shift from governments serving corporations to governments serving people and communities, a process which is easier at the local level but vital at all levels of government.

We use the terms "new democracy" and "living democracies" in part because "democracy" is equated in so many minds with elections alone. We would like to focus more attention on the dynamic processes initiated by civil society organizations around the world to instill new energy and meaning into democracy movements. In some countries, primarily in the South, these movements focus on winning community control over natural resources. In other countries, mainly in the North, movements are striving to refocus government agendas on a citizens agenda of rights.

B. Favoring the Local/Subsidiarity

Economic globalization entails first, and foremost, de-localization and disempowerment of communities and local economies. A high percentage of people on the earth still survive through local, community-based activities: small scale farming, local markets, local production for local consumption. This has enabled them to remain directly in control of their economic and food security, while also maintaining the viability of local communities and cultures. Even in developed countries, most livelihoods have traditionally been connected to local economic production. Economic globalization is rapidly dismantling this, strongly favoring economies based on export, with global corporations in control. This brings destruction of local livelihoods, local jobs, and community self-reliance.

It is therefore necessary to reverse directions and create new rules and structures that consciously favor the local, and follow the principle of subsidiarity, i.e., whatever decisions and activities can be undertaken locally should be. Whatever power can reside at the local level should reside there. Only when additional activity is required that cannot be satisfied locally, should power and activity move to the next higher level: region, nation, and finally the world. Policies such as "site here to sell here" and the grounding of capital locally should be codified. Economic structures should be designed to move economic and political power downward toward the local, rather than in a global direction. (In Europe, calls by IFG members and others for globalization to be replaced by more emphasis on protecting and rebuilding local economies has had its first political success. United Kingdom Green Members of the European Parliament were elected in 1999 on a manifesto that called for the "Protect the Local, Globally" route to localization.)

C. Ecological Sustainability

Economic globalization is intrinsically harmful to the environment, as it is based on ever-increasing consumption, exploitation of resources, and waste-disposal problems. One of its most important elements, export-oriented production, is especially damaging as it directly increases global transport activity, fossil fuel use, refrigeration and packaging, while requiring very costly and ecologically damaging new infrastructures: ports, airports, dams, canals, etc. It also accelerates conversion to industrial-style agriculture with corresponding increases in pesticides, water and air pollution, and biotechnology. Such elements, combined with many other wasteful aspects of global trade, are also powerful contributors to the problems of global climate change, ozone depletion, loss of habitat, and unprecedented levels of pollution. Viable alternatives must be rooted in the principle of ecological sustainability.

D. Human Rights

In 1948, governments of the world came together to adopt the United Nations Universal Declaration on Human Rights, which established certain core rights, such as "a standard of living adequate for . . . health and well-being . . ., including food, clothing, housing and medical care, and necessary social services, and the right to security in the event of unemployment." Building on this Declaration, governments negotiated two covenants in subsequent decades, one on political and civil rights and another on economic, social, and cultural rights.

Much of the past half century has been a struggle by people to press their governments to advance these rights. These rights remain as central to human development today as they did 53 years ago. The goal of trade and investment should be to enhance the quality of life and the respect of core labor, social, and other rights.

We believe it is the duty of governments to insure these rights, not only the political and civil rights, but also the economic, social and cultural rights. This has major implications. For example, . . . we believe that every person has the right to clean and safe water. That leads us to conclude that water should not be commodified or privatized and that it is the obligation of government to manage municipal water supplies. We recognize that many governments are corrupt and unaccountable, but this does not lead us to the conclusion that the private sector is a better guarantor of rights. Rather, it reaffirms our resolve to press accountability on government at every level.

Some have suggested that this principle of human rights can come into conflict with the second principle: that of "favoring the local/subsidiarity." The reasoning is that some local societies have instituted laws that violate human rights, such as female genital mutilation and other violations of the right against gender discrimination. We believe that when these two principles clash, then universal human rights should trump local assertion of authority that violates those rights.

E. Jobs/Livelihood/Employment

The United Nations Universal Declaration on Human Rights affirms everyone's "right to work, to free choice of employment, to just and favorable conditions of work, and to protection against unemployment". It also affirms that everyone "has the right to form and to join trade unions." Over the past 8 decades, the UN International Labor Organization has elaborated over one hundred conventions that further specify basic labor rights. Yet that same organization points out that today around 30 percent of workers are unemployed or seriously underemployed. Many of those who work do so under brutally exploitative and dangerous conditions.

One of the most dynamic social movements confronting corporate-led globalization is organized labor, which has gathered over one hundred million workers around the world into trade unions. Millions more join together in associations of informal sector workers. These movements, rooted in a struggle for these core rights, are a cornerstone of the social movements that are creating economic alternatives.

Hence, sustainable societies must both protect the rights of workers and address the livelihood needs of the 30 percent of humanity that has no work or is seriously underemployed. The reversal of globalization policies that displace farmers from their land and fisherfolk from their coastal

ecosystems are central to the goal of a world where all can live and work in dignity.

F. Food Security and Food Safety

Communities and nations are stable and secure when people have enough food, particularly when nations can provide their own food. People also want safe food, a commodity that is increasingly scarce as global agribusiness firms spread chemical- and biotech-intensive agriculture around the world.

Some of the strongest citizen movements around the world are now fighting the juggernaut of globalized industrial agriculture. Monopoly control of food and seeds among a small number of corporations now threatens millions of farmers and tens of millions of peoples' food security and safety. Global rules of trade now strongly favor the industrial agriculture model, rapidly destroying small scale farmers who mainly produce staple foods for local consumption. Globalized industrial agriculture is driving small farmers off their lands and replacing them with pesticide and machine-intensive monocultures producing luxury items for export, at great environmental and social cost. And, biotechnology brings a host of new ecological and health risks.

Any new rules of trade must recognize that food production for local communities should be at the top of a hierarchy of values in agriculture. Local self-reliance in food production, and the assurance of healthful, safe foods should be considered basic human rights. Shorter distances and reduced reliance on expensive inputs which must be shipped over long distances are key objectives of a new food system paradigm.

G. Equity

Texas populist Jim Hightower often quotes his father: "Son, everyone does better when everyone does better." Greater equity reinforces both democracy and healthy communities. Economic globalization, under the current rules, has widened the gap between rich and poor countries and between rich and poor within most countries. The social dislocation and tension which result have become one of the greatest threats to peace and security the world over.

Reducing the growing gap between rich and poor nations requires first and foremost the cancellation of the illegitimate debts of poor countries. And, it requires the replacement of the current institutions of global governance with new ones that include global fairness among their operating principles.

Reducing income and wealth gaps within nations will involve a series of steps to both pull up the bottom and establish caps at the top. A century ago, U.S. financier J.P. Morgan insisted that a company's top executive should not make more than 20 times the lowest paid worker. In the year 2000 in the United States, the average CEO made 517 times the income of the average worker. There are a plethora of policy options to improve the incomes of both industrial and rural workers. And, there are sensible proposals to remove incentives that encourage excessive executive pay.

H. Cultural, Biological, Economic and Social Diversity

A few decades ago, it was still possible to leave home and go somewhere else where the architecture was different, the landscape was different, the language, lifestyle, dress, and values were different. Today, farmers and filmmakers in France and India, and millions of people elsewhere, are protesting to maintain that diversity. Tens of thousands of communities around the world had perfected local resource management systems that worked, but that are being undermined by corporate-led globalization. Cultural, biological, social, and economic diversity are central to a dignified, interesting, and healthy life.

Note

The drafting committee of the IFG Alternatives Task Force consists of Maude Barlow, Walden Bello, John Cavanagh, Tony Clarke, Edward Goldsmith, Randy Hayes, Colin Hines, Martin Khor, David Korten, Sara Larrain, Jerry Mander, Helena Norberg-Hodge, Simon Retallack, Vandana Shiva, Victoria Tauli-Corpus, and Lori Wallach.

The New Internationalism

John J. Sweeney

For the last two decades, U.S. economic policy has been devoted to the creation of the global market. Trade accords tore down barriers. Global agreements protected property and investment. Public institutions, from the IMF and the World Bank, to the Ex-Im Bank and OPIC, provided subsidy and incentive—carrots and sticks—to integrate countries into the process.

Today, we experience the blessings as well as the bane of that effort. Communication sends instant messages across the world. Transport girds the globe. Production, marketing, distribution networks are international in reach. This global market is dominated, not surprisingly, by a handful of great transnational corporations. They claim a steadily growing share of global commerce—one-third of all manufacturing exports, three-fourths of commodity trade, four-fifths of the trade in technology and services. The market is fueled and foiled by de-regulated capital transactions, with over a trillion dollars a day changing hands in foreign exchange markets, many times that needed to finance trade or real investment.

The power of this market is apparent. The totalitarian states of the Soviet bloc could not withstand it. Europe's social democracies, now seeking shelter in a European Union, retreat before it. The state capitalist tigers of East Asia—the poster children of the global economy—have been leveled virtually overnight by its changing tides.

I suggest to you that we are now at an historic turning. As the Asian collapse makes clear, the challenge now is no longer how to create a global market, but how to put sensible boundaries on the market that already exists. How to make the market work for the majority and not simply for the few. How to protect us from its excesses.

The drive to forge the global market was led primarily from the suites—the plush offices of banks and corporations, the comfortable seminar rooms of the foreign policy community. The new internationalism—the drive to make this economy work for people, to secure basic worker and human rights, environmental and consumer protections, sensible anti-trust and financial regulation—is being driven from the streets. And signs of that are everywhere.

In Chaing Mai, Thailand two months ago, thousands of children began a global march against child labor. Delegations came from the Philippines, Bangladesh, and Indonesia where 8 and 10 year olds work 14 hour days for eight to ten pennies an hour. They sew the shirts, and hammer rivets into the jeans worn by youngsters their own age in our country.

John J. Sweeney, AFL-CIO president, excerpt from "The New Internationalism," speech to the Council on Foreign Relations, New York, 1 April 1998, 1–7, www.aflcio.org/publ/speech1998/sp0401.htm.

In Michigan, mothers were stunned when their children grew sick from uninspected, imported vegetables. The Clinton Administration immediately scrambled to increase funding for America's food and drug agencies.

In Mexico, workers in Tijuana's Han Young truck assembly plant finally won recognition for an independent trade union. One of Mexico's notorious maquiladoras, the Han Young factory paid workers 4 dollars a day; for many just getting to and from the plant consumed one-third of their wages. Most were not given masks to protect themselves from suffocating smoke. The plant initially fired the labor activists. But after hunger strikes, legal action, U.S. demonstrations outside of Hyundai showrooms, and international protests, the company—and the Mexican Labor Ministry—are now being compelled to confront the legitimate demands for an independent union.

On Wall Street, investors wonder at the sudden decline of Nike. The "swoosh" is everywhere, hawked by Michael Jordan, Tiger Woods and gaggles of other celebrities. Yet, consumers are turning away from Nike shoes and choosing others like New Balance. Part of the reason for Nike's fall from grace may well be that consumers are voting against Nike's labor practices—given notoriety by Doonesbury cartoons, human rights campaigns, campus protests, and Internet alarms.

Now, at the height of the new global economy, those who know it best are the most worried, for they understand how close to global deflation we were and are. In the wake of the Asian collapse, thoughtful and independent men like George Soros have called for dramatic reforms to limit speculative capital flows.

Will U.S. leaders and the foreign policy community—and the policy elite of other governments—embrace a new internationalism, and make it a centerpiece of policy, thought, and social invention? Or will they continue to see it as a distraction or worse.

Too often, of course, the struggles to create a new approach have been dismissed as protectionist. Those who reach this too simple conclusion fail to understand that working men and women will no longer accept this intellectual double standard. Laws that protect property and copyright are deemed part of a free market system, but those that protect worker and human rights are labeled reactionary. Efforts to free up capital flows are viewed as essential, while efforts to limit their wanton excess dismissed as retrograde.

I believe this attitude must change—and change quickly. Foreign and economic policy makers must see themselves as "present at the creation"—to borrow from Dean Acheson—devising new, accountable ways to impose sensible rules for the global economy.

The new internationalism cannot long be deferred, for two central reasons.

First, an untrammeled global economy is morally, and ultimately politically, indefensible. Treasury Secretary Robert Rubin has correctly warned about the "moral hazard" of IMF programs that bail out profligate speculators from their bad debts, encouraging them to gamble again.

But too little has been said about the "immoral hazard" of forcing working people to pay for the follies of others. There is, I am aware, a furious debate about whether the global economy produces a race to the bottom, or provides the basis for sustainable development. For many years, the Asian tigers were held up as proof of the potential benefits of the latter. Now starvation and food riots plague Indonesia. Mass unemployment faces workers in Korea and Thailand. Wage gains of a decade have been wiped out in a moment.

But whatever you believe about economic development, the combination of competitive global corporations and weak governments leads to conditions—a return to the dark Satanic mills of the early industrial age—that cannot withstand scrutiny.

Recently, a Vice President of the AFL-CIO, also a former garment worker, Clayola Brown, returned from Bangladesh. There Tommy Hilfiger, the GAP, Wal-Mart and K-Mart are opening factories, in flight from the higher wages of Hong Kong, Thailand and even China. Over 2100 factories employ 1.3 million workers. 85% are women or young girls. Children as young as seven work twenty hours a day in garment factories. The minimum wage is 23 dollars a month, but employers are urging the government to devalue the currency to stay ahead of their Asian competitors.

Burma is now ruled by a grim military dictatorship that keeps its economy afloat with a mix of drug trafficking and forced labor, labor that is clearing the land in preparation for the construction of a major multinational gas pipeline.

In China, a recent report by the National Labor Committee documents the fact that U.S. companies actually lower standards in China, slashing wages, eliminating benefits, imposing forced overtime. Factories producing garments for export to the US require that workers labor 12 to 18 hour days, six and seven days a week, for 13 to 23 cents an hour.

Some argue that child labor is a necessity for poor countries, and that attempts to ban it are a form of Western chauvinism. Others claim that enforcing internationally recognized, core labor rights—the right to organize, to bargain collectively, to strike—is interventionist, while imposing U.S. defined rules of copyright, and corporate law is free trade

Here is the simple truth: No society benefits from exploiting its children rather than educating them. No society benefits from impoverishing its working men and women rather than empowering them. No culture or creed can long condone slave labor, sweatshop labor, the imprisonment of workers seeking to organize trade unions.

And civilized opinion will not long accept the smooth rationales and ignore the harsh realities.

The Asia collapse suggests a second, compelling reason why we must turn to a new internationalist vision of making the global economy work for working people. That reason is economic necessity.

Look around the world. Europe struggles with slow growth and high unemployment. Russia and the East have yet to recover from their deep depression. Africa is largely written off. Latin America witnesses rising inequality, and roller coaster instability. Asia—the one area of growth and buoyancy—is now reeling. Japan seems mired in stagnation. This global economy is not working very well for most people.

[. . .]

You don't have to believe we are on the verge of global deflation to understand that Henry Ford was right. A prosperous economy requires that workers be able to buy the products that they produce. This is as true in a global economy as a national one. Labor rights, environmental standards, human rights are morally compelling. But they are also economic imperatives.

This combination of moral outrage and economic necessity is already transforming the debate in Washington and elsewhere. From Seoul to Peoria, popular reaction is building. The cur-

rent, laissez faire, corporate defined internationalism cannot be sustained. If we fail to understand this political and social reality and continue to blindly follow the free market ideologues, we will reap a whirlwind of ugly, destructive reaction.

. . . [T]here were many, from the right as well as the left, who opposed the passage of any further trade accords. On the right, nationalists call for abandoning the World Trade Organization as a threat to sovereignty. The AFL-CIO and the new internationalists hold a different position. We argue that trade accords must enforce core labor rights and environmental standards. Last year, instead of forging a reform coalition, the administration and the business community tried to roll the opposition. They failed.

On new funding for the International Monetary Fund, there are many, conservative as well as liberal, who argue that the IMF is more quack than cure, that its prescriptions are spreading the very plague it claims to cure. Conservatives argue that the market can solve the Asian crisis on its own.

The AFL-CIO and most progressives understand that doing nothing is too big a risk. We support public intervention to avoid depression, and limit the damage to working people. But the IMF's current practices create both the moral and the immoral hazard I spoke of before. We urged reforms in the IMF as a condition of expanding its funding. The administration accepted some change begrudgingly, but to date has been blocked by growing opposition on the right.

[. . .]

I believe it essential the United States put its weight behind a new internationalist progressive reform agenda. The charisma of the president, the logic of the Treasury Secretary, the force of U.S. influence and creativity should be moving now to define basic reforms, to enlist other nations in supporting them and bolstering citizen and workers movements that are demanding them.

The U.S. should be leading the way in making basic internationally recognized worker rights, environmental and consumer standards central to the global trading and investment regimes. IMF conditionality, World Bank loans, OPIC and Ex-Im Bank activities, and A.I.D. programs should be under review as we seek ways to write new rules for the global market.

Secretary Rubin is right that we need a new architecture for global capital and currency markets. But greater transparency is merely a pre-condition, not an answer.

We need to find ways to regulate capital flows as George Soros and others have suggested, and to slow short-term speculation, perhaps with a small transaction tax, as Nobel prize winner James Tobin has argued.

The U.S. should be pushing its European and Japanese allies to join with us to define new regulations—enforceable codes of conduct—on global corporations' behavior abroad. We should be aiding governments, worker and citizen movements to stand up for sensible rules, not forcing them to back down.

We have faced similar challenges before. At the beginning of this century, the great corporations and trusts forged a national market and an industrial economy. Then as now, the wrenching transition produced stark accumulations of wealth and power, generated booms and busts, displaced workers and farmers, sparked upheaval and protest.

Progressives of that era joined to organize unions, extend democracy, and impose new rules to make the economy work for people— food and drug standards, antitrust regulation, fair labor standards, a ban on child labor—and eventually, labor rights, social security, consumer and environmental standards.

These reforms did not come easily. They were not granted by the generosity of those Roosevelt called the "malefactors of great wealth." They met fierce resistance. They required worker organizing, citizen movements, a crusading press, leaders willing to challenge powerful trusts. We now face that same challenge once again, only this time at a global level.

All this may sound impossible. But we have seen the power of an idea whose time has come. We saw it in Selma, Alabama. We saw it in Gdansk. In Soweto. In recent months, we've seen it on the streets of Paris, of Bonn, of Brasilia. In the support given public workers in France and UPS workers in the US. In the courage of the Korean unions. In the shining faces of the children marching for the right to a childhood. Across the world, working men and women are striving to defend their dignity in the face of those who know the price of everything and the value of nothing. Now, American creativity and resourcefulness should enlist in furthering their quest, not frustrating it.

1.8

General Principles and Gender
Hemispheric Social Alliance

The Hemispheric Social Alliance brings together a broad range of organizations from throughout the Americas united by the conviction that any form of economic integration among our nations must serve first and foremost to promote equitable and sustainable development for all of our peoples. The members of the HSA, whether labor unions or environmentalists, family farmers or scholars, have been working for years to oppose the implementation of neoliberal policies in our respective countries. In addition to our shared critique of the negative impacts of that model, we are united by our conviction that we must move forward with both feet, combining protest with proposal, developing a common vision about what an alternative form of integration might look like. This document expresses our determination to construct an alternative to the Free Trade Area of the Americas (FTAA) based on the proposals described herein.
[. . .]

General Principles

No country can nor should remain isolated from the global economy. This does not mean, however, that the current "neo-liberal" or free market approach to globalization is the only, much less the best, form of economic integration.

This dominant free market approach (embodied in the North American Free Trade Agreement, large multinational corporations' negotiating agenda for the Free Trade Area of the Americas, the World Trade Organization, and the failed Multilateral Agreement on Investment) argues that the global market on its own will allocate and develop the best possibilities for each country. Thus, free trade does not simply involve opening ourselves to global trade; it also entails renouncing our role as active subjects in determining our future, and instead allowing the market to decide the future for us. According to this view, it is unnecessary for us to envision the kind of nation we want to be or could be. We only need to eliminate all obstacles to global trade, and the market itself will take on the task of offering us the best of all possible worlds.

The difference between this dominant approach and the alternative vision presented in this document lies not in whether we accept the opening of our economies to trade. The two fundamental differences are the following: 1) whether to have a national plan we can fight for or let the market determine the plan, and 2) whether capital, especially speculative capital, should be subject to international regulation. The recent trend has been to allow all capital, even speculative capital, free rein, and let the world follow capital's interests. We argue

Hemispheric Social Alliance, "General Principles" and "Gender," in *Alternatives for the Americas*, prepared for the Second People's Summit of the Americas (Quebec City, April 2001), 1, 6–7, and 64–69.

that history has demonstrated that the market on its own does not generate development, let alone social justice. In contrast, we propose a world economy regulated at the national and supra-national levels in the interest of peace, democracy, sustainable development and economic stability.

[. . .]

We are not opposed to the establishment of rules for regional or international trade and investment. Nor does our criticism of the dominant, externally imposed form of globalization imply a wish to return to the past, to close our economies and establish protectionist barriers, or to press for isolationist trade policies. But the current rules have not helped our countries overcome, nor even reduce, our economic problems. We propose alternative rules to regulate the global and hemispheric economies that are based on a different economic logic: that trade and investment should not be ends in themselves, but rather the instruments for achieving just and sustainable development. Our proposal also promotes a social logic that includes areas such as labor, human rights, the environment, and minorities—that is, previously excluded issues and people.

While our critique and proposal have a technical basis, they also spring from an ethical imperative. We refuse to accept the market as a god which controls our lives. We do not accept the inevitability of a model of globalization which excludes half or more of the world's population from the benefits of development. We do not accept that environmental degradation is the inevitable and necessary evil accompanying growth. We will not easily come to the position that economic measures applied in recent years throughout the Americas are the only way to set an economy on the right path.

A profound ethical imperative pushes us to propose our own model of society, one supported by the many men and women united in hope for a more just and humane society for themselves and future generations.

[. . .]

Gender

The process of globalization, financial integration, freer trade, and investment has profoundly transformed the lives of women in the Americas.

Globalization policies have been preceded by national adjustment proposals, the privatization of state enterprises, the restructuring of the employment policies from secure employment to flexible, temporary work, the relaxation of labor laws, the relaxation of tariffs and quotas which leads to the opening of markets (which tend to benefit Northern companies and bring "free" trade to countries of the South). The World Bank (WB) and the International Monetary Fund (IMF) have created an unjust packet of neoliberal policies called Structural Adjustment Policies (SAPs) that they have imposed as a model on poor nations.

Women in the Americas (both North and South) have seen their wages decline and their workloads double because of trade liberalization. Women are not only affected by global trade rules but are affecting the process of global trade by the ways in which they participate: as workers, producers, and consumers. The ways in which they participate are affected by class, race, ethnicity, sexual orientation, age, ability, religion and other aspects of identity as well as by nation and gender. Yet, in many ways, globalization and freer trade have exacerbated existing gender inequalities and deepened asymmetrical power relations between men and women in the Americas.

Trade rules are based on traditional neoliberal economic theories and macro-economic policies that are gender-blind and fail to take into account women's unpaid household work or unequal access to resources such as credit, land, education, and health services. The United Nations estimates that the global value of women's unpaid work is equal to 11 trillion dollars a year. This unpaid work—maintaining a household, caring for children and the elderly, and building community ties—is extraordinarily valuable. The fact that women's contributions are unrecognized in the market/formal sector leads to their being over-worked. Failure to recognize the economic and social contributions of women's unpaid work affects women's opportunities in public life, their status in society, their social development and their ability to exercise their human rights.

IMF/WB SAPs depend upon women's unpaid labor to cushion the impact of these adjustment policies. Governments have cut their domestic expenditures in order to pay off their loans. These cuts, largely in social spending, have led women to increase their workloads to respond to increasing prices of household goods and declining domestic food production. For example, women spend more time shopping for cheaper items, cultivating home gardens to supplement purchased goods, or walk rather than take public transport. Classical economic theories also assume that women's labor is "flexible," positing that women can be hired when the economy expands and dismissed when the economy contracts. This is because of an assumption that women are secondary wage-earners whose income supplements a household budget rather than supports it.

In the labor force, global trade rules offer both new opportunities and new problems for women. Much of the success of export-oriented growth is due to the large influx of women workers. Yet studies have shown that the transition to market economies is associated with a rise in occupational and sectoral segregation by sex. In Export Processing Zones (EPZs), women workers represent approximately 90 percent of the workforce although in some high-tech factories women are being dismissed and replaced by male workers. In the United States, 55 percent of temporary workers are women and 70 percent of all part-time workers are women.

Export-led growth strategies promoted in trade agreements in the Western Hemisphere employ a largely female workforce in low-paying, tedious, and precarious jobs. Women workers in the EPZs assemble garments, electronics, and other items for export abroad. Women work as many as 50–80 hours a week and earn just 56–77 cents an hour. These wages are often below the national minimum wage and are far below what a worker needs to provide food, electricity, and shelter for a family. Despite national economic growth in Mexico and El Salvador, wages have fallen for women workers in the EPZs.

These jobs often lack basic social protections and fail to uphold basic labor rights. Union organizing and women maquila workers who organize fellow workers are often barred in EPZs. Moreover, women workers in many factories have reported physical abuse, sexual harassment and violence, as well as mandatory pregnancy testing as a condition for employment. Yet because of the large pool of available low-waged labor, employers' have a great deal of power— any demands that women workers make could cost them their jobs.

Women also comprise the majority of workers in the lower levels of the service sector and are heavily concentrated in clerical, sales, financial, and service jobs that are regarded as "female" occupations. These jobs are considered less desirable than "male" jobs and pay lower wages.

Although women are entering the formal labor market in record numbers, they still face gender-based discrimination on many levels. On a basic level, too many women are concentrated in low-paying, low-skilled jobs that mirror tasks performed at home (cleaning, sewing, cooking, etc.). Regardless of what types of jobs women hold, they earn on average 75 percent of what men earn for comparable work around the world. The gap between men and women's wages varies widely. For example, men earn 25 percent more in the United States, 47 percent more in Brazil, 30 percent more in Chile, and 3 percent more in Costa Rica. Studies have shown that gendered wage differences remain even when men and women are similar in age, education, and years of work.

Many women, unable to afford child-care or failing to gain secure work in the formal sector, turn to the informal sector. In this sector, women can combine work and child-care although the work is poorly paid and tenuous. Workers in the informal markets range from street vendors to micro-entrepreneurs to crafts producers. Women vendors and crafts producers are vulnerable to global and national economic changes. Higher costs for materials and/or the influx of cheap imports as a result of new trade rules have decimated many women's craft sales.

Trade liberalization has also led to increased out-sourcing of work, where women will work out of their homes for a company and are paid a certain amount for each piece they complete. This type of work blurs the lines between formal and informal labor. These "home-based workers" are often paid less than EPZ workers and are not protected by national labor laws.

In rural areas as well, trade liberalization often strains women's ability to care for their families. Transnational corporations tend to promote one type of crop for export. This strategy of export promotion can destabilize the family farm, reduce the number of plants a family can grow for its own consumption, and cause men to emigrate from the rural areas to cities or other countries to find new jobs. While men move in search of jobs, women are left in the countryside to care for their families, work the farm, and maintain the household.

Women are also under-represented in decision-making structures that ratify multilateral trade policies. In Latin America and the Caribbean, women legislators comprise 9 percent of the seats in parliament (UNDP, 1999). In the United States, women comprise 12 percent and in Canada 23 percent of the seats in parliament. The dearth of women in decision-making positions severely limits their ability to influence the trade agreements which will have a large impact on their lives. In the WTO Dispute Settlement Body, only 12 (7.5 percent) are women.

Sustainable trade policies must reflect women's needs and concerns. Even World Bank studies show that rectifying gender inequities leads to economic growth, reduces market inefficiencies, and results in greater macroeconomic growth. Moreover, investing in women's welfare also positively impacts the lives of their families. Numerous studies have shown that as women's earnings increase, they invest a greater proportion of their earnings than men do into improving their children's nutrition, education, and general welfare. By investing in women today, we also invest in the next generation.

[. . .]

Guiding Principles

1. Structures and processes must be developed by trade negotiators to ensure women and representatives of women's organizations from all levels of society are included and engaged in trade debate. Women should be included in trade delegations and on dispute-resolution panels. Civil society groups, including women's groups, must be able to have their concerns reflected in the trade debate.

2. Women are affected differently by trade policies. The needs and concerns of all women, from various classes, ethnicities, races, geographical backgrounds, ages, sexual orientations, abilities and religions must be incorporated into the trade debate to ensure equitable trading policies leading to sustainable development. Therefore, it is important to guarantee access to a plurality of women's groups, including women's caucuses in labor unions, women's labor unions, and other grassroots organizations.

3. Political space to develop and propose alternatives to the current global trading model needs to be developed. Alternatives that reflect broader priorities than the market should be part of an on-going dialogue between trade negotiators, civil society organizations, and citizens about the goals and rules for global trade. For example, an official FTAA working group that examines how trade will affect women, social development, and human rights should be formed. This consultative group should rectify negative impacts of trade for women and relate to and inform all other FTAA Working Groups.

4. Trade agreements should not supercede international norms, covenants, and agreements which many countries have signed (such as the UN Convention to Eliminate All Forms of Discrimination Against Women (CEDAW), the UN Platform for Action from the UN Fourth Conference on Women, and the UN Declaration of Human Rights). Should there be a conflict between trade language and international treaties, then the international covenants should trump trade negotiations.

5. Women's myriad economic and social roles as well as women's cultural roles and women's paid and unpaid work need to be recognized.

6. Trade and investment should result in upwards harmonization for women and should be evaluated on a micro and macro level to assess the shifting balance of power and resources. This can result in increased benefits for all persons, including women and other previously underrepresented persons.

7. The positive benefits (externalities) of women's work caring for the household and children and elders should be factored into national GDP accounts or in "shadow" accounts.

Specific Objectives

Governments should:

1. Implement the UN 20/20 Initiative. The 20/20 Initiative requires each developing country to allocate 20 percent of its domestic budget, and every donor country to al-

locate 20 percent of its foreign aid to a country's social development programs including health care, education, access to safe water, basic sanitation, and basic reproductive health for all people.

2. Undertake a gender impact assessment of trade policy on women [. . .]
3. Integrate gender concerns, particularly the platform from Beijing and human rights treaties into all negotiations around and agreements on, investment and trade. In particular, include the Beijing Platform in Trade and Investment, which recognizes the economic, social, and cultural roles of women, especially regarding safeguards, intellectual property rights, economic authorship, and both paid and unpaid work. Gender should not be limited to one section of the negotiations, but rather, should be addressed as an overarching theme throughout investment and trade negotiations.
4. Government negotiators should develop and implement formal mechanisms for dialogue with women's groups about the impact of trade on women's lives and to accept their proposals for changes to agreements.
5. Establish policies and programs that ensure that child-care is affordable, accessible, and safe so that women with children who have to work outside of the home will be able to do so.
6. Develop and enforce laws, policies, and programs to remedy sexual harassment in the workplace. Foreign investors should be held accountable to domestic laws on sexual harassment, sex and pregnancy discrimination, job and/or wage discrimination, and other labor issues. Foreign investors should comply with international human rights standards.
7. Develop and enforce policies and laws that assure that women enjoy the full protection of civil, labor, reproductive, sexual, and human rights.

8. Increase communication and collaboration among women's bureaus, trade bureaus, labor bureaus, community groups, and other relevant parties when drafting trade agreements.
9. There should be concerted efforts to ensure that women benefit from some of the positive effects of globalization, such as the ability to communicate through the Internet, email, and other methods. It is imperative that women have increased access to computers, technology, and training.

Trade agreements and governments should:

1. Provide technical and development assistance that promotes education, technological training, capacity building, and skills development for women, particularly women who are displaced, or lose their livelihoods as a result of trade liberalization. Funds should be allocated to education, health, and labor programs that specifically have a gender component in a systematic and planned way.
2. Provide technical aid and development assistance to ensure that women have equal access to resources such as credit, technological training, as well as assets such as land.
3. Provide an analysis and assessment of how trade liberalization might affect women working in the informal sector.
4. Trade agreements should include mechanisms that protect small businesses from the influx of cheap imports.
5. Compensatory schemes, including retraining and capacity development should be included to support displaced workers.
6. Require foreign investors to comply with international codes of conduct and human rights standards and establish effective monitoring and enforcement of multi-national corporations that includes broad civil society participation.

1.9

The Death of the
Washington Consensus?

Robin Broad and John Cavanagh

Between the early 1980s and the late 1990s, an elite consensus swept the globe that unfettered free markets provided the formula to make rich countries out of poor. In policy circles, this formula came to be known as the "Washington Consensus."[1]

As we approach a new century, however, deep cracks have appeared within this consensus. Its legitimacy has come into question in the face of an increasingly effective citizens' backlash in North and South, and there is growing dissension within the ranks of its backers, as the effects of the financial crisis of the late 1990s are felt around the globe. While not yet dead, the consensus has been wounded—and potentially fatally so.

[. . .]

Hot Money

Over this past decade, the World Bank, the IMF, and the U.S. Treasury expanded their initial focus from the free trade and long-term investment stand of the consensus to the financial planks, pressing governments around the globe to open their stock markets and financial markets to short-term investments from the West.

Robin Broad and John Cavanagh, excerpt from "The Death of the Washington Consensus?" *World Policy Journal* 16, no. 3 (Fall 1999): 79, 82–85, and 87.

The resulting quick injections of capital from mutual funds, pension funds, and other sources propelled short-term growth in the 1990s, but also encouraged bad lending and bad investing.

Between 1990 and 1996, the amount of private financial flows entering poorer nations skyrocketed from $44 billion to $244 billion. Roughly half of this was long-term direct investment, but most of the rest—as recipient countries were soon to discover—was footloose, moving from country to country at the tap of a computer keyboard.

In mid-1997, as the reality of this short-sighted lending and investing began to surface, first in Thailand, then in South Korea, and then in several other countries, Western investors and speculators panicked. Their "hot money" fled much faster than it had arrived—leaving local economies without the capital they had come to depend on. Currency speculators like George Soros exacerbated the crisis by betting against the local currencies of the crisis nations, sending local currency values to new lows.

IMF advice seemed only to quicken the exodus of capital. Currencies and stock markets from South Korea to Brazil nosedived; and as these nations slashed purchases of everything from oil to wheat, prices of these products likewise plummeted. The financial crisis stalled production and trade in such large economies as Indonesia, Russia, South Korea, and Brazil, leaving in its wake widespread pain, dislocation, and environmental ruin. Exact figures are hard to come by, but the main international trade union federation estimates that, by the end of 1999, some 27 million workers in the five worst hit Asian countries—Indonesia, South Korea, Thailand, Malaysia, and the Philippines—will have lost their jobs.[7]

As economies collapsed, elite support for the Washington Consensus began to crumble. In the pages of the *Wall Street Journal*, former secretary of defense Robert McNamara likened the crisis to the Vietnam War, implying that then treasury secretary Robert Rubin, his deputy (and successor) Lawrence Summers, IMF managing director Michel Camdessus, and the other top managers had lost control.

Elite Dissent

Two sets of elite actors began launching critiques at [the U.S. Treasury and the IMF]—not quietly, but in a very public and vocal fashion, using the op-ed pages of the *New York Times*, the *Wall Street Journal*, and the *Washington Post* to make their cases. One group, led by such highly regarded free-trade economists as Jagdish Bhagwati of Columbia University, Paul Krugman of MIT, and World Bank chief economist Joseph Stiglitz, supports free markets for trade but not for short-term capital. (The group also includes such well-known Washington figures as Henry Kissinger.) Bhagwati argued that capital markets are by their nature unstable and require controls. Krugman outlined the case for exchange controls as a response to crisis.

However, as dramatically interventionist as some of their proposals are and as heated as the debate may sound, these critics largely seek to repair the cracks in the consensus—by allowing national exchange and/or capital controls under certain circumstances—not to tear down the entire edifice.

Some within this first set of consensus reformers have focused more on the folly of IMF policies during the crisis. Some prominent economists, such as Harvard's Jeffrey Sachs, himself once a proponent of "shock therapy" in Russia, faulted the IMF for prescribing recessionary policies that transformed a liquidity crisis into a full-fledged financial panic and subsequently into a collapse of the real economy in an expanding list of countries. "Instead of dousing the fire," Sachs wrote last year, "the IMF in effect screamed fire in the theater."[8] While still subscribing to the goal of free trade, Sachs and others argue that the IMF needs to revise its standard formula for economic reform, make its decisionmaking more transparent, and become more publicly accountable for the impact of its policies.

A second set of consensus dissidents goes further in criticizing the IMF, arguing for its abolition. The critique of this group is rooted in an extreme defense of free markets, and its members faulted the IMF for interfering in the markets. They charge that IMF monies disbursed to debtor governments end up being used to bail out investors, thus eliminating the discipline of risk (or "moral hazard") in private markets. This group is led by such long-time free trade supporters as the Heritage Foundation and the Cato Institute (whose opposition to publicly funded aid institutions is nothing new), but its ranks have recently swelled with such well-known, vocal converts as former Citicorp CEO Walter Wriston, former secretary of state George Shultz, and former secretary of the treasury William E. Simon.

These two camps of elite dissent within the consensus in the United States have their counterparts in other rich nations and among some developing country governments. West European economies, while not in the dire straits of Japan and much of the rest of the world, continue to be plagued by high unemployment, and their new joint currency, the euro, has gotten off to a shaky start. The European Union has also been involved in widely publicized trade disputes with the United States, several involving the European public's growing skepticism over genetically engineered foods.

As a result, a number of politicians in new center-left governments in Europe have raised their voices to question parts of the consensus. Even Clinton's closest ally, British prime minister Tony Blair, has a reform plan that includes a new intergovernmental global financial authority to help prevent future financial crises. Most West European governments support at least limited capital controls. And some members of the Canadian parliament are supporting an international tax on foreign currency transactions to discourage speculative transactions.

Japan is also looking for openings to rewrite parts of the consensus. The Japanese government has been both weakened and disillusioned by a decade of recession. Over the past two years, it has waged high-profile fights with the

United States over Japan's proposal to create an Asian economic fund to help countries in crisis (Japan lost), and over whether a Thai candidate backed by Japan and much of Asia, or a New Zealander backed by most of the West, should lead the World Trade Organization (a compromise was worked out).

In the developing world, there have also been a number of recent instances where elite actors have departed from specific aspects of consensus policies. In Hong Kong, long heralded by consensus adherents as a supreme example of free-market trade and finance policies, the government reacted to the crisis spreading through Asia by intervening in the stock market and acting to prevent currency speculation. Malaysia grabbed the world's attention in 1998 by imposing a series of capital and exchange controls that were successful in stemming short-term speculative flows. Several developing country governments have moved beyond their discontent over certain IMF prescriptions to openly question whether the World Trade Organization should heed American and European calls for new trade talks to further liberalize foreign investment rules and agricultural protections among member states.

The combination of these criticisms and actions has begun to influence even the IMF and the World Bank. In Indonesia, where the crisis has been particularly brutal, the IMF implicitly acknowledged that there were occasions when the costs of consensus policies were likely to be unacceptably high. Initially the IMF hung tough—until riots greeted the removal of price subsidies on fuel and precipitated a chain of events that actually led to the fall of the long-reigning Indonesian dictator Suharto.[9] In its dealings with the post-Suharto government, the fund responded to the pleas of the Jakarta government for increased social spending and the maintenance of subsidized prices for fuel, food, and other necessities.

The World Bank's president, James Wolfensohn, has taken small steps to distance himself and his institution from the more orthodox policies of the IMF. In 1997, he agreed to carry out a multicountry review of the bank's structural adjustment policies with several hundred NGOs led by the Development Group for Alternative Policies. And more recently, Wolfensohn's speeches and the bank's publications have included what amounts to blistering attacks on the social and environmental costs of consensus policies.

In the final analysis, however, these elite dissenters share a strategic goal: to salvage the overall message of the Washington Consensus while modifying the pillar of free capital flows. Indeed, the heat of the debate between these elite critics and consensus adherents Michel Camdessus of the IMF and Secretary of the Treasury Summers over capital mobility has made it easy for observers to overlook a key reality: the consensus still largely holds with respect to trade policy.

Cracks in the Consensus

Even though it is not the goal of the elite dissenters to kill the consensus, the appearance of any dissent at all is significant. Dissent from within ranks had been unheard of in the last two decades. Now, in their tinkering with the ten commandments of the consensus, and in their desire to capture the limelight, elite critics are not only undermining the legitimacy and credibility of the consensus but are also unwittingly opening the door to broader mass-based anti–free trade criticism. These elite critiques have opened cracks in the consensus in three key areas, cracks that could become deadly fissures at the hands of outside critics.

First, there is the question of in whose interests consensus policies are sculpted. The language some use in their elite critiques raises questions about the narrow interests that the consensus serves. Free-trade champion Jagdish Bhagwati, writing in *Foreign Affairs*, has decried free capital mobility across borders as the work of the "Wall Street-Treasury complex" (a term that builds on President Eisenhower's warnings of a "military-industrial complex").[10] Bhagwati points fingers at individuals who have moved between Wall Street financial firms and the highest echelons of the U.S. government and who, in Bhagwati's words, are "unable to look much beyond the interest of Wall Street, which it equates with the good of the world."[11] This should create ammunition for the outsider critique: if the U.S. Treasury (and international financial institutions) are not able to look beyond such narrow "special interests" in terms of capital, why should they be trusted to do so with broader economic policies?

Second, what goals should economic policies serve and who should determine these goals? One of the elite critics, the World Bank's Joseph Stiglitz, has recently begun to call for a "post-Washington Consensus" that moves beyond the narrow goal of economic growth to the more expansive goal of sustainable, equitable, and democratic development.[12] In speeches that have surprised many observers, Stiglitz argues that the debate over national economic policies and the debate over the new global economy must be democratized. For example, workers must be invited to sit at the table when their country's economic policies are being discussed in order to be able to argue against policies that hurt them. Outside critics need to push for Stiglitz's words to be turned into action. Why not invite workers—and environmentalists and farmers and others—who represent the broader national interests to participate?

Third, the elite dissenters are reigniting the Keynesian belief that the state has a legitimate role in development. Indeed, whatever comes of the global financial crisis, the widespread fear of an unregulated global casino that can devastate individual economies overnight is negating the consensus rejection of an activist state role. While most elite critics allow for a government role only in the realm of short-term financial flows, outside critics should exploit this crack to open up a larger debate about government intervention. With the acknowledgment that government is needed to check the markets on one front, there can be more intelligent debate over the role of government in other areas. The development debate, so lively in the 1960s and 1970s and so stifled in the 1980s and 1990s, can be revived.

[. . .]

Much as we would like to be town criers heralding the death of the Washington Consensus, such news is premature. Too many members of the policymaking elite, particularly in the United States, still cling to the precepts of the old consensus. While another global economic downturn would no doubt lend weight to the outsider critique, the future of these opposition proposals depends in the final analysis on the political sophistication of their proponents. Can citizen movements translate growing discontent into effective political pressure both at a national level and jointly in the WTO, the IMF, and the World Bank? Can they shift the debate beyond the confines of the free market dogma of the Washington Consensus?

In the closing months of the Second World War, a small group made up primarily of men from the richer countries sketched the architecture of the postwar global economy. The institutions they created are no longer serving the needs of the majority of people on earth. In the closing months of the twentieth century, there is at last the opportunity for a larger, more representative group to create new global rules and institutions for the twenty-first century. Indeed, since the Washington Consensus swept the globe two decades ago, the possibility of reading its obituary has never been greater.

Notes

1. The ten areas of consensus in terms of neoliberal, free-market policies, as noted by Williamson, are: "fiscal discipline" (i.e., policies to combat fiscal deficits); "public expenditure priorities" (to cut expenditures through the removal of subsidies, etc.); "tax reform"; "financial liberalization" (toward market-determined interest rates); competitive "exchange rates"; "trade liberalization" (to replace licenses with tariffs and to reduce tariffs); "foreign direct investment" (i.e., removing barriers); "privatization"; "deregulation" (of impediments to competition); and "property rights." See John Williamson, *The Progress of Policy Reform in Latin America*, Policy Analyses in International Economics, no. 28 (Washington, D.C.: Institute for International Economics, January 1990).

[. . .]

7. International Confederation of Free Trade Unions, *ICFTU Online*, January 21, 1999.

8. Jeffrey Sachs, "The IMF and the Asian Flu," *American Prospect*, March–April 1998, p. 17.

9. See Michael Shari, "Up In Smoke," *Business Week*, June 1, 1998, p. 66.

10. Jagdish Bhagwati, "The Capital Myth: The Difference Between Trade in Widgets and Dollars," *Foreign Affairs*, vol. 77 (May/June 1998), p. 7.

11. Bhagwati, "Capital Myth," p. 12.

12. Joseph Stiglitz, "More Instruments and Broader Goals: Moving toward the Post-Washington Consensus," 1998 World Institute for Development Economics Research annual lecture, Helsinki, Finland, January 7, 1998.

For Further Reading

There are several recently published readers that introduce the **debate between loosely defined "anti" and "pro" globalization forces** through reprints of published, secondary sources. *The Globalization Reader*, edited by Frank J. Lechner and John Boli (Malden, Mass.: Blackwell Publishers, 2000), does so by dividing globalization into economic, political, and cultural spheres. Another such introductory reader is *Globalization and the Challenges of a New Century* (Bloomington: Indiana University Press, 2000), edited by Patrick O'Meara, Howard Mehlinger, and Matthew Krain.

The following readings focus on specifics of the "worldviews" (and subsets within) analyzed in the introduction to this part: On current **protectionist** views, for an expansion of Patrick Buchanan's views, see his *A Republic, Not an Empire: Reclaiming America's Destiny* (Washington, D.C.: Regnery Publishing, 1999). For a **historical look** comparing "protectionism" in India and the early United States, see J. Ann Tickner's *Self-Reliance versus Power Politics: The American and Indian Experiences in Building Nation States* (New York: Columbia University Press, 1987). For a historical sweep that includes Frederick List and the German economic system, the United States and East Asia, see James Fallows's *Looking at the Sun: The Rise of the New East Asian Economic and Political Systems* (New York: Pantheon, 1994). For a reading on the history of the debate in the United States, see Dana Frank's *Buy American: The Untold Story of Economic Nationalism* (Boston: Beacon Press, 1999). And for a fascinating primary source, see Henry Clay's impassioned two-day speech extolling the virtues of protectionism ("Speech on Tariff," 30–31 March 1824 in *The Papers of Henry Clay*, vol. 3: *Presidential Candidate, 1821–1824*, edited by James F. Hopkins and Mary W. Hargreaves (Lexington: University of Kentucky Press, 1963), 683–730. Part II of the current book will include related sources on "import substitution industrialization" and on the so-called new international economic order.

One of the easiest ways to follow the **Washington Consensus and the mainstream free-market school** is through the web sites of the major institutions of economic globalization: the World Bank (www.worldbank.org), the IMF (www.imf.org), and the WTO (www.wto.org), as well as the key think tanks such as the Institute for International Economics (www.iie.org). Also illuminating are speeches and press releases from the U.S. Treasury Department (www.ustreas.gov). Writings by those I have termed the **ultra–free traders**, such as Meltzer, can be found through the web sites of think tanks such as the Cato Institute (www.cato.org), the American Enterprise Institute (www.aei.org), and the Heritage Foundation (www.heritage.org).

Thomas L. Friedman's *The Lexus and the Olive Tree: Understanding Globalization* (New York: Farrar, Straus, & Giroux, 1999) is often cited as the "classic" among the recent pro-globalization books. Nicholas D. Kristof and Sheryl WuDunn make an even more specific defense of "sweatshops" using China as a case study in *Thunder from the East: Portrait of a Rising Asia* (Knopf, 2000).

To follow the **"cracks" in the Washington Consensus**, see not only these "ultra–free traders" but also the much-discussed articles and speeches by Joseph Stiglitz, Stanford economist, former chief economist at the World Bank, and winner of the 2001 Nobel prize in economics. As of this writing, his work can still be found at www.worldbank.org/knowledge/chiefeconomist/stiglitz; among his key writings are "Back to Basics" (challenging the Washington Consensus regarding the East Asian crisis) and "Towards a New Paradigm" (in which he calls for a "post-Washington Consensus"). In addition to his more academic writing, see his scathing critique of the IMF in *The New Republic* (www.thenewrepublic.com/041700/stiglitz041700). The other mainstream economist who has authored useful critiques of the Washington Consensus is Harvard's Dani Rodrik: *Has Globalization Gone Too Far?* (Washington, D.C.: Institute for International Economics, 1997) and *The New Global Economy and Developing Countries: Making Globalization Work* (Washington, D.C.: Overseas Development Council Policy Essay no. 24, 1999), the latter distributed by Johns Hopkins University Press.

More detailed sources on the **citizen backlash** can be found in Parts III–V, as well as in the web site listing at the end of the book. A number of **more theoretical academics** provide a critical look at globalization, its limits, and the resistance to it. Notable is Richard Falk, who coined the term "globalization from below" for what I am calling the global citizen backlash; in addition to Falk's numerous works, see his *Predatory Globalization: A Critique* (Malden, Mass.: Blackwell, 1999). To read one of the most recent—and acclaimed—books, turn to Antonio Negri and Michael Hardt's *Empire* (Cambridge, Mass.: Harvard University Press, 2000). Also useful on this theoretical level are James Mittelman's *The Globalization Syndrome: Transformation and Resistance* (Princeton: Princeton University Press, 2000) and a book he edited, *Globalization: Critical Reflections* (Boulder: Lynne Reiner, 1996). The latter includes articles by academics such as Robert Cox and Stephen Gill who write on this subject. See also Barry Gills, ed., *Globalization and the Politics of Resistance* (New York: St. Martin's Press, 2000); and David Held and Anthony McGrew, *The Global Transformations Reader: An Introduction to the Globalization Debate* (Cambridge: Polity Press, 2000). From Europe, see also the journals *New Political Economy* (started in 1996), *Review of International Political Economy* (RIPE), and *Third World Quarterly*.

Two other books worth reading for theoretical foundations are Manfred B. Steger, *Globalism: The New Market Ideology* (2001), which has an especially good bibliography and Robert Schaeffer's *Understanding Globalisation: The Social Consequences of Political, Economic, and Environmental Change* (1997), both published by Rowman & Littlefield.

For updates on the International Gender and Trade Network and writings by Maria Riley, Peggy Antrobus, and others connected to it, see its web site (www.genderandtrade.net) or the web site of the Center of Concern, where the network's secretariat is based (www.coc.org/igtn.htm). Additional excellent academic work on **trade and gender** includes Caren Grown, Diane Elson, and Nilufer Cagatay, "Introduction to the Special Issue on Growth, Trade, Finance, and Gender Equality," *World Development* 28, no. 7 (July 2000); Maria Fontana, Susan Joekes, and Rachel Masika, "Global Trade Expansion and Liberalization: Gender Issues and Impacts," Report Commissioned by the Department for International Development, BRIDGE Report no. 42, Institute of Development Studies, University of Sussex, Brighton, January 1998; Gunseli Berik, "Mature Export-Led Growth and Gender Wage Inequality in Taiwan," *Feminist Economics* 6, no. 3 (November 2000); Lourdes Beneria and Amy Lind, "Engendering International Trade: Concepts, Policy, and Action," in *A Commitment to the World's Women*, ed. Noeleen Heyzer (New York UNIFEM, 1995); and Maria Sagrario Floro, "Women, Work, and Agricultural Commercialization in the Philippines," in *Women's Work in the World Economy*, edited by Nancy Folbre, Barbara Bergmann, Bina Agarwal, and Maria Floro (New York: New York University Press and Macmillan Press, 1992), 3–40. See also *ICDA Journal* of the International Coalition for Development Alternatives, Uppsala, Sweden.

A few **backlash leaders and activists** have put together their own readers. Kevin Danaher of Global Exchange does this regularly; his latest, published by Common Courage Press in Monroe, Maine, include *Globalize This! The Battle against the World Trade Organization and Corporate Rule* (edited with Roger Burbach, 2000) and *Democratizing the Global Economy: The Battle against the World Bank and the IMF* (2001). Sarah Anderson, John Cavanagh, and Thea Lee provide a guide to the world economy in their *Field Guide to the Global Economy* (New York: New Press, 2000). *The Case against the Global Economy* edited by Jerry Mander and Edward Goldsmith (San Francisco: Sierra Club, 1996) includes articles by members of the International Forum on Globalization and allies. To find articles by Southern authors who are part of the citizen backlash, see the journal *The Ecologist* (distributed by MIT Press) and *Third World Resurgence* (by Third World Network). Another good source is the UK journal *The New Internationalist*, which also publishes *No-Nonsense Guides*, including *The No-Nonsense Guide to Globalization* (by Wayne Ellwood, 2001) and *The No-Nonsense Guide to Fair Trade* (by David Ransom, 2001).

Both educational and fun are two **popular education sources**: Miriam Ching Louie with Linda Burnham, *Women's Education in the Global Economy* (Berkeley: Women of Color Resource Center, 2000); and Carol Barton and other members of the Economic Literacy Action Network (ELAN) Steering Committee, *Unpacking Globalization: A Popular Education Tool Kit* (Economic Literacy Action Network, April 2000), available through the Highlander Research and Education Center in New Market, Tennessee.

Part II

THE HISTORICAL CONTEXT

Part II

The Historical Context

Before moving forward into the global backlash's proposals, initiatives, and debates (in Parts III–V), let us step back in time. Too often, both proponents and opponents of the current corporate-dominated economic globalization articulate their visions and their proposals as if there were no historical precedents. The debate outlined in the first section did not begin in the modern period of so-called globalization; indeed, it has antecedents through history. The slave trade, colonialism, and imperial expansion set up economic, social, and environmental dynamics that still play out in today's global economy. Nearly every country's economy was reshaped substantially between the fifteenth century and the Second World War by the activities of colonial authorities and their corporate extensions such as the Dutch East India Company. And, as the citizen backlash argues, this has continued since World War II as newer private and public global economic actors have exercised a major impact on poor countries and on vulnerable populations within all countries, be they rich or poor.

The purpose of this section is to take a brief glance back, to enrich our understanding of the shoulders on which today's global citizen backlash—knowingly or unknowingly—sits. This sweeping glance at history will also help elucidate the debates within today's global backlash to change economic globalization. I have selected the readings in this section to offer a number of insights from history: (1) that economic integration not only pre-dates the period of so-called globalization from the 1990s onward but goes back centuries; (2) that as long as that economic integration has been occurring, so too have critics been pointing out its adverse economic, social, and environmental impacts; (3) that those adverse impacts have catalyzed resistance in various shapes and forms, governmental and nongovernmental, that also goes back centuries; and, finally, (4) that from those critics and that resistance have come proposals (again, both governmental and nongovernmental) to change the way economic integration works, proposals that can be compared and contrasted with today's citizen proposals in aim as well as content.

The eight readings in this section divide rather neatly into three historical periods: pre–World War II, the quarter century after the war, and the debates of the 1970s. (Parts III through V of this book concentrate on the post-1990s period.)

During the first of these periods, beginning with the initial significant overseas economic exchanges some five centuries prior to World War II, many economies were integrated into the global economy in ways that served the needs of the colonial powers over those of the colonies and local populace. Popular resistance to slavery and colonialism erupted at different times in different parts of the world.

We then move from the colonial times to look at the period from World War II through the 1970s. During and after World War II, the three public multilateral institutions that would govern the global economy were set in place. At the same time, modern transnational (or multinational, as some call them) corporations emerged in the post–World War II period as the key dynamic private institutions driving the integration of global production, consumption, and financial chains. However, not all were pleased with this growth of public and private institutions. As we will see, in the post–World War II period, the 1970s especially established a benchmark of concern and counterproposals: developing country governments banded together to pose alternative rules and institutions, and popular resistance to different aspects of economic globalization spread in many nations.

In expanding on this overview, Part II aims not to repeat the broad debate among proponents and opponents of corporate globalization laid out in Part I, but rather to lay the groundwork for understanding the roots of the critique and how current proposals, initiatives, and debates within the citizen backlash build on these historic critiques and proposals and how they break with them.

Pre–World War II

Economic integration among countries is hardly new; the era of significant economic interactions among countries goes back at least to Columbus's voyages beginning in the late fifteenth century. Before 1492, most of the regions of the world were largely self-sufficient. Most of what people ate, wore, and used was produced locally. But this was changed over the next two to three centuries, as a few colonial powers built fleets and militaries and began to claim large parts of the rest of the world under their rule. During this earlier era of economic integration, the central driving force was colonialism. Once the colonizers took over a territory, they began to transform economic activity. As Cecil Rhodes, British colonial founder of Rhodesia, put it rather bluntly, "We must find new lands from which we can easily obtain raw materials and at the same time exploit the cheap slave labour that is available from the natives of the colonies. The colonies would also provide a dumping ground for the surplus goods produced in our factories."[1]

This economic transformation was anything but benign. Excerpts from two classics detail this brutal creation of a "colonial division of labor," and its winners and losers. In the first excerpt, the late Walter Rodney provides an articulate voice of outrage at "how Europe underdeveloped Africa" through trade patterns that began before formal colonialism with the slave trade. Rodney, a native Guyanese who received a doctorate from the London School of Oriental and African Studies at age 24 and was banished from Jamaica for political activities in 1968, wrote the book while teaching in Tanzania during the reign of Julius Nyerere. As a memorial essay to Rodney recalled, "Rodney's most well-known book, *How Europe Underdeveloped Africa*, . . . was greeted with relative silence by African experts at universities in North America and Europe" given "the sense of outrage in the academy at a book which deliberately undermined [the then-prevailing] paradigms on Africa." Eventually, however, Rodney's book "was an enormous success on the continent where it became essential reading at most universities."[2] Indeed, Rodney's 1972 book (excerpted in Reading 2.1) became one of the best-known chronicles of the pre-colonial and colonial history of Africa; it remains a time-honored classic.

Other researchers and critics have analyzed not only the colonial period itself but also the impact of colonial patterns on contemporary problems such as environmental degradation and hunger. The equivalent analysis for Latin America is Eduardo Galeano's *Open Veins of Latin America*, with its economic, social, and environmental critique:

> Latin America is the region of open veins. Everything, from the discovery until our times, has always been transmuted into European—or later United States—capital, and as such has accumulated in distant centers of power. Everything: the soil, its fruits and its mineral-rich depths, the people and their capacity to work and to consume, natural resources and human resources.[3]

In the second excerpt (Reading 2.2), Frances Moore Lappé and Joseph Collins explicitly link this transformation of the colonies' agricultural sector to the legacy of modern hunger. At the time they penned *Food First* from which this reading is excerpted, Lappé was well-known as the author of bestseller *Diet for a Small Planet*, a book that provided analysis of and sample recipes for environmentally sustainable, protein-rich nutrition. In 1975, she and *Food First* coauthor Joe Collins had cofounded the California-based Institute for Food and Development Policy, better known today as Food First after their well-circulated and much-discussed book.

The history of the transformation of "the international division of labor"—how different countries relate to the world economy—suggested by these two readings is crucial to understanding the evolution of today's trade and investment patterns. Free-market economists, with their concept of "comparative advantage," write as if a country's trade and investment patterns are almost God-given, rather than the results of historical forces (combined, of course, with the realities of climate, etc.). But it is inaccurate to think of Ecuador, for example, as exporting bananas or Ghana cocoa simply because of a comparative advantage that resulted from the workings of the invisible hands of "free" market forces. That the Philippines should become the world's primary exporter of coconut products, for instance, was not merely a matter of climate and advantage; rather, the Spanish colonizers required each Filipino "indio" to plant a certain number of coconut trees.[4] The point is that broad historical events, shaped by governments and even individuals, created colonial trade and investment patterns that laid the groundwork for today's trade and investment patterns. Moreover, these patterns were created to serve narrow economic and political interests.

This historical foundation will be useful later in comprehending why the global backlash believes that these patterns can be changed, as well as in judging the effectiveness of various contemporary proposals to render trade, investment, and financial flows more socially and environmentally responsible. In fact, just as economic integration began centuries ago, so did innovative local, regional, and transnational resistance to economic globalization.

In a third reading (Reading 2.3), public educator and activist Zahara Heckscher makes this crucial point by analyzing five such resistance movements between the late eighteenth century and the early twentieth century. Each movement addressed different negative impacts of economic integration; each brought forth a unique kind of resistance. But as Heckscher analyzes the five case studies, she finds she has unearthed historical "antecedents to today's international campaigns against corporate globalization." (A note on this excerpt: This is the one reading that is not a reprint but was "commissioned" for this book. Heckscher began her inquiry into the history of resistance against economic integration as my graduate research assistant. After months of searching, we discovered that a suitable, integrative reading that made this point did not seem to exist—a fascinating commentary on the backlash's relative lack of historical perspective. Thus, we decided that she should write it herself. She was, at that point, already active in local and global social justice organizations and an accomplished author.)

World War II and the Early Postwar Years

With that broad sweep of almost 500 years of economic integration and resistance prior to World War II, this section now examines the public and private institutions that manage and dominate the post–World War II global economy.

First, the public institutions. To understand the mandates of the new public institutions—the World Bank, the IMF, and the General Agreement on Tariffs and Trade (GATT)—that were set up in the 1940s to govern the postwar world economy, one actually has to go back to the 1920s and the 1930s and the Great Depression. In the decade leading up to World War II, there was a total breakdown of the global economic order. First came financial panic—the so-called stock market crash; this sent production into a tailspin. Countries protected dwindling production and jobs in part by launching trade wars and implementing "beggar-thy-neighbor" policies (through policies such as competitive "cut-throat" devaluations) to protect their own markets while trying to out-export their rivals.

The Depression years and the world war that ensued were crisis times for the global economy—so trying that while the war was still raging (indeed, before it was at all clear which side would be victorious), some of the leading economic thinkers from the richer countries (including Britain's renowned Lord John Maynard Keynes, the father of modern macroeconomics, which serves as the foundation for modern macroeconomic policy) began to exchange drafts of visions for the postwar public multilateral institutions. The goal of the drafters was to create multilateral institutions that would not only rebuild the postwar world economy and manage trade, production, and finance, but also prevent future global economic breakdown. In 1944, at Bretton Woods, New Hampshire, as Dean Acheson wrote (Reading 2.4), he was "present at the creation" of two of these institutions: the World Bank and the International Monetary Fund. Acheson, who was then assistant secretary of state for economic affairs, subsequently became President Truman's secretary of state. His excerpt is meant to provide a kind of "we were there" look at these institutions.

It is also meant to be a reminder that there were lofty goals and intricate planning that went into the public institutions that manage today's world economy. In finance, the IMF was created to oversee an orderly exchange rate system and to provide short-term loans for countries that experienced unexpected shocks to their balance of payments. To stimulate production and the rebuilding of war-ravaged nations, a World Bank (officially the International Bank for Reconstruction and Development) was created to offer long-term, low-interest loans for "reconstruction" for Europe and "development" of Third World countries. (Over a 150-year time span from the 1800s through World War II, most of the Third World ceased being colonies.) In addition to these "Bretton Woods twins," the GATT was set up to oversee the reduction of tariff barriers to trade in manufactured goods. (GATT was the least powerful of the trio and in 1995 was subsumed by a more powerful World Trade Organization, as discussed in Part III. More detail on these institutions is found in Reading 2.8.)

In addition to gearing up production, finance, and trade, these post–World War II public institutions created an atmosphere ideal for the growth and global spread of large private corporations, the twentieth century's version of the East India Company and the like. As barriers to trade and investment fell in the decades following World War II, several hundred large private corporations began to weave global webs of production, consumption, finance, and culture. More and more of what people around the globe ate, drank, wore, drove, and entertained themselves with became the product of global assembly lines.

Proposals to Close the Gap between North and South

The rapid growth and influence of both modern global corporations and the public "multilateral" institutions over the development process elicited debate over other possible routes to development. The multilateral economic institutions increasingly counseled developing countries to open up their economies to the world economy through free trade and investment flows that seemed to benefit transnational corporations while exacerbating the gap

between "developed" and "developing" countries. The controversy surrounding the free-market advice offered by these institutions fed into a debate about
how developing countries should relate to the world economy. Likewise, the
global expansion and enlargement of modern multinational corporations
elicited a debate over whether they should be allowed to move around the
globe freely or whether there should be "checks" placed on them (and who
should place those checks and how to do so).

From Latin America starting as early as the late 1950s came a Southern "homegrown," influential critique and alternative development program; the "structuralists" sought to restructure developing countries' positions in the world economy. The structuralists' critique focused not on environmental or social and other
distributional issues within a country, but rather on the question of why "development" was disproportionately benefiting richer "core" countries rather than
poorer "periphery" ones and why the gap between the two appeared to be growing rather than shrinking. Argentine Raul Prebisch, the father of "structuralism,"
counseled that, as long as countries in the "periphery" relied on commodity exports and manufactured imports (i.e., as long as they were mired in the colonial
division of labor), their economies would be exploited to the benefit of the "core"
countries. Indeed, Prebisch and others at the Chilean-based UN Economic Commission for Latin American (set up in 1948) suggested that the very development
of the core depended on the underdevelopment of the periphery—to the extent
that periphery countries were actually moving backwards economically as the
value of their commodity exports fell relative to the value of their manufactured
imports (or "declining terms of trade").

To break out of this bind, Prebisch—and fellow structuralists Celso Furtado and
Hans Singer (among others)—instead suggested temporarily delinking parts of an
economy from the world economy to build up industrial capacity and internal
markets through a concerted, multi-tiered plan of import-substitution industrialization geared to move a country into ever-higher value-added manufactured
goods. Only when it had built up the capacity for industrial exports, according to
Prebisch, could a country in the periphery reinsert itself on an equal basis in the
world economy. This was more than an academic debate. Indeed, Prebisch and
structuralism changed both national policies and the global debate. Prebisch's vision led Southern countries across the globe—from Brazil to the Philippines—
to try import substitution over the course of the 1950s and 1960s.

Then came the 1970s. The 1970s witnessed a significant increase in transnational
corporations' "global reach," as Richard Barnet and Ronald Müller so aptly
phrased it in their writing, which culminated in one of the first books to chronicle
the expansion of these corporations—and the transnational banks that funded
them—into the Third World.[5] With the rise of transnational corporations (TNCs)
in the 1970s came increasing concern over TNCs' economic and political power
vis-à-vis Third World governments.

A major scandal with one TNC became the poster child for these concerns. Allegations arose in the early 1970s that the U.S.-based multinational International Telephone and Telegraph (ITT) had offered funds to the U.S. government to prevent the

democratically elected socialist government of Salvador Allende from taking power in Chile in 1970. Using that allegation as a starting point, the U.S. Senate Subcommittee on Multinational Corporations of the Senate Foreign Relations Committee, under Senator Frank Church, convened a multi-year inquiry into "Multinationals and United States Foreign Policy," interviewing dozens of expert witnesses to look at the power and practices of U.S. corporations in the developing world. The result was seventeen riveting volumes that offer a more thorough examination of corporate practices overseas than any other inquiry of this (or perhaps any) era. Reading 2.5 draws from Senator Church's opening remarks at three of the hearings: one in 1973, another in 1974, and the third in 1975. The subcommittee existed from 1972 to 1976, when it was "neutered" (in the words of its then-staff director) by being converted into a subcommittee on international economic policy.[6]

Energized by such public revelations of irresponsible TNC behavior, educated by Raul Prebisch and his structuralist theory, and emboldened by the economic success in the early to mid-1970s of the oil-exporting nations belonging to the Organization of Petroleum Exporting Countries (OPEC), a number of Southern governments found a collective voice to demand a different set of rules for the world economy and its players. And so it was that structuralist theory was transformed into the core of the "new international economic order" (NIEO) demands that Southern governments brought to the United Nations in the early 1970s. Centered on proposals to raise and stabilize raw material prices (i.e., to mediate the conundrum of declining terms of trade) and to increase Southern exports of manufactured goods (i.e., to break out of the colonial division of labor), the NIEO focused on how to get the economic benefits from interaction with the world economy to the Southern nation states. The UN General Assembly declaration establishing this new international economic order is excerpted in Reading 2.6.

Using the new pulpit and power afforded the South by OPEC's economic success, Southern governments succeeded in pushing the United Nations not only to pass the NIEO declaration but also to create new institutions: (1) the United Nations Conference on Trade and Development (UNCTAD), which was to initiate the core programs of the NIEO with Prebisch as its first head, and (2) a United Nations Commission on Transnational Corporations (UNCTC). For close to a decade and a half after its establishment in 1975, the UNCTC oversaw a failed attempt to negotiate a UN Code of Conduct on Transnational Corporations, which spelled out norms for corporate "rights" and "responsibilities." Included in the code's provisions, for example, is the requirement that "corporations shall respect human rights and fundamental freedoms in the countries in which they operate. In their social and industrial relations, transnational corporations shall not discriminate on the basis of race, colour, sex, language, social, national and ethnic origin or political or other opinion."[7] So too, in this era of 1970s corporate exposés and vociferous Southern demands, did both the International Labor Organization (ILO) and the Organization of Economic Cooperation and Development (OECD) issue their own corporate codes of conduct, in 1977 and 1978 respectively—basically nonenforceable documents that most observers agree did little to effect change in corporate behavior or public opinion.

Thus far this subsection has chronicled an era in which Southern governments, individually and collectively, attempted to reform the workings of the world economy and its key actors—or, to employ language I used in describing today's global backlash in Part I, to "reshape" the rules and institutions of the world economy to benefit the Southern states. But the 1970s also saw nongovernmental actors push for change. Indeed, catalyzed by the new international economic order debate and the ITT scandal, citizen campaigns for more specific corporate codes grew rapidly across borders to challenge various corporate abuses: corporate support for apartheid, unethical marketing practices by infant formula corporations such as Nestlé, and exploitative marketing practices by global pesticide, alcohol, and tobacco companies, to name a few of the key campaigns. Rather than delineating an overall code of conduct for corporate "rights" and "responsibilities" in the pattern of the UN code, these campaigns focused on specific instances of egregious corporate behavior. While some of these campaigns were local and most were less grandiose than the UN code initiative, several were sophisticated global efforts that succeeded in changing fundamentally the public perception of infant formula and other corporations, if not to alter the on-the-ground realities.[8]

World Bank, IMF, and the Birth of Resistance over the 1970s

On a parallel front, governments and citizen groups began to take on the World Bank, the IMF, and other public institutions. On the one hand, Southern governments through their NIEO demands called for expanded governmental and multilateral assistance to poorer countries. On the other hand, a series of exposés in the 1970s began to suggest that aid—be it bilateral assistance from governments or multilateral assistance from the World Bank and IMF—often had more deleterious than beneficial effects. On the ground, of course, local people had been witness to the impact of these loans in prior decades, but the fact that this criticism became more global in the 1970s reflects both the era and the growth of these institutions over the 1970s. (The World Bank, for example, increased its lending more than tenfold from 1968 to 1981.)[9]

In essence, these exposés said: When you look at aid on the ground and listen to what local people have to say, you discover that loans often coddle dictators and the well-off at the expense of the poor and a country's growth and development. According to these scholars and practitioners, by the 1970s aid was invariably geared toward pushing a free-trade development model that encouraged either (1) expansion of traditional primary-product exports (cementing a colonial division of labor) or (2) entry into labor-intensive, low value-added manufacturing exports such as apparel and electronics (creating what academics termed a "new international division of labor"[10]). In the latter case, the critics claimed, what donor money and concomitant advice promoted was not anything like the structuralist version of industrialization in less developed countries (LCDs), but rather "enclaves" of exploitative, import-dependent manufactured exports that gave the lion's share of the profits to TNCs for repatriation to their home countries. Furthermore, the exposés continued, aid consisted seldom of grants but typically of loans whose repayment would burden the vulnerable populations.

Part of this critique built on structuralist analysis. In looking at who benefits and who loses within countries, however, these critiques went beyond a NIEO focus and, indeed, foreshadowed the focus of today's citizen backlash on specific sectors (labor and environment, or women and indigenous communities, for example) *within* North and South.

Interestingly enough, women researchers and authors dominated the initial 1970s exposés and critiques that were published in the North; their books' titles summarize their theses.[11] From Europe came Teresa Hayter's *Aid as Imperialism* and Susan George's *How the Other Half Dies*. In 1974, Cheryl Payer wrote one of the first critiques of the IMF in her path-breaking work: *The Debt Trap*. Through detailed case studies, Payer outlined the devastating impact of IMF policies on poorer nations, locking them into a development model based on debt that subsequently forced them into more borrowing, more faulty development, and more debt.

The first extensive country case study of World Bank lending was that of the Philippines (a World Bank "country of concentration" and one of its top ten loan recipients at that point in time).[12] Over the late 1970s to early 1980s, Philippine scholar and activist Walden Bello (now a leading figure in the global backlash) and a group of his colleagues (including myself) amassed a wealth of evidence to provide a detailed case study of how World Bank aid bolstered dictator Ferdinand Marcos while restructuring the Philippine economy to serve the interests of global corporations and the global market. While research in the Philippines was crucial to this documentation, much of the evidence came from "confidential" documents supplied by increasingly disillusioned World Bank employees.

When the exposés began to appear in the North, the audience and the number of protesters were still small. It was the impact of this World Bank lending on indigenous communities around the world that brought environmental issues into the critique and Northern environmentalists into the protests. Reading 2.7 concerns one of the very first large-scale infrastructure projects to jump from being protested by indigenous, local inhabitants to garnering international attention and protest: the Chico dam project in the northern Philippines. The reading excerpts testimony that local indigenous leader Wada Taw-il (pseudonym) gave in 1980 in Antwerp, Belgium. His testimony was offered on behalf of indigenous communities in the Cordillera mountain region in the northern Philippines whose ancestral land was to be inundated by the Chico dam project. The project was partially funded in the initial stages by the World Bank.

In fact, five years earlier in 1975, some of the affected indigenous communities had written to World Bank president Robert McNamara, beseeching him to stop the funding: "We, the Bontocs and the Kalingas affected by the Chico River Basin Development Project, object most strongly to any assistance from the World Bank . . . to the Philippine government for this project. The reason is simple: the project would wipe us out as a people! At least ten Kalinga settlements and six Bontoc settlements will be devastated as a result of this dam project."[13]

This letter and Wada Taw-il's testimony (Reading 2.7) were significant; this was before the days when a World Bank president received such complaints regularly. For the local inhabitants the protests described in Wada Taw-il's testimony were somewhat successful (the World Bank eventually pulled out of further funding), but extremely risky given the excesses of the Marcos dictatorship. As Wada Taw-il explains, several local inhabitants were killed, including the community's revered spokesperson Macli-ing Dulag.

The major legacy of Chico, foreign-funded dam projects in India, and other infrastructure projects affecting indigenous communities and involving large-scale resettlement of local populations was the awakening of Northern environmental groups to the connections between the aid money and environmental degradation. This led to the campaigns launched by major U.S.-based environmental groups, starting in the early to mid-1980s, to reform the World Bank. Over the course of the 1980s, development and human rights advocates joined in—at times building on Hayter, Payer, Bello, and other broader political economic critics of the 1970s but often not even knowing of them. So too in the last decades of the century, would religious and other activists take on the IMF and World Bank in campaigns on Third World debt around the world. As will be seen in Parts III through V, by the 1990s, the resistance had grown to encompass more issues—building from development to include environment and justice, from aid to include trade and investment, from the World Bank to the IMF and then to include the World Trade Organization.

To capture this dynamic, I end with a more contemporary piece by Canadian Jacques Gélinas (Reading 2.8) to complement Acheson's period piece (Reading 2.4). Through Gélinas's critical eye, the excerpt provides more detail on the three institutions that managed the world economy from their birth through more recent decades. He captures the essence of the reality of how these institutions work as well as why their activities have, since the 1970s, garnered such resistance.

In Brief

As we move in subsequent sections of this book to contemporary proposals of the global citizen backlash, we will continually encounter concerns regarding these public and private institutions—the international economic and financial institutions and the private transnational corporations (including transnational banks). But, overall, the history of public and private institutions brings us to questions of the development models they push with their focus on unfettered trade and investment flows. As we shall see as we move into the rest of the book, the questions asked of these institutions in the twenty-first century move beyond those of North-versus-South so prevalent in the NIEO debates of the 1970s. Are the public institutions that govern the world economy equipped to deal with "sustainable development"? With environmental issues? With democracy and grassroots participation? And even with the basic economic problems that characterize today's world economy—a world apart from the economic problems that plagued a post-

Depression world economy? And, so too, these questions need to be applied to the thousands of transnational corporations that dominate today's world economy—and their investment, capital mobility, technology, and overall corporate practices.

But, as we move into the current period, we must not forget the threads that link what is new and innovative with what has been said or tried before. NIEO and UNCTAD proposals and the Nestlé campaigners were in essence trying to *reshape* the rules of the world economy. So too the 1970s had its *rollback* proponents, including Teresa Hayter protesting the "imperialist" aspects of foreign aid and Wada Taw-il's moving call against the building of dams.

This overall historical sweep is also meant to remind us that, just as individuals built the public institutions, so too presumably can individuals rebuild these institutions or construct other ones. Indeed, Dean Acheson (Reading 2.4) begins his book with an epithet from a thirteenth-century king of Spain that is equally fitting today: "Had I been present at the creation, I would have given some useful hints for the better ordering of the universe." That better ordering is the subject of the rest of the present book, as we turn to initiatives by the citizen backlash. Indeed, we are, in many ways, present at the re-creation of the world economy and the public and private institutions that manage it.

Notes

1. Quoted in "The Uruguay Round: Gunboat Diplomacy by Another Name," editorial, *The Ecologist* 20, no. 6 (November/December 1990): 202.

2. David Jackson (professor of African history, City College, City University of New York), "Walter Rodney Remembered (1942–1980)," *Trinidad Guardian*, 13 June 2000. This can be found on www.walterrodney.org. On returning to his native Guyana, Rodney was assassinated in 1980.

3. Eduardo Galeano, *Open Veins of Latin America: Five Centuries of the Pillage of a Continent* (New York: Monthly Review Press, 1973), 12.

4. This began in "1642, when a Spanish edict required each 'indio' [a Spanish colonial term for any Christian of "pure" Malay-Filipino descent] to plant 100–200 coconut trees to provide caulk and rigging for the colonizers' galleons." James Boyce, *Of Coconuts and Kings: The Political Economy of an Export Crop,* Working Paper Series, Working Paper 1991–13, Department of Economics, University of Massachusetts, Amherst, Mass., 1991, 4–5.

5. Richard J. Barnet and Ronald Müller, *Global Reach: The Power of Multinational Corporations* (New York: Simon and Schuster, 1974).

6. Jerome Levinson to Robin Broad, email correspondence, 10 September 2001. Levinson thought the verb I had originally used—"disbanded"—was somewhat too tame.

7. Quoted in Lance Compa and Tashia Hinchliffe-Darricarrere, "Enforcing International Labor Rights through Corporate Codes of Conduct," *Columbia Journal of Transnational Law* 33, 663 (1995): 670. See pages 670–71 for a summary of the OECD and ILO Codes.

8. See Robin Broad and John Cavanagh, "The Corporate Accountability Movement: Lessons and Opportunities," a study for the World Wildlife Federation's Project on International Financial Flows and the Environment, 30 July 1997; and Kathryn Sikkink, "Codes of Conduct for Transnational Corporations: The Case of the WHO/UNICEF Code," *International Organization* 40 (Autumn 1986): 815–40.

9. See Barend A. de Vries, *Remaking the World Bank* (Cabin John, Md.: Seven Locks Press, 1987), 13–14; and Robin Broad, *Unequal Alliance* (Berkeley: University of California Press, 1993), chapters 2 and 3.

10. On the new international division of labor, work by members of then–West Germany's Max Planck Institute stands as a classic: Folker Fröbel, Jürgen Heinrichs, and Otto Kreye, *The New International Division of Labor: Structural Unemployment in Industrialized Countries and Industrialization in Developing Countries*, trans. Pete Burgess (Cambridge, UK: Cambridge University Press, 1980; trans. of original edition, Hamburg: Rowohlt Taschenbuch, 1977).

11. For bibliographic details about these books, turn to For Further Reading at the end of Part II.

12. The quote is from Michael Gould, then the World Bank's Philippine division chief, in the confidential World Bank document: World Bank, "Philippines—Country Program Paper" (Washington, D.C., 26 March 1976), 17.

13. The Bontoc and Kalinga Delegates to the Vochong Conference on Development, letter to Robert S. McNamara, President, World Bank, 12 May 1975, reprinted in *Mortgaging the Future: The World Bank and IMF in the Philippines*, ed. Vivencio R. Jose (Quezon City: Foundation for Nationalist Studies, 1982), 167.

2.1

How Europe Underdeveloped Africa
Walter Rodney

It has been shown that, using comparative standards, Africa today is underdeveloped in relation to Western Europe and a few other parts of the world; and that the present position has been arrived at, not by the separate evolution of Africa on the one hand and Europe on the other, but through exploitation. As is well known, Africa has had prolonged and extensive contact with Europe, and one has to bear in mind that contact between different societies changes their respective rates of development. To set the record straight, four operations are required:

1. Reconstruction of the nature of development in Africa before the coming of Europeans.
2. Reconstruction of the nature of development which took place in Europe before expansion abroad.
3. Analysis of Africa's contribution to Europe's present "developed" state.
4. Analysis of Europe's contribution to Africa's present "under-developed" state.

Walter Rodney, excerpt from *How Europe Underdeveloped Africa*, rev. ed. (Washington, D.C., 1982), 33 and 75–79. Copyright © 1972 by Walter Rodney, copyright © 1981 by Vincent Harding, William Strickland, and Robert Hill; reprinted with the permission of The Permissions Company, P.O. Box 243, High Bridge, N.J. 08829, USA, on behalf of Howard University Press. All rights reserved.

The second task has already been extensively carried out in European literature, and only passing references need be made; but the others are all deserving of further attention.

[. . .]

How Europe Became the Dominant Section of a World-Wide Trade System

. . . . Western Europe and Africa had a relationship which insured the transfer of wealth from Africa to Europe. The transfer was possible only after trade became truly international; and that takes one back to the late fifteenth century when Africa and Europe were drawn into common relations for the first time—along with Asia and the Americas. The developed and underdeveloped parts of the present capitalist section of the world have been in continuous contact for four and a half centuries. The contention here is that over that period Africa helped to develop Western Europe in the same proportion as Western Europe helped to underdevelop Africa.

The first significant thing about the internationalization of trade in the fifteenth century was that Europeans took the initiative and went to other parts of the world. No Chinese boats reached Europe, and if any African canoes reached the Americas (as is sometimes maintained) they did not establish two-way links. What was called international trade was nothing but the extension overseas of European interests. The strategy behind international trade and the production that supported it was firmly in European hands, and specifically in the hands of the sea-going nations from the North Sea to the Mediterranean. They owned and directed the great majority of the world's sea-going vessels, and they controlled the financing of the trade between four continents. Africans had little clue as to the tri-continental links between Africa, Europe, and the Americas. Europe had a monopoly of knowledge about the international exchange system seen as a whole, for Western Europe was the only sector capable of viewing the system as a whole.

Europeans used the superiority of their ships and cannon to gain control of all the world's waterways, starting with the western Mediterranean and the Atlantic coast of North Africa. From 1415, when the Portuguese captured Ceuta, near Gibraltar, they maintained the offensive against the Maghreb. Within the next sixty years, they seized ports such as Arzila, El-Ksar-es-Seghir, and Tangier, and fortified them. By the second half of the fifteenth century, the Portuguese controlled the Atlantic coast of Morocco and used its economic and strategic advantages to prepare for further navigations which eventually carried their ships round the Cape of Good Hope in 1495. After reaching the Indian Ocean, the Portuguese sought with some success to replace Arabs as the merchants who tied East Africa to India and the rest of Asia. In the seventeenth and eighteenth centuries, the Portuguese carried most of the East African ivory which was marketed in India; while Indian cloth and beads were sold in East and West Africa by the Portuguese, Dutch, English, and French. The same applied to cowry shells from the East Indies. Therefore, by control of the seas, Europe took the first steps towards transforming the several parts of Africa and Asia into economic satellites.

When the Portuguese and the Spanish were still in command of a major sector of world trade in the first half of the seventeenth century, they engaged in buying cotton cloth in India to exchange for slaves in Africa to mine gold in Central and South America. Part of the gold in the Americas would then be used to purchase spices and silks from the Far East. The concept of metropole and dependency automatically came into existence when parts of Africa were caught up in the web of international commerce. On the one hand, there were the European countries who decided on the role to be played by the African economy; and on the other hand, Africa formed an extension to the European capitalist market. As far as foreign trade was concerned, Africa was dependent on what Europeans were prepared to buy and sell.

[. . .]

From the beginning, Europe assumed the power to make decisions within the international trading system. An excellent illustration of that is the fact that the so-called international law which governed the conduct of nations on the high seas was nothing else but European law. Africans did not participate in its making, and in many instances, African people were simply the victims, for the law recognized them only as transportable merchandise. If the African slave was thrown overboard at sea, the only legal problem that arose was whether or not the slave ship could claim compensation from the insurers! Above all, European decision-making power was exercised in selecting what Africa should export—in accordance with European needs.

The ships of the Portuguese gave the search for gold the highest priority, partly on the basis of well-known information that West African gold reached Europe across the Sahara and partly on the basis of guesswork. The Portuguese were successful in obtaining gold in parts of West Africa and in eastern Central Africa; and it was the Gold Coast which attracted the greatest attention from Europeans in the sixteenth and seventeenth centuries. The number of forts built there was proof to that effect, and the nations involved included the Scandinavians and the Prussians (Germans) apart from other colonial stalwarts like the British, Dutch, and Portuguese.

Europeans were anxious to acquire gold in Africa because there was a pressing need for gold coin within the growing capitalist money economy. Since gold was limited to very small areas of Africa, as far as Europeans were then aware, the principal export was human beings. Only in a very few places at given times was the export of another commodity of equal or greater importance. For instance, in the Senegal there was gum, in Sierra Leone camwood, and in Mozambique ivory. However, even after taking those things into account, one can say that Europe allocated to Africa the role of supplier of human captives to be used as slaves in various parts of the world.

When Europeans reached the Americas, they recognized its enormous potential in gold and silver and tropical produce. But that potential could not be made a reality without adequate labor supplies. The indigenous Indian population could not withstand new European diseases such as smallpox, nor could they bear the organized toil of slave plantations and slave mines, having barely emerged from the hunting stage. That is why in islands like Cuba and Hispaniola, the local Indian population was virtually wiped out by the white invaders. At the same time, Europe itself had a very small population and could not afford to release the labor required to tap the wealth of the Americas. Therefore, they turned to the nearest continent, Africa, which incidentally had a population accustomed to settled agriculture and disciplined labor in many spheres. Those were the objective conditions lying behind the start of the European slave trade, and those are the reasons why the capitalist class in Europe used their control of international trade to insure that Africa specialized in exporting captives.

[. . .]

The fact that Europe was the first part of the world to move from feudalism towards capitalism gave Europeans a headstart over humanity elsewhere in the scientific understanding of the universe, the making of tools, and the efficient organization of labor. *European technical superiority did not apply to all aspects of production, but the advantage which they possessed in a few key areas proved decisive.* For example, African canoes on the river Nile and the Senegal coast were of a high standard, but the relevant sphere of operations was the ocean, where European ships could take command. West Africans had developed metal casting to a fine artistic perfection in

many parts of Nigeria, but when it came to the meeting with Europe, beautiful bronzes were far less relevant than the crudest cannon. African wooden utensils were sometimes works of great beauty, but Europe produced pots and pans that had many practical advantages. Literacy, organizational experience, and the capacity to produce on an ever expanding scale also counted in the European favor.

European manufactures in the early years of trade with Africa were often of poor quality, but they were of new varieties and were found attractive. Estaban Montejo, an African who ran away from a Cuban slave plantation in the nineteenth century, recalled that his people were enticed into slavery by the color red. He said:

> It was the scarlet which did for the Africans; both the kings and the rest surrendered without a struggle. When the kings saw that the whites were taking out these scarlet handkerchiefs as if they were waving, they told the blacks, "Go on then, go and get a scarlet handkerchief" and the blacks were so excited by the scarlet they ran down to the ships like sheep and there they were captured.

That version by one of the victims of slavery is very poetic. What it means is that some African rulers found European goods sufficiently desirable to hand over captives which they had taken in warfare. Soon, war began to be fought between one community and another for the sole purpose of getting prisoners for sale to Europeans, and even inside a given community a ruler might be tempted to exploit his own subjects and capture them for sale. A chain reaction was started by European demand for slaves (and only slaves) and by their offer of consumer goods—this process being connected with divisions within African society.

2.2

Why Can't People Feed Themselves?

Frances Moore Lappé and Joseph Collins

In the very first speech I, Frances, ever gave after writing *Diet for a Small Planet*, I tried to take my audience along the path that I had taken in attempting to understand why so many are hungry in this world. Here is the gist of that talk that was, in truth, a turning point in my life:

> When I started I saw a world divided into two parts: a *minority* of nations that had "taken off" through their agricultural and industrial revolutions to reach a level of unparalleled material abundance and a *majority* that remained behind in a primitive, traditional, undeveloped state. This lagging behind of the majority of the world's peoples must be due, I thought, to some internal deficiency or even to several of them. It seemed obvious that the underdeveloped countries must be deficient in natural resources—particularly good land and climate—and in cultural development, including modern attitudes conducive to work and progress.
>
> But when looking for the historical roots of the predicament, I learned that my picture of these two separate worlds was quite false. My "two separate worlds" were really just different sides of the same coin. One side was on top largely because the other side was on the bottom. Could this be true? How were these separate worlds related?
>
> Colonialism appeared to me to be the link. Colonialism destroyed the cultural patterns of production and exchange by which traditional societies in "underdeveloped" countries previously had met the needs of the people. Many precolonial social structures, while dominated by exploitative elites, had evolved a system of mutual obligations among the classes that helped to ensure at least a minimal diet for all. A friend of mine once said, "Precolonial village existence in subsistence agriculture was a limited life indeed, but it's certainly not Calcutta." The misery of starvation in the streets of Calcutta can only be understood as the endpoint of a long historical process—one that has destroyed a traditional social system.
>
> "Underdeveloped," instead of being an adjective that evokes the picture of a static society, became for me a verb (to "underdevelop") meaning the process by which the minority of the world has transformed—indeed often robbed and degraded—the majority.

That was 1972. I clearly recall my thoughts on my return home. I had stated publicly for the first time a world view that had taken me years of study to grasp. The sense of relief was tremendous. For me the breakthrough lay in realizing that today's "hunger crisis" could not be described in static, descriptive terms. Hunger and underdevelopment must always be thought of as a *process*.

Frances Moore Lappé and Joseph Collins, "Why Can't People Feed Themselves?" in *Food First: Beyond the Myth of Food Scarcity* (Boston: Houghton Mifflin Company, 1977), 75–85.

To answer the question "why hunger?" it is counterproductive to simply *describe* the conditions in an underdeveloped country today. For these conditions, whether they be the degree of malnutrition, the levels of agricultural production, or even the country's ecological endowment, are not static facts—they are not "givens." They are rather the *results* of an ongoing historical process. As we dug ever deeper into that historical process for the preparation of this book, we began to discover the existence of scarcity-creating mechanisms that we had only vaguely intuited before.

We have gotten great satisfaction from probing into the past since we recognized it is the only way to approach a solution to hunger today. We have come to see that it is the *force* creating the condition, not the condition itself, that must be the target of change. Otherwise we might change the condition today, only to find tomorrow that it has been recreated—with a vengeance.

Asking the question "Why can't people feed themselves?" carries a sense of bewilderment that there are so many people in the world not able to feed themselves adequately. What astonished us, however, is that there are not *more* people in the world who are hungry—considering the weight of the centuries of effort by the few to undermine the capacity of the majority to feed themselves. No, we are not crying "conspiracy!" If these forces were entirely conspiratorial, they would be easier to detect and many more people would by now have risen up to resist. We are talking about something more subtle and insidious; a heritage of a colonial order in which people with the advantage of considerable power sought their own self-interest, often arrogantly believing they were acting in the interest of the people whose lives they were destroying.

The Colonial Mind

The colonizer viewed agriculture in the subjugated lands as primitive and backward. Yet such a view contrasts sharply with documents from the colonial period now coming to light. For example, A. J. Voelker, a British agricultural scientist assigned to India during the 1890s, wrote

> Nowhere would one find better instances of keeping land scrupulously clean from weeds, of ingenuity in device of water-raising appliances, of knowledge of soils and their capabil-

ities, as well as of the exact time to sow and reap, as one would find in Indian agriculture. It is wonderful, too, how much is known of rotation, the system of "mixed crops" and of fallowing. . . . I, at least, have never seen a more perfect picture of cultivation."[1]

None the less, viewing the agriculture of the vanquished as primitive and backward reinforced the colonizer's rationale for destroying it. To the colonizers of Africa, Asia, and Latin America, agriculture became merely a means to extract wealth—much as gold from a mine—on behalf of the colonizing power. Agriculture was no longer seen as a source of food for the local population, nor even as their livelihood. Indeed the English economist John Stuart Mill reasoned that colonies should not be thought of as civilizations or countries at all but as "agricultural establishments" whose sole purpose was to supply the "larger community to which they belong." The colonized society's agriculture was only a subdivision of the agricultural system of the metropolitan country. As Mill acknowledged, "Our West India colonies, for example, cannot be regarded as countries. . . . The West Indies are the place where England *finds it convenient* to carry on the production of sugar, coffee and a few other tropical commodities."[2]

Prior to European intervention, Africans practiced a diversified agriculture that included the introduction of new food plants of Asian or American origin. But colonial rule simplified this diversified production to single cash crops—often to the exclusion of staple foods—and in the process sowed the seeds of famine.[3] Rice farming once had been common in Gambia. But with colonial rule so much of the best land was taken over by peanuts (grown for the European market) that rice had to be imported to counter the mounting prospect of famine. Northern Ghana, once famous for its yams and other foodstuffs, was forced to concentrate solely on cocoa. Most of the Gold Coast, too, became dependent on cocoa. Liberia was turned into a virtual plantation subsidiary of Firestone Tire and Rubber. Food production in Dahomey and southeast Nigeria was all but abandoned in favor of palm oil; Tanganyika (now Tanzania) was forced to focus on sisal and Uganda on cotton.

The same happened in Indochina. About the time of the American Civil War the French decided that the Mekong Delta in Vietnam would be ideal for producing rice for export. Through a production system based on enriching the large landowners, Vietnam became the world's third largest exporter of rice by the 1930s; yet many landless Vietnamese went hungry.[4]

Rather than helping the peasants, colonialism's public works programs only reinforced export crop production. British irrigation works built in nineteenth-century India did help increase production, but the expansion was for spring export crops at the expense of millets and legumes grown in the fall as the basic local food crops.

Because people living on the land do not easily go against their natural and adaptive drive to grow food for themselves, colonial powers had to force the production of cash crops. The first strategy was to use physical or economic force to get the local population to grow cash crops instead of food on their own plots and then turn them over to the colonizer for export. The second strategy was the direct takeover of the land by large-scale plantations growing crops for export.

Forced Peasant Production

As Walter Rodney recounts in *How Europe Underdeveloped Africa*, cash crops were often grown literally under threat of guns and whips.[5] One visitor to the Sahel commented in 1928: "Cotton is an artificial crop and one the value of which is not entirely clearly to the natives . . ." He wryly noted the "enforced enthusiasm with which the natives . . . have thrown themselves into . . . planting cotton."[6] The forced cultivation of cotton was a major grievance leading to the Maji Maji wars in Tanzania (then Tanganyika) and behind the nationalist revolt in Angola as late as 1960.[7]

Although raw force was used, taxation was the preferred colonial technique to force Africans to grow cash crops. The colonial administrations simply levied taxes on cattle, land, houses, and even the people themselves. Since the tax had to be paid in the coin of the realm, the peasants had either to grow crops to sell or to work on the plantations or in the mines of the Europeans.[8] Taxation was both an effective tool to "stimulate" cash cropping and a source of revenue that the colonial bureaucracy needed to enforce the system. To expand their production of export crops to pay the mounting taxes, peasant producers were forced to neglect the farming

of food crops. In 1830, the Dutch administration in Java made the peasants an offer they could not refuse; if they would grow government-owned export crops on one fifth of their land, the Dutch would remit their land taxes.[9] If they refused and thus could not pay the taxes, they lost their land.

Marketing boards emerged in Africa in the 1930s as another technique for getting the profit from cash crop production by native producers into the hands of the colonial government and international firms. Purchases by the marketing boards were well below the world market price. Peanuts bought by the boards from peasant cultivators in West Africa were sold in Britain for more than *seven times* what the peasants received.[10]

The marketing board concept was born with the "cocoa hold-up" in the Gold Coast in 1937. Small cocoa farmers refused to sell to the large cocoa concerns like United Africa Company (a subsidiary of the Anglo-Dutch firm, Unilever—which we know as Lever Brothers) and Cadbury until they got a higher price. When the British government stepped in and agreed to buy the cocoa directly in place of the big business concerns, the smallholders must have thought they had scored at least a minor victory. But had they really? The following year the British formally set up the West African Cocoa Control Board. Theoretically, its purpose was to pay the peasants a reasonable price for their crops. In practice, however the board, as sole purchaser, was able to hold down the prices paid the peasants for their crops when the world prices were rising. Rodney sums up the real "victory":

> None of the benefits went to Africans, but rather to the British government itself and to the private companies . . . Big companies like the United Africa Company and John Holt were given . . . quotas to fulfill on behalf of the boards. As agents of the government, they were no longer exposed to direct attack, and their profits were secure.[11]

These marketing boards, set up for most export crops, were actually controlled by the companies. The chairman of the Cocoa Board was none other than John Cadbury of Cadbury Brothers (ever had a Cadbury chocolate bar?) who was part of a buying pool exploiting West African cocoa farmers.

The marketing boards funneled part of the profits from the exploitation of peasant producers indirectly into the royal treasury. While the Cocoa Board sold to the British Food Ministry at low prices, the ministry upped the price for British manufacturers, thus netting a profit as high as 11 million pounds in some years.[12]

These marketing boards of Africa were only the institutionalized rendition of what is the essence of colonialism—the extraction of wealth. While profits continued to accrue to foreign interests and local elites, prices received by those actually growing the commodities remained low.

Plantations

A second approach was direct takeover of the land either by the colonizing government or by private foreign interests. Previously self-provisioning farmers were forced to cultivate the plantation fields through either enslavement or economic coercion.

After the conquest of the Kandyan Kingdom (in present day Sri Lanka), in 1815, the British designated all the vast central part of the island as crown land. When it was determined that coffee, a profitable export crop, could be grown there, the Kandyan lands were sold off to British investors and planters at a mere five shillings per acre, the government even defraying the cost of surveying and road building.[13]

Java is also a prime example of a colonial government seizing territory and then putting it into private foreign hands. In 1870, the Dutch declared all uncultivated land—called waste land—property of the state for lease to Dutch plantation enterprises. In addition, the Agrarian Land Law of 1870 authorized foreign companies to lease village-owned land. The peasants, in chronic need of ready cash for taxes and foreign consumer goods, were only too willing to lease their land to the foreign companies for very modest sums and under terms dictated by the firms. Where land was still held communally, the village headman was tempted by high cash commissions offered by plantation companies. He would lease the village land even more cheaply than would the individual peasant or, as was frequently the case, sell out the entire village to the company.[14]

The introduction of the plantation meant the divorce of agriculture from nourishment, as the notion of food value was lost to the overriding claim of "market value" in international trade. Crops such as sugar, tobacco, and coffee were selected, not on the basis of how well they feed people, but for their high price value relative to their weight and bulk so that profit margins could be maintained even after the costs of shipping to Europe.

Suppressing Peasant Farming

The stagnation and impoverishment of the peasant food-producing sector was not the mere by-product of benign neglect, that is, the unintended consequence of an overemphasis on export production. Plantations—just like modern "agroindustrial complexes"—needed an abundant and readily available supply of low-wage agricultural workers. Colonial administrations thus devised a variety of tactics, all to undercut self-provisioning agriculture and thus make rural populations dependent on plantation wages. Government services and even the most minimal infrastructure (access to water, roads, seeds, credit, pest and disease control information, and so on) were systematically denied. Plantations usurped most of the good land, either making much of the rural population landless or pushing them onto marginal soils. (Yet the plantations have often held much of their land idle simply to prevent the peasants from using it—even to this day. Del Monte owns 57,000 acres of Guatemala but plants only 9000. The rest lies idle except for a few thousand head of grazing cattle.)[15]

In some cases a colonial administration would go even further to guarantee itself a labor supply. In at least twelve countries in the eastern and southern parts of Africa the exploitation of mineral wealth (gold, diamonds, and copper) and the establishment of cash-crop plantations demanded a continuous supply of low-cost labor. To assure this labor supply, colonial administrations simply expropriated the land of the African communities by violence and drove the people into small reserves.[16] With neither adequate land for their traditional slash-and-burn methods nor access to the means—tools, water, and fertilizer—to make continuous farming of such limited areas viable, the indigenous population could scarcely meet subsistence needs, much less produce surplus to sell in order to cover the colonial taxes. Hundreds of thousands of Africans were forced to become the cheap labor source so "needed" by the colonial plantations. Only by laboring on plantations and in the mines could they hope to pay the colonial taxes.

The tax scheme to produce reserves of cheap plantation and mining labor was particularly effective when the Great Depression hit and the bottom dropped out of cash crop economies. In 1929 the cotton market collapsed, leaving peasant cotton producers, such as those in Upper Volta, unable to pay their colonial taxes. More and more young people, in some years as many as 80,000, were thus forced to migrate to the Gold Coast to compete with each other for low-wage jobs on cocoa plantations.[17]

The forced migration of Africa's most able-bodied workers—stripping village food farming of needed hands—was a recurring feature of colonialism. As late as 1973 the Portuguese "exported" 400,000 Mozambican peasants to work in South Africa in exchange for gold deposited in the Lisbon treasury.

[. . .]

Perhaps the most insidious tactic to "lure" the peasant away from food production—and the one with profound historical consequences—was a policy of keeping the price of imported food low through the removal of tariffs and subsidies. The policy was double-edged: first, peasants were told they need not grow food because they could always buy it cheaply with their plantation wages; second, cheap food imports destroyed the market for domestic food and thereby impoverished local food producers.

[. . .]

Many colonial governments succeeded in establishing dependence on imported foodstuffs. In 1647 an observer in the West Indies wrote to Governor Winthrop of Massachusetts: "Men are so intent upon planting sugar that they had rather buy foode at very deare rates than produce it by labour, so infinite is the profitt of sugar workes. . . ."[20] By 1770, the West Indies were importing most of the continental colonies' exports of dried fish, grain, beans, and vegetables. A dependence on imported food made the West Indian colonies vulnerable to any disruption in supply. This dependence on imported food stuffs spelled disaster when

the thirteen continental colonies gained independence and food exports from the continent to the West Indies were interrupted. With no diversified food system to fall back on, 15,000 plantation workers died of famine between 1780 and 1787 in Jamaica alone.[21] The dependence of the West Indies on imported food persists to this day.

Suppressing Peasant Competition

We have talked about the techniques by which indigenous populations were forced to cultivate cash crops. In some countries with large plantations, however, colonial governments found it necessary to *prevent* peasants from independently growing cash crops not out of concern for their welfare, but so that they would not compete with colonial interests growing the same crop. For peasant farmers, given a modicum of opportunity, proved themselves capable of outproducing the large plantations not only in terms of output per unit of land but, more important, in terms of capital cost per unit produced.

In the Dutch East Indies (Indonesia and Dutch New Guinea) colonial policy in the middle of the nineteenth century forbade the sugar refineries to buy sugar cane from indigenous growers and imposed a discriminatory tax on rubber produced by native smallholders.[22] A recent unpublished United Nations study of agricultural development in Africa concluded that large-scale agricultural operations owned and controlled by foreign commercial interests (such as the rubber plantations of Liberia, the sisal estates of Tanganyika [Tanzania], and the coffee estates of Angola) only survived the competition of peasant producers because "the authorities actively supported them by suppressing indigenous rural development."[23]

The suppression of indigenous agricultural development served the interests of the colonizing powers in two ways. Not only did it prevent direct competition from more efficient native producers of the same crops, but it also guaranteed a labor force to work on the foreign-owned estates. Planters and foreign investors were not unaware that peasants who could survive economically by their own production would be under less pressure to sell their labor cheaply to the large estates.

The answer to the question, then, "Why can't people feed themselves?" must begin with an understanding of how colonialism actively prevented people from doing just that. Colonialism

- forced peasants to replace food crops with cash crops that were then expropriated at very low rates;
- took over the best agricultural land for export crop plantations and then forced the most able-bodied workers to leave the village fields to work as slaves or for very low wages on plantations;
- encouraged a dependence on imported food;
- blocked native peasant cash crop production from competing with cash crops produced by settlers or foreign firms.

Notes

1. Radha Sinha, *Food and Poverty* (New York: Holmes and Meier, 1976), p. 26.

2. John Stuart Mill, *Political Economy*, Book 3, Chapter 25 (emphasis added), 1848.

3. Peter Feldman and David Lawrence, "Social and Economic Implications of the Large-Scale Introduction of New Varieties of Foodgrains," Africa Report, preliminary draft (Geneva: UNRISD, 1975), pp. 107–108.

4. Edgar Owens, *The Right Side of History*, unpublished manuscript, 1976.

5. Walter, Rodney, *How Europe Underdeveloped Africa* (London: Bogle-L'Ouverture Publications, 1972), pp. 171–172.

6. Ferdinand Ossendowski, *Slaves of the Sun* (New York: Dutton, 1928), p. 276.

7. Rodney, *How Europe Underdeveloped Africa*, pp. 171–172.

8. Ibid., p. 181.

9. Clifford Geertz, *Agricultural Involution* (Berkeley and Los Angeles: University of California Press, 1963), pp. 52–53.

10. Rodney, *How Europe Underdeveloped Africa*, p. 185.

11. Ibid., p. 184.

12. Ibid., p. 186.

13. George L. Beckford, *Persistent Poverty: Underdevelopment in Plantation Economies of the Third World* (New York: Oxford University Press, 1972), p. 99.

14. Ibid., p. 99, quoting from Erich Jacoby, *Agrarian Unrest in Southeast Asia* (New York: Asia Publishing House, 1961), p. 66.

15. Pat Flynn and Roger Burbach, North American Congress on Latin America, Berkeley, California, recent investigation.

16. Feldman and Lawrence, "Social and Economic Implications," p. 103.

17. Special Sahelian Office Report, Food and Agriculture Organization, March 28, 1974, pp. 88–89.

[. . .]

20. Eric Williams, *Capitalism and Slavery* (New York: Putnam, 1966), p. 110.

21. Ibid., p. 121.

22. Gunnar Myrdal, *Asian Drama*, vol. 1 (New York: Pantheon, 1966), pp. 448–449.

23. Feldman and Lawrence, "Social and Economic Implications," p. 189.

2.3

Long before Seattle: Historical Resistance to Economic Globalization

Zahara Heckscher

Trade across borders is at least as ancient as the book of Genesis, which refers to a caravan of camels bearing gum, balm, and myrrh being transported from Gilead to Egypt when Joseph was sold into slavery by his brothers.[1] Throughout the millennia, extensive regional trade took place on all continents, from the Chinese dynasties to the Roman Empire, from the complex society of Great Zimbabwe to the astonishing Aztec markets of Mexico. In the past 500 years, regional trade has become global trade, tightly connected to European colonialism in Africa, Asia and the Pacific, the Middle East, Latin America, and the Caribbean.

Just as the current system of international trade dates back hundreds of years, so does the current resistance to exploitative forms of global trade.[2] Many early expressions of resistance to European commercial and labor practices were individual and small-group acts of non-cooperation or sabotage. In virtually every society the Europeans invaded, people rose up to protest the cruelty of slavery, theft of land, and plunder of resources. Some communities retreated into less accessible territories rather than submit to the devastation of European colonialism. Many captured Africans rebelled or committed suicide rather than become

slaves. Native Americans practiced guerrilla warfare in hundreds or even thousands of incidents of armed rebellion. A few Europeans, including Columbus's outspoken contemporary and chronicler, Bartolomé de Las Casas, used their power and privilege to protest the worst abuses of the colonial trade and labor practices.

Eventually, out of these isolated incidents, organized social movements developed in an attempt to control, transform, or abolish perceived injustices of international trade in goods and labor. Most of these movements were local and national, but a few were transnational. These early transnational alliances can be seen as the antecedents to today's international campaigns for global justice. This article will briefly explore five of the most dynamic examples of organized transnational resistance to economic integration between the 1780s and the early 1900s: the Tupac Amaru II uprising in Peru, the anti–slave trade movement, the campaign against colonization of the Congo, the First International Workingmen's Association, and the U.S.-based anti-imperialist movement.

The Tupac Amaru II Uprising

The Tupac Amaru II uprising of 1780–1781 in what is now Peru can be seen as a bridge between local anti-colonial rebellion and transnational social movements against exploitative

Zahara Heckscher, "Long Before Seattle: Historical Resistance to Economic Globalization" (Washington, D.C., September 2001).

economic integration.[3] The uprising was sparked in part by the free-market reforms imposed by the Spanish government through the colonial regime in the mid-eighteenth century. These changes opened trade between all the Spanish colonies and Spain. They were also designed to increase taxes while ending the extreme abuses of the forced labor and tax collection practices of the colonial administration. The introduction of these reforms benefited some elites, but disrupted trade patterns and flooded the textile market with cheap imports from Britain, devastating local industry and exacerbating economic inequality. The increase in taxes generated widespread resistance. Ultimately, the reforms failed to end the colonial abuses, and alienated a broad range of sectors, from Spanish and mestizo merchants to indigenous people, including José Gabriel Condorcanqui, a *curaca* (traditional leader), trader, and descendant of Tupac Amaru I, the last Inca to rule an Andean state.

Frustrated with the economic reforms and brutality of colonial government, José Gabriel changed his name to Tupac Amaru II and organized an army of 6,000. Like previous rebellions, the uprising was violent, and drew its inspiration in part in looking back to a vision of cultural, spiritual, and economic systems from before the European conquest. Like the social movements that followed it, the uprising was inspired in part by European Enlightenment ideas of self-governance, freedom, and "natural rights." The movement was intercultural, and could even be considered to be international, spreading from Lower Peru to Upper Peru (now Bolivia), and involving Spaniards as well as mestizos, creoles (whites born in the Americas), Afro-Peruvians, and indigenous people of various nationalities. While church officials perpetrated some of the abuses that sparked the rebellion, a handful of priests initially supported Tupac Amaru II. Women played an extremely important leadership role in the rebellion, especially Tupac's wife, Micaela Bastidas Puyucahua, Commissar of War.

The uprising ultimately failed for two reasons. First, it lost the battle of propaganda, when the colonial regime convinced whites and mestizos that the movement was a race war against them, and convinced the Pumacahua clan and their allies to remain loyal to the Spanish side. Then the uprising lost militarily (after Tupac failed to follow his wife's tactical advice); Tupac was captured, then tortured and killed, after being forced to watch the execution of his wife and family. Despite the lack of military success, the uprising is credited by some as contributing to the independence movement that gained power in the coming years and led to Peru's independence in 1821.

The International Movement against the Atlantic Slave Trade

While Tupac mobilized his forces in Peru, a movement against the Atlantic slave trade was gaining strength in Europe and North America.[4] At its peak, from 1787 to 1807, the movement was strongest in the United Kingdom, where numerous sectors of society were mobilized, from the textile workers of Manchester to Methodist Church founder John Wesley, from artisans in small Scottish towns to wealthy businessmen in London, from rural housewives to prime ministers. The movement involved significant collaboration among the British, the Americans, the French, and people of African origin, including black sailors of various nationalities, sons of African royalty sent to Europe to round out their education, and free European and American blacks. Olaudah Equiano and other former slaves from the Americas also played an important role.

Some have argued that the anti–slave trade movement was the first modern social movement, and the innovator of social change methodologies used by virtually every social movement that followed it.[5] Indeed, the tactics used by the campaign would sound surprisingly familiar to the organizers of the Seattle demonstrations against the World Trade Organization: popular theater, speaking tours and rallies, political poetry, pins, letter-writing campaigns, direct lobbying, petitions, electoral politics, and commercial boycotts. International networking was essential to the success of movement. For example, former slaves from the United States went on speaking tours in the United Kingdom, providing firsthand testimonies about the cruelties of the slave trade and bringing thousands of new supporters into the movement. British religious denominations shared their strategies with their counterparts in the United States, which helped to strengthen the movement here.

The movement eventually succeeded beyond the dreams of its originators; not only was the trade banned in the United Kingdom and the United States, but also the English Navy was used to intercept ships off the coast of Africa, search them, and send any Africans found back to Africa. The banning of the slave trade also helped create momentum for the abolition of slavery itself. The movement thus permanently altered the rules of the global economy and set a precedent for social movements promoting the value of human rights above the value of commerce.

European Workers and the First International Workingman's Association

The same radical ideas of justice and equality that spurred the abolition movement also led to an international movement focused on the rights of workers in the globalizing economy of mid-nineteenth-century Europe. In the 1800s, as a result of the industrial revolution, an increasing number of Europeans worked in factories in dire conditions: excessive work hours, low wages, abusive bosses. The global economy brought in new technologies that threatened jobs, and foreign-made goods that threatened domestic production.[6] European labor unions, which had developed out of craftsmen's guilds, began using strikes, work slowdowns, and destruction of machinery to fight for better wages, better work conditions, and protective tariffs. In England in the 1850s, factory owners fought back by importing workers from poorer European countries to replace striking workers, including cigar makers, tailors, and builders.

In response, the European workers developed an international strategy. The more radical unions, along with their intellectual supporters and associations of nonunionized workers, formed the First International Workingman's Association in 1864. The First International successfully intervened in 1866 to prevent the bosses of striking tailors in England from hiring strikebreakers from Belgium, France, and Germany. In 1867, a delegation of striking Parisian bronze workers visited London to seek support for their right to unionize; the International subsequently sent financial support from British unions and contributed to the success of the strike. While the First International lasted only until 1872, it played a key role in the development of national labor unions and working-class consciousness in Europe. In turn, these new unions and new ideas

made significant changes not only in labor conditions, but also in national policies, from freedom of speech laws to the extension of voting rights to people who did not own property. Many union activists, recognizing parallels between the exploitation of workers in Europe and the enslavement of Africans in the Americas, also played a role in the eradication of slavery overseas, along with veterans of the anti–slave trade movement. In short, like the current global justice movement, the international workers' movement was a multi-issue movement that included domestic as well as global goals.

Early Human Rights Activists: Working against Colonization of the Congo

The movement against Belgian King Leopold II's colonization of the Congo provides additional evidence of continuity between the social movements of the nineteenth century and the current global justice movement. From 1890 to 1910, an incredibly cruel form of colonization took root in the Congo; the Belgians used kidnapping and torture to force Africans to gather rubber in the jungle, murdered Africans for sport, and ordered soldiers to chop off the hands of adults and children they had killed to prove that they had used their bullets effectively.[7] The movement against colonization was sparked, in part, by a manager from an English shipping company, who recognized that his company's trade with the Congo was not really free or equal trade. Edmund Morel observed, as he supervised the loading and unloading of ships in Belgium, that a great wealth of ivory and rubber was being imported from the Congo, but only soldiers and guns were being exported in return. Assisted by exposés from two African Americans who had lived in the Congo, and with the support of a gay Irish Republican, Morel led a solidarity movement that eventually included large numbers of activists in England and the United States with supportive events in distant countries such as Australia. Hundreds of Congolese participated by sharing their stories with missionaries and movement activists, risking their lives in order to help activists publicize the atrocities internationally. Tens of thousands more lost their lives when they openly resisted colonial rule.

Morel and his colleagues saw governments as their key targets. While they had limited power to confront the Belgian state directly, they attacked it by pressuring non-Belgian states to sanction King Leopold II, much as today's human rights activists pressure their own governments to apply sanctions to countries that grossly abuse human rights.

New technologies played a large role in the development of the movement. Transportation developments and the telegraph made international communication and cooperation more feasible, the camera was used to document the atrocities, and slide-shows helped spread these images to a wide audience. These developments in information technology played the role the Internet currently plays in informing and mobilizing mass movements of activists. Like today's multinational corporations, the king fought back with his own information campaign: he financed newspapers that carried strategically placed articles on the Congo, distributed brochures and booklets to elite decision makers, and sponsored lobbyists in the United States, England, and Germany. Eventually, however, the activists succeeded in tarnishing the king's reputation, and portraying the injustices of his rule as "crimes against humanity," a term that African American journalist and historian George Washington Williams coined to describe Leopold's lethal role in the Congo.[8]

The movement's success in education did not translate into a complete change in policy, but gradually, some reforms were made, and the worst abuses of the colonial regime began to end with the death of King Leopold II. Morel and other members of the movement can be seen as early human rights activists; they used information as a political tool[9] and appealed to the concept of universal rights in order to exert moral, political, and economic pressure to change a regime that used immoral labor practices in the name of commerce.

The Anti-imperialist Movement: U.S.–Philippine Solidarity

The anti–slave trade, workers, and Congo reform movements directly fueled the dynamic U.S. anti-imperialist movement, which, to a degree, worked in solidarity with the Philippine independence movement.[10] The U.S. government, led by Presidents William McKinley and Teddy Roosevelt, had observed the European nations grabbing territories in Africa, Latin America, and Asia. With no remaining land in North America, and determined to access trade opportunities in China, the United States decided that the Philippines would be a perfect colony. The Filipinos were fighting against brutal Spanish colonizers. The United States sided with the Filipinos only long enough to defeat Spain in 1898—then turned its guns on the local population in 1899.

The transformation of the United States into a colonial power catalyzed a dynamic anti-imperialist movement and generated a fiery debate that divided the country. The movement included elderly activists who had previously been involved in the movement against slavery. It also included many African Americans, who saw the lethal racism in United States treatment of the Filipinos; among other forms of repression, the United States used "reconcentration camps" and "water torture" in the Philippines in an attempt to suppress the independence fighters.[11] Union leaders in the United States, including Samuel Gompers, opposed imperialism because they believed that the poor would bear the cost of empire through higher taxes, loss of life in war, and lower wages due to competition with the exploited labor force of the colonies. Intellectuals such as William James argued that empire was incompatible with the ideals expressed in the Constitution, and was a threat to democracy at home as well as abroad. Congo activist Edmund Morel visited the United States to help strengthen the anti-imperialist movement (and anti-imperialist Mark Twain helped build the U.S. branch of the Congo reform movement).

Most anti-imperialists supported the idea of Filipino self-government as articulated by Emilio Aguinaldo, the leader of the independence movement. The American Anti-imperialist League wrote that "We maintain that governments derive their just powers from the consent of the governed. . . .We earnestly condemn the policy of the present National Administration in the Philippines. It seeks to extinguish the spirit of 1776 in those islands."[12] Collaboration between the U.S. activists and the Aguinaldo movement was difficult because of the logistics of war and communication, but the U.S. anti-imperialists found ways to communicate directly with the Filipino rebels, as shown by secret documents captured by the U.S. Army. Many U.S. citizens, including disillusioned soldiers who had returned from combat in the Philippines, spoke publicly in favor of the Filipinos, although their actions prompted others to label them as traitors and even threaten them physically. Several African American soldiers went even further; they defected from the U.S. Army and joined the Filipino side. Corporal David Fagan, one of the defectors, became an officer in the guerrilla army and helped lead Filipino troops in their war against the U.S. occupation.

In many ways, the anti-imperialist movement failed; the Philippines was granted independence from the United States only in 1946. Since then, the United States has continued to exert "neocolonial" rule, propping up pro-U.S. presidents including dictator Ferdinand Marcos and promoting economic reforms in the interest of U.S. businesses, through the World Bank and other multilateral institutions. The anti-imperialist movement, however, did raise the political cost of empire to the point that the United States ceased trying to gain new territories overseas, preferring to use indirect methods of control. The anti-imperialists also set a precedent of grassroots U.S. support for democracy movements overseas, even when those movements were actively opposed by the U.S. government, a tradition that continued with support for the Spanish Republicans in the 1930s and the Nicaraguan Sandinistas in the 1980s, as well as various liberation movements in Africa from the 1950s to the present.

Today's activists, therefore, as they plan protests against the World Trade Organization, International Monetary Fund, World Bank, and transnational corporations, should not think that they represent the spontaneous generation of a new protest phenomenon. Certainly, some aspects of the current movement are new—such as the use of the Internet for informing and organizing. But the protests, from Seattle to Genoa, from Argentina to South Africa, have deep roots. Changes in technology, innovative protest styles, and analytical advances have been utilized for hundreds of years by organized groups of people seeking to oppose the devastating effects of global trade on local communities in Africa, Asia, Latin America, and beyond. The current protests would not be possible without the precedents set by earlier activists. And we can be confident that future activists will build on the analysis and tactical innovations, as well as the successes and failures, of today's movement for global justice.

Notes

The author would like to thank the following individuals for their comments on earlier drafts of this paper: Waskar Ari, John Cavanagh, Robert Crews, Jamie Foster, Bill Freese, Adam Hochschild, Joseph Horgan, Michael Kazin, Peter Klarén, Bill Minter, Jim O'Brien, Michael Prokosch, Richard Tucker, and David Walls. The initial research for the article was conducted for Professor Robin Broad of American University; she provided the questions that this article answers, as well as helpful commentary on earlier drafts and much encouragement. Any errors are my own. The footnotes of this article have been condensed. A version of the article with complete footnotes is available at www.volunteeroverseas.org through the link to Zahara Heckscher's biography.

1. Genesis 37:25–28.

2. While "international" here is somewhat ahistorical since the nation-state did not exist in its current form until relatively recently, I will stretch the terms "international" and "transnational" to include trade and activism among different cultures, kingdoms, and continents as well as among different nations.

3. The principal source on the Tupac Amaru uprising is Peter Flindell Klarén, *Peru: Society and Nationhood in the Andes* (New York: Oxford University Press, 2000). Klarén's definitive analysis includes an insightful bibliographical essay on the uprising and related events. Additional sources include Leon G. Campbell, "Social Structure of the Tupac Amaru Uprising in Cuzco, 1780–81," *Hispanic American Historical Review* vol. 64, no. 61 (1981): 675–693; Leon G. Campbell, "Church and State in Colonial Peru: The Bishop of Cuzco and the Tupac Amaru Rebellion of 1780," *Journal of Church and State* 22, no. 2 (1980): 251–270; and Leon G. Campbell, "Women and the Great Rebellion in Peru 1780–1783," *Americas (Academy of American Franciscan History)* 42, no. 2 (1985): 163–196.

4. The main sources of the anti-slave trade movement examples are Seymour Drescher, "Whose Abolition? Popular Pressure and the Ending of the British Slave Trade," *Past and Present*, no. 143 (May 1944) 136–166; Roger Anstey, *The Atlantic Slave Trade and British Abolition 1760–1810* (N.J.: Humanities Press, 1975); Clare Midgley, *Women against Slavery: The*

British Campaigns, 1780–1840 (London: Routledge, 1992); Olaudah Equiano, *The Interesting Narrative of the Life of Olaudah Equiano, Written by Himself* (Boston: Bedford Books, 1995 [first published 1789]; J. R. Oldfield, *Popular Politics and British Anti-slavery* (Manchester, U.K.: Manchester University Press, 1995); Wylie Sypher, "The African Prince in London," *Journal of the History of Ideas* vol. 2, no. 2 (April 1941): 237–247; Herbert S. Klein, *The Atlantic Slave Trade* (Cambridge, U.K.: Cambridge University Press, 1999).

5. The analysis of the anti–slave trade movement as precursor to today's social movements was informed by Margaret Keck and Kathryn Sikkink, *Activists beyond Borders: Advocacy Networks in International Politics* (Ithaca, N.Y.: Cornell University Press, 1998).

6. It was in this context that Karl Marx wrote the Communist Manifesto. The examples of the European trade union internationalism are from Susan Milner, *The Dilemmas of Internationalism* (New York: Berg, 1990).

7. The source of the Congo reform movement examples and analysis is Adam Hochschild's outstanding history of the colonization of the Congo, *King Leopold's Ghost* (Boston: Houghton Mifflin, 1998).

8. Williams's letter to the U.S. Secretary of State is quoted in Hochschild, *King Leopold's Ghost*, 112.

9. Keck and Sikkink, *Activists beyond Borders*, 18–22.

10. The principal sources of the anti-imperialist movement examples are Daniel B. Schirmer and Stephen Rosskamm Shalom, eds., *The Philippines Reader: A History of Colonialism, Neocolonialism, Dictatorship, and Resistance* (Boston: South End Press, 1987); Philip Foner and Richard Winchester, eds., *The Anti-imperialist Reader (Volume I): A Documentary History of Anti-imperialism in the United States, from the Mexican War to the Election of 1900* (New York: Holmes and Meier, 1984); and Philip Foner, *The Anti-imperialist Reader (Volume II): The Literary Anti-imperialists* (New York: Holmes and Meier, 1986).

11. Glenn A. Mann, "Corporal Daniel J. Evans Describes the 'Water Cure,' 1902" and "War and Disease in the Battle for Batangas," in Thomas G. Paterson and Dennis Merrill, *Major Problems in U.S. Foreign Relations, Volume I* (Boston: Houghton Mifflin, 2000), 387–389, 393–401.

12. "Platform of the American Anti-imperialist League, 1899," in Schirmer and Shalom, *The Philippines Reader*, 29–31.

2.4

Present at the Creation: The Bretton Woods Agreements

Dean Acheson

Agriculture and relief were simple matters compared to international monetary arrangements. The period of gestation of the latter about doubled that of elephants. Conceived in May 1941 in the lend-lease talks with Maynard Keynes, the agreements were brought forth in July 1944. For nearly two years the treasuries of the two countries, with Maynard Keynes leading for the British and Harry Dexter White for us, exchanged drafts and ideas. From time to time State and other agencies participated in a subsidiary way, our interest being directed chiefly to commercial policy and commodity agreements. . . .

By the spring of 1943 the White draft of an international monetary fund, with Keynesian amendments, cleared with Parliament and congressional committees, was distributed for study and further discussion in Washington. Nineteen of the governments sent experts to meet in June and make a report. An Anglo-American group in the autumn added sections on commercial policy, commodity agreements, cartels, and employment. The work of both groups emerged in the spring of 1944 as a "Joint Statement of Technical Experts on the Establishment of an International Monetary Fund." Meanwhile, the Treasury also conferred

with congressional committees and then published a draft outline of a proposed International Bank for Reconstruction and Development. In May the State Department issued invitations to forty-odd governments to meet on July 1 at Bretton Woods, New Hampshire, "for the purpose of formulating proposals of a definite character for an international monetary fund and possibly a bank for reconstruction and development."

Henry Morgenthau deserves the same high praise that has been given Mr. Hull regarding the United Nations Charter for the patience and thoroughness with which he prepared with Congress, foreign governments, and the public these intricate and most important agreements. They could not have been put through without his special quality of leadership. The field, especially of the Monetary Fund, was so technical that is necessitated picking a highly qualified lieutenant to do the technical work and backing him to the hilt. The field of monetary arrangements itself evoked very little popular and no congressional interest. Here Morgenthau's capacity for almost obsessive concentration on the matter in hand became of great importance. Harry White, so far as I could observe, served Secretary Morgenthau with complete loyalty and great skill. In later years it was charged that he had Communist sympathies. I have often been so outraged by Harry White's capacity for rudeness in discussion that the charges made against him would have seemed mild compared to expressions I have used, but he could be equally pleasant and amusing, as I well

Dean Acheson, "The Bretton Woods Agreements," in *Present at the Creation: My Years in the State Department* (New York: W. W. Norton, 1969), 81–84. Copyright © 1969 by Dean Acheson, reprinted with permission of W. W. Norton & Company, Inc.

remember from an evening when we joined the Keyneses for dinner at the Whites'. I have often differed, sometimes violently, with his policies, but they were usually policies that I knew were strongly favored by his chief. He died suddenly in 1948, and time has mellowed for me the harsher side of his nature. I say to his restless spirit with kindliness, *"Requiescat in pace."*

By the time invitations to the conference went out, I had been left without competitors as State's representative in the enterprise. Bretton Woods had been chosen both for the beneficent climate of the White Mountains and the availability there of a summer hotel of adequate size and condition. However, having been closed for three years, it presented problems of staffing and operation in wartime that had not been fully considered. Having at least recognized them, I did not stay in the hotel myself but in a comfortable inn at nearby Crawford Notch. The transportation problem was solved by appropriate attention to the military police assigned to guard our privacy and well-being.

Henry Morgenthau put me on the delegation despite an argument I had with him over its selection. He wished to include in it the ranking majority and minority members of the Banking and Currency committees of the two houses. However, Senator Charles Tobey of New Hampshire, the ranking Republican on the Senate committee, was reputed to be an extreme isolationist, and Morgenthau wanted to bypass him in favor of the next Republican. To have been pointedly excluded from a conference held in his own state when he was running for re-election would have been an insult Senator Tobey could not have overlooked. The sacred rights of seniority would have ranged his colleagues on his side and an enterprise that needed all the congressional support it could get would have been launched with a bitter partisan row. This, I told Morgenthau, could prove its death warrant; I might be a novice in international monetary arrangements, but I was a professional in senatorial ones. Reluctantly, he backed away from this folly and Tobey became one of the most effective supporters in the Congress of the international bank and fund. He also became a devoted and loyal friend to me.

While we were battling the disorganization during the opening weekend at Bretton Woods, Senator Tobey came to me with a request. The Fourth of July and the need for an address at the conference were hard upon us. So was the Republican primary in New Hampshire, where he faced opposition. If he could make the Independence Day address, he would receive most gratifying publicity throughout the state. With the help of Fred Vinson it was arranged, and our relations were forever cemented.

The evening of our arrival at Bretton Woods, unknown to me, proved to be the five-hundredth anniversary of the concordat between King's College, Cambridge, and New College, Oxford. Maynard Keynes, a devoted Kingsman, had arranged a celebration into which he poured his exuberant enthusiasm. Overcoming the near anarchy in the kitchen and wine cellar, he had organized a dinner for seven or eight representing the two colleges as well as Yale University, with which King's had a special relation, originating when a Kingsman, Charles Seymour, became President of Yale. H. H. Kung, the Chinese Finance Minister, who had recently received an honorary degree from the university, Oscar Cox, and I represented Yale. In private Keynes disrespectfully referred to His Excellency as "the old Mandarin" and in public delighted in asking his views on the most complicated monetary problems. But "H.H.," who had married a sister of Mme. Sun Yat-sen and Mme. Chiang Kai-shek, was quite able to hold his own in any company. He did so that evening, when Keynes was at his most charming and brilliant on the subject of the contribution of universities to civilization.

For nearly four weeks the work of the conference went on all day and often far into the night. Keynes thought that the pressure was "quite unbelievable," though by our standards it did not seem unusual. After attending some night sessions, contrary to his doctor's orders, he suffered a heart attack and forswore them. An effort to keep Keynes's illness quiet proved unsuccessful and led to the usual investigations of who leaked the story to the press. It appeared that on the evening of his attack an alarmed Lady Keynes, looking for someone to fetch a doctor, found a most helpful young man who, of course, turned out to have been a newspaper correspondent.

The chief work and arguments of the conference concerned the International Monetary Fund, where the State Department's interest in maintaining the freedom of trade from legal or monetary restraints was watched over by Pete Collado and Leo Pasvolsky. Under the monetary conditions existing at the end of the war, what Mr. Hull had always opposed as impediments to trade were seen by the Treasury as discriminations against the United States and just as vigorously opposed. My own duties and interest centered in the work of Committee II on the international bank, to which under Keynes's chairmanship I had been assigned and put in charge of drafting the bank's charter. Years later George Woods, then President of the bank, expressed his gratitude for its flexibility and broad powers. As contrasted with the fund, whose charter was largely dictated by monetary experts and narrowly hedged about, the bank management could do anything it wanted to. This restrictiveness of the fund document, mistakenly attributed by Keynes to the lawyers, was what he had in mind when he said in the final plenary session of July 22: "I wish that [the lawyers] had not covered so large a part of our birth certificate with such very detailed provisions for our burial service, hymns and lessons and all."

Keynes did not like lawyers. He thought the United States "a lawyer-ridden land" and believed that "the *Mayflower*, when she sailed from Plymouth, must have been entirely filled with lawyers." However, he paid our little band at Bretton Woods a handsome compliment for approaching his ideal lawyer: "I want him [a lawyer] to tell me how to do what *I* think sensible, and, above all, to devise means by which it will be lawful for me to go on being sensible in unforeseen conditions some years hence. . . . Too often lawyers are men who turn poetry into prose and prose into jargon. Not so our lawyers here in Bretton Woods. On the contrary, they have turned our jargon into prose and our prose into poetry. And only too often they have had to do our thinking for us."

In our discussions of the bank in Committee II we ran into three substantive issues, which in the end were worked out by private negotiation. The first of these grew out of the competing claims for loans of war-torn and undeveloped areas. Keynes and I favored equitable consideration of both, the criteria being the need for and efficacy of the project rather than the cause of it. White disagreed. The solid weight of the Latin American delegations threw the decision our way. More difficult was the desire of all delegations, led by the Russians closely followed by the Latin Americans, for much lower subscriptions to the capital of the bank than to that of the fund. The reason, of course, was that drawings

upon the fund were related to subscriptions and quotas, while borrowings from the bank would be unrelated to ownership of the capital stock. However, a general failure to subscribe would mean either no bank or one financed largely by the United States. Henry Morgenthau put a great effort into getting the Soviet Union to raise its subscription to the bank to the level of its quota in the fund. He was able to announce the achievement of this goal at the final plenary session. It was, however, a short-lived success, since the Soviet Union did not ratify either agreement.

Eddie Miller and I had more enduring success with the American republics. This involved many and long discussions with the principal delegations, followed by meetings with the whole group. One problem was to find a place spacious but private enough for so large and so confidential a meeting. My so-called office was clearly not that, as a more or less enclosed corner of the ballroom, now the plenary-session hall, had been turned over to me. It had once been a bar and still had the curtain that had been pulled across at closing time. Into this small spot of happier memories Miss Evans moved her typewriter and used the sink designed for washing glasses as a filing cabinet. She soon adopted other officeless waifs, including a spaniel, which frequently added its comments to the debates in progress on the other side of the curtain. We found other places to meet with our Latin American friends, who soon succumbed to Eddie's charm and persuasiveness in Spanish, Portuguese, and English.

The third issue was solved by changing our minds. The British had wanted the bank's lending power to be limited to the amount of its capital and surplus, while we had advocated a high ratio of loans to assets. However, our commercial-banker member, Ned Brown, pointed out to us that we would be defeating our own purposes in taking this view. The bank's bonds could not, at least initially, be sold without some guarantee by the United States Government, and our proposed original position would have required an open-ended commitment from the United States. We hastily joined the British in their position.

Toward the end of July the Bretton Woods conference ended amid mutual congratulations and we returned from our White Mountain resort to the muggy heat of a Washington August.

2.5

Multinational Corporations and United States Foreign Policy

Senator Frank Church

The International Telephone and Telegraph Co. and Chile, 1970–71

In May 1972, the Senate Foreign Relations Committee voted to conduct an investigation of assertions that the International Telephone and Telegraph Co. sought to enlist the cooperation of the U.S. Government in preventing Dr. Salvador Allende Gossens from taking office as President of Chile in 1970 and, subsequently, proposed policies to U.S. Government officials designed to bring about Mr. Allende's downfall.

These allegations arose out of the publication of a number of articles by Jack Anderson, the syndicated columnist, and others, based upon purported letters and memoranda written by various executives of ITT.

The committee felt, however, in order to insure a fair and balanced investigation, it was advisable to postpone any hearings until after the U.S. presidential election.

Scope of Study

The committee also voted to look beyond this particular case and undertake a broad examina-

tion of the role of multinational corporations, their influence on U.S. foreign policy and their economic impact. This study will take several years to complete. It will be comprehensive in scope, and it will seek to answer, among others, such questions as the following:

Do the activities of the multinational corporations advance the interests of the people of the United States taken as a whole? Are they exporting jobs which might otherwise be kept at home? Do they prefer to invest rather than export abroad because of the demands of the world market, or do our own government's policies skew the options in favor of investing? How do we achieve an increasingly open world economic system, and, at the same time, guarantee our own people that they will be gainfully employed? To what extent have our foreign aid programs been used to service the special needs of American-owned corporations abroad and to what extent should they be? Are investment incentives offered by the Federal Government to induce foreign investment by private capital either necessary or desirable in today's developing world? Finally, we shall seek to determine to what extent there is a coincidence of interest between the multinational corporations and U.S. foreign policy in selected key areas of the world.

In this hearing, we shall seek to ascertain whether the ITT corporation and the Central Intelligence Agency cooperated in an effort to prevent Salvador Allende Gossens from being

United States Senate, Committee on Foreign Relations, Subcommittee on Multinational Corporations, "Opening Statements by Senator Frank Church," *Multinational Corporations and United States Foreign Policy*, 93rd and 94th Congresses, Part 1 (20 March 1973), Part 4 (30 January 1974), and Part 12 (16 May 1975).

elected President of Chile in 1970; whether the company sought to induce other U.S. corporations to cooperate with it in bringing pressure upon U.S. Government officials to adopt policies which would make life more difficult for Mr. Allende's government; whether the ITT company proposed to U.S. Government officials policies designed to bring pressure on Mr. Allende's government, and, possibly, to lead to Mr. Allende's downfall; whether, as Mr. Allende has alleged, there was a credit embargo imposed on Chile by U.S. banks.

The telephone properties of the ITT company were guaranteed against expropriation by an insurance policy originally issued by the Agency for International Development. This policy is now administered by the Overseas Private Investment Corporation. The Chilean Government has intervened in the properties of the company. In the event the company is entitled to compensation, the potential liability for OPIC, which is federally financed, is an estimated $96.5 million.

The answers to the above questions may have a bearing on whether the company is entitled to be paid compensation under the insurance policy.

The multinational corporation is a relatively new phenomenon. It has only recently become a part of the American public consciousness, despite the fact that American overseas investment has had an explosive growth in the years following World War II. This growth is not limited to Latin America. The American presence abroad is pervasive and geographically widely distributed. It plays a significant role in such diverse areas as Australia, Canada, and the European Economic Community as well as Latin America.

In all of these areas, we can discern a rising tide of nationalism, which increasingly bears upon the role of the multinational corporations, largely U.S.-owned, in the economies and societies of these countries. It may be critical for the survival and viability of these corporations, that there be agreed upon standards of conduct in the countries in which they operate.

[. . .]

Multinational Petroleum Companies and Foreign Policy

. . . We are today opening a public hearing into the relationship of the multinational petroleum companies and U.S. foreign policy and whether, and to what extent this relationship has contributed to the energy crisis with which we are all so familiar. That experience now encompasses long lines at local gas stations, confused and daily changing statements by Government officials as to the dimensions, scope, and characteristics of the crisis; major consuming countries, allied to the United States, strike out on their own "to cut a deal" with the Arab Governments in what, increasingly has all of the characteristics of a mad scramble for the petroleum which comes out of the desert sands of the Middle East. Above all, there is a pervasive suspicion among the American people of oil companies, Government officials and, yes, the U.S. Congress. Indeed, anyone who has had anything to do with the decisions which affect international oil is today suspect in the public mind.

In part, industry and government have no one to blame but themselves. They have enveloped the government-industry relationship with a curtain of secrecy which inevitably has led to the most far-reaching suspicions. The first imperative in any inquiry into the causes of the energy crisis is thus to set aside, finally and definitively, this curtain of secrecy and allow the American people to understand what were the basic decisions which have a bearing on the present crisis, how these decisions were made, what were the alternatives, and what the effects have been. Only then can we rationally begin to formulate policies for the future which will have the requisite amount of public support.

Consequently, we initiate this inquiry with the intention of providing the American people with a comprehensive explanation of those foreign policy decisions, which are critical to an understanding of how we arrived at where we are today with respect to international oil. In so doing, we are dealing with corporate entities which may have many of the characteristics of nations. Of the 15 largest multinational corporations in the world today, 7 are petroleum companies. These seven companies—Exxon, Gulf, Texaco, Mobil, Standard Oil of California [SoCal], Royal Dutch-Shell and BP—British Petroleum—have annual sales which are in excess of the gross national product of such nations as India, Poland, Brazil, Sweden, and the German Republic. The smallest of the American "sisters," SoCal, has assets exceeding $8 billion. Thus, it should surprise no one that, in the course of these hearings, it may well appear, when we speak of corporate and Government relationships, the language will be that which is appropriate to dealings between sovereigns.

[. . .]

Reflection Upon the Extent United States Can Depend on Multinational Corporations

Moreover, we must realistically recognize that what we see in oil today may well be reproduced with respect to other major commodities. These hearings then are not only an examination of the relationship of multinational petroleum companies and U.S. foreign policy, but they also deal with a more far-reaching issue: To what degree this country can and ought to depend upon the multinational corporations to assure us of a secure source of raw materials at reasonable prices? We are today faced with a situation in which the U.S. national security is truly at issue and which calls for a clear perception of where lies the national interest and to what extent that interest coincides or diverges with the interests of private oil companies.

At bottom, that is the central issue that we seek to explore in these hearings.

[. . .]

Political Contributions to Foreign Governments

Gulf Oil Corp.

In the course of the Watergate Committee hearings and the investigation by the Special Prosecutor, it became apparent that major American corporations had made illegal political contributions in the United States. More recently, the Securities Exchange Commission has revealed that several multinational corporations had failed to report to their shareholders millions of dollars of offshore payments in violation of the Securities laws of the United States. The Gulf Oil Corporation, before us today, has admitted making $4.8 million in domestic political contributions and at least $4.3 million in overseas political payments.

The Securities and Exchange Commission is understandably concerned that the disclosure requirements of U.S. laws are complied with. This subcommittee is concerned with the foreign policy consequences of these payments by U.S.-based multinational corporations.

This is not a pleasant or easy subject for the corporations involved or U.S. Government officials to discuss in a public forum. This subcommittee deliberated long and hard as to whether it should pursue this matter, and, if so, in what fashion. It decided by a unanimous vote to initiate this investigation and to do so in open public hearings. For what we are concerned with is not a question of private or public morality. What concerns us here is a major issue of foreign policy for the United States.

No one has put it more succinctly than Gunnar Myrdal in his brilliant book "Asian Drama." Describing what he calls the "soft state," Myrdal writes:

> Generally speaking, the habitual practice of bribery and dishonesty tends to pave the way for an authoritarian regime, whose disclosures of corrupt practices in the preceding government and whose punitive action against offenders provide a basis for its initial acceptance by the articulate strata of the populations. The Communists maintain that corruption is bred by capitalism, and with considerable justification they pride themselves on its eradication under a Communist regime.
>
> The elimination of corrupt practices has also been advanced as the main justification for military takeovers. Should the new regime be unsuccessful in its attempt to eradicate corruption, its failure will prepare the ground for a new putsch of some sort. Thus, it is obvious that the extent of corruption has a direct bearing on the stability of governments.

It follows that, if a substantial number of multinational corporations bribe or attempt to gain influence through huge campaign contributions or agent's fees which find their way into the hands of foreign government officials, these very corporations may, in the long run, be the losers. Eventually, indigenous forces of reform or revolution will turn on these companies and make them the targets of radical measures.

Furthermore, illicit corporate contributions, bribes, and payoffs create unfair conditions for scrupulous competitors. Foreign officials looking for money are unconcerned about the quality of the product or service being offered. The company which slips the most under the table will get the most favored treatment.

Under such circumstances, a company which tries to maintain higher ethical standards finds itself up against the unfair competition of companies that resort to large-scale bribery. Ethical corporations will be squeezed out of many foreign markets and even the unethical firms will find their profits diminished.

Thus, we must know from our witnesses here today what were the circumstances which led them to make these payments. In what country were they made? Were they illegal in the country in which they were made? If the corporation was reluctant, did it bring the matter to the attention of the U.S. Embassy? If not, why not? Does the United States have a foreign assistance program in the country in which the payment was made? Was the company's investment in the country guaranteed, in whole or in part, by our Government's Overseas Private Investment Corporation? Was the U.S. Embassy aware of such payments? If not, why not?

Finally, this subcommittee will consider what legislation, if any, is warranted. Much has been written about codes of conduct governing multinational corporations. Many of the issues—transfer prices, expropriation—are complex and controversial. But there should be no controversy about this issue: if the developing countries are sincere in their desire to define acceptable rules of conduct for multinational corporations, then they should be willing to agree that corporations that do business in their country should be free from extortion. The corporations, if they are serious about wanting the rules of the game defined, should be willing to agree that they will refrain from making questionable payments to obtain competitive advantages. And the administration, if it is genuinely concerned about this problem, ought to take the lead in seeking a consensus around these elementary propositions.

In short, we cannot close our eyes to this problem. It is no longer sufficient to simply sigh and say that is the way business is done. It is time to treat the issue for what it is: a serious foreign policy problem.

2.6

Declaration on the Establishment of a New International Economic Order

United Nations General Assembly

We, the Members of the United Nations,
Having convened a special session of the General Assembly to study for the first time the problems of raw materials and development, devoted to the consideration of the most important economic problems facing the world community,

Bearing in mind the spirit, purpose and principles of the Charter of the United Nations to promote the economic advancement and social progress of all peoples,

Solemnly proclaim our united determination to work urgently for THE ESTABLISHMENT OF A NEW INTERNATIONAL ECONOMIC ORDER based on equity, sovereign equality, interdependence, common interest and co-operation among all States, which shall correct inequalities and redress existing injustice, make it possible to eliminate the widening gap between the developed and the developing countries and ensure steadily accelerating economic and social development for present and future generations.

1. The greatest and most significant achievement since the foundation of the United Nations has been the independence from colonial and alien domination of a large number of peoples and nations which has enabled them to become members of the community of free peoples. Technological progress has also been made in all spheres of economic activities in the last three decades, thus providing a solid potential for improving the well-being of all peoples. However, the remaining vestiges of alien domination, colonialism, foreign occupation, racial discrimination, *apartheid* and neo-colonialism in all its forms continue to be the greatest obstacles to the full emancipation and progress of the developing countries. The benefits of technological progress are not shared equitably by all members of the international community. The developing countries which constitute 70 per cent of the world population account for only 30 per cent of the world's income. It is not possible to achieve an even and balanced development of the international community under the existing international economic order. The gap between the developed and the developing countries continues to widen in a system that was established at a time when most of the developing countries did not even exist as independent States and which, by all its elements, perpetuates inequality.

2. The present international economic order is in direct conflict with current develop-

United Nations General Assembly, "Declaration on the Establishment of a New International Economic Order," Sixth Special Session, 1 May 1974, UN General Assembly Resolution 3201.

ments in international political and economic relations. Since 1970, the world economy has experienced a series of grave crises which have had severe repercussions, especially on the developing countries because of their generally greater vulnerability to external economic impulses. The developing world has become a powerful factor that makes its influence felt in all fields of international activity. These irresistible changes in the relationship of forces in the world necessitate the active, full and equal participation of the developing countries in the formulation and application of all decisions that concern the international community.

3. All these changes have thrust into prominence the reality of interdependence of all the members of the world community. Current events have brought into sharp focus the realization that the interests of the developed countries can no longer be isolated from the interests of the developing countries; that there is close interdependence between the prosperity of the developed and the growth and the development of the developing countries, and that the prosperity of the international community as a whole depends upon the prosperity of its constituent parts and international development is a shared and common responsibility of all countries. Thus the political, economic and social well-being of present and future generations depends more than ever on co-operation between all members of the international community on the basis of sovereign equality and the removal of the disequilibrium that exists between them.

4. The new international economic order should be founded on full respect for the following principles:

(a) Sovereign equality of States, self-determination of all peoples, inadmissibility of the acquisition of territories by force, territorial integrity and non-interference in the internal affairs of other States;

(b) Broadest co-operation of all the member States of the international community, based on equity, whereby the prevailing disparities in the world may be banished and prosperity secured for all;

(c) Equal participation of all countries in the solving of world economic problems in the common interest of all countries, bearing in mind the necessity to ensure the accelerated development of all the developing countries. While devoting particular attention to the adoption of special measures in favour of the least developed, landlocked and island developing countries as well as those developing countries most seriously affected by economic crises and natural calamities, without losing sight of the interests of other developing countries;

(d) Every country has the right to adopt the economic and social system that it deems to be the most appropriate for its own development and not to be subjected to discrimination of any kind as a result;

(e) Every country has the right to exercise permanent sovereignty over its natural resources and all economic activities. With this principle in mind:

  (i) Every country has the right to exercise effective control over its natural resources and their exploitation with means suitable to its own situation, including the right of nationalization or transfer of ownership to its nationals;

  (ii) The right of all States, territories and peoples under foreign occupation, colonial rule or *apartheid*, to restitution and full compensation for the exploitation and depletion of, and damages to, the natural resources, as well as the exploitation and manipulation of the human resources of those States, territories and peoples;

  (iii) Nationalization is an expression of the sovereign right of every country to safeguard its resources; in this connection, every country has the right to fix the amount of possible compensation and mode of payment, while possible disputes have to be solved in accordance with the domestic laws of every country.

This principle may be applied according to the national interests and laws of each country. It shall in no way affect the right of all States to conclude, in the free exercise of their sovereign will, agreements consonant with the purposes and principles of the United Nations;

(f) Control of the activities of transnational corporations by taking measures in the interest of the national economies of the countries where such transnational corporations operate on the basis of the full sovereignty of those countries;

(g) Right of the developing countries and the peoples of territories under colonial and racial domination and foreign occupation to struggle for their liberation and for the purpose of regaining effective control over their natural resources and economic activities;

(h) Extending of assistance to developing countries, peoples and territories under colonial and alien domination, foreign occupation, racial discrimination, or *apartheid*, or which are subjected to coercion, economic aggression or political pressure and neo-colonialism in all its forms and which have established or are endeavouring to establish effective control over their natural resources and economic activities that have been or are still under foreign control;

(i) Establishment of a just and equitable relationship between the prices of raw materials, primary products, manufactured and semi-manufactured goods exported by developing countries and the prices of raw materials, primary commodities, manufactures, capital goods and equipment imported by them with the aim of improving their terms of trade which have continued to deteriorate;

(j) Extension of active assistance to developing countries by the whole international community;

(k) Establishment of a new international monetary system one of whose main objectives is the promotion of development of the developing countries;

(l) Improving the competitiveness of natural materials facing competition from synthetic substitutes;

(m) Preferential and non-reciprocal treatment for developing countries in all fields of international economic co-operation, wherever possible;

(n) Securing favourable conditions for the transfer of financial resources to developing countries;

(o) To promote the transfer of technology and the creation of indigenous technology for the benefit of the developing countries in forms and in accordance with procedures which are suited to their economies;

(p) Necessity for all States to put an end to the waste of natural resources, including food products;

(q) The need for developing countries to concentrate all their resources for the cause of development;

(r) Strengthening—through individual and collective actions—of mutual economic, trade, financial and technical co-operation among the developing countries on a preferential basis;

(s) Establishment and strengthening by developing countries of producers associations in respect of major primary commodities of importance to the world economy.

5. The unanimous adoption of the International Development Strategy for the Second United Nations Development Decade was an important step in the promotion of international economic co-operation on a just and equitable basis. The accelerated implementation of obligations and commitments assumed by the international community within the framework of the Strategy, particularly those concerning imperative development needs of developing countries, would contribute significantly to the fulfillment of the aims and objectives of the present Declaration.

6. The United Nations is the only universal organization capable of dealing with problems of international economic co-operation in a comprehensive manner and ensuring equally the interests of all countries. It must have an even greater

role in the establishment of a new international economic order. The Charter of Economic Rights and Duties of States, for the preparation of which this Declaration will provide an additional source of inspiration, will constitute a significant contribution in this respect. All the member States of the United Nations are therefore called upon to exert maximum efforts with a view to securing the implementation of this Declaration which is one of the principal guarantees for the creation of better conditions for the present and future generations to live in peace and well-being worthy of human dignity.

7. This declaration on the Establishment of a New International Economic Order shall be one of the most important bases of economic relations between all peoples and all nations.

2.7

We Are to Be Sacrificed: Indigenous Peoples and Dams

Wada Taw-il

I am Wada Taw-il, an Igorot from the Cordillera of Northern Luzon in the Philippines. I have come as a representative of my people and as a witness against the systematic atrocities of exploitation and oppression inflicted upon us as a people.

Including our Muslim brothers and sisters, we number around six and a half million people, or 16 to 18 percent of the total Philippine population. We are composed of more than 60 distinct groups. We are the Igorots of the Mountain Provinces of Kalinga-Apayao, Bontoc, Benguet and Ifugao; the Tinggians of Abra; the Manobos, Subanon, Bilaan, Bagobo, Ata, T'boli, Tagakaolo, Higaonon, Tiruray, Mandaya, Mansaka of the South; the Mangyans of Mindoro; the Gaddangs, Ikalahans and Dumagats of Nueva Vizcaya; the Ibanag of Cagayan Valley; the Negritoes of Zambales, and others.

Our lands are in the remote interiors throughout the length of the Philippine archipelago. We are dependent on our lands in many ways. As farmers, the land is the basis of our survival. We are skilled in our farming practices and have few other options for successful livelihood. We cannot compete in the cities or labor markets as equals.

Wada Taw-il, "We Are to Be Sacrificed: Indigenous Peoples and Dams," in *Philippines: Repression and Resistance—Permanent Peoples' Tribunal Session on the Philippines* (Utrecht, Netherlands: Philippine-European Solidarity Center–Komite ng Sambayanang Pilipino [PESC-KSP], 1980), 184–91.

The land means much to us! Our history is bound to our lands. Fields handed down through generations are both economic assets and a statement of tribal history—a link with past ancestors. The forests and fields have spiritual significance for us, as the homes of powerful natural forces that are to be respected and cherished. They are also the resting place and homes of our ancestors.

The development and improvement of our lands are the fruits of the collective efforts of deceased ancestors. We, the living, have the grave responsibility to care for the land and the dead. Allowing the submersion or destruction of our land means a breaking of this awesome responsibility, an act of desecration against grave-sites and homes of the spirits. But what is more frightening is that it means our death as a people.

We have developed our own extensive and complex system of political organization, including the peace pact—which we have used as an effective deterrent against intruders. From the coming of the Spaniards to the eventual takeover of the Americans, we resisted all forms of foreign invasion.

[. . .]

Today . . . we believe that our culture, beliefs, traditions, indeed our very survival and existence as a people are threatened. We believe that the government is pursuing policies that can only be described as genocidal. . . .

One of the most far reaching and damaging parts of [Marcos] government policy which affects minorities is its energy program. The government has existing plans to build more than 40 major dams. Almost all of these dams are to be built on lands at present occupied by national minorities. The dams will submerge our best farmland, the settlements, graveyards and sacred sites of many peoples. It is estimated that more than one and a half million minority Filipinos and another half million poor farmers will be impoverished and dislocated by these dams.

These dams would not only displace communities of people, but would destroy the whole tribal economy of some peoples. The government has now passed special regulations empowering the National Power Corporation to restrict or even prevent farming within the watershed of dams, and to forcibly expel anyone breaking these rules. These rules would deny the people the means of basic subsistence that has been theirs for centuries. In my home—the Cordillera—the government has immediate plans for eight dams and further proposals for at least seven more. Already the Ifugao people who number more than 100,000 and live in the watershed of the Magat Dam are being prevented from clearing new mountain farms. They are forced instead to plant trees on their old clearings. This will being hunger to the Ifugao. But at the very time that the ordinary people are being prevented from continuing their farming practices, new logging concessions are given within the watershed. Local officials, including the governor and assemblyman of Ifugao, now have commercial logging concessions within the area. So, control over the cutting of trees is only imposed on the poor farmers but not on the rich concessionaire.

The energy program for the next ten years was planned to cost more than $14.5 billion but recently Marcos made an announcement that this program must be implemented in only five years. So our situation has become even more critical.

The proposed energy supply increase is not to meet local needs but is planned as an incentive to foreign investment. The whole program is heavily financed and backed by the World Bank, Asian Development Bank and USAID. Most of the Bank money is being spent on construction and equipment paid straight out to foreign heavy engineering contractors. In the Cordillera, on the Ambuklao dam, it was Guy Atkinson and Co of the USA; on the Magat Dam it is Voest

Alpine and Brown Boveri from Europe; on the Chico, it is Lahmeyer of Germany.

The government makes propaganda that these dams are a sign of progress and prosperity for the nation and will improve the quality of life, especially for the rural poor. But we in the Cordillera ask, "Whom does it really help?" We know it does not help us and we are the most neglected sector of the rural poor. We gain no share in the benefits of these dams, while our livelihood and culture are to be destroyed. We are to be sacrificed. Even Marcos says this.

In 1956 the Ambuklao Ibaloy were moved off their land. There was no adequate compensation, no place for relocation. After 25 years when the dam is already choking to death with silt the people still have no land. When they were on their land, they were promised relocation but when the dam was built and they were no longer a threat, there was no relocation.

The government says that dams will bring electricity and irrigation to the lowland peasants but these people still live in poverty. They cannot afford the high costs of electrical appliances or even irrigation pumps and rentals. The benefit is only to rich landlords in the Cagayan Valley, men like Defense Minister Enrile, Local Government and Community Development Minister Rono, President Marcos and a handful of others, all of whom have large tracts of land in the Cagayan Valley that will be irrigated by the Chico and Magat dams.

The dam program that has been worked out for the Philippines by the World Bank has come to be priority only under martial law conditions. When the Chico was first considered for damming in the 1960s the project was indefinitely shelved because of the social costs involved. But by 1973 under martial law when the people had no voice, it was no longer thought necessary to even ask for the people's opinion or even inform them. In Kalinga and Bontoc, we first learned of the project when survey teams invaded the valley. The people angered by such deceit, ejected the teams.

In July 1974 the survey teams came back with a military escort and abused the people, especially in Cagaluan, Kalinga, where three boys were lined up and soldiers used submachine guns to shoot coconuts off their heads.

We tried petitions and legal appeals to the government and the World Bank, thinking that no one would knowingly destroy the culture and livelihood of the 80,000 people of the Chico. But Marcos avoided meeting our delegations. He made excuses and one delegation that went to Manila to plead for their land was turned away because the President was too busy they said "with the preparations of the *Miss Universe* contest"!

Only when it was clear that the people would fight for their land and would have support in Manila and elsewhere did Marcos take notice. The people adopted the tradition of our peace pact which is strong among us to call for unity in the defense of our lands.

It was at this point that the attempts to trick and deceive and divide us really began. Marcos' Minister Melchor announced the suspension of all work in the Chico Valley and the indefinite postponement of Chico II dam in the heart of the mountains. But it is clear now that this was a conscious trick. There has been no attempt to bring the issue of Chico II up for further discussion but plans for its construction have gone ahead. Construction is now scheduled to begin within 3 years.

At the time of Minister Melchor's announcement the government had fears that the Chico would become another minority problem which could spark off an all out war like that of the Muslims in the south. Marcos has an agency, the PANAMIN (Presidential Assistance on National Minorities), to deal with its minority problem but like the government it does not represent the people but the big business that seeks to exploit their lands. Who the PANAMIN serves is very clear by looking at the people who control it. These people are some of the biggest capitalists in the Philippines like Elizalde, Ayala, Soriano & Cabarrus, and working for them are both serving and retired military officers including those who have been trained in Vietnam in counter-insurgency programs.

PANAMIN was established without even one representative of a national minority as a member. It does not represent or serve the interests of the minority people. Under martial law it has become the government's instrument of repression against minorities. The documents we present show that the PANAMIN, like the state it serves, has had to resort increasingly to armed oppression; and that now, the major item of the

PANAMIN Budget is for its own security not for minority development.

[. . .]

We approached World Bank representatives in Manila who repeated the promise of Robert McNamara that the World Bank would not fund the Chico project in the face of opposition from the people; but they lied and they have continued to fund the project despite our opposition. They have also funded other projects like that on the Magat river and elsewhere.

The people's fight for their rights against the Marcos government has taught them many bitter lessons. The resistance of the Kalinga gives hope to other people in the Philippines, thus the government has to send its troops into the province to silence us.

There have been many and horrible abuses against my people. Many of these abuses are documented and show that contrary to the government's assertion that military abuse is rare and incidental, in fact it is common and systematic. None of the soldiers identified to have committed the severest abuses of murder, torture, arson and rape have ever been made to pay.

[. . .]

In April 1980, Macli-ing Dulag, the spokesman of the Kalingas was murdered by the 44th Infantry Battalion. Macli-ing was a powerful opposition spokesman and the best known of our leaders. He was shot down inside his own house in the night by men since identified and admitted by the government to be members of the 44th Infantry Battalion under the leadership of Lieutenant Adalem. On the same night in the same village an attempt was also made on the life of Pedro Dungoc, another of the Kalinga opposition spokesmen.

Macli-ing was well known to the government for his opposition. His village had hosted two major Peace Pact celebrations called to discuss the dam problem and unite the people and strengthen them in their opposition. He had been offered bribes by Elizalde which he refused.

His murder was a further proof to us that we could not expect justice within the present system where even our most respected spokesmen are just gunned down like animals. The people all know that we must be prepared to defend our land if we are to survive.

2.8

The Pillars of the System

Jacques B. Gélinas

The Bretton Woods Agreement

In the early 1940s, as the guns of war were thundering in Europe, the Allies—mainly the USA and the UK—began designing a new international economic order encompassing currency control, foreign investment, free trade and unimpeded access to raw materials.

Coming out of the war unscathed, overcapitalized and controlling over half the world's industrial production and 80 per cent of all gold reserves, the US took the lead in this process. In July 1944, it convened an international conference, attended by the Allied nations, including the USSR,[1] at Bretton Woods, a New Hampshire resort, to redefine the rules of the post-war trade and monetary game. The leading lights of capitalist economics attended, including the famous British economist John Maynard Keynes and the Undersecretary to the US Treasury, Harry Dexter White. Keynes's proposal involved the creation of an international currency, the *bancor*, administered by a central international bank. That system would have produced a more stable and fair world economy by automatically recycling trade surpluses to finance trade deficits, but it did not suit the United States' interests,

and the latter had sufficient clout to secure approval for its own plan. Recognized as an international currency, the dollar was proclaimed 'as good as gold'. In short, the conference was invited to ratify the crowning of Washington as the world economy's new capital, replacing London after a reign of over two centuries. *Ipso facto*, the US Federal Reserve Board became the world currency issuer.[2]

Underlying all the discussions was an unswerving belief in the universal principle of free trade and free competition upon which the United States had resolved to found the new economic order. This principle gave absolute priority to the market for the allocation of resources and distribution of wealth. Power having spoken, the economists and other experts readily followed suit in celebrating the virtues of the market.

From Bretton Woods sprang the three pillars, as they were then called, of the new international economic edifice: the International Monetary Fund (IMF), the International Bank for Reconstruction and Development, or the World Bank, and, in 1947, the General Agreement on Tariffs and Trade, better known as the GATT.

The International Monetary Fund

The IMF was given the mandate of instituting an international monetary order based on currency

Jacques B. Gélinas, "The Pillars of the System," in *Freedom from Debt: The Reappropriation of Development through Financial Self-Reliance*, trans. Arnold Bennett and Raymond Robitaille (London: Zed, 1998), 46–58.

stability. All currencies were declared exchangeable at fixed rates against the dollar, which itself was indexed to gold at the fixed rate of $35 an ounce. Together with the central banks, the IMF's job was to guarantee this stability. Its specific role was to defend currency parity against market pressures by providing support, primarily through short- and medium-term loans, to economies afflicted by a budget deficit or temporary financial instability.

In August 1971, the United States suspended the convertibility of the dollar, that is, the possibility of trading it for gold at a fixed rate. By that very fact, the IMF lost its *raison d'être* because the replacement of fixed rates with generalized currency floating made its currency stabilization role insignificant. Instead of disappearing, however, the IMF found a new calling: restructuring the economies of the underdeveloped countries, whose debt levels were beginning to cause concern.

Today, the IMF is riding high with 181 members—almost every country in the world—and 2000 employees at its headquarters, not far from the Capitol in Washington, DC. In the early 1990s, it saw its role confirmed as the international monetary system's main pillar, when it required its members to boost their shares substantially so that it could enhance its role in refinancing the debt-ridden countries. The G7 approved the expansion of the IMF's lending capabilities, bringing the Fund's capital to $200 billion. At its recent meetings, the G7 agreed to double this amount in order to set up a new Emergency Financing Mechanism to support countries confronted with a 'Mexico-type crisis'.[3] In so doing, the industrialized countries acknowledged the IMF's role as the pillar of the debt system. Perceiving the absurdity of the process, some renowned economists have suggested that the IMF 'give up this role, since it can never be strong enough to support a mountain of debt'.[4] The IMF will never act on this suggestion since no handsomely paid and well-maintained bureaucracy has ever undermined itself or even reformed on its own initiative.

IMF policies are decided upon by the member countries, whose voting rights, and shares, are proportional to the size of their GDP. The OECD group holds about 60 per cent of the voting rights, the G7 countries 45 per cent and the United States alone 17 per cent. Third World countries thus have a negligible influence on IMF decisions.

The IMF is more authoritarian and more powerful than its sister institution, the World Bank. It is also more secretive. It does not have to bother about development, the environment and social parameters. It pretends to abide by strict monetary rules which are noble, absolute and immutable. This is why the IMF transcends all these terrestrial problems. Its experts are never at fault. The satirist hardly exaggerated when he had one of these experts reply to criticism: 'That's fine in practice, but it doesn't work in theory.'

The World Bank Group

As indicated by its official name, the International Bank for Reconstruction and Development, the World Bank's mission initially involved two aspects: reconstruction of war-ravaged European countries and development financing. It began lending in 1946, first concentrating on rebuilding Europe, but the USA undercut it in 1948 by launching the Marshall Plan.

Seeing its primary role significantly reduced from the start, the Bank adjusted its aim and focused on the underdeveloped world. From 1948 on, it opened its coffers to the Latin American countries, starting with Chile, Mexico and Brazil. Its objectives have steadily evolved in this direction. The media often attribute a humanitarian role to the World Bank, but in fact its stated goals are: (1) to finance development by lending money while seeking maximum profits as circumstances dictate; (2) 'to promote private foreign investments'; (3) 'to promote the long-range balanced growth of international trade'.[5] It has regularly reported profits over the past decade, accumulating over $16 billion in reserves, with its present rate of profit at around $1 billion a year.

Be that as it may, aid from the Bank translates into loans, at low or regular interest, only on the basis of the customer's capacity to repay and under strict conditions, with freedom of trade and investment topping the list. As one international aid specialist explains: 'the Bank is in the *business* of lending money for development. If it stops doing that, then it ceases to have a role. Conversely, the more lending it does the more important its role becomes. This creates a pressure within the institution to make loans big and to make them quickly.'[6] In the past few years, the pace of lending, instead of declining due to the over-indebtedness of many countries, has tended to accelerate. Since 1991, total loans granted each year have fluctuated between $20 and $24 billion. Approximately 25 per cent of these loans go to the forty-six least developed countries (LDCs).

The IBRD does not tolerate any delay in repayment and never allows its customers to reschedule their debts. This apparent contradiction seeks to maintain the principle prevailing in the 'serious' financial world that once a debt is contracted, it constitutes a sacred commitment that no individual and, above all, no government can elude. Deviating from this principle would encourage bad borrowers. (Some cynical observers with an opposing view have suggested that it would be only logical for over-indebted countries to refuse to repay their debts in order to discourage the bad lenders who extended credit under such lax conditions.)

In addition to the IBRD itself, the World Bank Group includes the International Finance Corporation (IFC), the International Development Association (IDA) and the Multilateral Investment Guarantee Agency (MIGA).

Created in 1956, the IFC's purpose is to encourage holders of local and foreign capital to invest in the private sector in underdeveloped countries. It has helped a large number of multinational corporations establish themselves in underdeveloped countries.

Founded in 1960, the IDA specializes in the granting of long-term loans, at very preferential rates. These loans are often new money to pay back old debts, sometimes to the IBRD itself.

The MIGA, the latest addition to the World Bank Group, was established in 1988 to offer private investors technical assistance and insurance against losses incurred because of non-commercial risks.

With its 181 members, 11,000 employees, offices in sixty-five countries and fifteen headquarters buildings covering 3 million square feet in Washington, DC, the World Bank is indisputably the biggest IFI. It is the flagship of the entire foreign aid business. According to a non-written convention, the president of the World Bank is a US citizen designated by the President of the United States. He is assisted by twenty-four full-time board members, eighteen vice-presidents, four managers and sixty department directors. These decision-makers are among the best paid in the world, with salaries that are al-

ways well into six figures and all kinds of perks. Women are practically absent from this very macho club of improvised bankers; they can easily be counted on the fingers of one hand and hold the least important management positions. Occasionally, a woman may be appointed to one of the eighteen vice-presidencies.

Regional development banks—the Inter-American Development Bank (1959), the African Development Bank (1964), the Asian Development Bank (1965) and the Caribbean Development Bank—support the World Bank's mission by faithfully following its policies. Between them, they lend around $11 billion annually.

The GATT/World Trade Organization

The birth of the GATT proved to be more difficult, since the United States wanted to consolidate the principle of absolute freedom in international trade in this third pillar. The first version of an international trade agreement, put forward by the United Nations and signed in Havana on 24 March 1948, went against this orientation by calling for the introduction of a legal principle: 'the obligation to take into account the unequal development of different States.'[7] This draft established a criterion of positive discrimination in favour of the weakest countries, so contrary to the US non-discrimination doctrine, under which the transnational Del Monte of California is supposed to compete fairly, on a level playing field, with a communal *ejido*[8] of Chiapas peasants.

The US Congress therefore aborted the Havana Charter creating the International Trade Organization (ITO), and instead approved the General Agreement on Tariffs and Trade (GATT), a provisional protocol signed in Geneva in 1947.

From the day it was established, the GATT has always fought systematically and bitterly to liberalize trade throughout the world. It finally succeeded on 15 April 1994 with the signing of the Marrakesh Agreement which embodied the results of the Uruguay Round trade negotiations. The Third World countries agreed, even though they had been excluded from the wheeling and dealing between the USA and Europe. As the representative of Mauritius in Marrakesh stoically declared at the session's end: 'We lost everything, but we will put our head on the block with dignity.'[9]

Following the Marrakesh decisions, the GATT was replaced by the World Trade Organization on 1 January 1995. The WTO already has 120 member countries and 30 more have applied for membership. Its orientation does not correspond in any way to that of the Havana Charter. The WTO's mission is to enforce all the agreements arising from the successive GATT negotiations. Its Charter contains no social, ecological or cultural clause that could help establish equitable terms of trade between industrialized and weak economies. The Marrakesh Conference only recommended the creation of a Committee for Trade and Environment that would report to the Ministers' biannual meeting. At the Ministers' first meeting in Singapore in December 1996, the environment was hardly mentioned. The Committee tabled its report which 'proved to be so lacking in substance that the environmental organizations present called for the Committee's dissolution. . . . The subjects of interest to the South, were practically swept under the carpet'.[10]

The Third World's commercial downfall is even more evident if one considers that the strongest countries respect the principles of free trade only when they benefit from them. In the textile and clothing sector, for example, where underdeveloped countries have a comparative advantage, the industrialized countries maintain high tariff barriers. A 1992 UNCTAD study revealed that in these two fields 'the industrialized countries, in violating principles of free trade, are costing the developing countries an estimated $50 billion a year—nearly equal to the total flow of foreign assistance'.[11] Overall, unequal trade currently costs the underdeveloped countries about $500 billion per year.

Structural Adjustment

Towards the end of the 1970s, thanks to a situation that they themselves had helped to create, the Bretton Woods institutions, clearly deviating from their original role, decided that it fell within their competence completely to reshape the Third World economies in order to 'adjust' them to the requirements of the global market. Most of the underdeveloped countries, having benefited from a virtually unlimited supply of capital, were now heavily in debt. Trapped by credit-based development, they had no other choice, if they wished to continue down the same road and obtain new loans, than to submit themselves to the 'conditionalities' of the Bank and the Fund.

These conditions were presented in a kind of package deal known as Structural Adjustment Programmes (SAP). Robert McNamara,[12] the World Bank's earnest president from 1968 to 1981, inaugurated in 1979 the 'structural adjustment' era and established its ideological foundations.

The structural adjustment policy is based on one indisputable observation: Third World economies are not adapted to the world economy as it exists today. Since it is out of the question for the world economy to adjust to the economic structures of underdeveloped countries, it is necessary to proceed in the opposite direction: adjust these outmoded structures to the international system whether the interested parties like it or not. According to the IMF and Bank experts, adjustment leads to development but begins with debt repayment: *first things first*. In their view, everything holds together: to be able to repay their debts, the Third World countries must restructure their economy, sector by sector. As one observer remarked: the SAPs are a foreign-controlled coup in slow motion. In other words: a remote-controlled unilateral adjustment.

Carrying out these reforms has become the main task of the Bretton Woods institutions, now vested by the international financial community with the trusteeship of the underdeveloped countries. The Bank and the IMF base their actions on common documents, concocted in Washington and secretly negotiated with the credit-seeking governments. These 'confidential' protocols, called 'Policy Framework Papers', serve as economic and social policies for in-depth structural reforms.

The adjustment policy is implemented through two kinds of loans. First, the structural adjustment loans (SALs) that have three specific objectives: (1) to cushion the debt crisis by cutting the deficit and spending; (2) to increase exports by converting the country's natural resources into exportable goods, in a context of globalization . . . and debt repayment; (3) to help multinational corporations establish themselves in closed economies considered to be too inward-looking.

Second, the sectoral adjustment loans (SECALs) are mainly intended to support the transformation of a given sector. They are very flexible. Governments can use part of the money received as they wish, provided that the desired adjustments—price deregulation, currency devaluation, elimination of the minimum wage, and so on—are duly implemented. Thus, the World Bank plays a key role in government decision-making and helps docile politicians to get rich quickly.

Generally formulated in obscure jargon, the IMF and Bank requirements come down to two points: export more, spend less. In real terms, the SAPs signatory countries commit themselves to the following measures:

- *the elimination of customs barriers* to do away with locally produced goods and services made unprofitable by international competition; thus, if Egyptian peasants cannot produce cereal crops more cheaply than Canadian farmers, they will have to abandon their farms and move to the shantytowns of Cairo, as candidates for food aid
- *incentives to export* in order to obtain the currency needed to discharge the debt and balance the budget; this means reorienting the economy to modernize the export product sectors, such as coffee, cocoa, bananas, sugar and peanuts; this restructuring often brings new investment for which the Bank readily provides credit, adding to the debt burden
- all-round *deregulation of prices* (especially agricultural products), wages, interest rates and exchange rates, and *liberalization of legislation* (especially laws controlling foreign investment and profit transfers)
- *privatization*, because the economy must be organized by the market's 'invisible hand' and not by politicians and bureaucrats
- *public spending cuts*, which are tantamount to forcing governments to trim the more easily reduced items of the budget, namely the 'unproductive' social services: education, health and housing.

Women under the SAP Yoke

These policies have proven to be disastrous for ordinary citizens, particularly in the LDCs, but also in countries with apparently less fragile economies such as Venezuela, Mexico and Brazil, where riots and even revolts have erupted in protest against the IMF-dictated measures. International experts admit that immediate results are often disappointing. This is not because the theory is wrong, they explain, but because it is not applied strictly enough.

By imposing the production and consumption standards of advanced capitalism on poor countries, Structural Adjustment Programmes are widening the gap between the rich, connected to the import-export sectors, and the popular classes, driven down by the merciless laws of competition and the debt service through lost purchasing power, wage cuts and rural exodus.

Women are at the bottom of this foreign-controlled production line. They suffer the consequences of the big lending institutions' anti-social and even anti-economic policies. According to very sound estimates, women already perform 75 per cent of subsistence labour in Third World countries.[13] Their situation is worsened by male migration to plantations. The industrial priorities of development, which mainly concern men, make life more difficult for women because they must continue to handle domestic tasks, health care and children's education. Ayesha Iman, a Nigerian social-researcher, summed up the situation in a terse remark: 'SAP is really sapping us.' (Nigeria has been implementing the SAPs since 1986). She explains:

SAPs advocate the transfer of costs from the public sector to the private market-ruled sector. This means effectively from paid to unpaid sectors and from the state to households—in other words to women. Thus, for example, the reduction in health services means that the sick must be cared for (attended, cleaned up after, cooked and served meals and medicine) by mothers, sisters and aunts, rather than by paid workers in hospitals. Higher food prices have meant a switch to cheaper or unprocessed foods which require longer preparation time before consumption—work which has also fallen to women. Extra hours of work are thus added to women's working day, with consequent extra fatigue and health stress. [. . .]

SAPs have failed in Africa even on the IMF and World Bank's own narrow terms of economic and budgetary performance. They have resulted in the increased physical vulnerability of people (especially of children, the poor and women) to malnutrition, fatigue and disease. These horrific physical effects of structural adjustment have led the UN Economic Commission for Africa to express its fear of the 'real danger of a systemic break-down'.[14]

Despite these disastrous results observed throughout the Third World—or rather because of what is considered in high places as an exemplary performance—these three pillars of the world economy recently received recognition at the highest levels for their mission to integrate the underdeveloped economies into the global market. In 1996, for the first time ever, the top executives of the World Bank (James Wolfensohn), the IMF (Michel Camdessus) and the WTO (Renato Ruggiero) were officially invited to participate in the discussions at the annual G7 meeting in Lyons, France. At the summit, the three protagonists of the adjustment of the Third World received an official blessing from the 'political bureau' of the developed world and were given the green light to carry on regardless with their neoliberal policies.

Notes

1. Forty-four countries participated in the Bretton Woods Conference, twenty-seven of them from the 'underdeveloped areas'. There were 169 official delegates, all men except Miss Mabel Newcomer, a professor of economics. The USSR also participated but finally chose not to join the Bretton Woods institutions. The Eastern European countries followed its lead.

2. See Terence R. Hopkins, Immanuel Wallerstein et al., *The Age of Transition: Trajectory of the World-System 1945–2025* (London and New Jersey: Zed Books, 1996), pp. 210–11.

3. In reference to the second great financial crisis that shook Mexico, in December 1994/January 1995. A drain out of Mexico of speculative capital forced the United States, the IMF and the Bank of International Settlements (BIS) to run to the rescue of the Salinas de Gortari government with a $50-billion stand-by credit financed with public funds—and guaranteed with Mexican oil—a real gift from the taxpayers to a handful of rich speculators. This was, according to Michel Camdessus, Director of the IMF, 'the first great

crisis of our new world of global markets'. (See H.-P. Martin and H. Schumann, *The Global Trap*, p. 93.) After Mexico came Thailand where the IMF was given the opportunity, in July 1997, to use its brand-new Emergency Financing Mechanism with a credit of $17 billion and renewed 'conditionalities'.

4. P. Fabra, 'FMI: la dangereuse métaphore du pilier', *Le Monde,* 15 May 1990.

5. World Bank, *Articles of Agreement* (as amended effective 16 February 1989), art. 1.

6. Graham Hancock, *Lords of Poverty: The Free-wheeling Lifestyles, Power, Prestige and Corruption of this Multi-million Dollar Business* (London: Macmillan, 1989), p. 143.

7. Camara Ismaël, *Comprendre le GATT* (Sainte-Foy, Québec: Le Griffon d'Argile, 1990), pp. 3–4.

8. Traditional community agricultural system of Mexico's indigenous peoples.

9. Quoted by P. Leymarie, 'La Banque mondiale en Afrique. Moins d'État pour une "bonne politique"', *Le Monde diplomatique*, September 1994.

10. Rainer Falk, 'Multilateral Forum or Rich Men's Club?', *Development and Cooperation* [C+D], Berlin, March–April 1997.

11. UNDP, *Human Development Report 1994*, p. 66.

12. This is the very man who, as US Defense Secretary from 1961 to 1968, applied the principle of 'cost-effectiveness' in the conduct of the Vietnam War. In his memoirs, he confesses that the war, in which 4 million Vietnamese and 58,000 Americans died, was a serious mistake. 'We were wrong, terribly wrong', he writes in *In Retrospect* (p. xvi). The US knew nothing, he admits, of Vietnamese history, culture and nationalism. In 1968, when he became the president of the World Bank, he apparently still had not learned anything; he set out with the same zeal to wage war on poverty, riding on the same principle: *cost-effectiveness*.

13. See 'closing the Gender Gap in Development', in *The State of the World 1993, A Worldwatch Institute Report. Toward a Sustainable Society*.

14. A. Iman, 'SAP is really sapping us', in *New Internationalist*, July 1994.

For Further Reading

Aconcise few pages of further readings for more information on more than a 500-year period is a daunting task. Needless to say, what follows is anything but comprehensive.

Numerous books chronicle **colonial transformations**. On Latin America, for example, there is Eduardo Galeano's *Open Veins of Latin America: Five Centuries of the Pillage of a Continent* (New York: Monthly Review Press, 1973) quoted in the introduction to this part. Country-specific case studies include Renato Constantino's *History of the Filipino People* (New York: Monthly Review Press, 1975). For a compelling firsthand account of colonial exploitation in the Indonesian coffee trade, hunker down with Multatuli (pseudonym of Eduard Douwes Dekkar), *Max Havelaar or the Coffee Auctions of the Dutch Trading Company* (New York: Penguin, 1987), translated by Roy Edwards, which was first published in 1860 (or watch the movie *Max Havelaar*). Historian Richard Tucker has written insightful environmentally focused looks at colonialism, including his chapter-length trip through "Five Hundred Years of Tropical Forest Exploitation" in *Lessons of the Rainforest* edited by Suzanne Head and Robert Heizman (San Francisco: Sierra Club, 1990). See also his *Insatiable Appetite: The United States and Ecological Globalization of the Tropical World* (Berkeley: University of California Press, 2000).

The sources listed above also touch on resistance, at least briefly. A good complement is recent literature on **transnational NGO movements**, which typically includes a historical chapter. The book to start with is the already seminal *Activists beyond Borders: Advocacy Networks in International Politics* by Margaret Keck and Kathryn Sikkink (Ithaca, N.Y.: Cornell University Press, 1998).

In terms of the **history of economic integration**, an intriguing recent addition argues that the current period of so-called globalization is not the most economically integrated period in history. See the first chapter of Paul Streeten's *Globalisation: Opportunity or Threat?* (Copenhagen: Copenhagen Business School Press, 2001).

"Structuralist" literature is vast and especially so if you also move into the sub-sequent **"dependency"** literature, which builds on structuralism but argues that trade with developed countries is so inherently anti-development that a more permanent "delinking" is necessary. Much of what Raul Prebisch wrote was published in the *CEPAL Review*, the publication of the UN Economic Commission for Latin America and the Caribbean (www.eclac.org) and UNCTAD (www.unctad.org). Prebisch's seminal work is *The Economic Development of Latin America and Its Principle Problems* (New York: UN Department of Economic Affairs, 1950). Other key structuralist writing includes Hans Singer's "The Distribution of Gains between Investing and Borrowing Countries," *American Economic Review* 40 (1950): 473–85; and Celso Furtado's *Development and Underdevelopment: A Structural View of the Problems of Developed and Underdeveloped Countries*, published by the University of California Press in 1967. For more on import-substitution industrialization to build up domestic manufacturing, see Albert Hirschman's *The Strategy of Economic Development* (New Haven, Conn.: Yale University Press, 1959). To move more into dependency theorists, start with André Gunder Frank, "The Development of Underdevelopment," *Monthly Review* (September 1966): 111–23. See also Immanuel Wallerstein, *The Modern World System* (New York: Academic Press, 1974); and Paul Baran, *The Political Economy of Growth* (Harmondsworth, UK: Penguin Books, 1957).

For more detail on the **NIEO** demands, see Group of 77 (G-77) documents, such as Group of 77, Third Ministerial Meeting, "Manila Declaration and Program of Action," which was drafted in Manila between 26 January and 7 February 1975 as the G-77 document for UNCTAD IV (which was held in Nairobi, 5–31 May 1976). An excellent source for such UN documents is a series published by OCEANA Publications called *The Third World without Superpowers*. The NIEO declaration (Reading 2.6) and its attached "programme of action," for instance, can be found in Karl P. Savant and Joachim W. Müller, *The Third World without Superpowers*, 2nd series, vol. 20: *The Collected Documents of the Group of 77* (New York: OCEANA Publications, 1995), 337–54. On the 1970s UN and other external codes of conduct, see Lance Compa and Tashia Hinchliffe-Darricarrere, "Enforcing International Labor Rights through Corporate Codes of Conduct," *Columbia Journal of Transnational Law* 33, 663 (1995): 665–71; and the work of Harris Gleckman (former chief of the UNCTC's Environmental Unit), including Gleckman and Riva Krut, *Business Regulation and Competition Policy: The Case for International Action*, published in 1994 by Christian Aid, World Development Movement, and other London-based NGOs.

The literature on **TNCs** is now also vast. But this was not the case when Barnet and Müller wrote the path-breaking *Global Reach*. (See Part I, note 5.) Around that same time from UNCTAD came the pioneering work of Frederic F. Clairmont, such as *The Marketing and Distribution System for Bananas* (Geneva: UNCTAD, 1973). For the companion to *Global Reach* and a look at TNCs at the end of the twentieth century, see Richard J. Barnet and John Cavanagh, *Global Dreams: Imperial Corporations and the New World Order* (New York: Simon & Schuster, 1994). Other important books that look at TNCs' global ventures include Mark Green and Robert Massie Jr., *The Big Business Reader* (New York: Pilgrim Press, 1980); and more recently William Greider, *One World Ready or Not* (New York: Simon &

Schuster, 1997); David Korten, *When Corporations Rule the World* (West Hartford, Conn.: Kumarian, 1995); and, on corporations and the global labor force, Richard C. Longworth, *Global Squeeze: The Coming Crisis for First-World Nations* (New York: Contemporary Books, 1998). On the impact of corporate-led globalization on American workers, read Barbara Ehrenreich's *New York Times* bestseller: *Nickel and Dimed: On (Not) Getting By in America* (New York: Holt, 2001).

Moving on to the **World Bank and IMF**, the full citations for the books mentioned in my text are the following: Teresa Hayter, *Aid as Imperialism* (Middlesex, England: Penguin Books, 1971); Cheryl Payer, *The Debt Trap: The IMF and the Third World* (New York: Monthly Review Press, 1974; Middlesex, England: Penguin Books, 1974); and Susan George, *How the Other Half Dies* (Montclair, N.J.: Allanheld, Osmun & Co., 1977). The Philippine case study was turned into two books: Walden Bello et al., *Development Debacle: The World Bank in the Philippines* (San Francisco: Institute for Food and Development Policy, 1982), and Robin Broad, *Unequal Alliance: The World Bank, the International Monetary Fund, and the Philippines* (Berkeley: University of California Press, 1983). Chapter 2 of that last book includes historical references on the Bank and Fund in the 1940s onward. For an original source, consult the prolific Keynes: Donald Moggridge, ed., *The Collected Writings of John Maynard Keynes*, vol. 26: *Activities 1941–1946, Shaping the Post-war World: Bretton Woods and Reparations* (Cambridge, UK: Macmillan and Cambridge University Press, 1979).

Beginning in 1986, NGOs held an **annual NGO meeting** to coincide with the annual autumn Bank and Fund meetings and to focus on developmental and environmental critiques. In the beginning, these were coordinated at least partially by the Environmental Defense Fund, Friends of the Earth, National Wildlife Federation, Development Group for Alternative Policies, and the Bank Information Center. See Bank Information Center, ed., *Funding Ecological and Social Destruction: The World Bank and the International Monetary Fund* (Washington, D.C., September 1989) for the global NGO submissions to the September 1989 International NGO Forum on World Bank and IMF Lending, held in Washington, D.C., and plenary resolutions from the earlier fora.

Also published in 1989, *An NGO Guide to Trade and Finance in the Multilateral System* (Ross Hammond and Michael McCoy, eds.) by the UN Non-Governmental Liaison Service provides an excellent "reference guide" that juxtaposes information on the public institutions with NGO views before trade, investment, and finance became a central campaign issue.

The classic **environmental critique** of the World Bank as well as the story of the campaigns to change it is by Bruce Rich, who was one of the environmentalists who launched the Washington end of those campaigns: *Mortgaging the Earth: The World Bank, Environmental Impoverishment, and the Crisis of Development* (Boston: Beacon, 1994). A more academic companion by Robert Wade—written as part of an authorized but independent history of the Bank with access to Bank papers, files, and personnel—does a good job of detailing that history: "Greening the Bank: The Struggle over the Environment, 1970–1995" in *The World Bank: Its First Half Century* vol. 2: *Perspectives*, edited by Davesh Kapur and John P. Lewis (Washington, D.C.: Brookings Institution, 1998).

Part III

REALIGNING TRADE RULES

Part III

Realigning Trade Rules

With the context provided by Parts I and II, Parts III through V focus on the specifics of today's global citizen backlash. These parts explore in greater detail contemporary citizen strategies and proposals to transform trade and investment, either by rendering them more socially and environmentally responsible (Parts III and IV), or by stopping certain aspects of them (Part V). Each part also examines key debates that have erupted among citizen groups about specific strategies and proposals. As we will see in Part III, changing the rules for trade and investment can encompass regulatory (i.e., mandatory) changes promulgated and enforced by governments or international (multilateral) organizations to which governments belong. These proposals involve legally binding rules to govern corporate or government behavior at national and international levels. Alternatively, as we will see in Part IV, changing the rules can involve voluntary changes by corporations themselves through "self-governance."

Let us now turn to proposals to change the rules that govern corporate behavior through governmental or intergovernmental regulations. A central mechanism that citizen groups have identified to advance environmental and social ends involves reforming "trade and investment agreements." These agreements are negotiated among governments, typically to lower barriers to trade in goods and services and to ease corporate entry into new production sites and new markets. As such, the conventional trade and investment agreement, unadorned by environmental or social considerations, focuses on protections for corporate investors and traders. Those protections are backed up by enforcement mechanisms written into the trade agreement to ensure the countries abide by what they agree to or to impose sanctions on the signatories if they do not.

Some within the citizen backlash have seized upon trade and investment agreements as a focus for reform precisely because each such agreement has provided "a corporate bill of rights," as some backlash members phrase it, without concomitant social and environmental responsibilities. But it is the power of trade sanctions that makes the use of trade and investment agreements so appealing as a potential instrument for environmental and social objectives to some within the citizen backlash, and so repugnant to others. In this section, we look at two case studies of the citizen backlash's attempts to change the rules through changing the focus of trade and investment agreements. The first covers the environmental and labor "side agreements" attached to the North American Free Trade Agreement, signed in 1993 by the United States, Canada, and Mexico; the second centers on proposals to create binding labor and environmental protections in the World Trade Organization.

Social Clauses Prior to the 1990s

Before turning to these two specific cases, it is useful to sketch the history of attempts to "adorn" trade and investment agreements and institutions with social or environmental concerns or both.

In the United States, the effort to put a social face on trade policy has roots in both interstate and international trade policy, going back more than 100 years. As early as the late nineteenth century, workers and worker rights advocates in the United States fought successfully to link respect for worker rights to trade benefits through federal legislative initiatives. The first of these was the McKinley Tariff Act of 1890, which banned the import of goods made by "convict labor."[1] During Franklin D. Roosevelt's "New Deal" administration, as capital fled from "Northern" unionized states to "Southern" non-union states, the focus was on federal legislation to regulate social aspects of trade policy *within* the United States. Thus came the 1937 Fair Labor Standards Act, which stated boldly: "Goods produced under conditions that do not meet rudimentary standards of decency should be regarded as contraband and ought not to be allowed to pollute the channels of interstate commerce."[2]

There were attempts to extend this logic to international commerce. As has been argued in Part II, the focus of backlash antecedents prior to the 1990s was primarily on changing global rules to increase the share of economic benefits going to the Third World overall. But the past 50 years and more of negotiations of global trade rules have also included attempts to try to link trade benefits to a given country's respect for specific labor rights. When countries came together in the 1940s to build a trade organization to complement the World Bank and the International Monetary Fund, there were among the framers some vocal proponents of what they called a "social clause" to protect worker rights. None other than the eminent Lord John Maynard Keynes envisioned the General Agreement on Tariffs and Trade (GATT) as one small part of a broader "International Trade Organization" (ITO) which would have lowered trade barriers in the larger context of pressing for full employment and social protections. Indeed, the Havana Charter, the draft document for the International Trade Organization, actually included a worker rights clause.[3] (See Reading 2.8 by Gélinas for more details.)

In the end, however, because of lack of support in the U.S. Senate, the ITO with its social clause did not prevail. Instead of the more grandiose International Trade

Organization pushed by Keynes and others, a smaller GATT secretariat was established with the limited mandate of reducing tariff barriers in trade in manufactured goods. Rather than totally ignoring the question of how exploited labor conditions can lead to unfair trade advantages, however, the GATT did include a prohibition on trade in goods made by prison labor—leaving the door open to a broader social clause, some proponents of such a clause have argued.

Work on linking worker rights to trade was revived in a major way in the 1980s. In Europe, the campaign was led by the largest overarching global confederation of unions, the International Confederation of Free Trade Unions (ICFTU) to which the U.S. national trade union federation (the AFL-CIO) belongs. In the United States, under the leadership of Pharis Harvey (a former missionary in Asia), labor, human rights, and religious activists created the International Labor Rights Fund (ILRF; originally called the International Labor Rights Education and Research Fund) in Washington, D.C., in 1986. Working with allies in key Southern countries such as India, the participating groups studied seventy years of deliberations in the International Labor Organization (ILO), the UN agency where employers, worker representatives, and governments from North and South have negotiated over 150 conventions on labor rights and standards. The ILRF culled from these ILO conventions a set of basic worker rights that it argued were internationally recognized: freedom of association, the right to collective bargaining, bans on child and forced labor, nondiscrimination, and minimum standards with respect to wages, working conditions, and health and safety.[4]

With support from key U.S. unions and religious organizations, the ILRF and other groups helped craft federal legislation to link U.S. trade and investment privileges to our trading partners' respect for these core labor rights. The majority of the U.S. corporate community, viewing the various pieces of legislation as an infringement on its freedom to profit from differences in labor conditions and rights across countries, fought the linkage. They derided labor rights (and environmental standards) as unwanted "hitchhikers" on agreements centered on trade and investment.[5] Yet, on several notable occasions since 1984, the worker rights proponents prevailed and the U.S. Congress passed legislation that conditioned trade benefits for countries on respect for worker rights. First, in 1984, the U.S. Generalized System of Preferences (GSP, a program that reduces tariffs on exports from many poorer countries to the United States) was amended to deny benefits to a country found in violation of the specified internationally recognized worker rights. Over the 1980s and 1990s, similar amendments were attached to legislation concerning the Overseas Private Investment Corporation (which provides U.S. firms insurance on overseas investment), the Caribbean Basin Initiative (which grants trade benefits to Caribbean countries), and the Trade Act of 1988.[6]

A Social Clause for NAFTA

The focus on U.S. legislation in the 1980s gave "social clause" proponents initial successes and valuable experience. But even with the shield of ILO conventions, it also opened U.S. groups up to criticism that these were not the results of bilateral or multilateral negotiations, but were unilateral initiatives that reflected U.S. values and protectionist objectives. This was especially the case since the U.S. government had a tendency to implement the legislation prejudiciously against countries that were political adversaries (e.g., Sandinista Nicaragua and socialist Romania) while failing to act against gross violators such as Indonesia and Malaysia where U.S. corporate involvement was strong. The intergovernmental negotiations first on a U.S.-Canada Free Trade Agreement (which went into effect in 1989) and then on an expanded trinational U.S.–Canada–Mexico North American Free Trade Agreement (NAFTA, on which negotiations began in 1990) gave the citizen backlash its opportunity to move from its unilateral focus to a regional one. As the three governments met to negotiate NAFTA, citizen groups launched parallel nongovernmental negotiations, with two agendas: a defensive one to critique the governmental agenda as having unacceptable costs for citizens and the environment in all three countries and a more sophisticated, offensive one to propose an alternative agenda. "Not this NAFTA" became their rallying cry.

What might an alternative integration plan, acceptable to citizen groups in all three countries, look like? During these meetings, participating NGO coalitions from all three countries began drafting such a collaborative document. The historic document, excerpted in Reading 3.1, spells out the trilateral NGO view of the "grand bargain" that a more expansive trade and investment agreement encompassing economic, environmental, and social goals should entail. It was an exercise that not only forced the backlash to articulate its shared vision, but also pushed groups to grapple with the fact that there was not always one clear and easy backlash agenda. Many citizen groups in all three countries opposed the pact outright; others, including a significant portion of the environmental community, argued for inclusion of enforceable worker rights, environmental standards, or both.

To be effective, the backlash sought unity wherever possible—North and South, labor, environment, religious, farm, and other social sectors. As seen in Reading 3.1, they rooted their integration proposals in conventions of both the ILO and the UN Universal Declaration of Human Rights; given no equivalent for internationally recognized environmental rights, they suggested building on basics such as "the right to know (about public environmental threats) and the right to a toxic-free workplace and living environment." At the same time, the groups sought compromise on contentious issues. For instance, groups in the United States had to grapple with the fact that Mexican groups wanted increased aid and debt relief. Likewise, labor and environmental groups were forced to think hard about how to overcome the trade-off that some assumed existed between jobs and a clean environment.

The trinational NGO campaigns and protests hounded the governmental negotiations and grabbed media attention. In the media, stories of footloose factories abandoning one exploited labor force to take advantage of a more exploited and lower paid (but often just as productive) labor force merged with health and environmental stories of toxic dumps and babies born without brains along the U.S.–Mexico border. And, although hundreds of TNCs banded together in a corporate alliance (USA*NAFTA) to push for NAFTA, public-opinion polls in the United States showed more people opposed to it than supportive.[7] In the middle of the trinational governmental negotiations, Bill Clinton became U.S. president; in his campaign he had reached out to labor and environmentalists and embraced some of their critique of NAFTA. Accordingly, the Clinton government led negotiations for social and environmental language to be added as social clauses tacked onto NAFTA.

The result was the North American Agreement on Environmental Cooperation (NAAEC) and the North American Agreement on Labor Cooperation (NAALC). The "side agreements" divided the citizen backlash, with some key environmental groups wooed to the U.S. administration's side. For the most part, U.S. labor, as exemplified by the AFL-CIO, remained critical. But the cover offered by the side agreements, in addition to political vote-buying by the administration, was enough to squeak NAFTA through the U.S. Congress.[8] With U.S. congressional approval, Mexico and Canada followed suit—and the NAFTA and its side agreements became a reality.

Rather than enforcing internationally recognized labor rights, the side agreements focus on the implementation of national law and are applicable to a "persistent pattern of failure by the Party complained against to effectively enforce" the relevant labor and environmental law.[9] Were these side agreements attached to NAFTA a step forward or not? To this day, the citizen backlash is divided in its assessment of the side agreements, as shown in the divergent views of Lance Compa and Jerome Levinson (Readings 3.2 and 3.4).

Taking a more positive view is Lance Compa, a law and labor rights professor, a former union organizer and lawyer, and a participant in the NGO negotiations for "A Just and Sustainable Development Initiative for North America" (reprinted in Reading 3.1). He was appointed by then-U.S. labor secretary Robert Reich to serve as the top U.S. official in the NAFTA labor commission created by the NAALC (1995–97). In Reading 3.2, Compa urges his fellow NAFTA critics to take "another look" at the labor side agreement. Distinguishing the ideal from the practical (i.e., negotiable), he revisits key criticisms to tally up the pros and cons of the side agreement as well as the bureaucracies it built. How fatal, for instance, is NAALC's avoidance of international norms? And how should we judge the three governments' desire to sculpt an agreement that does not impinge upon each nation's sovereignty. Compa uses as the basis for his review not only the negotiations but also the first six cases that have been reviewed under the NAALC.

Cornell professor Maria Lorena Cook (Reading 3.3) sees another unintentional positive impact of the side agreements as far as the citizen backlash is concerned: the cross-border organizing that they have catalyzed. Cook is a leading U.S. expert on the Mexican labor movement and the independent union sector that has built up close ties with many U.S. unions and NGOs.

Juxtaposed to Compa and Cook is Jerome Levinson, the former staff director of the 1973 U.S. Senate "Church Subcommittee" (discussed in Part II in connection with Reading 2.5), former general counsel of the InterAmerican Development Bank, and currently distinguished lawyer in residence at American University's

Washington College of Law. Levinson's pro-bono legal work has included serving as counsel for complaints under the labor side agreement. In Reading 3.4,
Levinson provides a specific case study of a dispute brought under the labor side
agreement: that of a Sony subsidiary in Nuevo Laredo, Mexico. Levinson uses
that case to argue that the glass is half empty with regard to the power of the side
agreement to correct unfair labor practices. It is a case that Levinson knows well
as he provided the pro-bono legal defense for the Mexican workers. The reader
can feel Levinson's frustration as he discusses how he won the case, only to discover that winning brought no benefits to the wronged Mexican workers and no
reprisals to Sony. As Levinson was quoted as saying in the *Journal of Commerce*,
"The record of the side agreement is dismal. . . . [The Sony case] shows the limits
of the side agreements and why they don't work."[10]

It is worth reading Compa, Cook, and Levinson carefully to weigh their points.
A few details are probably worth reiterating: First, as discussed above, the side
agreements focus not on international rights or standards but on the enforcement
of existing domestic law. Second, as Compa explains, the labor side agreement
does not treat all infringements of labor rights equally: only some labor violations
can lead to monetary fines or sanctions; infringements of the other key rights cannot. Which brings us back to the Sony case: Since this case involved freedom of
association (the right to form an independent union at Sony's plant in Mexico),
the highest level of review involved the three ministers or secretaries of labor,
who decided the complaint was valid. Since the complaint was against the Mexican government (and not Sony), it was the Mexican government that had to do
penance—by holding public meetings to review labor rights available under
Mexican law and by further study of how to avoid this "persistent" problem of
nonenforcement.

How are we to assess this and, indeed, weigh Compa's and Levinson's assessments? While they agree on what happened and in fact probably agree on overall
goals, Compa sees opportunity while Levinson finds a charade. But both arguments have validity. Looking through Levinson's prism, one finds wrist-slapping
at best for the Mexican government with no reprisals for Sony and no compensation for the wronged workers.[11]

All true, Compa or Cook would likely reply, but would also quickly add: let us
accept that this is the reality of the side agreement and let us push it as far as we
can. And, in fact, some Mexican NGOs saw the case in positive terms, arguing that
in the U.S. context such public meetings may seem insignificant, but in the Mexican context, public questioning of officials is a rare phenomenon. And, even in the
Sony case, one saw a ripple effect, with Ford in Mexico agreeing to the establishment of an independent union partly because it did not want the bad publicity
that Sony received.

While Compa and Levinson focus on the labor side agreement, controversies
around amending trade and investment agreements extend to the environmental
side agreement. A case in point is the 1996 complaint brought under the environmental side agreement by the Mexican Center for Environmental Law (among others) about an incomplete environmental impact assessment for a new pier being con-

structed off the coast of Cozumel, Mexico. On the one hand, the complaint was successful; the final ruling was that Mexico had indeed ignored its own environmental laws. On the other, the verdict did nothing to stop the pier's construction. The case produced a "beautiful" report, according to Cozumel lawyer Dora Uribe, "but there isn't one recommendation."[12] To many observers, it seemed a tragic comedy of sorts: Not only was the pier almost fully constructed by the time the negative final report was issued, but construction continued after it was issued. The side agreement gave no power to stop construction.[13]

The debate over the NAFTA side agreements continues into the twenty-first century as governments across the Western Hemisphere attempt to spread NAFTA to the hemisphere in a Free Trade Area of the Americas. (On the FTAA, refer to Reading 1.8.)

A Social Clause for the World Trade Organization?

In the late 1990s and early 2000s, the debate over social clauses returned to the multilateral level. In 1994, the completion of a new round of GATT negotiations (the Uruguay Round launched in 1986) transformed the global trade body into a more powerful World Trade Organization (WTO). With expanded dominion over trade in agriculture (which ironically the U.S. government now sought after having opposed it in the ill-fated ITO negotiations) in addition to manufacturing and with entry into services and investment, the establishment of the WTO was a victory for corporate interests. (For more background on the WTO, see Gélinas, Reading 2.8.)

In the 1980s, the GATT and the topic of world trade in general had seemed like an amorphous target for the backlash, almost impossible to turn into a sound bite that would resonate with non-experts and catalyze wide opposition. But once the WTO opened its door for business in 1995, its secretive "dispute resolution panels" began issuing decisions that continually put free-trade goals above environmental and social ones. While WTO defenders found logical arguments within each of these decisions (or at least rationales that demonstrated how the decisions meshed with the WTO charter and precedents), the citizen backlash found its voice in attacking an organization whose decisions seemed to enshrine free trade above all else. Indeed, the cases were almost too good to be true as sound bites for WTO critics to exploit in public relations campaigns. The WTO as much as proclaimed: "Keep importing that tuna, USA; you are not allowed to try to save the dolphins." Or, "Europe, stop your preferential treatment of bananas from your former Caribbean colonies (as enshrined in the long-established Lome Convention); U.S. giant Chiquita wants you to buy its Central American bananas instead." Or, "a pox on the U.S. Clean Air Act; the attempt by the U.S. Environmental Protection Agency to make imported gas comply is wrong." And so on.

By November–December 1999, when ministers of the WTO members met in Seattle, Washington, ostensibly to launch a "Millennium Round" of negotiations to push further a global free trade and investment agenda, the backlash was at its strongest. Some 40,000–50,000 protesters—among them, environmentalists, workers, peasants, indigenous people, women, students, religious activists, and human rights advocates, North and South—held teach-ins and protests. Environment and labor groups presented a united front and marched side by side.

The movement's critique of the WTO is fairly unified, North and South, social and environmental. It is on the question of what should be done that the backlash remains divided. One contentious debate surrounds whether a social clause, added onto the existing WTO structure, would be a step forward.

Organized labor across the globe is largely supportive of such a social clause. Indeed, one key group among those taking the lead in proposing a specific social clause for the WTO is the Brussels-based International Confederation of Free Trade Unions (ICFTU). The ICFTU actually was formed in 1949 from key groups who had been pushing a version of a social clause in the 1946–47 negotiations to build an international trade organization out of which came GATT in 1948 (without a social clause). Today, the ICFTU has 221 affiliated organizations representing about 155 million members in over 140 countries and territories. About two-thirds of the ICFTU's affiliates are from developing countries, comprising half the total number of workers the ICFTU represents.[14] Reading 3.5, culled from a long booklet by the ICFTU, begins with a multi-pronged rationale for a social clause in the twenty-first century to protect human rights (with those of children, women, and workers specifically mentioned). The ICFTU then moves on to articulate a sophisticated rendition of a worker-rights-clause mechanism that would link the WTO to the ILO.

Countering the pro-social-clause position of groups such as the ICFTU is Martin Khor of the Malaysia-based Third World Network and a leading spokesperson for the global backlash. Khor articulates his position in Reading 3.6, excerpted from a publication written for Seattle. Khor's and his allies' arguments are essentially three-pronged: (1) that the WTO is deeply flawed because of Northern governments' (notably the United States') ability to control it to serve their own economic and geopolitical interests; (2) that environmental and social clauses would be used by the United States and other Northern members of the WTO to camouflage their own protectionist goals and/or as a stick to further weaken Southern states with independent economic agendas, such as Malaysia; and (3) that backing up such social and environmental goals with the power of trade sanctions ultimately will hurt poorer countries and leave richer ones relatively unscathed. The citizen backlash, in this argument, should focus its attention on a more fundamental restructuring to democratize or replace the WTO or on alternative arenas for its environmental and social agenda. Khor's reading offers arguments against both a social and an environmental clause in the WTO and provides his alternatives.

The critiques of a WTO social clause by Khor and the Third World Network, Walden Bello and his Bangkok-based Focus on the Global South, and other groups and individuals mirror most Southern governments' refusal to consider attaching a social clause to the WTO. (A notable exception is the government of South Africa.) And, the U.S. government, under pressure from U.S. labor and other

NGOs, has since the days of George H. W. Bush reluctantly taken a lead in raising the topic of labor and environmental rights within the WTO. As a result, the widespread perception in the media is that the North is for a social clause and the South against it. But this gross generalization—of "South" versus "North"—makes the faulty assumption that the interests of nation states and subnational actors in either North or South necessarily mesh. Likewise, the generalization misses the subtleties of the citizen backlash. A survey of Southern and Eastern European NGOs and trade unions conducted by Swiss-based development groups Bread for All and Berne Declaration suggests a more varied opinion among Southern backlash groups. While those who responded to the survey "overwhelmingly said yes to the introduction of a social clause in international trade . . . inseparable from an ecological clause," differences emerge as to the role of the WTO as well as to the role of trade sanctions.[15]

Indeed, within North and South, as one further disaggregates beyond national-level interests, one finds a divergence of opinion among backlash groups and discovers the complexities of assigning "Northern" or "Southern" interests to a social clause. Reading 3.7 provides a revealing case study of this by analyzing the debate over a social clause in India, the country with the world's second largest workforce. It is written by Rohini Hensman with the Union Research Group, a research and education group in Bombay (Mumbai). Hensman is active in both trade union and women's movements, and her two hats show in her analysis. She details arguments in the Indian trade union and NGO community against social clauses. She then counters with arguments for some kind of social clause made by women workers and by women activists whose work supports labor unions, as well as by male workers (such as plant-level activists from independent unions) and NGO activists on child labor. She provides additional food for thought, such as the complexities of social clause debates in a country where the overwhelming majority of workers toil outside the formal sector and the question of why social clauses thus far have not penalized the companies themselves.

Moving from labor union groups such as the ICFTU, worker-support groups such as Hensman's, and multi-faceted research/advocacy groups like Martin Khor's, where do self-proclaimed environmental groups, North and South, stand in the social clause debate? Echoing Khor, most environmental groups critique the WTO as undermining environmental laws. Most share Khor's concern with an institution that, by definition, deems illegal those environmental protections based on "production process method" (PPM, i.e., whereby a country importing shrimp is not permitted to protect turtles killed in the harvesting process). And when the European Union put a ban on beef containing bovine-growth hormone, it passed the WTO's "production process method" test (i.e., the good protected was the good traded—beef) and the WTO's "nondiscrimination test" (i.e., treating both domestic and imported beef the same), but it failed on another basis for WTO rulings that baffles most environmentalists: the WTO seems unwilling to accept a reasonable version of the "precautionary principle" for acting to protect public health; instead its rulings require that a country's actions be based on near certain scientific proof, which is almost never available. Environmental critiques also highlight the WTO's seeming disdain for allowing consumers to have full information via mandated environmental labeling.

But, once again, the shared critique among environmental groups in the backlash does not bring forth a unified "environmentalist" position on a social clause. Some environmental groups focus on incorporating changes regarding PPM and the precautionary principle into the WTO's governing mandate to reform the WTO's charter to put environmental goals ahead of free-trade goals—in essence adding a social clause.

Hilary French of the U.S.-based Worldwatch Institute lists her views of the "priorities for reform": "clearly incorporating the precautionary principle into WTO rules, protecting consumers' right to know about the health and environmental impact of products they purchase by safeguarding labeling programs, recognizing the legitimacy of distinguishing among products based on how they were produced, providing deference to multinational environmental agreements in cases where they conflict with WTO rules, ensuring the right of countries to use trade measures to protect the global commons, and opening the WTO to meaningful public participation."[16]

The majority, however, want to remove these environmental decisions from the WTO. They call for the hundreds of international environmental treaties to take precedence over the WTO, should the two conflict. In fact, this was done in NAFTA, which explicitly cedes power to the Montreal Protocol on Substances That Deplete the Ozone, the Basel Convention on the Control of Transboundary Movements of Hazardous Wastes and Their Disposal, the Convention on International Trade in Endangered Species of Wild Fauna and Flora (CITES), and a series of specified multilateral environmental agreements.[17]

Others on the "remove" side want to build an environmental equivalent of a strengthened ILO. This is the view of Lori Wallach, director of Ralph Nader's Public Citizen's Global Trade Watch: "We don't want to put the environment in the hands of an organization whose charge and worldview is commercial. . . . We need to have an entity of equal stature, and we need the WTO to be cut out of national and international environmental policies."[18]

In Brief

Whatever the outcome of the debate within the backlash about attaching social clauses to bilateral, regional, and multilateral trade and investment agreements, a few things are clear. First, we will never return to the days when government trade experts could meet in relative obscurity to negotiate the technical details of trade and investment agreements that focused solely on a free-trade, pro-corporate economic agenda. This is a victory won by the citizen backlash over the last decade—thanks both to the movement's work and to the on-the-ground reality that such free-trade agreements brought unacceptable environmental, economic, and social costs.

Second, this backlash victory is reverberating to change the shape of actual trade agreements. A case in point is the bilateral free-trade agreement between the United

States and Jordan, signed in October 2000 in the waning months of the Clinton administration. While the agreement uses language reminiscent of NAFTA's side agreements to link the trade and investment benefits to both countries' enforcing their own labor and environmental laws, this is not relegated to a side agreement. Rather, it marks the first time that a U.S. bilateral trade agreement includes within its core text "social clauses" covering labor and the environment. I reprint the preamble to the agreement and the sections on labor and the environment (Reading 3.8).[19]

A third point is also clear: on social clauses, the backlash has been able to disagree on a specific tactic without becoming divided. Backlash proponents and opponents of a WTO social clause worked together in the Seattle, Quebec, and other protests, acknowledging their disagreement, while not letting it divide them.

Notes

1. As the Committee on Ways and Means report on the bill noted, the bill's "Section 24 contains an important provision never before enacted in any American tariff law. It declares that all goods, wares, articles and merchandise manufactured wholly or in part in any foreign country by convict labor shall not be entitled to entry [into the USA] . . . and the importation thereof is hereby prohibited." Quoted in William McKinley, *The Tariff in the Days of Henry Clay and Since: An Exhaustive Review of Our Tariff Legislation* (New York: Kraus Reprint Company, 1970 reprint), 109–10. Note that this book was originally printed by the Henry Clay Publishing Co., New York, in 1896. See also chapter XI, "McKinley Tariff and Billion-Dollar Congress, 1889–1893" in Davis Rich Dewey, *National Problems, 1885–1897* (New York: Greenwood Press, 1968. First printing Harper & Brothers, 1907), 173–87.

2. Quoted in "Fair Labor Standards Act: The New Deal Fight for a Wage and Hour Law," *Congressional Digest* 79, no. 3 (March 2000): 71. See U.S. Senate Committee on Education and Labor and U.S. House Committee on Labor, *Fair Labor Standards Act of 1937: Joint Hearings Before the Committee on Education and Labor, U.S. Senate, and Committee on Labor, U.S. House of Representatives*, 75th Congress, 1st Session, 2–5 June 1937: 1–1222.

3. International Confederation of Free Trade Unions, *Building Workers' Human Rights into the Global Trading System* (Brussels, Belgium: ICFTU, 1999), 49.

4. See Terry Collingsworth, "An Enforceable Social Clause," *Foreign Policy in Focus* 3, no. 28 (October 1998): 1–4. As Cornell professor Lance Compa cautions, "The ILRF's 1980s delineation of 'core' rights should not be confused with the ILO's 1998 Declaration, which is as of now the authoritative definition of 'core' standards." Lance Compa to Robin Broad, e-mail correspondence, 2 September 2001.

5. For a similar argument from the World Bank, see World Bank, *Global Economic Prospects and Developing Countries 2001*, chapter 3: "Standards, Developing Countries, and the Global Trading System."

6. See John Cavanagh et al., *Trade's Hidden Costs* (Washington, D.C.: International Labor Rights Education and Research Fund and the Institute for Policy Studies, 1988).

7. See, for instance, Gerald F. Seib, "Clinton Needs to Sway the Public on NAFTA Issues as Poll Shows That Many Oppose the Agreement," *Wall Street Journal* (15 September 1993): A24.

8. Sarah Anderson, Marc Bayard, et al., "Who Benefits from Fast Track? A Study of the Corporate Free Trade Lobby," report released by the Institute for Policy Studies, Washington, D.C., and United for a Fair Economy, Boston, Mass., 23 October 1997, 1–4. On the legal "vote-buying," see "NAFTA Pork: Free Lunch for Corporations and Congress," *CovertAction* (Winter 1993–94): 25, (which is based on information compiled by Public Citizen and Citizens Trade Campaign).

9. Article 28 of the environmental side agreement and article 27 of the labor side agreement, quoted in Jack Garvey, "Trade Law and Quality of Life—Dispute Resolution under the NAFTA Side Accords on Labor and the Environment," *The American Journal of International Law* 89 (1995): 442.

10. Quoted in Tim Shorrock, "NAFTA Side-agreement Slips into Fast-Track Spotlight," *Journal of Commerce* (18 September 1997): 3(A).

11. In addition, as Levinson stresses to me, contrast the ineffectual side agreement enforcement provisions with those which chapter 11 of NAFTA itself gives to foreign investors: "An investor can drag the Mexican government, a state or municipality, into binding international arbitration, where the result is backed up with monetary penalties and, ultimately, trade sanctions." Jerome Levinson to author, e-mail communication, 10 September 2001.

12. Quoted in Susan Ferriss, "Oversight Group Coexists Uneasily with NAFTA—Feeling Helpless, Environmentalists Grow Frustrated," *Atlanta Constitution*, 2 August 1998, 14(A).

13. North American Commission for Environmental Cooperation, "Final Factual Record of the Cruise Ship Pier Project in Cozumel, Quintana Roo," October 1997, 1–58; "Cozumel Factual Record a Victory for Transparency, If Not for Environment," *Border Lines* 5, no. 11 (December 1997), www.irc-online.org/borderline/1997/b141; and Tim Duffy, "Coalition Wants Cozumel Pier Stopped," *The News* (Mexico), 31 October 1997.

14. Information provided by James Howard, director, Employment and International Labour Standards, ICFTU, e-mail to author, 5 October 2001; and Peter Bakvis, director, ICFTU/ITS Washington Office, e-mail to author, 1 October 2001. For updated statistics on ICFTU membership and other matters, see the ICFTU web site (www.icftu.org).

15. Michele Egger and Catherine Schümperli, "Social Clause: Survey among NGOs and Trade Unions of the South," (Berne, Switzerland: Déclaration de Berne and Pain Pour le Prochain, 1996), 1–8. Quote is from p. 8. See also the original, longer version of the survey (*Clause Sociale: Sondage auprès des ONG et Syndicats Européens et du Sud*) which is in French.

16. Hilary French, "Coping with Economic Globalization," in *State of the World 2000*, ed. Lester R. Brown et al. (New York: W. W. Norton, 2000): 194.

17. Justin Ward and Jared Blumenfeld, "GATT and the Global Environment: The Road Ahead," Paper for the Conference on Trade and the Environment, Pacific Basic Research Center, John F. Kennedy School of Government, Harvard University, 29–30 April 1994, 27. The authors are with the National Resource Defense Council, a U.S. environmental group, and are referring to NAFTA Article 104.

18. Lori Wallach in Doug Henwood, ed., "Whose Trade?" *The Nation*, 6 October 1999, 15.

19. State Department official (anonymity given), discussion with author, Washington, D.C., 13 July 2001; and International Labor Rights Fund, "Briefing Paper: ILRF and Trade-Related Advocacy, paper for the Board of Directors and Council of Advisors Meeting, July 2001, 2.

While the agreement, as excerpted in Reading 3.8, was signed by the U.S. executive branch on 24 October 2000, legislation to implement it was approved by the U.S. Congress in 2001.

3.1

A Just and Sustainable Trade and Development Initiative for North America

Mexican Action Network on Free Trade, Alliance for Responsible Trade, and Citizens Trade Campaign, with Action Canada Network

On March 25–27, 1993, representatives of citizens' organizations from Mexico, the United States, and Canada met in Washington, D.C., to discuss proposals for a new social and economic agenda for the continent. The meeting included representatives from environmental, labor, religious, consumer, and farm groups. It was the fifth trinational gathering during the past two years in which we have developed common understandings about the impact of accelerated integration on our respective peoples.[1] The following is a summary of the just and sustainable development initiatives for North America that have emerged from our ongoing discussions.[2] They are offered as ideas to help stimulate a more democratic debate on alternatives to NAFTA.

The signatory networks have closely studied and discussed the hastily negotiated NAFTA and the side agreements on labor and the environment. We have concluded that this NAFTA package promotes a brand of economic integration that benefits a small sector in each of our countries at the cost of rising inequalities and continued degradation of the ecosystems on which we and future generations depend. We advocate the

rejection of the NAFTA package and the initiation of new negotiations to craft rules that encourage mutually beneficial trade, investment, and development activities. Our countries *can* reduce trade barriers and remove some obstacles to investment, as long as we embrace a new framework of initiatives for our continent and for the world that steer trade and investment to promote fair paying jobs, democratic and self-reliant communities, and a healthy environment.

The initiatives outlined below are either absent or inadequately addressed in NAFTA and the side agreements on labor and the environment. Hence the slogan of some [of] our members: "Not this NAFTA." The initiatives outlined below are based on sound principles. Respect for basic human rights, the promotion of democracy, citizen participation in decision-making, environmental sustainability, and the reduction of economic inequalities among and within our countries should be the foundations on which North American development is built.[3]

Clashing Visions

North America contains almost 14 percent of the world's land, 7 percent of its people, and 30 percent of its measured economic activity. From its indigenous peoples to the diverse array of Mexican, Canadian and U.S. communities, the continent is rich in cultures and natural resources. For

Mexican Action Network on Free Trade, Alliance for Responsible Trade, and Citizens Trade Campaign, with Action Canada Network, excerpt from "A Just and Sustainable Trade and Development Initiative for North America" (28 November 1993), 1–2, 4–6, and 10.

centuries, rivers and waterways, trading routes, travel, and war have brought our people in contact with one another. For centuries some of this contact has enriched us all while other relations have enriched some at the expense of others.

The economic integration of our continent has greatly accelerated over the past quarter century, especially since the mid-1980s with the advent of the U.S.-Canada Free Trade Agreement and the economic liberalization in Mexico that has accompanied that nation's entry into the General Agreement on Tariffs and Trade (GATT). Canada and the United States now trade more goods and services with one another than any other two nations, and Mexico has been the fastest growing trading partner of the United States. (For Mexico, the United States accounts for 70 percent of its trade.)

Today, we are faced with a fundamental choice over the future integration of our continent. Two visions that are fundamentally at odds with one another have been placed in the public debate.

The first vision is expressed in the proposed North American Free Trade Agreement signed on December 17, 1992, by George Bush, Brian Mulroney, and Carlos Salinas—an agreement that would remove most trade and investment barriers between our nations. The "free trade" or "neoliberal" vision offered by the NAFTA's promoters claims to be one of accelerated economic integration in the name of enhancing U.S. competitiveness against Asia and the European Community.

The alternative vision offers a democratic program for North American integration based on principles of justice and sustainability. This vision is emerging from citizens' dialogue across the continent. These two visions clash on three levels:

- **Process:** The NAFTA was negotiated in total secrecy by government officials, aided by advisory panels dominated by large transnational corporations. By contrast, the new vision is emerging from a democratic process of dialogue that includes all segments of society.
- **Policies:** The clash of policies is laid out within this document. One vital difference is that NAFTA policies focus exclusively on the movement of goods, services, and capital. The alternative vision focuses on policies that address social and environmental realities as well as the movement of people,

or immigration, that accompany the flows of goods, services, and capital. NAFTA policies try to restrict the role of government in society; the alternative vision acknowledges the positive role that government should play in social welfare and in providing incentives to steer market forces toward social gains.
- **Politics:** The three national governments and the corporate backers of the NAFTA have attempted to pass the NAFTA by buying support—and buying off the opposition. The political vision of the just and sustainable option is one of building consensus among a rich diversity of communities and social sectors.

As an alternative to the NAFTA, the signatory organizations from Mexico, the United States, and Canada commit ourselves to the long-term process of constructing more just and sustainable development initiatives in all nations of North America. This task will be much easier if NAFTA is not approved. New initiatives will address the inequalities among and within our countries, create public accountability for corporate integration, and strive to make economic development beneficial to the greatest number of people. These initiatives address the problems not only of the U.S.-Mexico border, but of other areas where large corporations have failed to meet environmental health and social needs. We also open the discussion to the creation of new regional political institutions to address the social consequences of economic integration; we should study the European Community and the European Parliament for lessons on this process.

While these proposals emerge from an ongoing dialogue among three North American nations, we believe that they have relevance to the entire world. The initiatives described here pertain to all nations that subscribe to the criteria of just and sustainable development. We invite other organizations and our governments to work with us in this effort.

[. . .]

The Question of Fairness: Addressing Inequalities

Central to the problems of integration are the enormous economic disparities among the nations of North America. Mexico's citizen groups have accordingly placed the issue of "compensatory financing" at the core of their alternative development proposals. The experience of the European Community reinforces this emphasis. By providing tens of billions of dollars in structural and regional development funds, the EC has stimulated economic activity in relatively less developed sectors and countries. With these funds, some countries have been able to reduce social and economic inequalities and to strengthen cohesion and infrastructure within their borders and throughout the region. Certain EC projects have had adverse ecological consequences, however, offering both positive and negative lessons for future initiatives.

In North America, several proposals have been put forward to create a North American Development Bank. Some of the proposals offer nothing more than a reinforcement of the same top-down, unsustainable model of development that has characterized industrialization on the U.S.-Mexico border. Some of the proposals also falsely claim that such a bank could be largely self-financing, when in reality much of the environmental cleanup and worker training that is needed will not pay for itself. We do support the development of new regional financing mechanisms, including a new regional bank, as long as such mechanisms address the needs of poor areas and poor people in all three countries. In addition, new institutions should be managed transparently and democratically with broad social, governmental, and private participation.

Currently, less funds are available in North America than in Europe for this kind of compensatory financing effort. In addition to new funding mechanisms, however, there are three steps that would help reduce inequalities. Billions of dollars provided to Mexico through multilateral institutions could be better used; billions of dollars that flow from Mexico to the United States in debt service could be reduced; and some existing, small-scale funding mechanisms could be enhanced to address the needs of the poorer majority in Mexico.

A. Reform Multilateral Institutions

Over the past three years, the World Bank and the Inter-American Development Bank have committed about $8 billion in loans to Mexico, more than has been provided to any other nation

in Latin America. The conditions of the loans promote the export-oriented, privatization model common to these two institutions, conditions that have often deepened the inequalities and exploitation in that country; the loans have not succeeded in narrowing the gap between Mexico and its neighbors to the north.

Our nations should take the lead in thoroughly reviewing the operations of the existing lending institutions, with the long-term goal of reforming them to address inequalities and poverty in countries such as Mexico. We should then jointly call for the United Nations to convene a meeting that would focus on democratizing the institutions that govern the world economy and would explore the need for new institutions to promote equitable, sustainable, and participatory development.

B. Reduce Debt

Mexico remains the second largest debtor nation in the developing world. Payments to service this debt are a major drain on the country's resources. No development strategy can achieve significant progress without substantial debt reduction. Realistic debt reduction plans that are not tied to International Monetary Fund (IMF) and World Bank conditionalities would free resources to fund development initiatives. Debt reduction schemes should steer the payment of debt service in local currency into a development fund that is administered in a democratic manner. The Mexican Action Network on Free Trade has designed proposals for such funds that, in addition to debt swaps, could be financed through domestic and foreign contributions, and would be administered with substantial participation of nongovernmental organizations.

The NAFTA does not address the need for debt reduction. Large foreign debts in both the United States and Canada are also an issue, but since debt restructuring schemes in these countries do not involve World Bank and IMF conditionalities, the debt debate differs significantly from that of Mexico.

C. Support Small-Scale Development Foundations

In recent years, small-scale community foundations have emerged to improve living conditions for poor Mexicans by supporting high-impact social service projects. These foundations have successfully involved poor Mexicans in designing, planning, and executing innovative projects. We need to share the lessons of the more successful of such ventures in Mexico and in other countries, and encourage governments and the private sector to assist these foundations. The Mexican Action Network on Free Trade has also proposed the creation of a publicly managed environmental fund to rehabilitate forests, rivers, lakes, and other areas adversely affected by past commercial activities.

D. Trade Adjustment Assistance

None of our three countries has a plan for assisting the millions of small farmers and campesinos displaced by farm concentration and economic integration. In Mexico, this land concentration process has been speeded by the reform of Article 27 of the Mexican constitution, which now permits the sale of ejido lands. Nor has any of the three countries adequate programs to assist workers displaced as a result of increased integration. A new guaranteed funding source should be established in each country to supplement the inadequate trade adjustment assistance funds for job retraining and agricultural and infrastructural development in communities, industries, and companies affected by growing integration.

Such assistance must be accompanied by a broader package of programs designed to discourage concentration of businesses and land in the hands of a few large corporations and to encourage support for small and family-owned farms and businesses. Experience worldwide has shown that such efforts are at the heart of sustainable development and lead to the creation of stable jobs at reasonable wages.

International Rules

While the power and mobility of large, private firms to shift jobs, capital, factories, and goods across borders have increased—and would increase further under the NAFTA—the ability of our governments to protect the basic economic and social rights of our people has decreased. As governments find it harder to meet citizens' needs for employment and other necessities,

corporations have not filled the gap. We must address this shift in power, pressing our governments to create the necessary checks and incentives to ensure that corporate activity contributes to the common good.

There are several areas, detailed below, in which action is needed.

A. Enforceable International Worker Rights and Labor Standards

A new trinational agreement should incorporate comprehensive, multilateral protection of workers' rights and workplace health and safety standards. Such protection will enable all people to benefit from the economic activity generated by North American development. It will also make the growth of workers' income, including average industrial wages, commensurate with growth in productivity, and advance workplace standards and workers' rights throughout the region. We acknowledge that the form this protection takes must address the uneven levels of development among our nations and the disparity in power among our three governments. As a first step, the labor-related provisions of the UN Universal Declaration on Human Rights and ILO conventions are the appropriate standards to be enforced by each country as an essential element of regional economic integration.

Once these standards are recognized, a central feature of any new agreement is making international workers' rights enforceable through a fair, and reasonably swift trinational process. The three countries would negotiate the precise composition of "internationally recognized" workers' rights, including, at a minimum, the ILO conventions of the right to free association and to organize, the right to collective bargaining, and the right to strike, as well as protections against child labor, prison or forced labor, and all forms of discrimination.

Any government or private party with pertinent information could bring complaints about violations of these rights to the relevant enforcement bodies.[6] We must strive to create a dispute resolution process that restricts fines to the guilty parties.

We should also develop mechanisms that will, over time, raise wages worldwide toward the highest prevailing rates. In the context of a new North America agreement, the minimum wage in the traded goods sectors of the two lower wage countries should move as quickly as possible toward that of the highest wage country.[7] Minimum wages in each country should allow for a decent quality of life.

B. Environmental Rights and Standards

There is no international equivalent to the International Labor Organization in the field of the environment. As a result, no code exists for international environmental standards. As a first step in this direction, we advocate the trinational negotiation of a set of basic continental environmental rights, such as the right to know (about public environmental threats) and the right to a toxic-free workplace and living environment. We also support launching a process to define minimum regional (or international) environmental standards. As with workers' rights and standards, these safeguards would be set as "floors" rather than ceilings and enforced with fines or other appropriate trade measures. Our governments should also clarify their commitment to existing international environmental treaties and the inability of trade agreements to override them.

Further, any new North American agreement should be preceded by impact assessments for labor and the environment in the United States, and equivalent assessments in Canada and Mexico.

C. Codes of Conduct

Historically, most trade agreements have enhanced the ability of corporations to shift investment and goods across borders without imposing responsibilities on firms to address the harmful social or environmental effects of these activities. As companies become more global, we need new codes to increase the public accountability and corporate responsibility of private firms. Listed below are several key existing and potential mechanisms for codifying corporate behaviors.

1. *United Nations Code of Conduct:* Beginning in the mid-1970s, the United Nations began negotiating a code of conduct on transnational corporations that prohibited bribery of public officials, required corporate disclosure of potential dangers of products and production processes, banned the ex-

port of goods or factories deemed unsafe in one country, and several other measures. The Reagan administration played a prominent role in politicizing the negotiations; by the early 1990s, the negotiations deteriorated into gridlock. The process should be revived and its scope broadened to include many of the standards and principles enumerated above.

2. *Maquiladora Code of Conduct:* A binational coalition of religious, environmental, labor, Latino and women's organizations are pressing U.S. corporations on the U.S.-Mexico border to adopt a set of standards in their plants that will ensure a safe environment on both sides of the border, safe working conditions, an end to sexual and physical harassment, and a livable wage for workers.

3. *Individual Corporate Codes:* In recent years, Levi Strauss, Sears, and a few other firms have begun to respond to union and public pressure by adopting their own corporate codes of conduct, committing the companies and their subcontractors to certain labor practices. These codes should be standardized and expanded to all firms that operate internationally, with each industry adopting appropriate standards.

4. *Fair Trade Marketing:* Alternative trade organizations in Europe and the United States have for years been promoting international trade with an emphasis on establishing a fair relationship between poor producers and consumers in the developed world. These organizations have spearheaded efforts in the European Community to adopt a new "green seal" program that will alert consumers to products that meet environmental standards at all stages of the production, packaging, and disposal process. This could serve as a model for a North American system, with the addition of respect for worker rights and labor standards as part of the "seal" process.

5. *Foreign Environmental Practices Act:* Several groups on the U.S.-Mexico border have proposed a U.S. law that would require U.S.-based corporations working in Mexico and other countries to follow U.S. environmental standards, except when the standards of the host country are more stringent.[8]

Notes

1. See MODTLE, "Development and Trade Strategies for North America," Washington, D.C., 1992; and "U.S. Citizens' Analysis of the North American Free Trade Agreement," December 1992.

2. In addition to those at the tri-national meeting, useful comments have been provided by Common Frontiers, the Canadian Centre for Policy Alternatives, the Action Canada Network, the Ecumenical Coalition for Economic Justice, the Inter-Hemispheric Education Resource Center, the Texas Center for Policy Studies, the Border Ecology Project, the Development GAP, the Center of Concern, the Institute for Policy Studies, Greenpeace, the Economic Policy Institute, ACTWU, ILGWU, UAW, UFCW, the Institute for Agriculture and Trade Policy, the Mexican Action Network on Free Trade, and certain Congressional staff and other individuals.

3. The Action Canada Network has prepared its own publication on alternatives and is working on a "Fair Trade and Investment Act." During and after the negotiations on NAFTA and the supplemental agreements, the Mexican Action Network on Free Trade (RMALC) has been presenting proposals on labor, environment, human rights, and other issues to the Mexican government. See Bruce Campbell, "Sustaining Canada: A Fair Trade and Investment Act," in August 1993 Action Canada Dossier on Alternatives, coordinated by the Canadian Centre for Policy Alternatives and the International Labor Rights Research and Education Fund. See also, Ian Robinson, "North American Trade: Continental Economic Integration as if Democracy Mattered," Canadian Centre for Policy Alternatives, September 1993.

[. . .]

6. See International Labor Rights Education and Research Fund, "Protecting Labor Rights in Connection with North American Trade," Washington, D.C., 1993.

7. Richard Rothstein, "Setting the Standard: International Labor Rights and U.S. Trade Policy," *Economic Policy Institute Briefing Paper*, 1993, p. 12.

8. Texas Center for Policy Studies, "NAFTA and the U.S./Mexico Border Environment: Options for Congressional Action," Texas, September 1992, pp. 1–4.

3.2

Another Look at NAFTA

Lance Compa

"**W**eak," "toothless," "worthless" and "a farce"—these were some of the epithets applied to the North American Free Trade Agreement (NAFTA) labor side accord negotiated by the United States, Mexico, and Canada in 1993. Trade unionists and labor rights supporters were upset, first by the text of the North American Agreement on Labor Cooperation (NAALC) when it appeared, then by early experiences after it went into effect on January 1, 1994. But those wanting progress on labor rights and standards in international trade should be careful of making some idealized "best" the enemy of the good.

The Text

When the side accord was completed in mid-1993, critics cited three main problems with the text. First, it did not create common norms for the three countries. Instead, the negotiators preserved national sovereignty in the formulation of labor laws and the setting of standards, making "effective enforcement" of domestic law the focus of the accord. What good is an agreement, said critics, that leaves weak laws and standards

in place instead of pulling them up to higher, harmonized levels?

The second major criticism involved the bureaucracy, procedural maze, and seeming cross-purposes built into the agreement. NAALC creates separate domestic agencies in each country's Labor Department, called the National Administrative Offices (NAO), which are responsible for a first review of labor law matters in *another* country. This means that complainants must turn to another government, often in another language, to raise their concerns.

The agreement sets up a council of ministers and a permanent, trinational secretariat that together make up a "Commission for Labor Cooperation." The secretariat conducts research and reporting on comparative labor law and labor market issues and staffs *ad hoc* advisory groups, evaluation committees, and arbitration panels composed of nongovernmental experts from each of the countries.

Each of these bodies has complicated jurisdictional reach, and among them they combine various research, reporting, reviewing, consulting, advising, and decision making powers. Timetables for different levels of review, consultations, evaluations, and arbitrations make for a minimum of several months, and as much as two to three years, before procedures could be exhausted.

The side agreement also called for a broad program of cooperative activities on labor law and

Lance Compa, "Another Look at NAFTA," *Dissent* 44, no. 1 (Winter 1997): 45–50.

labor market matters among governments. Critics said this feature might make governments reluctant to question or criticize each other's law enforcement under the agreement's review, evaluation, and dispute resolution mechanisms.

The third objection addressed the division of NAALC's eleven "Labor Principles"—basic labor rights to which the governments commit themselves in making the deal—into three categories or tiers of treatment. The first tier involves so-called "industrial relations" subjects covered by the first three labor principles: (1) freedom of association and the right to organize, (2) the right to bargain collectively, and (3) the right to strike. Though they lie at the heart of international labor rights, these issues get the lowest level of treatment under the NAALC—the first-level "review" process, with optional ministerial consultations.

Eight labor principles covering prohibition of forced labor, nondiscrimination, equal pay for men and women, workers' compensation, migrant labor protection, child labor, minimum wage, and occupational safety and health issues can proceed from review to evaluation. Only the last three of these are susceptible to the full range of treatment that includes review, evaluation, and arbitration, with possible application of sanctions in cases of a "persistent pattern of failure to effectively enforce" laws in those areas. Critics argued that narrowing the funnel as issues move forward only chokes off possibilities for enhancing labor rights in North America.

Since it took effect at the beginning of 1994, six cases have been treated under the NAALC. Four involved alleged interference with independent union organizing at Mexican maquiladora factories, one concerned union members' rights in a Mexican government ministry, and one dealt with a shutdown by Sprint of a California facility in the midst of a union organizing campaign. These cases left labor rights advocates frustrated and disappointed because they did not lead to what complaining parties sought: reinstatement of fired workers or new union formation at each of the workplaces. Moreover, because each of these cases involved the right to organize, one of the three "first-tier" labor principles, they could not proceed to evaluation or arbitration.

These criticisms should not be discounted. A "level playing field," at least for irreducible "core" standards on such issues as freedom of association, nondiscrimination, and forced labor, for example, and strong, rapid enforcement against violators is the goal of everyone who advocates labor rights in international trade. However, criticism should be measured not against an ideal but against the reality of international trade and labor negotiations in the current regional and global economy. Even then, judging the effectiveness of the NAALC should await a broad experience of the agreement's potential uses. In this light, the scorn directed at the NAALC reflects more impatience than analysis.

Common Standards, Bureaucracy, and Tiers

It's easy to hold in principle that a labor rights clause in a trade agreement ought to provide for universal standards. But it's not so easy in practice, particularly when there is wide economic disparity among the negotiating countries, and when a single country accounts for 85 percent of the economic activity in the trade area.

In the NAFTA context there is also a sensitive problem of sovereignty concerns in all three countries. These are not just concerns of government officials; they are deeply held in all sectors of society, including trade unions and social activist communities. Many Mexican and Canadian labor policy analysts look at the state of U.S. labor law and the U.S. labor movement, and recoil at the prospect of homogenized labor laws. They are not about to give up laws created by their own representatives, administered by agencies accountable to their own executive branches, and reviewed by their own judiciary, to a new supranational agency that might be dominated by the economic interests of the United States.

U.S. trade unionists ought to be equally skeptical about solving their own labor law problems through some kind of international legerdemain. Could the NAFTA side agreement overturn the frequently proclaimed deficiencies in U.S. law—National Labor Relations Board (NLRB) election rules, the striker replacement doctrine, contingent workers' lack of protection, and others—without action by Congress? These are issues for American workers to address through their own organizing and political action, not by demanding some "silver bullet" in the NAALC.

Another problem with creating trinational labor norms lies in the fundamental labor law jurisdiction of each country. Mexican labor law is primarily based in the federal Constitution and federal statutes, with a large state role in enforcement. Most of the maquiladora factories come under state government jurisdiction in the five border states of Mexico, for example. U.S. labor law is also federal, but with a constricted role for the states. State moves to ban striker replacements, for example, have been struck down by the courts as pre-empted by federal law. In contrast, Canadian labor law is almost totally provincial, not federal. Each province enjoys its own sovereignty in fashioning and enforcing labor laws, and is not disposed to let the federal government hand over these matters to a trinational agency.

These differences did not just happen. They result from national histories replete with anticolonial wars, civil wars, constitutional crises, regional conflicts, and class struggles. With three ministries of labor sitting down to negotiate the first labor agreement connected to a trade pact, it is unrealistic to expect them to undo these differences and defer to a supranational power.

The approach taken in the NAFTA side deal, emphasizing "effective enforcement" of domestic labor law, is a more practical starting point than attempting to fashion common norms. Any system of law is really only as good as its system of enforcement. U.S. experience with a resurgent sweatshop industry in major American cities should give pause to demands that Mexico or any developing country "raise" its standards to the levels of industrialized countries before enforcement is strengthened in every country.

Instead of yielding sovereignty over their labor laws and standards, the NAFTA countries shaped the NAALC to open themselves up to trinational scrutiny of their enforcement regimes. Such scrutiny is conducted under the NAALC's review process, through special studies by the secretariat, and through evaluation and dispute resolution by independent, nongovernmental experts who are free to reach their own conclusions about the effectiveness of each country's labor law enforcement. This represents an extraordinary candor in international relations, in contrast to traditional sovereignty rules. It should not be scorned because it fails to achieve a supposed ideal of international fair labor standards and swift, sure punishment powers.

As for bureaucracy, it is true that the NAFTA labor side accord sets up a complex structure and procedures. But this is typical of international agreements. Anyone who ever brought a labor rights case to the International Labor Organization (ILO), to the Organization for Economic Cooperation and Development (OECD), or to the Organization of American States (OAS) or the United Nations Human Rights Commissions can attest to their complex links, slow turns, and elliptical conclusions. For that matter, American trade unions and employers who have been through the mill of NLRB proceedings and their judicial appeals should hardly be disappointed in the world's first international trade and labor agreement's red tape.

Similarly, a "tiered" approach to labor issues is not unusual in the international context. The European Union (EU) also divides the twelve elements of its Social Charter into three tiers of treatment, much like those of the NAFTA labor pact. To be precise, the same subjects susceptible only to first level review in the North American scheme—rights of association and organizing, collective bargaining (as distinct from consultation with "works councils," which are something else in the EU scheme), and the right to strike—are specifically *excluded* by the Maastricht Treaty from any form of Europe-wide legislation. For now, these issues are so central to national identity, history, and workplace culture that no society accepts changes forced from outside its own body politic.

The Cases

The first cases under NAALC provided an important forum for public discussion of labor conditions in NAFTA countries. Such matters had usually been taken up by anonymous officials in obscure proceedings. Now they are subjected to a formal, public review with cleansing sunshine effects.

While the first maquiladora cases ended with no follow-up ministerial consultations, publicity surrounding them prompted reinstatement of several workers, and widespread instructions from U.S. firms' headquarters to their Mexican subsidiaries to comply carefully with Mexican labor laws.

Ministerial consultations in the other cases led to a wide range of trinational contacts and events that illuminate labor law realities in the three NAALC countries. One discussion, for example, compared Mexico's union registration system, the U.S. NLRB election system, and several Canadian provinces' "card-check" systems for union certification. In the Sprint case, the three labor ministers held a widely publicized public forum and instructed the trinational labor secretariat to conduct the first-ever comparative study of the effects of plant closing on workers' freedom of association and right to organize in the three countries. Such mutual efforts are indispensable for creating a knowledge base for progress in trinational treatment of labor rights issues.

Continued reviews can encourage governments to strengthen their enforcement efforts and encourage businesses to turn toward voluntary codes of conduct or some other form of self-regulation on workers' rights and labor standards. Where trade union actions are implicated in a review, efforts to strengthen democratic participation in union affairs may result.

NAFTA's labor side agreement contains several positive features for labor rights advocacy that ought to be appreciated, or at least tested over a long term, before drawing any conclusions about its worth. Used creatively, the agreement provides an opportunity for advancing workers' rights in the globalizing economy. It can be used in all three countries by trade unionists and labor rights advocates, by government officials responsible for labor standards, and by enterprises looking to a "high road" employment relations strategy. The challenge for labor rights supporters is to find such creative uses, not to lament lost opportunities for the perfect agreement.

The agreement's positive features include the establishment of the labor rights-trade linkage as a matter of policy in trade agreements; the wide range of the agreement's "Labor Principles," compared to the narrower definition of international labor rights in most other trade and labor contexts; and the variety of cross-border avenues and arenas that it opens up for international cooperation in support of workers' rights.

The Principle of the Thing

A strong reaction is underway against the very idea of a labor rights-trade link, also known as

the "social clause" in trade discourse. The prime minister of Malaysia, for example, has repeatedly attacked labor rights proposals as an attempt to impose "Western values" and "Western concepts of trade unions" on developing Asian countries.

The ILO, the OECD, the World Bank, the World Trade Organization (WTO) and other international bodies have all shied away from linking trade and labor rights. In this light, the NAALC is a unique accomplishment of the governments of Canada, Mexico, and the United States. It backs up the linkage of labor rights and trade policy with mechanisms for cross-border reviews and potential sanctions when workers' rights are violated and governments fail to enforce their laws. Critics should appreciate just how big a breakthrough it was for the North American trade negotiators to reach this point, compared to progress on the "social clause" in other contexts.

The Scope of the NAALC's "Labor Principles"

Another important breakthrough in the NAFTA side agreement lies in its movement beyond the usual formulation of "core" labor standards. Even while they reject a labor rights-trade link, the ILO, the European Union, the World Bank, and the OECD limit their debate to a labor rights "core" embracing freedom of association and the right to organize while barring forced labor and discrimination (sometimes adding child labor).

In contrast to these three or four issues, NAALC specifies eleven Labor Principles that run the length and breadth of workers' concerns. They include all those mentioned in other attempts to define a "core," and add a forthright endorsement of the right to strike—something most international instruments avoid (there is no ILO Convention on the right to strike, for example). NAALC goes on to embrace matters usually untreated in labor rights discourse but vitally important to workers—minimum wages, hours of work, overtime pay, workers' compensation, protection of migrants, occupational safety and health. The fact that these issues are opened up to cross-border treatment gives the agreement a concrete content often lacking in vague "core" labor rights definitions.

Untested Forums

The cases raised thus far under the NAALC all involved the first of the agreement's eleven principles: freedom of association and the right to organize. No cases involving any of the other ten principles has been initiated. The agreement's independent evaluation procedure has not been invoked, nor has the arbitration mechanism been put to the test.

In sum, one subject matter—organizing—has been treated at the stage-one review level, when the potential exists for three subjects—organizing, bargaining, and striking—to get such first-level treatment. Five other subjects—forced labor, equal pay, nondiscrimination, workers compensation, and migrant labor—can get two levels of treatment: review and evaluation. Three more—child labor, minimum wages, and safety and health—can get all three levels of treatment: review, evaluation and arbitration. Experience with just one of a possible twenty-two combinations of subject and treatment is hardly the basis for conclusions about the agreement's worth.

The potential use of an Evaluation Committee of Experts (ECE) is especially interesting. Eight topics are susceptible to an evaluation under the NAALC. The ECE procedure is deliberately nonaccusatory. It can be initiated by one government alone, as long as it is willing to open up its own enforcement record in the subject matter being evaluated. But now it is not government officials undertaking the evaluation. It is an independent panel of experts from the three countries who can undertake their own comparative analysis, reports, and recommendations. This could be a powerful tool for promoting effective labor law enforcement. Interested unions, employers, or other groups could call to their government's attention problems that might lend themselves to a ministerial request for an ECE. Collaborating across borders, such groups could encourage all the governments to undertake an ECE in a recognized area of common concern. Beyond that, they could ask for cases implicating child labor, minimum wage, or occupational safety and health issues to advance beyond evaluation to the dispute resolution level of treatment, if two governments agree to carry such cases forward.

Another key outgrowth of the NAFTA labor side accord is the process of exchange, communication, and collaboration among labor rights advocates at the trinational level [see Reading 3.3]. Under the agreement's unusual cross-cutting procedures, issues involving practices in one country must be initiated in or by another country. Thus, trade unionists and their allies are compelled to collaborate across North American borders to use NAALC mechanisms.

Labor rights advocates need to view the side agreement not as a chariot of fire righting all wrongs against labor, but as one that creates new space for governments, employers, and unions to honor workers' rights. This "opening up" of labor rights debates in both domestic and international forums is one of the most important results of NAALC.

Any number of idealized "social charters" with universal standards and swift, powerful enforcement powers could be drafted by critics of the labor side agreement. But the agreement had to be negotiated by sovereign governments, each with its own swirling, often clashing, business, labor, and political currents.

The result is a hybrid agreement. It preserves sovereignty, but creates mutual obligations. It sets up new domestic agencies as well as a trinational secretariat. It combines broad cooperation and consultation programs alongside review, evaluation, and dispute resolution mechanisms. But above all, the agreement promotes *engagement* on labor rights and labor standards on an unprecedented international scale. It's worth becoming a player, not just a critic.

3.3

Cross-Border Labor Solidarity

Maria Lorena Cook

Even before NAFTA, the United Electrical Workers union (UE) and the Mexican *Frente Auténtico del Trabajo* (FAT) fashioned a strategic organizing alliance targeting "runaway" General Electric plants in the maquiladora region. The Teamsters union and the FAT undertook similar efforts at a Honeywell plant without the formality of a written agreement. The Communications Workers of America (CWA) has developed close ties with the *Sindicato de Telefonistas de la Republica Mexicana* (STRM), the national telephone workers union of Mexico.

The International Ladies Garment Workers Union and the Amalgamated Clothing and Textile Workers Union, now joined in the new union UNITE, have carried out joint programs with unions in Mexico and Canada. In one "twin plant" setting with unionized shops in Eagle Pass, Texas, and Piedras Negras, Coahuila, for example, the UNITE local collaborated with its Mexican counterpart to achieve key contract gains in both factories. On a broader scale, the Texas state AFL-CIO has formed a Border Solidarity Committee to work with Mexican unions in the border region. Outside organized labor, a multitude of labor-allied nongovernmental organizations in the three countries have been con-ducting a series of trinational conferences, workshops, research projects, and other bridge-building efforts for the past five years to press for a strengthened social dimension in North American economic integration. Few of these efforts would have been undertaken outside the NAFTA context.

The UE, the Teamsters, and the CWA filed NAFTA labor cases with the U.S. National Administrative Office on behalf of Mexican workers involved in FAT and STRM organizing efforts. Another case was filed by a coalition of four groups—the Washington-based International Labor Rights Fund, the Texas-based Coalition for Justice in the Maquiladoras, the American Friends Service Committee Maquiladora Project, and the Mexican National Association of Democratic Lawyers—for a democratic union group in a Sony plant.

The assistance flows both ways. The Mexican STRM filed the Sprint case complaint on behalf of workers being organized in California by the CWA. In 1995 FAT organizers helped the UE win an organizing victory at a large manufacturing plant in Milwaukee, Wisconsin with a high complement of Mexican-American workers.

Mexican workers, union organizers and labor lawyers testified in public hearings in the U.S. on the G.E., Honeywell, and Sony cases. Mexican, U.S., and Canadian labor, democracy, and human rights advocates spoke out at public forums held by the U.S. and Mexican labor

Maria Lorena Cook, "Cross-Border Labor Solidarity," *Dissent* 44, no. 1 (Winter 1997): 49.

departments on union registration as part of the Sony case consultation. U.S. and Mexican unionists were joined by leaders of the Canadian, German, and British telephone workers unions in the public forum inspired by the Sprint case under the NAALC.

Even now, trade unionists in the United States, Mexico, and Canada are examining potential new submissions under the NAALC. All these steps required careful coordination to shape common positions. As those involved know each other better, they find new ways to link their movements. Although it is not *only* the labor side agreement driving these actions, the NAALC creates a framework for concrete work—developing strategies, drafting submissions, planning testimony, mounting press conferences, setting up demonstrations, meeting with government officials, participating in the agreement's cooperative activities program and events that flow from ministerial consultations, and all the learning about each other's countries and labor movements that takes place in the process.

3.4

NAFTA's Labor Agreement: Lessons

Jerome I. Levinson

This is the story of the attempt, in Mexico, by 21-year-old Alma Rosa Huerta and her worker colleagues to elect union officials of their own choosing through truly democratic elections, and form a union independent of government control. Huerta and her friends were employed by the Mexican maquiladora subsidiary, Magneticos de Mexico (MDM), of Sony Electronics, Inc., (Sony) an American subsidiary of the multi-billion dollar Japanese conglomerate, the Sony corporation. Maquiladoras are plants, generally located in Mexico along the border with the United States, which transform U.S. products into more advanced stages, and then, under favorable customs arrangements, send the more advanced products back to the United States. The great majority of the maquiladora plants are owned by U.S. corporations.

It is the story of how the workers' efforts were frustrated by the Mexican Government and the official union which only nominally represented the workers' interests. In Mexico, "official" unions are associated with the Mexican Workers Confederation (CTM), which has historically been closely tied to the Institutional Revolutionary Party (PRI) that has governed Mexico for the

Jerome I. Levinson, excerpt from "NAFTA's Labor Agreement: Lessons from the First Three Years" (Washington, D.C.: Institute for Policy Studies, and International Labor Rights Fund, 12 November 1996), 1–4 and 18–22.

past 70 years [until 2000]. Yet a growing number of "independent" unions are not affiliated with the CTM, or any other trade union confederation traditionally linked with the PRI.

As a condition of his support of the North American Free Trade Agreement (NAFTA), candidate Bill Clinton had assured American workers that he would negotiate a labor side agreement that would guarantee that the Mexican Government would enforce its own laws so as to protect core worker rights in Mexico, including the right of free association. Mexican workers would be enabled to negotiate effectively, through strong independent unions of their own choosing, with multi-national corporations (MNCs). The MNCs would be on notice that they could no longer depend upon official unions to assure a docile work force; productivity gains would have to be equitably shared with workers. The market for U.S. goods and services would be expanded; the wage gap between Mexican and U.S. workers, over time, would be narrowed. The glaringly regressive income distribution in Mexico would be gradually overcome, and political and social stability more likely be assured.

On August 16, 1994, four human rights and worker rights organizations filed a petition with the U.S. National Administrative Office (USNAO), alleging that the Government of Mexico had failed to enforce its own laws guaranteeing the right of freedom of association in connection with the attempt by Alma Rosa

Huerta and her colleagues at the MDM plant to form an independent union.[2]

The USNAO was established under the North American Agreement on Labor Cooperation (NAALC), of NAFTA. The NAALC reviews submissions concerning labor law matters arising in any of the three NAFTA countries. Mexico and Canada have established NAOs, which, like the USNAO, are empowered to consider submissions related to labor law matters in the territory of the two Parties other than their own.

The NAFTA is the only international trade and investment agreement where the Parties have attempted to establish a formal linkage between such an agreement and each Party's enforcement of its own labor (and environmental) laws. The linkage, however, is tenuous; there are no mandated legal consequences for the Parties to the NAFTA of a violation of the NAALC. Nor, under the NAALC, is there an effective remedy for a failure, as alleged in the MDM Submission, by Mexico to enforce its own laws guaranteeing the right of freedom of association, the most basic of all worker rights. The only recourse is a Consultation process among the Parties.

The USNAO determined that Alma Rosa Huerta and her worker colleagues had, indeed, been frustrated in exercising their right of free association: "In the end, despite pursuing every legal means of redress, the attempts to register an independent union failed. . . . Interested workers who signed the original petition were subsequently dismissed from their employment and remain unemployed to date. . . . It appears that such dismissals were intended as punishment and a warning to other Sony workers." (USNAO, Report on Ministerial Consultations, p. 10).

The dissident MDM workers who attempted to form an independent union were betrayed, then, not only by the Mexican Government, MDM and the CTM, all of whom joined to deny them their right of free association; they were betrayed, as well, by the NAALC, which was supposed to guarantee that such rights would be assured in Mexico. In failing to achieve that objective, the NAALC also betrayed U.S. workers, who must now do what Bill Clinton assured them they would not have to do: compete for investment capital against a Mexican labor relations system that is rigged to assure a compliant work force. (Clinton, 1992). And they are doubly disadvantaged, because that investment capital is primarily designed to produce goods for export to the United States, which absorbs approximately 70 percent of Mexican exports. Those exports often displace domestic U.S. production.

The Mexican government is engaged in a desperate attempt to attract foreign direct investment (FDI) to rescue a failed economic policy. In this effort it is supported by billions of dollars of loans from the Multilateral Financial Institutions (MFIs), the World Bank, the International Monetary Fund (IMF) and the Inter-American Development Bank (IDB), all with the enthusiastic endorsement of the United States Treasury. Each of these institutions, like the Mexican Government, the CTM and Mexican entrepreneurs, have a vested interest in seeing to it that Mexican workers are not represented by independent unions that would negotiate more aggressively with MNCs than would the CTM-affiliated unions, creating a climate less conducive to attracting investment.

The story of what happened to the MDM workers is thus much more than the simple story of a labor dispute in Mexico. It illuminates in graphic detail just how difficult it will be to assure core worker rights as part of the emerging open trading and investment regime that now constitutes the dominant economic orthodoxy.[3] But it is also vivid testimony as to how essential it is to assure respect for those rights as part of that regime.

What follows is a brief summary of the more important lessons to emerge from the USNAO consideration of the MDM matter. This is then followed by a more extensive analysis of why the NAALC has been so ineffectual in carrying out President Clinton's commitment to ensuring that Mexico would enforce its own labor laws.

[. . .]

The USNAO

On October 13, 1994, the USNAO accepted for review the Submission which had been filed on August 16 by the four NGOs alleging that Mexico had failed to enforce its own laws guaranteeing freedom of association.

A. IBT and UE Submissions (Honeywell and GE)

There had been two previous submissions accepted by the USNAO for review. Almost immediately after the NAALC took effect on January

1, 1994, the International Brotherhood of Teamsters (IBT) and the United Electrical, Radio and Machine Workers of America (UE)—filed complaints with the USNAO, alleging labor rights violations against two U.S.-based MNCs, Honeywell and GE. The Submissions were similar. They claimed that (i) both companies had dismissed employees who had engaged in an attempt to form independent unions; and (ii) the Mexican government had failed to intervene to assure the right of the employees to free association, in accordance with its own law, constitution and international commitments.

The USNAO's hearing on the IBT and UE submissions took place on September 12, 1994 at the U.S. Department of Labor headquarters in Washington D.C. The cost of bringing workers to Washington D.C. limited the number of workers who could travel to the hearing.

Neither GE nor Honeywell executives appeared at the hearing. The companies filed written statements, denying the allegations that workers had been fired because of their activities in trying to organize a union, and contesting the jurisdiction of the USNAO in even holding the hearing.

On October 12, 1994, the USNAO issued its public report on the IBT and UE submissions. The USNAO noted that there was disagreement about the events at each of the plants, namely whether workers were fired because of union activity or not, and declined to make a determination itself, although it noted the coincidence that the firings took place at the time of organizing drives at the plants. It gave equal weight to the company and worker versions of what transpired at the plants, despite the fact that the company did not appear at the hearing, whereas the workers were subject to questioning by the Secretary of the USNAO. (Under procedures adopted by the USNAO, only the Secretary could question the witnesses).

The USNAO declared itself not in a position to make a finding that the Mexican government failed to enforce the relevant labor laws, noting that the dismissed workers' acceptance of severance pay and the fact that two cases were still pending precluded the government of Mexico from coming to a conclusion on the matter. In the absence of a finding by the Mexican government, the USNAO observed that it could not come to an independent judgment. (USNAO Public Report IBT and UE, pp. 29–31).

In effect, this decision gave Mexico a veto over the scope of the inquiry by the USNAO: by not arriving at a decision on the merits of the allegations by the employees, Mexico precluded the USNAO from arriving at an independent judgment as to the merits of the claims.

B. The MDM Submission

The MDM submission differed in one important respect from the IBT and UE Submissions: The MDM dissident workers had attempted to obtain the registration of an independent union, an attempt which had been frustrated by an entity of the Mexican government, the CAB in Ciudad Victoria. The MDM submission, consequently not only alleged, as did the IBT and UE submissions, that the Mexican government had failed to intervene to protect the workers against the intimidation of the company, (and against the local and state police and a fraudulent election conducted by the official union); the government, through the local CAB, an entity established by the Mexican Constitution, and, therefore, a Mexican government authority, had wrongfully denied registration of an independent union. In so doing, the government of Mexico had failed to enforce its own law assuring the right of free association for the dissident MDM workers. (NGO MDM Submission, pp. 20–21).

The MDM submission put fully into play the registration requirement and the role of the CABs in frustrating the formation of independent unions. More than the IBT and UE submissions, it shifted the focus from the transgressions of the companies involved, to the action of the Mexican government. It placed squarely at issue the question addressed by Clinton's October 4, 1992 Raleigh speech, and the issue which the NAALC was designed to address: would the government of Mexico countenance the right of a group of Mexican workers to form a union of their own choosing, not affiliated with the CTM, and, if not, what consequences flowed from that denial?

In subsequent communications on behalf of the MDM workers, the NGOs requested that: (i) the USNAO hearing not take place in Washington, but in a venue closer to the border between Mexico and the U.S., so that more workers could participate in the process; (ii) simultaneous translation be provided so that the proceedings would be more meaningful for the participating workers; (iii) the USNAO lift its restriction upon radio and television coverage of the proceedings; (iv) the USNAO give greater weight to the testimony in the Hearing, where the Secretary of the NAO has an opportunity to test the credibility of the witnesses by asking questions, than to faceless written statements; and (v) that the NAO arrive at an independent judgment as to company intimidation of workers for union organizing, without the necessity for the Government of Mexico to make a prior determination as to whether the company had interfered with that right. (Harvey, 1994).

The USNAO scheduled a public hearing on the NGO MDM Submission for February 13, 1995 in the city of San Antonio, Texas, which is two hours driving time from Nuevo Laredo, Mexico, where the MDM maquiladora plant is located. The site of the hearing made it more accessible for the MDM workers who wished to testify. Moreover, the Secretary of the USNAO intervened with both MDM and the U.S. Embassy in Mexico City to facilitate the attendance at the Hearing by the MDM workers. The Embassy contacted the U.S. Border Patrol to advise the officials that the workers were crossing the border for the purpose of testifying at a U.S. government-sponsored hearing. The Secretary's intervention with MDM was to urge that MDM not obstruct the appearance of the workers before the USNAO.

Thirteen workers, twelve of them women, appeared before the USNAO in San Antonio and related their account, as described above, of MDM intimidation and collusion with the official union to prevent the formation of an independent union, and of their attempt to obtain registration of their union with the CAB in Ciudad Victoria. MDM, like Honeywell and GE, elected not to present any witnesses, but filed a letter with the USNAO, by its lawyers, denying the allegations in the MDM submission that the company intimidated employees for union organizing activity. (Epstein Becker, 1995).

On April 11, 1995, the NAO issued its report and findings on the MDM matter. It noted that it had "focused specifically on the Government of Mexico's compliance with its obligations under the NAALC. . . . As such, the NAO review has not been aimed at determining whether or not the company named in the submission may have acted in violation of Mexican labor law." (USNAO Public Report pp. 24–25).

Nevertheless, in contrast with the IBT and UE Submissions, the USNAO explicitly acknowledged the pressures upon Mexican workers to accept severance pay rather than contest alleged illegal dismissals:

"In the first report, it was specifically noted that many workers chose severance pay rather than pursue their legal remedies. This scenario is repeated in the instant situation, and the only explanation offered for this, outside of the economic circumstances discussed below, was the consistent testimony offered by workers that management personnel and CTM representatives pressured and intimated them into signing full releases and accepting severance as soon as it was offered so as not to risk losing it and/or to avoid being blacklisted in the maquiladoras." (Id at p. 26).

It also determined that there had been company intimidation of workers for union activities:

"Considering the duration of employment of the dismissed workers with MDM (ranging from four to fifteen years), their documented association with the opposition union movement, and the circumstances of their separation, it appears plausible that the workers' discharges occurred for the causes alleged, namely for participation in union organizing activities. . . . These workers generally do not have the financial resources to pursue reinstatement before the CABs, often opting for settlement of their complaints in return for money, as happened here in all but two instances. More importantly, the workers repeatedly articulated their concerns about impediments in obtaining impartial remedies." (Id at p. 27).

Concerning the denial of registration of the independent union by the Ciudad Victoria CAB, the USNAO observed that, . . . "expert testimony presented to the USNAO indicates that the CABs are specifically empowered to remedy these types of minor administrative deficiencies." (Id at p. 31). It concluded that, "serious questions are raised herein concerning the workers' ability to obtain registration of an independent union through the registration process with the local CAB." (Id at p. 32).

The USNAO, consequently, recommended that Ministerial Consultations are appropriate to "further address the operation of the registration process." (Id). Ministerial Consultation is the only remedy available under the NAALC, since Ambassador Kantor had agreed to eliminate sanctions as a possible remedy for a Party's failure to enforce its own laws relating to the right of freedom of association.

With respect to the company's dismissal of employees for union activities, of which it had found credible evidence, not even Ministerial consultations were possible.

Ministerial Consultations

On April 11, 1995, U.S. Secretary of Labor Robert Reich sent a letter, pursuant to Article 22 of the NAALC, to then Mexican Secretary of Labor and Social Welfare, Santiago Onate, requesting Ministerial Consultations on the union registration issue. Secretary Onate accepted the request.

The USNAO feared that the Mexicans might interpret Ministerial Consultation to mean nothing more than a cup of coffee between the two ministers. Hence, the USNAO was relieved when the Mexican Minister agreed to the following activities: (a) three joint seminars among the Parties to "better explain and improve implementation and public understanding of procedures regarding union registration and certification at the federal and state levels;" (b) a study dealing with union registration and its implementation, to be conducted by three independent Mexican labor law experts under the auspices of the Mexican Secretariat of Labor and Social Welfare (STPS); and (c) a series of meetings by STPS officials with (i) dissident MDM employees who had tried to form an independent union, (ii) the official CTM-affiliated union officials, (iii) MDM executives, and (iv) Ministry of Labor authorities in the Tamaulipas State, for the purpose of discussing the issues raised in the USNAO Public Report.

The first seminar, conducted in Mexico City, afforded Mexican workers and labor law practitioners, particularly those representing workers trying to obtain registration of independent unions, a public forum not previously available in Mexico for airing their grievances. Subsequent seminars illuminated the conflict of interest inherent in the present composition of the CABs. In Mexico, the seminars were perceived as opening up for public discussion a subject matter previously suppressed: the Mexican government's labor practices designed to frustrate the formation of independent unions. (Delgado).

The meetings with the MDM dissident workers were of little consequence.

The USNAO, which staged the seminars in conjunction with the Mexican NAO, was scrupulous to a fault in observing the diplomatic niceties: the seminars discussed labor law practices in the United States and Canada as well as in Mexico. Whatever the deficiencies in U.S. labor law and practice, however, and they are many, the NAALC was a consequence of President Clinton's concern with labor abuses in Mexico, and the threat they posed of unfair competition for American workers. The events at MDM gave graphic expression to those concerns. The ultimate test of the NAALC must be evaluated in terms of whether the NAALC has effected any significant change in those abusive practices. The harsh fact is that it has not.

The USNAO forthrightly stated the results of the MDM Submission:

> "In the end, despite pursuing every legal means of redress, the attempts to register an independent union failed . . . [t]he time consumed by the initial denial, and subsequent CAB denial of registration, caused irreparable harm. Interested workers who signed the original petition were subsequently dismissed from their employment and remain unemployed to date. While these workers may have been dismissed for "cause" and paid the appropriate severance allowances mandated by Mexican law their separation cannot be viewed as coincidental with their efforts to form an independent union. It appears that such dismissals were intended as punishment and a warning to other Sony workers." (USNAO Report on Ministerial Consultations, p. 10).

And it bluntly stated that, "[T]he labor representative on the CAB generally represents the incumbent or majority union—in the instant case a CTM affiliate. Therefore, at least one member of the CAB had a competing interest with the independent union seeking registration." (Id).

No sanctions could be taken against MDM; no workers were reinstated. The Mexican government, a Party to the NAALC and the NAFTA, could not be sanctioned for failing to assure workers at MDM their constitutional right of free association. The CABs continue to exist with their current composition and acknowledged conflict of interest. Nothing changed as a consequence of the NAALC.

Reflections

The story that emerges out of the MDM experience is a story of betrayal. Alma Rosa Huerta and her friends took seriously the Mexican Constitution's guarantee of freedom of association; they believed . . . that they would be able to compete in elections for the selection of union delegates to represent workers in the MDM plant. They believed that the NAALC could . . . be an effective instrument for redressing their grievances.

In each instance they were betrayed.

[. . .]

And, despite the courageous and candid reports of the USNAO, there is no effective action under the NAALC that can be taken on behalf of the MDM dissident workers.

Understood in retrospect, no other result should have been anticipated. The NAFTA and the NAALC were based upon different assumptions which cannot be reconciled. . . . [D]espite all of Mexico's reform efforts, and the Brady debt reduction deal, Mexico had not been able to attract the foreign investment it considered essential for its new economic strategy. The proposal for an FTA with the United States was a last desperate attempt to attract that capital. What Mexico had on offer for the MNCs was cheap labor and, through the CTM, a controlled labor force. These arrangements assured that the companies would have virtually a free hand in dictating the conditions of work. Disturbing the CTM domination of the labor force, which is guaranteed by the composition of the CABs, would have undermined Mexico as an attractive investment site.

The NAALC, however, was based on precisely the opposite assumption: that the denial of free association to Mexican workers constituted an unfair incentive for MNCs to invest in Mexico.

[. . .]

Lessons

1. President Clinton was right to link enforcement of core worker rights to NAFTA. Without this, countries face a strong temptation to compete for scarce investment capital by creating or maintaining a repressive labor relations system. Although the Administration's policy is riven with contradictions, the linkage of worker rights to an international trade and investment agreement, no matter how tenuous, is an important first step in institutionalizing that linkage.

2. The NAALC, without a clear legal bridge to NAFTA, is a fatally flawed agreement. Linkage is not enough. How that linkage is defined is important. An agreement on worker rights should be an integral part of a trade and investment agreement and not a side agreement with only a tenuous legal tie to the main agreement. The NAFTA should be re-negotiated so that worker rights are elevated to the same level of importance as the protection of corporate property rights. This can only be accomplished by placing the commitment to worker rights in the main body of NAFTA, where they are potentially subject to the dispute settlement procedures, including the possibility of sanctions against both offending companies and Parties. (The same reasoning applies to the environmental side agreement).

3. Where, as in Mexico, a repressive labor relations system is central to the government's economic program and the maintenance of the political party in power, the resistance to change will be enormous. Capacity to impose reform from the outside will be limited. But the United States should not make it more difficult for those within Mexico who are struggling to bring about changes in current labor relations. The U.S. Treasury's indiscriminate support of Mexico's economic program without reference to the labor abuses inherent in that program undermines the stated U.S. commitment to protecting worker rights.

4. In the Mexican context, calling for enforcement of existing laws is not sufficient. It is also necessary to change the institutions that have made it possible to maintain the present system which is designed to frustrate the formation of independent unions. For example, the requirement that unions be registered by Conciliation and Arbitration Boards (CABs), a form of labor tribunal, whose members, by the admission of Mexico's own leading labor law experts, have a direct interest in denying such registration, is incompatible with the obligations that Mexico assumed in the NAALC (NAALC, Article V, Par 4).

5. It should be the explicit policy of the United States that there will be no more international trade and investment agreements without specific provisions to enforce core worker rights. MNCs would then be on notice that the rules of

the game are being equalized. They will not be able to take advantage of jurisdictions which have a deliberate policy of suppressing free trade unions in order to gain competitive advantage in attracting foreign investment. And the international community would be on notice that this country does not accept that the concept of comparative advantage includes the suppression of core worker rights, particularly the right of free association, the foundation of all other worker rights.

6. The contradiction between U.S. support of worker rights through international trade and investment agreements and the World Bank's policy to undermine such efforts must be resolved. The World Bank has an almost paranoid pre-occupation with the "monopoly power" of unions to set wages and conditions of work in the present international environment, where core worker rights are barely respected. The emphasis on labor market flexibility and decentralized plant and enterprise collective bargaining are simply disguised attacks on the capacity of unions to negotiate effectively on behalf of their members. The U.S. Treasury's uncritical endorsement of these policies undermines the credibility of the stated U.S. goal of fortifying respect for worker rights.

7. The final lesson is related to the first six. Worker rights are only one aspect of the overall problem in re-defining the international trade and investment regime to restore some balance between the power of workers and management. But it has been asked to carry a disproportionate part of the burden of that re-definition.

It is time to re-examine the assumptions which have guided U.S. policy for the past four decades. There is no longer any reason, if there ever was one, for the U.S. government, through the Overseas Private Investment Corporation (OPIC) to guarantee companies against the risks—expropriation, currency inconvertibility, and war risk— of doing business abroad. OPIC should be abolished and the U.S. should withdraw from its multi-lateral counterpart, the World Bank Investment Guaranty Authority (MIGA). Similarly the tax preference provisions of the Internal Revenue Code that have historically favored the overseas investments of the MNCs, notably the foreign tax credit and the deferral of taxes owed to the U.S. Treasury, should be repealed.

Tax breaks and other incentives, such as OPIC, were enacted to encourage American overseas investments as part of a broader strategy of American economic expansion abroad, and of containing communism. We have not, however, cleared away the debris of policies that were enacted in a different time and which, in completely changed circumstances, continue to encourage MNCs to expand their overseas investments.

What is needed is a comprehensive approach which does not automatically assume that the interests of the MNCs are identical with the U.S. national interest. We can then begin to restore some reasonable balance between the power of these great companies and that of working men and women.

Notes

[. . .]

2. The International Labor Rights Education and Research fund, now the International Labor Rights Fund (ILRF); the National Association of Democratic Lawyers (Mexico); the Coalition for Justice in the Maquiladoras; and the American Friends Service Committee.

3. Core worker rights generally are understood to refer to freedom of association, the right to bargain collectively, and the right to strike. In the context of the negotiation of the NAALC, these rights are referred to as industrial relations. Additionally, the concept also refers to an adequate minimum wage, prohibition of child labor and the assurance of safe work-place conditions. This concept of core worker rights is embodied in individual Conventions of the International Labor Organization (ILO), and in various provisions of U.S. legislation dealing with trade, investment (the Overseas Private Investment Corporation (OPIC)) and U.S. support for the MFIs.

References

Clinton, Bill. 1992. "Expanding Trade and Creating American Jobs". *North Carolina State University*, Raleigh, North Carolina (October 4).

Delgado, Dora, 1996. "Side Accord Seen As Mechanism for Change in Mexico, Groups Say," *Special Report, (No. 156) Bureau of National Affairs*, (August 13).

Epstein Becker & Green. 1995. Letter to Irasema T. Garza, Secretary, United States National Administrative Office, re: Submission #940003. (January 19).

Harvey, Pharis. 1994. Letter and Memo to Irasema Garza, Secretary, National Administrative Office, *Subject Sony Submission and NAO Basis for Decisions in Honeywell and GE Cases.* (November 17).

North American Agreement on Labor Cooperation. 1993. Between the Government of the United States of America, the Government of Canada and the Government of the United Mexican States. (September 13).

U.S. National Administrative Office, North American Agreement on Labor Cooperation.

1994. *Public Report of Review, USNAO Submission #940001 (Honeywell) and Submission #940002 (GE).* Bureau of International Affairs, U.S. Department of Labor, (October 12).

U.S. National Administrative Office, North American Agreement on Labor Cooperation. 1995. *Public Report of Review, USNAO Submission #940003 (MDM de Mexico, Sony).* Bureau of International Labor Affairs, U.S. Department of Labor, (April 11).

U.S. National Administrative Office. 1996. *Report on Ministerial Consultations on NAO Submission #940003. (MDM de Mexico, Sony) under the North American Agreement on Labor Cooperation.* Bureau of International Labor Affairs, U.S. Department of Labor, (June 7).

3.5

Building Workers' Human Rights into the Global Trading System

International Confederation of Free Trade Unions

The Human Rights Case for a Workers' Rights Clause

The moral case for a workers' rights clause is unanswerable. Globalization promises a great deal, but delivers insecurity and cruelty to millions. The world cannot tolerate an economic system that depends on repression for profit; that exploits children and young women; and that makes slavery a sound business option. A workers' rights clause would create the potential for a different future, one that creates a basis for really achieving workers' rights and economic development and growth on the basis of respect for human rights and improvement in living and working conditions for all world citizens.

The international community already agrees that the global economy needs global regulation. That is the whole basis for the World Trade Organization; for international standard-setting; for laws banning the manufacture and sale of counterfeit goods and protecting intellectual property; and for the environmental initiatives following on from the Earth Summit. Many of the mechanisms set up to enforce these regulations are expensive for the compa-

nies to operate, and operate across the jurisdiction of nation-states.

[. . .]

There seems no justification for global regulation to protect property rights, while claiming that the same type of international regulation cannot operate to protect basic human and trade union rights.

[. . .]

Promoting Productivity and Encouraging Collective Bargaining

Much of the concern about a workers' rights clause is the result of a misunderstanding about what a workers' rights clause is and how it would work. A workers' rights clause is protective—it will help protect workers and children from exploitation—but it is not protectionist. Its aim is not to undermine economic competition, but to enhance it by removing unfair advantages. It will not restrict free trade, but will bring more people into the global economy. And it will work to close, rather than to widen, the gap between the developing and the developed world.

The aim of a workers' rights clause is to ensure that companies which trade agree to abide by seven basic rights, and these rights proposed by the international trade union movement are among the most highly ratified of the Interna-

International Confederation of Free Trade Unions (ICFTU), excerpt from *Building Workers' Human Rights into the Global Trading System* (Brussels, Belgium: ICFTU, 1999), 17–18, 33–36, 38, 40, and 44–45.

tional Labour Office (ILO). Six of the seven have been ratified by over 120 states. Universal adherence to these would not alter developing countries' legitimate comparative advantage but prevent the most extreme forms of cut-throat competition and exploitation.

What is crucial about the rights to organise and bargain is that they are enabling rights. They give workers and employers the means to negotiate improvements in wages and working conditions as trade and development expand.

In those negotiations, workers would obviously take note of how their employer was doing and how much their country could afford; negotiations don't take place in an economic vacuum. Unlike fly-by-night transnationals who are only interested in making cheap goods for a quick profit, workers have a long-term interest in their country's prosperity. They would expect a fair share when things are going well; and if they were allowed a genuine say in economic policy, they would be more likely to accept and carry out difficult decisions when there were problems.

There is no possibility that a workers' rights clause would bring about an international minimum wage that will drive the industries in poor countries to bankruptcy; split the world market into two camps and undermine global free trade. No one can seriously suggest that giving workers in the developing world the basic rights enshrined in a workers' clause will lead to their wage costs spiraling up to European levels. It just won't happen. Developing countries will still be able [to] enjoy comparative advantages from their abundant supply of labour. All that will happen is that governments will not be able to keep these costs down by oppressing their workers; and transnational corporations will not be able to bully countries into competitive repression.

In any event, it is not true that low wages will give countries a guaranteed competitive edge. Labour costs obviously figure in the final price of any product entering the world market. The exact weight of labour costs, however, depends on productivity; a poor country with low per capita income and low wages may still not have much competitive advantage on world markets because of low productivity. Likewise high wages matched by high productivity may make the output of rich countries very competitive.

The best way for developing countries to guarantee prosperity is to base their economies on high productivity and high skills; and the best way to do this is to allow workers and employers to set high standards, and fair wage levels. It makes sense that as trade and productivity grows, wages and other conditions of work also rise as national conditions permit, rather than be kept down by exploitation and repression.

[. . .]

Cheap labour is not all that developing countries have to offer the world. Not only is that an insulting picture of their economies; it is also inaccurate. To take just one example, India turns out 250,000 science graduates a year. Many of the world's leading companies are hiring Indian computer programmers to write their software and to process their data. Cost is a factor; but so are skill-levels. This is the kind of competition developing countries will have to offer in the information age. A workers' rights clause will give them the space to do that by easing the constant downward pressure on standards brought about by the present system.

It is surprising that the arguments against workers' rights in the WTO are being put forward with such fervour by governments in the developing world; and it is interesting that this view is not shared by the citizens of these countries. Workers in the developing world make up some of the most committed members of trade union organizations; their women workers are among the most passionate advocates of equal treatment; and the campaign against child labour and forced labour has strong roots in the developing countries.

Countries that take the high road to development will become more efficient, more competitive and more prosperous as long as their efforts are not undermined by countries who try to cut corners by exploiting their citizens. A workers' rights clause will help close off the short cuts.

[. . .]

Protecting Women's Rights through the WTO

Often the expansion of trade is based on access to low wage female labour. Historically trade liberalization in the least developed countries has tended to increase women's employment in labour intensive industries like manufacturing of electronics, clothing and textiles. Manufacturing [plants] are often located in special Export Processing Zones, where [standards] of health and safety are low, working hours are extremely long and workers have no rights to organise.

[. . .]

Through the introduction of a workers' rights clause the WTO could ensure that non-discrimination and equal pay was built into the world trading system. In countries where there are no laws to make sure women workers are treated equally to men, it would result in legislation to make sure that multinational corporations as well as domestic employers are required to apply ILO Convention 100 on Equal Remuneration, and Convention 111 on discrimination in employment.

Tackling Child Labour
in a Workers' Rights Clause

According to even the most conservative estimates there are now 250 million children working who should be given the chance to go to school and who should be replaced in the workforce with adults. Of these nearly half work full time, and at least 60 million children are engaged in extremely hazardous work.

[. . .]

So far, the WTO has not felt that it was within its remit to look at the inter-relationship between trade and child labour, even though at least 15 million children are producing goods for international markets, in agriculture and in industrial production. The WTO could begin work now by joining with the ILO to link programmes of assistance to measures to end child labour through WTO action on the basis of ILO Convention 138 (minimum age of employment) and the new Convention 182 (on the Worst Forms of Child Labour). With a workers' rights clause which outlawed child labour no country could be more competitive in one field than another country which did not use child labour.

[. . .]

Working Together, the WTO
and the ILO Could Get Countries
to Respect Workers' Rights

The aim behind a workers' rights clause is to ensure that the promotion of free trade goes hand in hand with the improvement of workers' rights. Implementation should therefore be a joint operation between the World Trade Organization (WTO) and the ILO. The ILO has obvious competence in setting standards and in supervising the application; and the WTO would make sure that failure to enforce the basic standards does not lead to unfair competition.

Our proposal is that a joint WTO/ILO Advisory Body could be set up to oversee the implementation of a workers' rights clause. This body would have the authority to undertake periodic reviews of how countries were applying the principles enshrined in a workers' rights clause; or to step in if there was a well-justified complaint.

This side of the operation would be the particular responsibility of the ILO team on the joint advisory body; the ILO already does much of this anyway, although there would be a need to reinforce its existing procedures.

The reviews would typically show either that the standards were being followed—in which case, no further action would be needed—or that the country concerned was in breach of its obligations, and certain changes in labour law and/or practice were necessary.

In the latter case, the ILO report would make recommendations to the country concerned on these changes and, if necessary, offer technical assistance and make additional resources available to help countries put things right.

The government of the offending country would then have a period of time in which to change its ways. We are suggesting two years, following which there would be a second report. This second report would typically reach one of three conclusions. It could show that the country was applying the standards; or that while the problem had not yet been solved, progress was being made; or that the government had failed to co-operate with the ILO and that the standards were still not being met.

So what exactly are the rights which would be included in a workers' rights clause? The clause contains seven of the most universally ratified conventions, universal standards applicable for all countries whatever their level of development. How they are translated into law and practice can vary according to the institutions and customs of the country concerned. The ILO in its supervision of the standards does not attempt to impose a global harmonization of labour laws; it examines whether the effect of laws and practice achieve the objective of ensuring that the principles are applied.

[. . .]

In terms of implementation, the ILO and not the WTO would be responsible for reviewing the respect of the core ILO Conventions concerned. The impartiality of the ILO and its expertise on international labour conventions in law and practice is beyond question. Because the ILO would have a key role in any workers' rights clause, that would give trade unions a right to launch complaints and representations about the violation of workers' rights.

3.6

How the South Is Getting a Raw Deal at the WTO

Martin Khor

Other Issues at the Door: Environment and Labor

A. Social and Environment Issues Seeking an Entrance

Another set of "new issues" is knocking on the door to enter the WTO system. Unlike other "new issues" that are pushed by the northern-based corporations, this set of issues is being advocated by social organizations (mainly in the North but also by some in the South) that are seeking ways to protect or promote their interests. The key issues in this category are environment and labor. There may be attempts in the future to introduce other issues, such as human rights and gender equity. Indeed, if environment and labor were to enter the WTO system as subjects for agreements, it would be conceptually difficult to argue why other social and cultural issues should also not enter.

The objectives of the social organizations in linking their particular causes to trade measures are different from the aims of corporations who seek linkages (in investment and procurement) to gain greater market access and market share, or (in [International Property Rights]) to protect

their domination and hinder potential new rivals. The social organizations are looking for more effective ways to protect their interests and believe that the instruments of trade measures or trade sanctions can be very effective. They believe that their causes (to defend animal rights, conserve the environment, or protect jobs and promote higher social standards) can most effectively be promoted if governments of countries that have "low environmental and social standards" are faced with the potential threat of trade measures and sanctions on products that are produced using the low standards.

In this, the social organizations concerned are seeking methods similar to those of the corporations, in that they are pressuring their governments and negotiators to make use of a strong enforcement mechanism (unilateral trade measures, or the dispute settlement mechanism of the WTO backed up with the possibility of trade sanctions).

Thus, trade measures have become methods of choice, and the WTO has become a vehicle for big corporations and some social organizations in promoting their interests.

B. Trade and the Environment

That there are links between trade and the environment cannot and should not be denied. Trade can contribute to environmentally harmful activities. Ecological damage, by making production

Martin Khor, excerpt from "How the South Is Getting a Raw Deal at the WTO," in *Views from the South: The Effects of Globalization and the WTO on Third World Countries*, ed. Sarah Anderson (San Francisco: International Forum on Globalization, 1999), 41–49.

unsustainable, can also have negative effects on long-term production and trade prospects. In some circumstances, trade (for example, trade in environmentally sound technology products) can assist in improving the environment.

What is of concern or relevance in looking at "linkages" is the advocacy of the use of trade measures and sanctions on environmental grounds. Some environmental and animal rights groups believe that national governments should be given the right to unilaterally impose import bans on products on the grounds that the process of production is destructive and that WTO rules should be amended to enable these unilateral actions.

Some groups, and some developed country members of the WTO, go further and have advocated a set of concepts linking trade measures in the WTO to the environment. These concepts are processes and production methods (PPMs), internalization of environmental costs, and eco-dumping. The three concepts are interrelated. The implication is that if a country has lower environmental standards in an industry or sector, the cost of that country's product is not internalized, making prices artificially low. Thus, when that country exports these products, it is practicing eco-dumping. As a result, an importing country would have the right to impose trade penalties, such as levying countervailing duties, on the goods.

This set of ideas poses complex questions relating to concepts, estimations, and practical application, particularly as they relate to the international setting and to the WTO. Developing countries are likely to find themselves at a great disadvantage within the negotiating context of the WTO, should the subject (which has already been discussed in the Committee on Trade and Environment) come up for negotiations.

One of the main issues is whether all countries should be expected to adhere to the same standard, or whether standards should be allowed to correspond to levels of development. The application of a single standard would be inequitable because poorer countries can ill afford high standards, thus, their products would become non-competitive. The global burden of adjustment to a more ecological world would be skewed inequitably toward the developing countries.

This is counter to the principle of "common but differentiated responsibility" of the UNCED or Earth Summit, which states that the devel-

oped countries, which take the greater share of blame for the ecological crisis and have more means to counter it, should correspondingly bear the greater responsibility for the global costs of adjustment.

Given the unequal bargaining strengths of the North and South in the WTO, the complex issues relating to PPMs, cost internalization, and trade-related environmental measures should not be negotiated within the WTO. If they are discussed at all, the venue should be the United Nations (for example, in the framework of the Commission on Sustainable Development) in which the broader perspective of environment and development and of the UNCED can be brought to bear.

Unilateral trade measures taken by an importing country against a product on the grounds of its production method or process are also fraught with the dangers of protectionism and the penalizing of developing countries. However tempting the route of unilateral import bans may be for the environmental cause, it is an inappropriate route as it will lead to many consequences and could eventually even be counter-productive.

Policies and measures to resolve environmental problems (and there are many such genuine problems that have reached the crisis stage) should be negotiated in international environmental forums and agreements. These measures can include (and have included) trade measures. However, the relationship between the WTO and the multilateral environmental agreements (MEAs) is the subject of much debate. On the one hand, developing countries fear that a system of blanket and automatic approval by the WTO of trade measures adopted by an MEA could lead to abuse and protectionism. A sticking point is what constitutes an MEA, as it may include not only truly international agreements convened by the UN and enjoying near-universal consensus, but also agreements drafted by a few countries that then invite others to join.

On the other hand, environmental groups and also developing country and some developed country governments genuinely fear that negotiations in new MEAs can be (and are being) undermined by the WTO. For example, a few countries argued against an International Biosafety Protocol on the grounds that WTO free-trade principles take precedence over environmental objectives. Such arguments are false, as the WTO already allows for trade measures agreed to in MEAs through the present Article XX. Nevertheless, this tactic was used to reject the proposals by the overwhelming majority of delegations to establish checks on the trade in genetically modified organisms and products. Blatant use of the slogan "free trade" to undermine vital health and environmental concerns contributes to the erosion of public confidence in free trade and the WTO system.

[. . .]

C. Trade and Labor Standards

The push for incorporating labor standards with trade measures in the WTO has come from labor unions in the North and international trade unions that also have affiliations in developing countries. However, some trade unions in some developing countries are opposed to including labor standards in the WTO. Proponents have linked the issue of labor standards to the broader concept of a "social clause," which could include the rights of various groups in society. Some political parties in developed countries also support this concept.

Advocates of a social clause may be motivated by various objectives. Many trade unions believe that transnational corporations are relocating from countries with higher labor standards to those with lower standards, and that this trend acts to depress labor standards by reducing the bargaining power of workers. They also believe that by linking the threat of trade sanctions to labor standards, there will be pressure to upgrade the level of standards in developing countries. They are careful to include only internationally recognized core labor standards and to exclude the issue of wage levels in the demands for linkage to trade and the WTO.

Other advocates believe that the linking of social issues (including, but not exclusively, labor standards) to the WTO and its sanctions system of enforcement is an effective way of countering the adverse social effects of trade and investment liberalization, by forcing corporations and governments to observe socially responsible policies.

Developing countries fear that the objectives of the northern and international trade unions, and of developed country governments that back the social clause demand, are mainly protectionist in nature, that they want to protect jobs in the North by reducing the low-cost incentive that attracts global corporations to developing countries. They argue that low labor costs in their countries are a function not of deliberate exploitation of workers but of the general low standard of living and the lower level of development, and that the low cost is a legitimate comparative advantage. They therefore have opposed the inclusion of labor standards in the WTO and argued successfully (as in the Singapore Ministerial Declaration) that the issue belongs in the ILO.

There is, of course, justification for public interest groups to be concerned about the social consequences of globalization and liberalization and to campaign to change the nature and effects of the present globalization trends. However, the issue is whether labor standards and social clauses in trade agreements are an appropriate route. Arguments to the contrary have merit for the following reasons:

i. Such an issue, when placed in the WTO context, would be linked to the dispute settlement system and the remedy of trade penalties and sanctions. In other venues, there is the option (which many would argue is more appropriate) of linking the improving of labor standards to positive incentives, rather than seeking punitive measures.

ii. Even though most advocates only demand minimum labor standards such as the right of association for workers, there is no certainty that the issue will be so confined in the future. Once the concept of social issues and rights enters the WTO system, it can be expanded within the particular issue (e.g., an extension to social security and wage levels within the issue of labor standards) and extended to other issues (such as the rights of children, women, and the disabled; human rights in general; the right to education, health, nutrition, etc).

iii. It is possible or even likely that once rights and social issues enter the WTO, countries with low social standards would be deemed to be practicing "social dumping" (or unfairly subsidizing its products by avoiding social costs) and importing countries could be enabled to impose countervailing duties.

iv. Developing countries are likely to bear the costs of a loss of competitiveness. The poor social conditions in the poorer countries are largely related to the low level of development and the lack of resources (although the waste and mismanagement of resources also do contribute significantly). Lower social standards are thus linked to (though not entirely caused by) lower levels of development. It is very possible that the linkage between social standards and trade measures in the WTO system would lead to placing additional pressures on developing countries and that many of their products would cost more and become noncompetitive, or face trade penalties, or both.

v. It is possible that the firms and products eventually affected will not be confined to those involving trade and exports but would include the firms (most of them small and locally owned) that cater to the local market. By not being able to remain competitive, some might close.

vi. It is also possible that the erosion of competitiveness and the higher costs (perhaps beyond what would normally prevail in countries at the existing stage of development) would cause loss of jobs, closure of firms and farms, and reduced investment, or the movement of some workers to more poorly paid jobs.

vii. The inclusion of labor standards would open the door to a much wider range of issues relating to social standards, social rights, and human rights. Many new "conditionalities" would be introduced, not only on trade at the border but also on domestic production and investment. The issues will be so complex and complicated that they will tie the WTO system in knots, and occupy the time and energy of diplomats and policy makers, not to mention the NGOs and social organizations, in an enterprise that is fraught with controversies and dangers, and with no clear guaranteed benefits.

viii. Finally, the efforts of NGOs and social organizations could be directed instead toward the sources of the social problems within and outside the WTO. For example, to offset problems caused by the WTO, those concerned about human rights and the livelihood rights of ordinary people could examine and campaign for changes to the existing agreements. . . . They could also try to prevent new agreements (such as those on investment, procurement, and industrial tariffs) that would affect the viability of local firms, the livelihoods of workers, and the people's right to development.

And to counter problems whose sources are beyond the WTO, there can be intensified campaigns for debt relief and reforms to the IMF and structural adjustment programs, a proemployment macroeconomic policy (rather than priority to restrictive monetary policy), as well as campaigns for improved human rights and against exploitative child labor and poor working conditions, etc. But the notion of linking social rights to a trade sanctions regime, though tempting at first, is likely to be counterproductive in results.

3.7

How to Support the Rights of Women Workers in the Context of Trade Liberalisation in India

Rohini Hensman

It is not at all surprising that the Indian government is opposed to the inclusion of a social clause in international trade agreements: the united opposition of all sections of employers in any attempt to link minimum labour standards with trade is sufficient explanation for the Indian government's stand. However the rejection of the social clause by all the national trade unions[1] is more surprising, and needs to be examined in greater detail. What accounts for this consensus between employers, government and national trade union leaderships? Does it represent the interests of rank-and-file workers? In particular, does it represent the interests of women workers? We shall look at these questions later. But first, a very brief summary of the background against which the debate is taking place.

Background

An estimated 8 percent of the labour force in India falls into the formal or organised sector which is protected by fairly comprehensive labour laws covering industrial disputes, unfair

dismissal, trade union rights, working conditions, health and safety, etc. etc. Restrictions on the employment of children and young persons, restrictions on night work for women, maternity benefits and workplace creches for the pre-school children of women workers are all covered by these laws. While employers may not necessarily respect these provisions, workers in this sector, who have traditionally been highly unionised, have used them to their advantage.

Employment of women has rarely gone above 11 percent of the formal sector labour force at most. Case studies indicate that once a workforce gets unionised and the legal provisions for women have been implemented, recruitment of women decreases or stops and their percentage in the workforce declines. This has happened, for example, in textiles and pharmaceuticals[2] and opencast iron-mining.[3] In all these cases, the reduction in the proportion of women was associated with technological change and rationalisation; in the case of the Indian Leaf Tobacco Division of ITC, 25,000 women engaged in manual leaf stripping lost their jobs when the operation was automated in the early 1980s.[4] The national and other trade unions in this sector have fought for maternity benefits and creche facilities for women, but not against the initial confinement of women to labour-intensive jobs and later exclusion from the workforce; for equal remuneration for the same work, but not for equal pay for work of equal value, nor for equal opportunities.

Rohini Hensman, "How to Support the Rights of Women Workers in the Context of Trade Liberalisation in India," in *Trade Myths and Gender Reality: Trade Liberalisation and Women's Lives*, ed. Angela Hale (Brussels, Belgium: International Coalition for Development Action; Uppsala, Sweden: Global Publications Foundation, 1998), 71–88.

Discrimination in employment has disadvantaged not only women, but also workers from scheduled castes (dalits) and religious minorities (especially Muslims), who are grossly under-represented in the formal sector compared to their proportion in the population.

It follows that the vast majority of these under-privileged workers, as well as children, are to be found in the informal or unorganised sector, where legal protection is minimal, and even those provisions which exist can rarely be implemented because it is so easy for employers to dismiss workers who try to form unions. More than 50 percent of the workers in this sector are women.[5] Despite the heavy odds against them, some workers in the informal sector have succeeded in forming unions, but until recently, there was no organisation representing them at a national level. However, in May 1995 the National Centre for Labour was formed, bringing together in a national federation unorganised sector workers in SEWA (Self Employed Women's Association), unions of fishworkers, construction workers, agricultural and forest workers, and many others.[6]

[. . .]

Opposition to the Social Clause from Trade Unions and NGOs

National trade union leaderships, Left parties and some NGOs have opposed the idea of labour standards linked to trade agreements for a variety of reasons. Going through reports and statements coming out of two national consultations on this issue, organised in Delhi (March 1995) and Bangalore (October 1995) by the Centre for Education and Communication, one can find the following arguments:

(1) The new WTO regime is more weighted in favour of the industrially advanced countries than the old GATT regime, and the social clause would provide a further basis for them to intervene against Third World countries.[13]

(2) The social clause is aimed at eroding the competitive edge of Third World exports.[14]

(3) The linkage of labour standards to multilateral trade agreements should be rejected along with WTO itself, since they are part of an exploitative international order.[15]

(4) The social clause is a protectionist measure.[16]

(5) Individual countries should decide on how to improve labour standards.[17]

(6) Trade-linked labour standards will function in the interest of MNCs.[18]

(7) The ideological function of proposing the social clause is to suggest that low labour standards in Third World countries are a result of internal problems like a weak democratic tradition and the indifference of trade unions, whereas the real reason is the centre periphery inequality of the international economic system.[19]

(8) Trade-linked labour standards are the least effective way of enforcing (or enabling trade unions to enforce) labour standards.[20]

(9) "Social clauses make bedfellows of Northern trade unions and their corporations to jointly police and undermine social movements in the South".[21]

(10) Since labour standards lie in the domain of the ILO, the social clause should become part of the ILO.[22]

[. . .]

Trade union bodies like the AFL-CIO and ICFTU are in favour of the social clause, at least partly because they feel that competition with cheap labour in Third World countries is causing job losses in Europe and North America. Some governments and parties in these countries—those who are more amenable to trade union pressure—support them. Others, like the British Conservative Party, are opposed to social clauses. The Dutch government and Dutch business are also opposed to the social clause, while the British Labour Party claims to support it. There is no evidence to suggest that MNCs support the social clause, and it seems logical to conclude from their anti-union behaviour in India that they would be opposed to any measure which enforces collective bargaining and trade union rights. The international financial institutions are against linking labour standards to trade because this would impose limits on the freedom of capital and the exploitability of labour; the World Bank's 1995 *World Development Report* says in so many words that "It is best to keep multilateral trade agreements confined to directly trade-related issues to prevent protectionist interests from misusing such links". And apparently the former Chairman of GATT, none other than Arthur Dunkel of the infamous Dunkel Draft, also feels that the social clause amounts to back door or disguised protectionism.[26]

What emerges is that far from being unanimous on this issue, labour and capital in the industrially advanced countries are sharply opposed to each other, while governments and political parties lean one way or the other depending on their own sympathies and whose pressure is stronger at the time.

Support for the Social Clause from Trade Union Activitists and NGOs

While the trade union leaders, Left parties and NGOs who reject the social clause try to dissociate themselves from the position taken by Indian capital and the Indian government, there is nonetheless an implicit assumption that what is bad for "India" or "the nation" is also bad for Indian workers. There could be many reasons for this nationalist position: for example, the powerful emotions aroused by accounts of the struggle for independence combined with ignorance of the changes in the nature of Indian capitalism since then, or a mistaken association of economic nationalism with a certain degree of state commitment to social justice, among others. By contrast the arguments in favour of the social clause below—by rank-and-file worker unionists, and activists working with organised labour, the informal sector, and child labour— represent a passionate rejection of any kind of compromise with Indian capital and a government which they see as having betrayed the interests of workers and the poor:

Sujata Gothoskar (woman activist of Workers' Solidarity Centre, working with formal sector unions in Bombay): The first argument is about "eroding the competitive edge of our country." *This competitive edge is supposedly the miserable wage levels of the workers, the bad living and working conditions and the denial to them of basic human rights.* Is it not shameful for us to argue about "our advantages" in such a cynical manner? . . . *With this argument, every struggle by the workers for a better life may be argued as eroding the competitive edge of our country.* Does this not negate the rationale and existence of the unions itself?

The second argument is about "individual countries deciding how to improve . . . labour standards."

Can workers and unions ever talk about individual countries deciding on improvement of labour standards? When countries decide, who or what exact sections decide? When TADA or other laws are made and used to arrest and harass workers, unionists or anybody protesting against injustice, who decides these laws and their implementation? . . . *Can we say India decides? Can we say workers decide? Unionists decide? People decide?*

The government is the biggest flouter of labour legislation, so how can they be trusted to implement it? There are dangers in linking the social clause to trade, but there's no other option.[27]

In fact, Ashim Roy shows that replacing child labour by adult labour in the carpet industry, for example, would hardly make any difference to the ultimate sale price because most of the markup occurs elsewhere. This is unlikely to hit exports, but it would result in somewhat lower profits for the employer. This supports Thomas Mathew's conclusion that "the social clause would not erode the competitive edge; it would rather impair the exploitative advantage".[28]

Srilata Swaminadhan (woman activist of the Rajasthan Kisan Sanghathan, working with the rural poor in Rajasthan): What the poor and toiling masses are being told to do by their ruling classes is to stand by their respective governments in fighting against linkages as that is what is the national interest.

While exposing the hypocrisy of the developed nations behind their demand for linking social clauses with [Multilateral Trade Agreements] it is equally important that we expose the hypocrisy of our own government and ruling classes (and those of all [LDCs]).

It is being borne home with every action of the government that "national interest" means only the interest of the minority rich who rule this country and control all its wealth and resources. . . .

Is it not the height of hypocrisy that our government should consider linking equal wages to men and women with trade, to be against the interests of the nation? Is it not revealing that it considers giving a guarantee to stop child labour as harmful to our country? . . .

So, the next question is—what do the toiling men, women and children of a country owe to its government and to its ruling classes that have so blatantly and shamelessly rejected them? . . . Do the poor of our countries have to abdicate all their rights and privileges in order to prove that they are loyal to the nation and are all the sacrifices for our "development" only to be made by the poor?[29]

Amrita Chhachhi (woman activist, describing the problems of women working in the electronics industry in Delhi): As a result of the current economic policy, even well-known TV firms are sub-contracting industrial work. This has resulted in a large number of small ancillary units where women are employed at below minimum wages. These units are so flexible that they can close down operations and relocate them at short notice. As a result, all attempts at organising women labourers have been failures. It has become extremely difficult to even trace the movement of these units from location to location. Unionisation is impossible in this scenario. "Therefore," she said, "there is very little possibility of a purely internal struggle or mechanism that could solve the problem. One may have to explore the idea of an international mechanism which includes trade sanctions . . ."[30]

Joseph Gathia (Centre for Concern for Child Labour): The quantum jump in child labour as a result of the new policies is particularly reflected in the carpet industry where there were around 30,000 children in 1979–80, but . . . 395,000 in 1993–4 . . . "In this context," he said, "the social clause is the only silver lining in an otherwise dismal scenario. We need to support the inclusion of a social clause and not allow the developed countries to use it in their favour." He felt that the current opposition to the social clause was not warranted . . . He also questioned the stand of trade unions, that enforcement of labour standards by ILO, and not by WTO, would be acceptable. He felt that the ILO had no teeth and our governments have not been listening to ILO . . .[31]

Murlidharan (worker unionist from Boehringer-Mannheim Employees' Union): It may be true that there are protectionist interests behind the social clause proposal. But the protectionist interests of the Lancashire mill-owners were behind most of our labour legislation, yet we have been able to use it to our advantage.[32]

Harish Pujari (worker unionist from Otis Elevator Employees' Union): The social clause can't be used against workers, and we may be able to use it to our advantage, so why should we oppose it?[33]

M. J. Pande (Bombay Union of Journalists): We all know that the U.N. is an organisation dominated by imperialist interests, yet we support its Human Rights Charter: couldn't we therefore support the social clause while rejecting the exploitative world order represented by the WTO?[34]

Bennet D'Costa (worker unionist from Hindustan Lever Employees' Union): Most of world trade consists of MNC products, so they will be hardest hit by the social clause. It must be linked to trade, otherwise there will be no way of enforcing it. But Third World workers must have a say in defining the social clause and putting what we want into it; we can't just accept what trade unions in the imperialist countries suggest. Did they ever protest against colonialism? They have benefited from imperialism, but they haven't raised their voice against it.[35]

Nima Sridhankar (woman worker unionist from Rhone-Poulenc Employees' Union): Why should we look at the social clause only in terms of what has been proposed already? We should make our own proposals. If Nike violates the rights of workers in Bangladesh or Indonesia, the company should be penalised. If a country discriminates against certain sections like women, Dalits or Muslims in, say, education, then the country should be penalised.[36]

The Way Forward

It is impossible in a paper this length to do justice to all the arguments which have been put forward on this issue, but the foregoing extracts give some idea of the range between the two extremes. Ultimately, the question is, as Sharit Bhowmik correctly poses it:[37] Is opposition to the social clause justified? And none of the arguments for opposition carries conviction. Granted the proposed social clause is inadequate, it needs to be modified, its implementation has to be monitored carefully, it needs to be supplemented by other forms of action locally, nationally and internationally; but if we look at it from the standpoint of workers—rather than a fictitious "national interest" which consolidates labour, capital and the state—then it seems that on balance the social clause could be used to help internal struggles, just as trade sanctions against apartheid South Africa supported internal struggles against the apartheid regime.

Perhaps it is only from the standpoint of those who are not struggling for collective bargaining rights for all workers, the abolition of child labour, and freedom from discrimination that the social clause looks so threatening? Do Indian trade union bureaucrats have the moral right to oppose the social clause when they have never seriously taken up the issues of child labour, the collective bargaining rights of over 90 percent of the labour force in the informal sector, and blatant discrimination against women, Dalits and Muslims in the formal sector? Surely they should ask themselves why they have landed up with such unsavoury bedfellows as the World Bank, Arthur Dunkel and the British Conservative Party? While it is certainly true that there are external causes of the low labour standards in India, this by no means rules out the existence of internal causes as well.

At the same time, there are good reasons for the scepticism frequently expressed about the bona fides of European and North American trade unions and the international union organisations dominated by them. [. . .]

Let us take the example of child labour. [. . .]

If trade unionists in Europe and North America want to convince us that they are genuinely concerned about these children and not just about their own jobs, they must help us to come up with creative solutions to this problem. Perhaps they could campaign for debt cancellation which is directly set off against government expenditure on rehabilitating and educating these children, and an immediate end to structural adjustment policies which lead to increases in child labour. Such proposals have to be part of any discussion of the social clause.

Putting together all the positive contributions to the debate on the social clause, I would propose the following:

Since the social clause has not yet come into being, there is scope for discussion and debate to modify the proposal. In the context of the conditions and debate in India, the following points should be considered:

- It does indeed seem to be unfair that if an MNC violates worker rights in a Third World country, it should get away scot free while the country alone is penalised. There should be some provision for penalising the company too—e.g. a worldwide trade boycott against its products. The company should also be held responsible for the conditions it imposes on its suppliers, if these allow or encourage violations.

- Most child labour is not in the export sector at all, so the problem would not be solved if child labour in export production alone were to be penalised. There should be penalties against violations of minimum standards even if these occur in non-export sectors.

- It is also worth considering the suggestion that if there is rampant discrimination in areas other than employment, that too should be penalised. In India, with its abysmal record on female literacy, education immediately comes to mind—especially since education has a bearing on employment opportunities too.

- The provisions for equal remuneration and non discrimination will certainly benefit women workers if they are implemented. But women would still be at a disadvantage in the labour market due to their extra burden of domestic labour. In a different context,[41] women worker activists proposed that men as well as women should be entitled to parental leave and childcare. It would make a very big difference to women workers if these provisions are included in the minimum standards—and would also eliminate child labour in the form of girls being kept at home to look after younger siblings. The problems of physical abuse and sexual harassment also need to be addressed.

- More generally, there could be a welfare or social wage component in the minimum standards.

- We should also consider including health and safety provisions. After our bad experience with the Bhopal disaster, it seems especially important to have some means of regulating the conduct of MNCs and penalising them for violations.

- International action in support of minimum labour standards should not be limited to blocking exports of a country. It can include (a) stopping its imports of arms and ammunition, and (b) positive incentives. This will also ensure that countries taking action are not merely being protectionist, but are willing to take action even if their own exports (e.g. of arms to Indonesia) suffer thereby.

- The overall mechanism whereby minimum labour standards are enforced should at every stage involve the workers in whose interests they are supposedly being implemented.

  a) They should be consulted about the standards themselves.

  b) The initiative in making complaints about violation of standards should come from them. It would be completely farcical, for example, if the government of the USA, which is responsible for the deaths of over half a million Iraqi children as a result of the Gulf War and economic sanctions, should pose as a champion of child workers; i.e. complaints from the US government about child labour in other countries should not be acceptable.

  c) The ILO, and trade union or NGO researchers working with them, could play a role in investigating complaints and recommending a course of action to the WTO. However here too, workers should be interviewed in confidence as part of the research exercise, in order to ensure that the action taken does not go against their interests.

- There are widespread fears that the WTO will be biased in the way it implements trade sanctions—e.g. that it will bow to the pressure and interests of powerful countries within it. There should be a mechanism for ensuring transparency and accountability in its decision-making.

Conclusion

There has to be much more debate on the social clause as well as other ways of enforcing minimum labour standards (e.g. international trade union action, publicity campaigns, consumer action), locally and nationally as well as internationally. A forum for the international debate needs to be created. We in India have some knowledge of what trade unions in Europe and the U.S. are saying, but very little idea of what trade unions, activists and women workers in other Third World countries are arguing and de-

manding. How can we get this information? And conversely, how can we make sure that the voices of grassroots activists and women workers from India (and not just those of trade union bureaucrats) are heard in other countries? Creating a forum where this information can be exchanged and the various points of view discussed is an urgent necessity.

Notes

1. See "An Appeal from the Central Trade Union Organisations of India to the fifth Conference of Labour Ministers of Non-Aligned and other Developing Countries", New Delhi, January 1995.

2. Rohini Hensman, "The Gender Division of Labour in Manufacturing Industry: A Case Study in India", *Discussion Paper 253*. Institute of Development Studies, University of Sussex, December 1988.

3. Ilina Sen, "Technology and Women: A Case Study from the Mining Sector in India", Paper presented to the United Nations University Institute for New Technologies, 1995.

4. Communication from a trade unionist in ITC, Hyderabad, September 1995.

5. See Gabriele Dietrich, "Women's Struggle for Production of Life: Public Hearings of Women Workers in Informal Sector", *Economic and Political Weekly*, 1.7.95, pp. 1551–54, for a description of the appalling conditions in which these women work. She also points out that lack of childcare leads to daughters being kept away from school to look after younger siblings at home.

6. Mohan Mani, "New Attempt at Workers' Resistance: National Centre for Labour", *Economic and Political Weekly*, 7.10.95, pp. 2485–86.

[. . .]

13. Anuradha Chenoy, "The Social Clause in the International Trading System", Centre for Education and Communication, New Delhi, 1995, p. 2 (mimeo).

14. Sujata Gothoskar, 1996, "The social clause—whose interest is it serving?" in J. John and A. Chenoy (eds.), *Labour, Environment and Globalisation*, Centre for Education and Communication, New Delhi, pp. 59–66.

15. Anuradha Chenoy, art. cit., p. 6.

16. Hindu Mazdoor Sabha (HMS) and All India Trade Union Congress (AITUC), quoted in

"Report of the Proceedings of the National Consultation on Social Clauses in Multilateral Trade Agreements", New Delhi, March 1995, p. 7.

17. The Centre of Indian Trade Unions (CITU), quoted by Sujata Gothoskar, op. cit., p. 62.

18. Ashim Roy, "Labour Standards in Multilateral Trade Agreements: An Overview", *Labour File*, Vol. 1, No. 2, p. 7, 1995.

19. Ashim Roy, op. cit., p. 10.

20. Ashim Roy, op. cit., p. 9.

21. Vandana Shiva, "North paying lip-service to social issues", *The Observer of Business and Politics*, 19/9/95.

22. Anuradha Chenoy, op. cit., p. 4.

[. . .]

26. See Martin Ferguson, "International Trade and Workers Rights", *International Union Rights*, Vol. 1, Issue 7, 1994, p. 4.

27. Up to *'People decide?'* is from Gothoskar, *op. cit.*, pp. 62–63. The rest is from an interview in December 1995.

28. Roy, *op. cit.*, p. 6; Thomas Mathew, "The Need for a Social Clause", in John and Chenoy (eds.), *Labour, Environment and Globalisation*, Centre for Education and Communication, New Delhi, pp. 67–69.

29. Srilata Swaminadhan, "Towards International Solidarity", in John and Chenoy (eds.), *Labour, Environment and Globalisation*, Centre for Education and Communication, New Delhi, pp. 55–58.

30. Amrita Chhachhi, quoted in V. Vivekanandan, 'Outright Rejection or Strategic Use? A Report', in John and Chenoy (eds.), *Labour, Environment and Globalisation*, Centre for Education and Communication, New Delhi, pp. 151–75.

31. Joseph Gathia, quoted in V. Vivekanandan, *op. cit.*, p. 167.

32. Discussion on the social clause at the Blue Star Workers' Union office, Bombay, April 1995.

33. Ibid.

34. May Day meeting of Trade Union Solidarity Committee, Bombay, 1995.

35. Ibid.

36. Discussion organised by the Workers' Solidarity Centre, Bombay, April 1995.

37. Sharit K. Bhomik, "Social Clause: Is Opposition to it Justified?" *Economic and Political Weekly*, 16/12/95, pp. 3199–3200.

[. . .]

41. See Rohini P.H., "Women Workers in Manufacturing Industry in India: Problems and Possibilities", in Haleh Afshar (ed.), *Women, Development, and Survival in the Third World*, Longman, London and New York, 1991, pp. 260–87.

3.8

Agreement on the Establishment of a Free Trade Area

United States of America and Hashemite Kingdom of Jordan

Preamble

The Government of the United States of America ("United States") and the Government of the Hashemite Kingdom of Jordan ("Jordan"),

Desiring to strengthen the bonds of friendship and economic relations and cooperation between them;

Wishing to establish clear and mutually advantageous rules governing their trade;

Aspiring to promote their mutual interest through liberalization and expansion of trade between their countries;

Reaffirming their willingness to strengthen and reinforce the multilateral trading system as reflected in the World Trade Organization, and to contribute to regional and international cooperation;

Recognizing that Jordan's economy is still in a state of development and faces special challenges;

Recognizing the objective of sustainable development, and seeking both to protect and preserve the environment and to enhance the means for doing so in a manner consistent with their re-

spective needs and concerns at different levels of economic development;

Recognizing that their relations in the field of trade and economic activity should be conducted with a view to raising living standards and promoting economic growth, investment opportunities, development, prosperity, employment and the optimal use of resources in their territories;

Desiring to foster creativity and innovation and promote trade in goods and services that are the subject of intellectual property rights;

Recognizing the need to raise public awareness of the challenges and opportunities offered by trade liberalization;

Wishing to raise the capacity and international competitiveness of their goods and services;

Desiring to promote higher labor standards by building on their respective international commitments and strengthening their cooperation on labor matters; and

Wishing to promote effective enforcement of their respective environmental and labor law;

HAVE AGREED AS FOLLOWS:

[. . .]

Article 5: Environment

1. The Parties recognize that it is inappropriate to encourage trade by relaxing domestic environmental laws. Accordingly, each

---

"Agreement between the United States of America and the Hashemite Kingdom of Jordan on the Establishment of a Free Trade Area," signed by the government of the United States of America and the government of the Hashemite Kingdom of Jordan, 24 October 2000, preamble, articles 5 and 6.

Party shall strive to ensure that it does not waive or otherwise derogate from, or offer to waive or otherwise derogate from, such laws as an encouragement for trade with the other Party.

2. Recognizing the right of each Party to establish its own levels of domestic environmental protection and environmental development policies and priorities, and to adopt or modify accordingly its environmental laws, each Party shall strive to ensure that its laws provide for high levels of environmental protection and shall strive to continue to improve those laws.

3. (a) A Party shall not fail to effectively enforce its environmental laws, through a sustained or recurring course of action or inaction, in a manner affecting trade between the Parties, after the date of entry into force of this Agreement.

   (b) The Parties recognize that each Party retains the right to exercise discretion with respect to investigatory, prosecutorial, regulatory, and compliance matters and to make decisions regarding the allocation of resources to enforcement with respect to other environmental matters determined to have higher priorities. Accordingly, the Parties understand that a Party is in compliance with subparagraph (a) where a course of action or inaction reflects a reasonable exercise of such discretion, or results from a *bona fide* decision regarding the allocation of resources.

4. For purposes of this Article, "environmental laws" mean any statutes or regulations of a Party, or provision thereof, the primary purpose of which is the protection of the environment, or the prevention of a danger to human, animal, or plant life or health, through:

   (a) the prevention, abatement or control of the release, discharge, or emission of pollutants or environmental contaminants;

   (b) the control of environmentally hazardous or toxic chemicals, substances, materials and wastes, and the dissemination of information related thereto; or

   (c) the protection or conservation of wild flora or fauna, including endangered species, their habitat, and specially protected natural areas in the Party's territory,

but does not include any statutes or regulations, or provision thereof, directly related to worker safety or health.

Article 6: Labor

1. The Parties reaffirm their obligations as members of the International Labor Organization ("ILO") and their commitments under the ILO Declaration on Fundamental Principles and Rights at Work and its Follow-up. The Parties shall strive to ensure that such labor principles and the internationally recognized labor rights set forth in paragraph 6 are recognized and protected by domestic law.

2. The Parties recognize that it is inappropriate to encourage trade by relaxing domestic labor laws. Accordingly, each Party shall strive to ensure that it does not waive or otherwise derogate from, or offer to waive or otherwise derogate from, such laws as an encouragement for trade with the other Party.

3. Recognizing the right of each Party to establish its own domestic labor standards, and to adopt or modify accordingly its labor laws and regulations, each Party shall strive to ensure that its laws provide for labor standards consistent with the internationally recognized labor rights set forth in paragraph 6 and shall strive to improve those standards in that light.

4. (a) A Party shall not fail to effectively enforce its labor laws, through a sustained or recurring course of action or inaction, in a manner affecting trade between the Parties, after the date of entry into force of this Agreement.

   (b) The Parties recognize that each Party retains the right to exercise discretion with respect to investigatory, prosecutorial, regulatory, and compliance matters and to make decisions regarding the allocation of resources to enforcement with respect to other labor matters determined to have higher priorities. Accordingly, the Parties understand that a Party is in compliance with subparagraph (a) where a course of action or inaction reflects a reasonable exercise of such discretion, or results from a *bona fide* decision regarding the allocation of resources.

5. The Parties recognize that cooperation between them provides enhanced opportunities to improve labor standards. The Joint Committee established under Article 15 shall, during its regular sessions, consider any such opportunity identified by a Party.

6. For purposes of this Article, "labor laws" means statutes and regulations, or provisions thereof, that are directly related to the following internationally recognized labor rights:

   (a) the right of association;

   (b) the right to organize and bargain collectively;

   (c) a prohibition on the use of any form of forced or compulsory labor;

   (d) a minimum age for the employment of children; and

   (e) acceptable conditions of work with respect to minimum wages, hours of work, and occupational safety and health.

For Further Reading

The ill-fated **ITO** with its social clause was mentioned in Parts II and III. A number of factors working together led to the United States' ultimate refusal to ratify the ITO charter: among them, the U.S. Congress was wary of international tinkering with domestic agriculture; the spirit of internationalism that led to its approval of the World Bank and IMF just a few years earlier had waned; some key U.S. business sectors lobbied strongly against the ITO for being too protectionist and others for not being protectionist enough. For more on this, see William Diebold, *The End of the ITO*, Essays in International Finance (Princeton, N.J.: Princeton University, 1952), 1–37; Patrick Low, *Trading Free: The GATT and U.S. Trade Policy* (New York: Twentieth Century Fund, 1993); and Stefanie Ann Lenway, *The Politics of U.S. International Trade* (London: Pitman Publishing Limited, 1985). See also the work of economic historian Susan Ariel Aaronson, including *Trade and the American Dream: A Social History of Postwar Trade Policy* (Lexington: University Press of Kentucky, 1996); and *Taking Trade to the Streets: The Lost History of Public Efforts to Shape Globalization* (Ann Arbor: University of Michigan, 2001). On Keynes's view of the ITO, see Hans Singer, "The Bretton Woods System: Historical Perspectives," *Third World Economics* (16–31 August 1993): 13–16.

Moving on to the more **current "social clause" initiatives**, a few books provide good overviews of the issues raised by the citizen backlash with regard to regulating trade and investment. For thorough but easy reading, see Hilary French, *Vanishing Borders: Protecting the Planet in the Age of Globalization* (Washington, D.C.: Worldwatch Institute, 2000); and Belinda Coote and Caroline LeQuesne, *The Trade Trap: Poverty and the Global Commodity Markets* (Oxford, UK: Oxfam, 1992, 1996 rev.). Jeremy Brecher, Tim Costello, and Brendan Smith's *Globalization from Below: The Power of Solidarity* (Cambridge, Mass.: South End Press, 2001) provides more of an insider's look (as do Brecher's and Costello's other writings).

There is a good deal of information available on **NAFTA's social clause**. A useful place to start is with the institutions built by NAFTA's side agreement: the United States' National Administrative Office, located in the U.S. Department of Labor (www.dol.gov), the Commission for Labor Cooperation in Dallas (info@naalc.org), and the North American Commission for Environmental Cooperation (www.cec.org); these sites provide a wealth of information about procedures and actual complaints.

Interestingly enough, most of the literature analyzing the side agreements is found in **law journals**. In addition to numerous articles by Lance Compa, see, for instance, Michael J. Kelly, "Bringing a Complaint under the NAFTA Environmental Side Accord: Difficult Steps under a Procedural Paper Tiger, but Movement in the Right Direction," *Pepperdine Law Review* 24, no. 71 (1996): 71–97; A. L. C. de Mestral, "The Significance of the NAFTA Side Agreements on Environmental and Labour Cooperation," *Arizona Journal of International and Comparative Law* 15, no. 1 (Winter 1998): 169–85; and Jack Garvey, "Trade Law and Quality of Life—Dispute Resolution under the NAFTA Side Accords on Labor and the Environment," *The American Journal of International Law* 89 (1995): 439–53.

Beyond law reviews: John Audley, program officer for the Sierra Club in Washington, D.C. from 1991 to 1993, analyzes environmentalists and NAFTA in his *Green Politics and Global Trade: NAFTA and the Future of Environmental Politics* (Washington, D.C.: Georgetown University Press, 1997). For an analysis based on interviews of organizations and government in all three NAFTA countries, see also Arturo Zárate-Ruiz, *A Rhetorical Analysis of the NAFTA Debate* (Lanham, Md.: Rowman & Littlefield, 2000). On the **Sony case**, see Dimitris Stevis with Eric Myers, "The Struggle for Union Democracy at Sony: A Report on the Sony Submission to the United States National Administrative Office," Coalition for Justice in the Maquiladoras, San Antonio, Texas, 16 May 1997.

For more on the **Free Trade Area of the Americas**, see the full Hemispheric Social Alliance publication excerpted in Reading 1.8. Links to the full text and other relevant publications can be found through the web site of the Alliance for Responsible Trade (www.art-us.org).

For more on **cross-border organizing** between U.S. and Mexican groups, see Mary E. Kelly, "Cross-Border Work on the Environment: Evolution, Successes, Problems, and Future Outlook," Texas Center for Policy Studies, July 1998; and Rachael Kamel and Anya Hoffman, eds., *The Maquiladora Reader: Cross-Border Organizing Since NAFTA* (Philadelphia, Pa.: American Friends Service Committee, 1999). Read Compa's "NAFTA Labor Side Agreement and International Labor Solidarity," *Antipode* 33, no. 3 (2001): 451–67. And, for an insightful view from Mexican women workers along the U.S. border, see Comite Fronterizo de Obreras (CFO or Border Committee of Women Workers), "Six Years of NAFTA: A View from Inside the Maquiladoras," published by CFO in cooperation with the American Friends Service Committee, Piedras Negras, Coahuila, Mexico, and Philadelphia, Pa., October 1999, available through www.afsc.org or CFO@comuni-k.com. See also the web site of Foreign Policy in Focus (www.fpif.org), a joint project of the Institute for Policy Studies and the Interhemispheric Resource Center.

Literature on the **WTO** (www.wto.org) is quickly becoming vast—both from academics and from NGOs themselves. Much of the NGO material was written for Seattle and subsequent WTO meetings and much of the academic literature was written after Seattle. Worth reading is the rest of *Views from the South* from which the Khor excerpt is taken, as well as other writings published by the UK-based Women Working Worldwide for which Hensman's article was initially written. The Third World Network's early concerns about the WTO are articulated in Chakravarthi Raghavan, *Recolonization: GATT, the Uruguay Round, and the Third World* (Penang, Malaysia: Third World Network, 1990), with a foreword by Julius Nyerere.

A lot of material exists on **citizen groups' web sites** (listed in the bibliography). Especially worth consulting are those of Public Citizen's Global Trade Watch (directed by Lori Wallach) and the AFL-CIO (much of which is authored by their top trade-policy specialist Thea Lee)—both have been key groups in the U.S.-based organizing on trade-related issues such as NAFTA and the WTO. Also see other publications of the International Forum on Globalization which has convened many of the "teach-ins" on economic globalization. For more on the **substance of a social clause**, see the Brussels-based ICFTU and the International Labor Rights Fund (for example, Terry Collingsworth's article cited in note 4 of my introduction to Part III). Canadian environmental lawyer Steve Shrybman, like Compa, has writing that spans a range of publications from law journals to backlash outlets, such as "The World Trade Organization: The New World Constitution Laid Bare," *Ecologist* 29, no. 4 (July 1999). Also see the work of David Batker and Isabel de la Torre, such as *WTO: But What Are We Trading Away?* (Seattle: Asia Pacific Environmental Exchange, 1999), with web site www.ban.org.

A **counterpoint** to the environmental critique of NAFTA and its side agreements that suggests how the WTO itself is capable of meeting the environmental challenge was authored by insider Gary Sampson, who spent a dozen years as director at the GATT and then at the WTO, including director of the WTO's Trade and Environment Division: *Trade, Environment and the WTO: The Post-Seattle Agenda*, Policy Essay no. 27 (Washington, D.C.: Overseas Development Council, distributed by Johns Hopkins University Press, 2000).

Part IV

CHALLENGING
CORPORATE CONDUCT

Part IV

Challenging Corporate Conduct

The new wave of anti-sweatshop campus activism since the late 1990s stands in part as a result of about a decade of backlash initiatives to make corporations "voluntarily" initiate measures aimed at increasing corporate social and environmental accountability. And that student activism has, in turn, helped catalyze an upsurge of corporate "self-regulation." Part IV turns to these voluntary initiatives—providing a contrast to Part III's examination of how the citizen backlash has sought to use the power of government to change rules to protect workers, communities, the environment, the poor, and other marginalized sectors of society. In Part IV, we examine proposals for corporate "self-regulation" primarily since 1990, focusing on "codes of conduct," "certification programs," and "alternative trade" or "fair trade" organizations. The aim is to present the trajectory of the citizen backlash initiatives and proposals in this arena, while highlighting innovations and debates over these innovations.

The 1980s and Alternative Trade Organizations

The roots of the explosion of voluntary corporate code activity over the past decade reach back to work done at the multilateral level in the 1970s. As discussed in Part II, governments, corporations, and citizen groups began to negotiate corporate codes of conduct at the United Nations level almost thirty years ago. A strong movement emerged among nongovernmental organizations, North and South, and among Third World governments advocating greater corporate accountability around the world through a combination of a global UN code and UN-brokered codes such as the one for the marketing of infant formula.

But the 1980s and the free-market triumphalism that marked the administrations of Ronald Reagan, George H.W. Bush, Margaret Thatcher, and Helmut Kohl

ushered in a far less propitious environment for the development of intergovernmental or multilateral codes. Momentum toward a UN Code of Conduct was
stopped dead in its tracks when the Reagan administration in the United States,
along with some European governments and Japan, shifted to oppose the effort in
the 1980s. Eventually even the UN Commission on Transnational Corporations
was dismantled. During this period when the free-market Washington Consensus
reigned (see Part I) and the very legitimacy of government regulation of corporate
affairs was called into question, the movement to enhance global governance of
corporations was set back significantly.

There was, however, one small beacon of light: "alternative trade organizations"
(ATOs), which were born in Europe in the 1960s and spread to the United States in
the 1970s. As opposed to attempts to use the United Nations to steer global investment in a sustainable direction, the ATO movement sought to create a voluntary, alternative route for international trade—a route that would shun traditional commercial trade and circumvent its profit-maximizing corporate actors. Instead, the
movement focused on providing alternative trade channels for goods whose production met small producers' needs, marketing coffee, crafts, and other goods directly to consumers, thus bypassing the profit-hungry "middleman" as well. Reading 4.1 looks at the history of alternative trade organizations, as well as some of their
more recent accomplishments. One of these accomplishments is the creation of coalitions of ATOs, including the Fair Trade Federation. The reading itself is an excerpt
from a booklet distributed by the Fair Trade Federation and authored by independent journalist Rose Benz Ericson, an "active volunteer" (her own words) for the Fair
Trade Federation and one of the founders of the Fair Trade Resource Network, which
serves as a clearinghouse for information on ATOs. This "alternative trade" movement was among the first to grapple with criteria—or codes of conduct—that producers had to meet in order to earn the title "alternative trade organization."[1]

Codes of Conduct in the 1990s: What and Why?

With the shattering of the 1970s and 1980s visions of more mandatory codes and
with the foundation provided by ATOs, the stage shifted to a new generation of
corporate codes of conduct in the 1990s that focused on "voluntary" codes
adopted by individual corporations.

By then, although regulatory attempts were still largely eschewed, the Washington Consensus free-market dominance became somewhat more muted as economic globalization left environmental, social, and economic crises in its wake. Increasingly, analysts wrote critical pieces on the abysmal conditions in the overseas
factories used by global corporations. In the second reading (4.2), Angela Hale follows in this tradition and examines the working conditions in the global production of garments (or apparel). Hale is director of Women Working Worldwide, a
United Kingdom–based organization that works with an international network of
organizations of women workers, mainly in Asia but also in other regions. Women
Working Worldwide is based at Manchester Metropolitan University where Hale

once taught. In this piece, Hale uses her insight as both scholar and activist to chart the transformation of the garment industry over recent decades into global production lines of literally thousands of wholly independent, nameless "subcontractors" whose sweatshops were, until the 1990s, beyond scrutiny. This analysis provides a good sense of the challenges involved in improving workers' lives along the far-flung apparel production chains. (The latter part of her piece, which I return to later in this introduction, provides a preview of some of the complex issues raised by the last decade of code of conduct work in this sector.)

Not surprisingly, as the kind of global assembly line analyzed by Hale spread, stories began to appear in the media across the globe about sweatshop conditions in the factories of Levi Strauss, Nike, and other apparel and footwear companies with brand-name recognition. Such exposés of sweatshop conditions led to renewed demands and campaigns for corporate regulatory oversight, which pushed some corporations to view "self-regulation" via voluntary corporate codes as a smart pre-emptive move against the possibility of regulation.

The first U.S. apparel company to promulgate its own, internal corporate code of conduct was Levi Strauss and Co. Levi's "Business Partner Terms of Engagement and Guidelines for Country Selection" was formulated in 1991 and approved in March 1992, followed by a Reebok code in 1992. I have chosen to reprint the original Levi Strauss code (Reading 4.3) because it was the first of these voluntary corporate codes, and it was promulgated by a company that prided itself on its socially responsible image.

In addition, the Levi's code illustrates the content of these initial codes—with vague details on environmental requirements and more details on labor rights. This was perhaps, in part, because it was harder to define a set of environmental rights that could be empirically measured. That is, a core labor right—such as no child labor or no prison labor—seemed much easier to measure and much less subjective than, say, the right to a clean environment. Accordingly, Levi Strauss agreed not to contract production to firms that used prison labor or committed other specified violations of worker rights. As the Levi's code reveals, these company-specific codes were (and often still are) typically timid in some respects. While Levi's goes beyond many codes that simply focused on prohibiting child labor, in its first code Levi's ignored the most fundamental of worker rights: "freedom of association" or the right to unionize. The glaring void was rectified as Levi's revised its code over the course of a decade, typically in response to "external" complaints.[2]

On the other hand, from its initial rendition onward, the Levi's code stands as one of the few codes to specify not only factory-specific standards but also country-level standards (initially "Guidelines for Country Selection" and later "Country Assessment Guidelines"). Thus, when Levi Strauss determined that China's persistent rights violations did not live up to the benchmarks set by its "Country Assessment Guidelines," it announced that it would phase out all production contracts in that country. Similarly, Levi Strauss stopped subcontracting in Burma [Myanmar] due to flagrant Burmese violations of human rights.

Most codes were adopted as the result of pressure from citizen campaigns. Levi's, for example, claims the promulgation of its code was but another step in the history of a responsible corporation. But it was undoubtedly no coincidence that the code's public appearance followed on the heels of an exposé of its operations in Saipan (located within the Northern Mariana Islands, a U.S. commonwealth in the Pacific) and a U.S. government investigation.[3]

In the United States, where the campaigns began with more fervor in the early 1990s than in Europe,[4] actions against individual corporations were orchestrated by a relatively small number of NGOs. In most campaigns, activists cleverly chose big name brands with big name recognition, especially among students: the Gap, Nike, Liz Claiborne, Disney, and so on. In addition to Pharis Harvey and the Washington, D.C.–based International Labor Rights Fund, among key individuals and U.S.-based backlash groups initiating these campaigns were Charles Kernaghan and the New York–based National Labor Committee, Medea Benjamin and Kevin Danaher and the San Francisco–based Global Exchange, and Jeff Ballinger and Press for Change. Chicago-based US/Labor Education in the Americas Project (US/LEAP, then called the Guatemalan Labor Education Project) and allied groups, working with organizations in Guatemala, tried to initiate the first agricultural code of conduct through a campaign to get Starbucks to adopt a code to govern conditions under which the coffee it sells is grown. Where no codes existed, groups pressed for codes; when codes were formulated, groups used national and international media to expose cases of noncompliance and push for better codes and better implementation.

In Europe, a Clean Clothes Campaign began in the Netherlands in 1990; UK-based groups included Christian Aid, the World Development Movement, and the New Economics Foundation. In Canada, corporate-code campaign groups included the Maquila Solidarity Network and the Wear Fair campaign.

Such backlash groups organized a small but vocal group of consumers to make the selected corporation hear the demands. Under banners and picket signs announcing boycotts of trendy apparel produced under sweatshop conditions, students and others picketed the Gap at holiday season and returned their sweat-produced sneakers to Nike in protest. These demonstrations of consumer concern over corporate abuses began to worry companies whose sales were based in part on brand-name recognition and started to place pressure on some corporations' bottom-lines. As garment industry consultant and self-described non–"do-gooder" David Birnbaum warned corporate readers of the *Wall Street Journal* in 1996: "I'm here to tell you that the tapping noise you hear on your door is your CPA [certified public accountant] coming to announce that . . . if you want to survive, now would be a good time to develop a social conscience."[5] Indeed, as early as 1992, Levi's vice president Robert Dunn left Levi's to found the nonprofit Business for Social Responsibility to engender discussion and initiatives on corporate responsibility among its member companies and demonstrate that corporations could act responsibly on their own.

North and South: Whose Codes? And Who Benefits?

Unlike Levi Strauss's broader focus, many of the exposés and many of the resulting corporate codes zeroed in on child labor. It was, after all, the specific labor rights violation that most easily struck a cord of outrage among Northern consumers. Who could turn the pages without a pang of outrage and remorse when, for instance, *Life* magazine featured a picture essay of Pakistani children as young as three stitching soccer balls for Northern children to play with?[6] In addition, to the extent that codes were a corporate response to NGO pressure, eliminating child labor was a modest concession by most corporations.

But the narrow focus on child labor engendered debate. Some backlash groups (especially in the South) found abolishing child labor too limited a goal and one that exposed Northern campaigners' biases. Should we really care about a human being's exploitation only until he or she reaches the legal working age? they asked. Most Southern groups seemed willing to put up with the photo-op focus on child labor as a tactical decision, as long as the strategic goal was a broader set of core labor rights. There were other issues of debate as well: many Southern groups, joined by some Northern development groups, were concerned that attempts to penalize firms for using child laborers would ultimately penalize the child workers and families dependent on their earnings for basic survival. Some pointed out that child workers were a reality for every country as they industrialized. Further, would not the "liberated" children have little choice but to turn to even more dangerous occupations such as prostitution or making bricks for domestic use?

On the other hand, responded advocates of such codes, how could poor families break out of the inter-generational cycle of poverty and marginalization unless children were moved from workplace to school? And, as then International Labor Rights Fund director Pharis Harvey noted, in a country such as India, child labor is reserved for the lowest caste.[7] In today's global economy, child labor does not eliminate poverty; it perpetuates it.

But the most convincing rebuttal came from the South. One brave spokesperson who proved that the outrage against child labor was not simply a Northern concern was a Pakistani boy named Iqbal Masih. Masih went from indentured ("bonded") servitude (in return for a loan—or "bond"—of $16 to his parents), weaving hand-loomed carpets for export from age 4 to 10 (by which point, with a daily salary of one rupee or $0.03, the loan had ballooned to over $400) to become perhaps the most eloquent spokesperson against child labor. With stunted growth from his years shackled to the loom and with a riveting story, Masih garnered worldwide attention as he asked Northerners to stop buying products made with child labor. "In my country," he said in a 1994 interview, "children think that America is to blame for our exploitation, because most of the things we make are exported to the U.S." I reprint the speech he gave at the acceptance of an international human rights award as well as the introductory remarks by actor Blair Underwood who presented the award to Iqbal (Reading 4.4). Sadly, in 1995, just months after accepting the award, he was brutally murdered in Pakistan; many suspect the killer was connected to the Pakistani carpet industry.[8]

While in his life and death Masih became the human face for why Northern consumers should care about child labor, other Southern advocates against child labor helped craft initiatives to try to ensure that his heartbreaking saga was not repeated. Since 1980 in India, Kailash Sartyarthi, and the Bonded Labour Liberation

Front which he heads, have been physically freeing child weavers from de facto slavery in the carpet industry—through the mid-1990s alone, some 29,000 children. And such anti–child labor groups are not only an Indian phenomenon; Sartyarthi's group is connected to the South Asian Coalition on Child Servitude, a coalition of dozens of similar groups in Bangladesh, India, Nepal, Pakistan, and Sri Lanka. Sartyarthi and the coalition once again confirm that this is not only a Northern concern. And it is dangerous work on the ground; Sartyarthi has spent time in prison and at least two of Sartyarthi's coworkers have been murdered.[9]

In the mid-1990s, Sartyarthi and his colleagues added an offensive, proactive program to this defensive one: they launched the "Rugmark" carpet-labeling initiative in India and Germany to label hand-loomed carpets woven without child labor. They subsequently forged Rugmark partnerships with groups elsewhere in Europe and then the United States, and expanded to other parts of South Asia. Through Rugmark, Sartyarthi and his colleagues brought innovations to code of conduct work, moving from simply trying to eliminate child labor to trying to improve the former child workers' lives by creative multifaceted programs that included schooling and other support services. Reading 4.5, by freelance writer Suzanne Charlé, details how Rugmark works.

Around the same time that Rugmark was launched, another initiative took the lead from groups in the South, this time focused on the production of toys. The majority of toys are made in Asia (and especially China) under subcontracts from such big-name toy companies as Mattel and Hasbro. Citizen backlash groups in Asia and the Pacific drafted a model "Charter on the Safe Production of Toys" as a vehicle for ending the exploitative work conditions in Asian toy factories and institutionalizing a broad set of worker rights. The urgency of their mission was heightened by yet one more tragedy caused by exploitative working conditions: in 1995, 188 workers were killed in Thailand when a fire decimated a toy factory with locked fire exits. Collaborating with the Catholic Institute for Industrial Relations, the World Development Movement and the Trade Union Congress in Britain, the Asian groups called on toy firms to adopt their model code. Leading toy manufacturers rejected the code but felt sufficient pressure to respond with their own narrower code.[10]

Sectoral Codes, Monitoring, and Certification

Rugmark and the toy code demonstrate a trend in corporate code of conduct work. As more and more companies developed individual codes, there began to be pressure to move beyond company-specific codes such as that of Levi Strauss.

One of the earliest attempts to make voluntary codes broader was a code adopted in 1992, around the same time that Levi's announced its company-specific code. This came out of the work of environmental activist Joan Bavaria and her Boston-based Coalition for Environmentally Responsible Economics (CERES). Rather than focus on creating codes for individual firms or even specific industries, CERES asks corporations to voluntarily sign on to its ten "CERES Principles" (originally called the Valdez Principles) of environmentally responsible corporate behavior, which range from "informing the public" to "energy conservation" to "management commitment" via "selecting our Board of Directors . . . consider[ing] demonstrated environmental commitment." In essence, the goal of CERES is to influence corporate behavior by creating uniform mechanisms for firms to submit information on their environmental practices and performances. Corporations report annually on progress toward meeting the principles. Notable among CERES's more than fifty signatories in the early 2000s were such large multinationals as Sun Oil (which in 1993 broke ranks with other big oil firms and Fortune 500 members to sign on), Polaroid, General Motors, Bethlehem Steel, and Bank of America.[11]

By the mid-1990s, it was becoming clear that—with the proper mix of media work against a company or sector (i.e., toys) in which corporations depended on their "good" brand name—even a small amount of consumer pressure could succeed relatively quickly in getting a company to promulgate its own code of conduct for labor rights. A key question was whether the codes were having any impact on the conditions of work. Levi's and most other companies were in charge of enforcing and monitoring their own codes. CERES, for instance, was dependent on reports generated by the corporations themselves. The weak implementation of these codes, and the ease with which investigative reporters and NGOs were able to find abuses by subcontractors, prompted some backlash groups to view voluntary codes as a flawed tool.

Other backlash groups, however, took up the challenge, defining the next stage in their work to be the invention of independent and effective mechanisms to monitor corporate codes. Going beyond questions concerning the contents of a code, new questions emerged: Once a company promulgates a code of conduct, who should do the monitoring? And how? The choices involve various kinds of internal (by the company) or external (by outside sources) monitoring. Citizen groups came to view internal monitoring with some suspicion and favor codes with external, independent, third-party certification by other members of civil society.

For backlash groups, the test case of independent, external NGO monitoring of an individual company's code came in 1995 and involved the Gap and one of its suppliers in El Salvador. Like Levi's, the Gap was a company that viewed itself as socially responsible and since 1993 had had its own voluntary code of conduct. But, the New York–based National Labor Committee, in collaboration with grassroots groups, uncovered egregious anti-union activities in a factory that subcontracted for the Gap (among other big-name companies) in El Salvador. The National Labor Committee skillfully used the case to generate widespread publicity around the Gap's inability and/or unwillingness to enforce its code. As religious, student, labor, and other activists in both the United States and El Salvador joined the chorus of disapproval in sermons and picket lines, the Gap announced it accepted the charges and intended to move its business out of El Salvador to suppliers elsewhere. To the Gap's surprise, activists responded by demanding that the Gap instead stay in El Salvador, pressure its subcontractor to respect basic worker rights, and allow independent NGO monitoring of that subcontractor. The Gap finally agreed, setting up a "pilot program" using a team of local labor rights and human rights NGOs (that became the Independent Monitoring Group of El Salvador or GMIES) for external, independent monitoring in that Salvadoran factory where worker rights violations had sparked the National Labor Committee campaign.[12]

While this case set a precedent for "independent, external monitoring" by local NGOs working in collaboration with Northern NGOs, it raised challenges for some in the backlash. How could it be replicated broadly in terms of the time, attention, and resources devoted to one relatively minor subcontractor? And, should NGO monitors be "advocate" monitors or more truly "independent" (i.e., nonaligned) monitors? Both sets of challenges gained urgency as the private sector discovered the potential profits to be made by moving into the fledgling field of social accounting; accounting groups with expertise on financial not social accounting suddenly jumped onto the social accounting bandwagon as well. For example, PriceWaterhouseCooper has been Nike's "worldwide independent monitor" since 1998 even though its status as Nike's auditor belies the term "independent."[13]

This was not what most backlash proponents of independent and external monitoring had in mind. Enter the formation of a different kind of NGO—whereby the individuals involved transformed themselves from advocates of social and environmental responsibility to trained and objective monitors of the compliance of local production sites to a code's given set of criteria. In Reading 4.6, Homero Fuentes and Dennis Smith present a case study of such a nonprofit organization which they helped to found: the Guatemala-based Commission for the Verification of Codes of Conduct (COVERCO).

How does the COVERCO model attempt to offer independence and objectivity? According to Smith, COVERCO consciously built a "methodology" of monitoring based on the concept of "non-substitutability" whereby "we will not substitute for management consultants . . . for a union . . . for participants in advocacy groups . . . or as agents of the government to attempt to enforce labor law." COVERCO also distinguished itself from monitors who claim that they can assess the on-the-ground reality in a week or so: "To identify patterns of non-compliance, you need to monitor in a non-crisis situation over time for six months or so."[14]

Like the Independent Monitoring Group of El Salvador (GMIES), COVERCO clearly demonstrates the ability of backlash organizations and individuals to put on new hats as initiatives evolved. In fact, COVERCO not only helps to train similar "independent monitors" elsewhere in Central America, but also has expanded its monitoring from apparel to other sectors, including coffee. Writes Aron Cramer, a vice president of the corporate member organization Business for Social Responsibility: "The lesson of some of the independent monitoring projects undertaken in Latin America . . . has been that civil society institutions' capacity to act without the presence or sponsorship of a multinational company has been strengthened."[15]

GMIES and COVERCO offered two new models of monitoring, but still other parts of the backlash pushed the experimentation with voluntary codes of conduct in different ways. Was there any way to merge NGO-based external, independent, third-party verification favored by most within the backlash with the industry-wide focus of CERES? How could voluntary codes be pushed beyond companies with name recognition, such as Reebok, into arenas where consumers did not shop by brand name—such as shrimp or paper clips or wood products? In a series of initiatives to improve upon the effectiveness and credibility of voluntary codes and monitoring, a number of nonprofits have created innovative "certification" programs that attempt to offer consumers assurances that goods are produced under certain specified conditions. Some strive to define production processes that are environmentally benign; others aim to certify absence of child labor; others offer assurances on other labor conditions; yet others do a combination.

Rugmark, discussed above, is one example of a certification effort against child labor via labeling, launched in South Asia, Europe, and the United States in the 1990s. Another advanced one with an even broader agenda is the international Forest Stewardship Council (FSC), based in Oaxaca, Mexico, which was established in 1993 and which offers certification that wood came from forests that were managed to meet FSC's very specific criteria of "sustainability." And coffee certified by a group named TransFair is yet another.

Two readings present certification cases in more detail. First, for an overview of certification with case studies of the Forest Stewardship Council and TransFair-certified coffee (which is now sold at Starbucks as well as in my university cafeteria), I excerpt from an article by Michael Conroy in Reading 4.7. Conroy is a former economics professor and now a Ford Foundation program officer working in the environment and development field. Following Conroy's excerpt, I include the actual FSC principles and criteria (Reading 4.8), which cover a good deal of terrain—from core environmental criteria to economic and social criteria including labor rights and the rights of indigenous communities. (Readers are encouraged to compare the contents of codes reprinted in this Part.) As of 2001, there were some twenty-five national FSC initiatives—in countries ranging from Cameroon to Finland, Papua New Guinea to the United States. The global FSC "principles and criteria" printed in full in Reading 4.8 stand as the principles and criteria that all national initiatives must observe, but the standards developed from these are different regionally.

Beyond forest products, coffee, and hand-loomed carpets, certification schemes are gathering momentum in other sectors as well. There now exists a comparable Marine Stewardship Council. In Europe, the TransFair seal is used to market not only fairly traded coffee, but also tea, honey, and commodities such as bananas; TransFair USA certifies tea, too. There are, around the globe, dozens of certification programs aimed at setting environmental and, often, socioeconomic standards for the burgeoning ecotourism and sustainable tourism industry.[16] And the fact that diamond revenues have funded wars in parts of Africa has led to an initiative to establish a scheme to certify "non-conflict" diamonds.[17]

Will the birth of so many different certification schemes cause confusion and rivalry? In an ambitious attempt to create an umbrella group for sector-specific certification schemes, the International Social and Environmental Accreditation and Labeling Alliance (ISEAL) was born in Mexico in 1999. In addition to the FSC, its members include the Marine Stewardship Council, Social Accountability

International (SAI, created by the New York–based Council for Economic Priorities), Fairtrade Labelling Organizations International (FLO, itself comprises TransFair, Max Havelaar, and others), the International Federation of Organic Agricultural Movements, the International Organic Accreditation System, and Conservation Agriculture Network.

Students Confront Sweatshops

Perhaps the best-known and most contentious effort to change corporate behavior in the United States concerns the apparel industry. College campuses have been host to a huge debate over monitoring and the role of NGO–corporate partnerships in this sector. Unfortunately, this is a case study of how a disagreement within the backlash turned into a serious division, although it has narrowed somewhat in recent times.

The first actor is the Apparel Industry Partnership (AIP) and its related Fair Labor Association (FLA). Its history in a nutshell: In mid-1996, a dialogue was launched in the United States among leaders from the apparel and footwear industries (including L.L.Bean, Liz Claiborne, Nicole Miller, Nike, Patagonia, Phillips-Van Heusen, and Reebok) and representatives from human rights and labor rights organizations. The goal was to get both sides—private companies and NGOs—to iron out an apparel code of conduct that was acceptable to both. (While the U.S. Department of Labor convened the meeting, it was acting not in its regulatory capacity but as a "cheerleader" to support the dialogue; it then largely stood to the side in the deliberations.) In April 1997, the group released its compromise Apparel Industry Partnership "Workplace Code of Conduct," which included guidelines on worker rights; a subsequent agreement established a "Fair Labor Association" (FLA) to enforce and monitor the AIP.

While the AIP/FLA negotiations began with fanfare, they quickly moved into controversy that opened a painful fissure in the U.S.-based backlash (a fissure that subsequently spread overseas to allied groups). By the time the FLA agreement was signed, the two union participants had pulled out, although respected pro-labor NGOs remained. The unions found the FLA deficient in at least two key areas: it lacked requirements for a "living wage" (which allows workers to meet basic needs for which minimum wages are often deficient) and for full public disclosure by corporations of the factory sites where their goods are produced. In essence, the debate revolved around the question of whether or not unions and NGOs were willing to compromise in order to get companies to sign on to a code. U.S. unions wanted no compromises on their list of essentials; perhaps more critically, as the AIP/FLA negotiations progressed, key U.S. union participants appeared to grow wary of corporate codes of conduct in general—viewing them as shifting the focus away from the centrality of union organizing.

Into this debate stepped a new and potent actor, the United Students Against Sweatshops (USAS) with its anti-sweatshop demands on college administrators. As mentioned at the start of this book, USAS was born out of a wave of activism that hit college campuses across the United States in the late 1990s, soon after the Apparel Industry Partnership was launched. College administrators responded with surprising speed, worried about being branded sweatshop supporters. By 1999, over a hundred U.S. and Canadian colleges and universities had joined the FLA. But by then USAS (which from its inception had strong ties to the AFL-CIO affiliate UNITE!, which organizes workers in the textile and apparel industries) echoed the unions' criticism of the FLA. USAS pressured colleges to pull out of the FLA and instead join an alternative anti-sweatshop group, the Worker Rights Consortium (WRC). (Unlike the FLA, the WRC covers only collegiate-licensed apparel carrying schools' logos.)

It is easy to get enmeshed in the differences between the two codes which can be found online. As opposed to the FLA, the WRC code on paper includes a living wage requirement and requires full public disclosure of the location of subcontractors. The WRC relies on a complaint-driven check on corporations, depending on workers themselves as the source of complaints. But the WRC came with its own set of weaknesses: How would living wages be calculated? Did its proponents have sufficient contacts and expertise and resources to make its worker-initiated system work across the globe? Would workers, toiling under the conditions that Hale chronicles (Reading 4.2) and living in countries where speaking out could bring reprisals, really come forward with complaints to relay to the U.S.-based WRC? How, for instance, would this work in China, a key player in the global apparel production line?

By the late 1990s and early 2000s, the FLA–WRC "disagreement" had grown acrimonious. Strong arguments buttress each side. On the FLA side: If one believes that various stakeholders including corporations need to participate in a given code affecting them, then one needs to expect the sort of compromises of the FLA. If one believes that the role of codes is to push for freedom for unions to exist and operate freely, then the living wage issue is less crucial to include up-front; rather, it is one of many issues that local unions can push for once core labor rights exist. Moreover, the technical side of living wage calculations has yet to be sorted out satisfactorily. On the WRC side: If one believes that a code of conduct's purpose is to ensure that goods have not been made in sweatshop conditions, then a code without a living wage is severely deficient. And, a company that is unwilling to provide full disclosure of factories presumably has something to hide.

This is likely to be a case in which the proof of the pudding is in the eating. As both the FLA and the WRC geared up operations in 2001, these divisive issues seem to me to be less crucial than they appeared earlier; the schism between the two in practice appears narrower than the initial schism in rhetoric. Examples: In its day-to-day operations, the WRC acknowledges its current inability to calculate a living wage; the FLA in turn acknowledges the validity of the living wage as a longer-term goal. Nike set a precedent as an FLA member by providing full, public disclosure of its production sites. The WRC admits the need to talk with corporations. Worker complaints may drive the WRC on paper, but the organization has also decided to conduct regular "proactive" investigations that resemble the FLA's monitoring. In reality, both codes have the potential to advance worker rights. With this logic, the American University (where I teach) and a few dozen other universities have decided to join both. Recall Hale (Reading 4.2)—it is a huge, exploitative global assembly line with literally hundreds of thousands of production sites. There is ample room for more than one model.[18]

In addition, in Readings 4.9 and 4.10, I reprint two sign-on letters to college and university presidents that put the FLA–WRC controversy in what should be the more important, broader context of the free market versus backlash debate. The first (Reading 4.9) was drafted by prominent free-trade advocates including Jagdish Bhagwati of Columbia University, Robert Stern of the University of Michigan, Harvard's Jeffrey Sachs, and Nobel laureate Robert Lucas and other members of the Academic Consortium on International Trade. That letter denigrates students for their naïve anti-sweatshop initiatives which, it alleges, actually make Southern workers worse off. The second (Reading 4.10) is a rebuttal by Robert Pollin of the University of Massachusetts, University of Texas economist James K. Galbraith, Lourdes Beneria at Cornell, Harvard's Dani Rodrik, and others who have created Scholars Against Sweatshop Labor. Also signed by a Nobel laureate in economics (Lawrence Klein), this second letter praises student actions to change sweatshop conditions. Each letter gathered hundreds of signatures. In grouping the FLA with the WRC, both letters should help refocus the debate on the larger common struggle of the two organizations against corporate-led globalization.

In Brief

Where does the voluntary code of conduct and certification effort stand at this juncture in the early years of the twenty-first century? For a view from backlash insiders, I turn to Pharis Harvey, Terry Collingsworth, and Bama Athreya of the International Labor Rights Fund, who summarize their sense of where the backlash stands in terms of the gains in this work and challenges that remain (Reading 4.11). For another assessment from within the backlash, turn to the last two subsections of Reading 4.2 for Angela Hale's perspective, informed by numerous workshops she has helped organize among women garment workers and their advocates around the world in her capacity as head of the UK-based nonprofit Women Working Worldwide.

As these two readings and this part as a whole suggest, the generation of voluntary corporate codes and certification initiatives born in the 1990s and early twenty-first century has had some impact. In several cases, it has begun to change public awareness. And, in some notable cases, with public pressure, such campaigns and initiatives have moved beyond merely heightening awareness to changing corporate behavior. Listen to the assessment by Aron Cramer, a vice president of Business for Social Responsibility:

> Five years ago . . . a company that had a code of conduct could be characterized fairly as a "leader" for having taken that step. These days, the test of leadership is far more demanding. . . . there are rumblings of new issues like "e-tailers," living wages, and the need for harmonisation of standards. . . . It has become commonplace for company personnel to say: "This issue is not going away."[19]

While many of the code and certification initiatives grew from activist and consumer concerns in the North, some of the more effective campaigns either involved intimate coordination with groups on the ground in the producing countries in the South or actually took their lead from Southern groups. New coalitions have been catalyzed and new actors have entered the effort. As they gather strength and learn from each other and as they innovate, they build momentum toward greater enforceability—a goal still largely unmet.

And so too does this decade of backlash campaigns for codes appear to have been successful in terms of eliciting activity by one long-dormant public actor: the United Nations. Indeed, a quarter century after the United Nations began its efforts to create a global code of conduct and a decade after those efforts were called off, UN Secretary-General Kofi Annan launched a new initiative on corporate responsibility in the summer of 2000, labeled the "Global Compact" (which he mentions in Reading 1.2). Through it, the United Nations announced it was partnering with dozens of the world's largest corporations to press for social and environmental responsibility. The compact lists nine "principles" of labor, environmental, and human rights drawn from United Nations conventions and agreements. Companies, by voluntarily joining the compact, agree to report on an annual basis their progress in advancing these rights.

But dozens of backlash leaders from across the North and South— from Nigeria, India, and Thailand, to Brazil, France, and the United States, among others—collectively cried foul. Many involved in the backlash work on codes would have welcomed the entry of the United Nations regulatory power into this arena. But they saw Annan's initiative as a step backwards from the gains they had made in pushing for voluntary corporate codes with teeth, including the more rigorous standards of monitoring (the compact has none) or of third-party certification (again, the compact has none). "Bluewash," they termed it (the UN flag is blue), emphasizing the fact that compact endorsers included firms with reputations for systematically violating basic rights.[20]

In sum, when put together, do these backlash campaigns and the resulting codes—from Levi-like company-specific codes to FSC-like certification to the United Nations voluntary compact—spell out a countervailing power to global corporate power? Is voluntary enough? Or are they a smokescreen for corporations to avoid the stronger teeth of regulation? Or, will a generation of voluntary efforts open the door to more regulatory efforts—perhaps even bringing us back to a United Nations code, but a more binding one?

Notes

1. As Ericson notes, at some point terminology changed; to many proponents, ATOs became "fair trade organizations." For my purposes, that latter term is somewhat confusing, given that proponents of social clauses and other initiatives likewise term themselves supporters of "fair trade." Thus I will stick to the term "ATO."

2. For the most recent version, see www.levistrauss.com.

3. Much of the information about Levi Strauss comes from an interview with two Levi executives (anonymity given) by the author, San Francisco, California, 11 October 1996. Regarding its history,

among other things I was told that Levi Strauss "kept workers on in the Great Depression . . . and was "one of the first to integrate factories in the South" of the United States in the 1940s and 1950s. See also Karl Schoenberger, *Levi's Children: Coming to Terms with Human Rights in the Global Marketplace* (Boston: Atlantic Monthly Press, 2000).

4. William Echikson, "It's Europe's Turn to Sweat about Sweatshops," *Business Week* (19 July 1999): 96. Note that Echikson is based in Brussels.

5. David Birnbaum, "Forget MFN [Most Favored Nation], the Consumers Are Coming!" *Wall Street Journal*, 9 April 1996. This was an op-ed piece.

6. Sidney Schanberg with photos by Marie Dorigny, "Six Cents an Hour," *Life*, June 1996, 38–46.

7. Pharis Harvey, "Where Children Work: Child Servitude in the Global Economy," *Christian Century* 112, no. 11 (5 April 1995): 363.

8. The quote is from Trudie Styler, "The Short, Tragic Life of Iqbal Masih" [An Interview with Iqbal Masih], *Harper's* no. 3413, April 1996, 210. The facts about Iqbal Masih are from Pharis Harvey, "Iqbal's Death," *Christian Century* 112, no. 18 (24–31 May 1995) 557-58; and David L. Parker with Lee Engfer and Robert Conrow, *Stolen Dreams—Portraits of Working Children* (Minneapolis: Lerner Publications, 1998) which includes a chapter entitled "The Story of Iqbal," pp. 9–18. The book is a combination of photos by David Parker and essays on child labor.

9. On Satyarthi and SACCS, see "The Tragedy of Child Labor: An Interview with Kailash Satyarthi," *Multinational Monitor* 15, no. 10 (October 1994): 24–25; and Kerry Kennedy Cuomo, *Speak Truth to Power: Human Rights Defenders Who Are Changing Our World* (New York: Crown Publishers, 2000), 213–15.

10. See the full issue entitled "Toy Story," *Asia Monitor Resource Center* [Hong Kong], no. 22 (April–July 1996); and Shada Islam, "If It's Broke, Fix It," *Far Eastern Economic Review* (20 June 1996): 67. Key to the campaign was the work of the Hong Kong Christian Industrial Committee.

11. The principles are quoted from CERES Board of Directors, "The CERES Principles," adopted on 28 April 1992 (available online at www.ceres.org). CERES, "Reaching a Critical Mass: A Strategic Plan for CERES," Boston, 1996; Theo Emery, "Boston Coalition Getting Companies to Volunteer to Be Ecologically Sound," *Boston Globe*, 14 January 1997; and Stan Hinden, "Joan Bavaria's Crusade for the Environment," *Washington Post*, 23 December 1990.

CERES has advanced the state of the art of environmental reporting, first by making many of its corporate environmental reports (the CERES Reports) available online and then by using its experience with the CERES Report to launch the Global Reporting Initiative (GRI) with the United Nations Environment Program in 1997. The goal of the GRI is to standardize environmental reporting. The members of GRI's international steering committee include the Council on Economic Priorities (U.S.), the Investor Responsibility Research Center (U.S.), the New Economics Foundation (UK), and General Motors, among others.

12. Information sources include a Gap corporate executive (anonymity given), interview by author, San Francisco, 10 October 1996; and Charles Kernaghan, executive director, National Labor Committee, telephone interview with author, 3 September 1996. *New York Times* op-ed writer Bob Herbert traveled to El Salvador in October 1995. During this period, according to Kernaghan, Herbert wrote six op-eds related to the GAP campaign on broader worker rights issues at "maquila" factories. See, for instance, "A Sweatshop Victory," *New York Times*, 22 December 1995.

13. Information on the auditor is from "Report of Independent Accountants" at the end of Nike's 2000 and 2001 *Annual Reports*. The information on monitoring is from "Independent Monitoring" on Nike's web site (www.nikebiz.com/labor).

14. Moreover, Smith stresses, COVERCO was able to build this model thanks to the "space and openness" offered by Liz Claiborne when it engaged COVERCO's services in Guatemala. Interview with Dennis Smith, Washington, D.C., 9 September 2001.

15. The quote is from Aron Cramer, "Ethical Sourcing: The Indicators of Serious Intent," in *Visions of Ethical Sourcing*, ed. Raj Thamotheram (London: Financial Times Prentice Hall for Shared View Social Responsibility Ltd., with financial support from Société Générale de Surveillance [SGS], 2000), 25. See COVERCO, "1st Public Report–Independent Monitoring Pilot Project with Liz Claiborne,

Inc.," 5 October 1999 (25 pages). For a similar initiative in Indonesia, see Insan Hitawasana Sejahtera (Social Science Research and Consultancy), "Peduli Hak: Caring for Rights–An Intensive Research, Evaluation and Remediation Initiative in Two Indonesian Factories Manufacturing Reebok Footwear," Jakarta, Indonesia, October 1999.

16. Martha Honey and Abigail Rome, "Protecting Paradise: Certification Programs for Sustainable Tourism and Ecotourism" (Washington, D.C.: Institute for Policy Studies, October 2001). This report (available from the publisher) grew out of the first international workshop on ecotourism and sustainable tourism certification schemes held at Mohonk Mountain House in New Paltz, New York, in November 2000. The workshop, attended by forty-five certification specialists from twenty countries, was sponsored by the Institute for Policy Studies (IPS) and supported by the Ford Foundation. For conference minutes, see the IPS Ecotourism Project page at www.ips-dc.org.

17. Physicians for Human Rights, "The Campaign to Eliminate Conflict Diamonds," 1–4 (www.phrusa.org/campaigns/sierra_leone/diam) accessed 20 September 2001. A very thorough forty-four-page report on "non-conflict diamonds" is available through Global Witness (www.oneworld.org/globalwitness/reports/conflict). For the UN General Assembly resolution on non-conflict diamonds, see www.un.org/peace/africa/Diamond.htlm.

18. To read the codes themselves: for the FLA, see www.fairlabor.org; for the WRC, see www.workersrights.org. Information on the WRC and FLA is partly from two briefings to the Workplace Conduct Advisory Group, American University, Washington, D.C., of which I am a member: (1) by FLA Executive Director Sam Brown and FLA university liaison Maureen Murtha, 1 March 2001; and (2) by WRC Executive Director Scott Nova, 29 March 2001.

19. Aron Cramer, "Ethical Sourcing: The Indicators of Serious Intent," in *Visions of Ethical Sourcing*, ed. Raj Thamotheram (London: Financial Times Prentice Hall for Shared View Social Responsibility Ltd., with financial support from Société Générale de Surveillance [SGS], 2000), quotes from pp. 21, 25, 26.

20. The Global Compact is available online at www.unglobalcompact.org. The backlash response can be followed on the web site of Corporate Watch (formerly the Transnational Resource Action Center), www.corpwatch.org. See two letters from citizen groups to UN Secretary-General Kofi Annan, dated 20 July 2000 and 21 July 2000.

4.1

The Conscious Consumer: Promoting Economic Justice through Fair Trade

Rose Benz Ericson

Long before the anti-sweatshop bandwagon began rolling, retail and wholesale groups called alternative trade organizations (ATOs) or fair trade organizations (FTOs) were providing models of economic justice. They work with disadvantaged artisans and farmers to market their wares directly to First World consumers, minimizing the cut taken by often-exploitative middlemen and returning substantial payments to the producers. These groups use the terms "alternative trade" and "fair trade" to distinguish themselves from traditional commercial trade operations, which typically focus on generating profits and benefiting buyers, rather than optimizing conditions for producers.

Worldwide, Fair Trade—the commerce of ATOs and FTOs—totals some $400 million in sales annually, according to *The New York Times* and the International Federation for Alternative Trade. Though a tiny percentage of the whopping $3.6 trillion in total goods exchanged globally, Fair Trade sales represent a significant effort toward reducing economic injustice.

Fair Trade organizations are those that adhere to a strict set of criteria regarding workers' pay, conditions and other terms, set forth by recognized groups like the Fair Trade Federation and the International Federation for Alternative Trade.

Across North America, more than 1,000 retailers, catalog operations, church groups and Web sites sell Fair Trade goods—coffee and tea, food products, home furnishings, clothing, jewelry, toys and crafts—accounting for about 10 percent of worldwide Fair Trade sales. Most shops and catalogs also feature photos and brochures to tell the stories of the Third World producers whose economic and social well-being has been dramatically improved through their access to First World markets.

[. . .]

What Is Fair Trade?

Fair Trade, or alternative trade, refers to the exchange of goods based on principles of economic and social justice. The key goals of Fair Trade are to empower low-income, disadvantaged or otherwise marginalized artisans and farmers around the globe to better their conditions, and to promote understanding between them and First World consumers.

Fair Trade Federation members pledge to:

- Pay a fair wage in the local context.
- Provide equal opportunities for all people, particularly the most disadvantaged.

Rose Benz Ericson, excerpt from *The Conscious Consumer: Promoting Economic Justice through Fair Trade* (Gettysburg, Pa.: Fair Trade Federation, 1999), 5, 7–13, and 18. Reprinted with permission of Rose Benz Ericson and the Fair Trade Resource Network. Order through the Fair Trade Resource Network at info@fairtraderesource.org.

- Engage in environmentally sustainable practices.
- Build long-term trade relationships.
- Provide healthy and safe working conditions.
- Provide financial and technical assistance to workers whenever possible.

While a "fair" price is often difficult to determine, Fair Trade advocates generally agree that the producer should earn enough not only to cover material and labor costs, but also to improve the standard of living for herself, her family, her cooperative and her community.

FTOs and ATOs can be either for-profits or not-for-profits, wholesale or retail. They work with producers—both cooperatives and nongovernmental organizations—to provide markets for farm products, textiles and handcrafts in developed nations. Because Fair Traders reduce the number of exploitative middlemen and keep overhead low, they typically return one-quarter to one-third of the retail price of items to artisans—in countries where hourly wages are counted in pennies. A portion of that return may take the form of job training, technical assistance, health care, access to loans and grants, and/or dividends.

For coffee farmers, partnership with a Fair Trade organization means guaranteed minimum prices and freedom from the hardships of the erratic world coffee market. Fair Trade organizations pay $1.26 U.S. for a pound of green beans, regardless of how low the market price goes. When the world price exceeds $1.26, ATOs pay their farmer-partners a floating rate that consistently exceeds the market figure.

Through Fair Trade, producers receive increased income to feed, clothe, shelter, educate and provide health care for their families; access to loans to buy land, livestock and materials; training and technical assistance; ownership of the means of production; and respect for their cultural traditions and native environments.

Buyers of Fair Trade products help to:

- Ensure that producers are paid a living wage.
- Provide working conditions that are safe, dignified and democratically run.
- Support community development in housing, health, education and appropriate technology.
- Encourage environmentally sound business practices that protect local resources.

- Preserve cultural diversity by supporting indigenous talents and family traditions.

Fair Trade supporters encourage villagers to remain in the countryside to earn a living, rather than migrate to overcrowded, disease-ridden urban areas.

How Fair Traders Differ from Commercial Importers

Fair Traders' goal is to benefit those on the short end of the trade stick, not maximize returns to stockholders. Though all Fair Trade organizations must sustain themselves, and some operate as for-profit businesses, their focus is not on generating profits at home. By reducing the number of middlemen and minimizing overhead, ATOs typically pay producers one-quarter to one-third the retail price of a product, in cash and/or other benefits. Fair Traders also frequently prepay for merchandise, so that producers have cash for materials and do not suffer hardship if items do not sell.

They frequently work with cooperatives, where producers have a say in how their items are created and sold. Cooperatives are encouraged to provide benefits such as health care, child care and access to loans. Fair Traders also work with non-governmental organizations, whose mission often is to benefit populations with the greatest disadvantages.

ATOs encourage producers to reinvest their profits in their communities—for health clinics, potable-water plants and other vital projects.

Fair Trade organizations aim to shift processing and packaging activities to the Third World, so that as much money as possible will remain in the producer country. Ten Thousand Villages, for example, buys certain promotional materials from artisan groups in Bangladesh and Egypt. In commercial trade, such activities typically are performed in the First World, depriving the neediest countries of the opportunity to boost their incomes.

Fair Trade groups work with producers overlooked by commercial distributors. These producers may be economically disadvantaged—and therefore neediest—because of political strife, social upheaval, distance from a population center, discrimination or physical disability. Fair Trade work enables women, in particular, to gain economic and social clout in societies that frequently consider them second-class.

Fair Traders strive for long-term partnerships, working with producers to resolve issues of sizing, quality control and timely delivery. ATOs negotiate with artisans to modify their designs to appeal to customers abroad, boosting sales potential. They also often provide training in business skills such as bookkeeping. Because the relationships are based on trust, producer partners have every incentive to offer Fair Trade organizations their best-quality coffee beans or handcrafted items.

They encourage producers also to sell their products domestically, and to find other markets on their own, reducing their reliance on one or two sources.

Fair Traders emphasize consumer education in their marketing. Some distributors put a tag on the products they sell, introducing the producer and describing the conditions under which he or she worked, creating a bridge across cultures. Mail-order ATOs use their catalogs to explain their missions, and to describe the challenges facing the Third World.

Some Fair Traders educate the buying public by selling at churches and schools. Development and wider use of Fair Trade seals will enable shoppers to know at a glance that an item was produced under empowering conditions.

The History of Fair Trade

Most alternative trade organizations began as missionary projects, humanitarian efforts or political/economic action statements. Linked to the Fair Trade movement are non-governmental organizations, which often leverage the marketing expertise of ATOs to enhance their efforts to aid Third World populations.

In North America, the church-related organizations are the oldest and among the largest alternative traders. Ten Thousand Villages (formerly SELFHELP Crafts of the World) is a Pennsylvania-based program of the Mennonite Central Committee. SERRV International of Maryland, originally a project of the Church of the Brethren, is now an independent organization. Both began buying handcrafts from European war victims after World War II and later switched their focus to Third World artisans. Together, these two ATOs in 1998 accounted for roughly $20 million in sales in North America, through catalogs, hundreds of retail outlets and thousands of church-run con-

signment sales. Ten Thousand Villages estimates that its sales represent the equivalent of 12,500 full-time jobs for artisans, and improved living standards for more than 50,000 villagers. Both SERRV and Ten Thousand Villages are posting steadily increasing sales.

Economic-development ATOs started in Europe in the 1960s, when the Dutch division of the group OXFAM opened its first shops selling goods produced by Third World cooperatives. By the mid-1980s, more than 1,000 Third World shops were operating in the United Kingdom and Switzerland. A decade later, Fair Trade employs some 1,500 people in Europe and reaches the public via 45,000 points of sale, according to Fair TradeMark Canada.

In North America, the 1970s and 1980s saw a surge in the creation of economic/political ATOs such as Global Exchange and Pueblo to People, often in response to strife in developing nations and a growing awareness that the gap between rich and poor was widening. The 1986 establishment of Equal Exchange, the United States' largest coffee ATO, was significant for its creation of a sustainable-business model that produces a high-quality version of a valuable commodity while making a political statement.

Today, some 100 Fair Trade organizations operate in North America, accounting for $35 million to $40 million in retail sales, according to the Fair Trade Federation, and recent articles in *The Wall Street Journal* and *The New York Times*.

As they move into the 21st century, Fair Traders are emphasizing synergy—with one another as well as with policy advocates, environmentalists, corporate watchdogs and labor rights activists. The creation of federations enables Fair Trade organizations to share resources and develop integrated strategies. The movement's current agenda also includes:

- Standardizing Fair Trade criteria.
- Expanding and/or developing certification and monitoring of production.
- Lobbying to make government policies friendlier to small farmers.
- Reaching a broader group of consumers.

Ten Thousand Villages, for example, has moved beyond the Mennonite community to open retail shops in upscale neighborhoods across the country, where customers expect quality and service worthy of the trendiest commercial outlets.

Fair Trade's Major Players

In North America, groups like Ten Thousand Villages, SERRV International, Equal Exchange, Global Exchange and Canada's Bridgehead Inc. have given the movement visibility. But equally vital are a variety of newer, smaller organizations like dZi-The Tibet Collection, African Market and MarketPlace-Handwork of India, which provide fresh direction to the Fair Trade movement.

Especially innovative is an organization called PEOPLink, which trains artisans from developing countries to use the Internet to market their products. PEOPLink's work recently caught the attention of U.S. President Bill Clinton, who at a 1998 e-commerce conference cited "the stories of people in Africa and Latin America lifting themselves from abject poverty through access to the Internet." Rapidly, Fair Trade organizations are embracing that venue to reduce the costs of printing and mailing catalogs.

Several umbrella organizations have formed to encourage resource sharing among players of all sizes, to nurture newer Fair Trade wholesalers and retailers, and to further Fair Trade as a movement. The U.S.-based Fair Trade Federation draws members from around the world, as does the International Federation for Alternative Trade, now based in the United Kingdom. The European Fair Trade Association, founded in 1990, has its headquarters in the Netherlands.

The most visible Fair Traders in Europe include OXFAM Trading, Traidcraft plc and Twin Trading, all based in the United Kingdom; Holland's Fair Trade Organisatie; and Germany's Gepa Aktion Dritte Welt Handel.

In addition, at least three Europe-based operations provide keys to the marketability of Fair Trade products by offering certification and monitoring for commodities—including coffee, tea, sugar, honey, cocoa, bananas and raisins. Producers who meet Fair Trade criteria pay licensing fees that allow them to display the seals on their products. TransFair International, founded in Germany, has licensee operations in Austria, Canada, Japan, Holland, Italy, Luxembourg and the United States. The Max Havelaar Foundation, based in Holland, licenses food items in Denmark and Switzerland as well. In Britain, the Fairtrade Foundation licenses coffee, tea and organic chocolate.

[. . .]

Looking Ahead

Educating and motivating consumers remains a major objective for Fair Trade advocates. In a world still governed by supply and demand, consumers retain the ultimate say in what goods will sell, for without buyers, there can be no profits. Increasingly, manufacturers are heeding consumers' growing knowledge about and demands regarding human rights and environmental sustainability.

History shows that, when consumers get organized, they get their way. The public's demand for automobile air bags and recycled paper have brought those products into the mainstream. Similarly, campaigns against tobacco and alcohol consumption have significantly altered society's attitude toward the manufacture and use of those products.

With the average consumer—who is older, more educated, more aware of global issues, more interested in socially responsible investing and more focused on values than they were a decade ago—the principles of Fair Trade are striking a chord. Increasing media attention on the Fair Trade movement belies a culture hungry to spend its money in meaningful ways.

As Fair Trade advocates continue to create alliances with church, political and business groups, and as consumers slowly embrace a system that makes commerce work for the disadvantaged majority, all move a step closer to a common vision: a world where all human beings have the opportunity to benefit from the fruits of their labor, and from the wealth of the planet.

4.2

What Hope for "Ethical" Trade in the Globalized Garment Industry?

Angela Hale

In the autumn of 1999, a major UK garment retailer joined the Ethical Trading Initiative (ETI) just as the media were announcing the loss of thousands of jobs in its UK factories. Joining the ETI means a commitment to the promotion of labour standards as embodied in ILO Conventions. Yet British workers' jobs are rapidly being lost to countries in Asia and Eastern Europe, where companies know that people are employed in conditions far below these standards. Companies overcome this apparent contradiction between pronouncement and practice by expressing their commitment in terms of the progressive implementation of a code of conduct rather than an immediate guarantee of acceptable standards. However, in the case of the garment industry, the implications of global restructuring are such that the hope of achieving this objective seems increasingly remote.

The Development of "Ethical Trade"

The Ethical Trading Initiative is a UK-based response to the growing public demand for corporate codes of conduct on labour standards. This demand has spread throughout North America and Europe on such a scale that it can be seen as one of the significant social movements of the 1990s. Public concern has grown over time as the media has revealed that reputable companies are selling everyday consumer goods made by exploited workers. One of the first scandals was revealed in 1992 when a report appeared in the *Washington Post* about the production of Levi jeans by Chinese prison labour on the island of Saipan. Levi Strauss immediately reacted by drawing up a code on labour standards for all its overseas suppliers. Walmart, the biggest retailer in the US, drew up a similar code in 1993, and soon almost all leading US garment retailers followed suit. Although European companies were slower to respond, many are now publishing codes. In the UK this includes C & A, Littlewoods, Next, Marks and Spencers, Burton, Pentland, Monsoon, the Co-op, Grattan, John Lewis, River Island, Tesco and Asda (now owned by Walmart). Some have drawn up their own codes; others have adopted the ETI base code.[1] The crucial question facing campaigners has been whether these company codes indicate real commitment or are merely public relations exercises.
[. . .]

The Changing Face of the Garment Industry

The pressures of globalisation are particularly strong in the case of the garment industry. The changing rules of world trade mean that more and more countries are integrated into a global market and encouraged to compete for exports. There has been massive relocation of garment production over the past 30 years, and more is predicted as the Multi-Fibre Arrangement (MFA) is phased out by January 2005.[2] Northern retailers and brand-based companies maintain overall control of the industry whilst shifting their production sites from one location to another. This has been made possible by the development of information technology which enables information, designs and orders to be communicated around the world twenty-four hours a day.

Probably the most significant factor in determining the direction of shifts in production sites is the relative cost of labour from country to country. During the first phase of relocation in the 1960s and '70s, European and US companies outsourced to countries such as Hong Kong, Singapore, and South Korea. Production was then relocated to lower wage economies, such as the Philippines, Indonesia, Thailand, and Mexico. Now it has shifted to Bangladesh, Central America, and more recently Vietnam and, above all, China. Sometimes workers from these countries are taken to other locations, e.g., from China to Mauritius and from South Asia to the Middle East. Companies in the more developed Asian economies have maintained a stake in the garment trade partly through subcontracting labour-intensive production processes to even lower wage economies: for example, Hong Kong and Taiwan are the main investors in China, and Korea has focused on Indonesia and Central America. This has produced a system of "triangular manufacturing" under which companies take orders from Europe and the US, contract them out to lower wage economies, and then ship the finished goods back to the buyers.

The shifting of production sites has been accompanied by other changes in company strategy. Internationalisation initially consisted of Northern manufacturers setting up similar factories in the South. However, there has since been a move towards outsourcing to independently owned factories. The extent of this shift is demonstrated by the emergence of "manufacturers without factories," companies such as Nike and Adidas which have built their success on the promotion of brand labels. They concentrate on increasing profit through design and marketing whilst reducing costs and risk

through outsourcing. Meanwhile, major retailers have changed their buying policies. Since the 1970s they have bypassed importers by sending their own buyers overseas. More recently, they have also begun to compete directly with brand-name manufacturers by promoting their own labels. They outsource the production of these labels; they may design the goods themselves or may contract out the design as well.

The changing demands of the fashion industry have also played their part in altering patterns of production. New technology at the point of sale has enabled retailers to monitor trends closely and to look for a quick response from manufacturers. The traditional two-season cycle has broken down, and design, fabric, and colour changes are being made more frequently. For manufacturers this means short lead times, short runs and the need for flexible production. To some extent this has acted against international sourcing, enabling some small domestic clothing manufacturers in higher-income countries to survive. Whereas basic goods can be easily produced in low-income countries, fashion items at the top end of the market may be supplied most efficiently in the country of sale.

Intense international and local competition, combined with the demands of the fashion industry, has meant that the garment industry of the 1990s has been characterised by a massive increase in subcontracting. Typically there are different levels of subcontracting. Buying companies contract major manufacturers who subcontract to smaller production units, who in turn increase their flexibility by bringing in temporary workers and putting work out to homeworkers. Homeworkers play a key role in these production chains, not only in low wage economies but also in industrialised countries of Europe, North America and Australia.

The advantages of subcontracting to manufacturers are fairly clear. Local manufacturers produce to order and the demand can fluctuate enormously. Later arrival of material, or last minute changes in fabric or colour, can also cause production delays. By reducing the regular factory workforce and using subcontractors, employers can react to these changes but keep costs to a minimum. Employers are also absolved from any responsibility for workers; indeed, subcontracting is sometimes used in response to worker demands for improved wages and conditions. There is evidence that subcontracting can enable manufacturers to reduce their labour and overhead costs by more than half. In some countries, such as the Philippines, up to 75% of output is contracted out (Green, 1998).

Downward Pressure on Labour Conditions

These changes in the garment industry have had the overall effect of increasing downward pressure on working conditions. As consumers shop around for the best buys, retail companies are in constant competition to maintain their profit margins. Contractors, agents, and trading companies feel the pressure to produce lower-cost goods. Meanwhile, with the increasing number of countries involved in export production, local manufacturers are locked into fierce competition for orders. Middlemen who have to meet the cost demands of the buying company maximise their own profits by squeezing manufacturers. Rather than turn down an order, local manufacturers accept unprofitable deals and make them work by increasing pressure on their own workforce through forced or unpaid overtime and by subcontracting to small workshops and to homeworkers, the lowest-paid workers at the end of the chain.

This growing pattern of international subcontracting means that the whole industry works on the basis of flexibility, short-termism, competition and insecurity. It is therefore no surprise that workers themselves are faced with these problems. As production is moved to cheaper locations, millions of workers in industrialised countries are losing their jobs, not only in Europe and North America but also in the newly industrialised countries of Asia. Even in low wage economies there is the constant threat of further relocation. The end of the MFA phaseout threatens to bring on a period of even more intense competition, increasing this feeling of insecurity.

Garment workers also face the daily insecurity of having their employment determined by fashion trends and market fluctuations. Even in larger factories, many employers have adopted ways of removing their responsibility for their workforce when work is scarce. Workers may be employed on a casual, part-time, temporary basis, and agencies that supply contract labour are being used more frequently. At the same time, competition between local manufacturers to re-

duce costs and complete orders results in an increase in work intensity. This is manifest in increased working hours, and reductions in the numbers of workers on production lines. Work intensity is at its highest when a particular production deadline has to be met and workers are typically kept in the factory until the order is complete. Employers may even persuade workers that this is in their interests, since jobs will be lost if orders are not completed.

The irony of this downward pressure is that companies at the top of international subcontracting chains are themselves creating the conditions that operate against attempts to implement codes of conduct. If the demand for flexibility translates into insecurity and periods of intense overtime, it is unrealistic to expect standards on working hours and proper working contracts to be adequately implemented. If competitive pressure is such that costs have to be cut, it may be impossible for local contractors to increase wage levels and bring health and safety measures up to international standards without going out of business. In any case, if they have no long-term stake in the business, their aim will be short-term profits rather than investment in improved working conditions. All these issues need to be addressed by any company genuinely committed to promoting ethical business practice.

The Challenge of the Supply Chain

Companies seeking to overcome these dilemmas also face practical problems associated with increasingly complex subcontracting chains. The first problem is actually knowing where their goods are produced. Most companies operate through agents, trading companies, or local contractors. These middlemen increase their power by providing as little information as possible. Often overseas companies do not know the names or locations of factories from which they are buying, and this information can change rapidly from one week to the next. Even if the factory itself is known, it is highly unlikely that local contractors will reveal the extent of outsourcing to smaller production units and homeworkers. Most companies buy from a range of local suppliers; even if the companies can locate these suppliers, it will be impossible to monitor them all. One US retailer is estimated to have over 13,000 suppliers who in turn source from up to 78,000 subcontractors (Kearney, 1999).

As part of their commitment to ethical trade, some larger companies insist that their own representatives visit at least some of the factories from which the companies source. Some are also setting up their own buying operations and establishing more direct relationships with local manufacturers. This is sometimes accompanied by a dramatic reduction in the number of suppliers. Such a closer working relationship does provide greater opportunity for monitoring the implementation of company codes by those particular companies. However, what are the implications for workers in the production units that are no longer used, and for homeworkers at the end of subcontracting chains? And what about workers who supply less responsible companies?

For companies the exercise is inevitably one of ensuring that their own house is in order, rather than of striving for any overall improvement of working conditions. However, trade unions and NGOs must have a wider agenda. The real issue is whether codes of conduct are an appropriate instrument for addressing the overall threat to labour standards in globalised industries. It is even conceivable that codes of conduct could be made to apply to workers as a whole, and if so, how can this be achieved? Even if all companies agreed to respect codes of conduct, can there ever be appropriate and sufficiently resourced procedures for monitoring their implementation? Is enough known about the ways in which the attempt to achieve this is impacting on workers themselves? Unless such issues are addressed, we cannot be sure that in the end it will be workers and not companies who will gain most from this exercise.

Ethical Trade Means Involving Workers

Another irony of the ethical trade movement is that, although it is fundamentally about workers' rights, workers themselves have not been part of the process. Codes are not negotiated between employers and workers, but are introduced in a top-down fashion by the employers themselves. Sometimes this occurs in consultation with NGOs and trade union officials, but this typically happens in the country where a given company is based, far removed from the actual workplace. In short, codes of conduct are being introduced on behalf of workers without their knowledge or consent. It is simply assumed that workers will see this initiative as being in their interest.

As a member of the NGO group of the ETI, Women Working Worldwide (WWW) has argued that codes of conduct can only have a significant impact if workers understand them and are able to use them as negotiating tools. WWW carried out a small research and consultation exercise with its partner organisations in Indonesia, the Philippines, Sri Lanka, Bangladesh, Pakistan, and India. This exercise clearly demonstrated that workers knew nothing about codes of conduct even when they were working in factories supplying well-known companies that had such codes, such as Nike and the Gap. When the concept was explained to them they showed a high level of scepticism, based on a distrust of anything introduced by management and on widespread experience of corruption. Many felt that even attempting to find out whether their companies had codes could lead to victimisation or dismissal. Nevertheless, they were curious to know more and they welcomed the WWW's suggestion of an educational programme on the issue of codes.

Workers demonstrated their willingness to explore the potential of codes by their involvement in this subsequent education programme. They gave up their few hours of leisure time for the programme; many feared victimisation so that the sessions were sometimes held in secret. At times Indonesia was in a state of political turmoil and Bangladesh was under floodwater. Nevertheless, groups in all six countries reported that the programme had been positive and productive. In part this was because the discussion of codes opened up more general issues such as the place of workers in international supply chains. Few workers had previously questioned where their products went after leaving the factory, and many became enthusiastic about using brand labels as a way of tracing supply chains. They began to see that codes of conduct could be a useful tool in confronting some of the problems of organising in the context of globalisation. They provided a link to workers working for the same company in other countries and to consumer campaigns in Europe and North America. As Shirin Akhter from Karmojibi Nari in Bangladesh reported, "Workers became aware that foreign consumers are trying to do something good for them. They have got the feeling that they are not alone. As a result their level of awareness and sense of their rights was raised" (Hensman and Hale, 1999:26).

However, the educational programme made it clear that workers did not see company codes as a solution to the struggle for workers' rights, even in factories that directly supplied the world market. There was a strong feeling that the impact of codes would be limited unless workers had proper work contracts and the right to organise. Although some codes might include these rights, workers had no confidence that these would be implemented unless workers themselves were in a position to act collectively. All groups viewed as crucial that workers representatives be involved in the implementation and monitoring of codes. It was felt that ideally this should be done through trade unions. However, most workers had limited experience of trade unions, except as remote and sometimes corrupt organisations. (Unions are banned in most Free Trade Zones, and rarely operate in smaller subcontracted units.) Nonetheless, everywhere the struggle for genuine trade unionism was seen as more important than the promotion of company codes.

Ultimately, only workers themselves can monitor the conditions in which they work and ensure that their rights are not being violated. Workers' own awareness and organisational ability is therefore essential to any attempt to improve labour conditions through codes of conduct. The problem is that the same processes that operate against the implementation of codes of conduct in the garment industry also operate against effective worker organisation. International subcontracting not only creates huge gaps between workers and their ultimate employers; it also divides workers from each other. Traditional forms of trade union organising based on secure factory employment will not work in the context of a casualised and dispersed labour force. And yet globalisation does provide new opportunities for international alliances between workers themselves, as well as between workers and those organisations that are campaigning on their behalf. There is an urgent need for new ways of organising that take into account the realities of global subcontracting chains and at the same time recognise the potential for action at an international level. Only then will the movement for ethical trade begin to have a significant impact.

Notes

1. The ETI base code was drawn up by representatives of member companies, NGOs and trade unions. It consists of a set of standards, based on core conventions of the ILO, which relate to health and safety, forced labour, maximum working hours, living wages, discrimination, child labour, regularisation of employment, and freedom of association and collective bargaining.

2. The MFA is a quota system set up in 1974 to protect the garment and textile industries of Europe and North America. Under the new Agreement on Textiles and Clothing, the MFA is being phased out to bring trade in textile and garments in line with WTO rules. Trade in garments will then be more determined by market forces, and it is predicted that whilst certain countries such as China and India will gain, other developing countries are in danger of losing their entire garment industry.

References

Green, D. (1998) Fashion Victims. London: CAFOD.

Hensman R., and A. Hale (1999) Women workers and codes of conduct: Report of educational programme in Asia. Manchester: Women Working Worldwide.

Kearney N. (1999) International Tailor Garment and Leather Workers Federation internal document.

4.3

Business Partner Terms of Engagement and Guidelines for Country Selection

Levi Strauss & Co.

evi Strauss & Co. has a heritage of conducting business in a manner that reflects its values. As we expand our sourcing base to more diverse cultures and countries, we must take special care in selecting business partners and countries whose practices are not incompatible with our values. Otherwise, our sourcing decisions have the potential of undermining this heritage, damaging the image of our brands and threatening our commercial success.

Business Partner Terms of Engagement

Our concerns include the practices of individual business partners as well as the political and social issues in those countries where we might consider sourcing.

This defines Terms of Engagement which addresses issues that are substantially controllable by our individual business partners.

We have defined business partners as contractors and suppliers who provide labor and/or material (including fabric, sundries, chemicals and/or stones) utilized in the manufacture and finishing of our products.

Levi Strauss & Co., "Business Partner Terms of Engagement and Guidelines for Country Selection" (San Francisco, formulated in 1991, approved in 1992). Reprinted with permission of Levi Strauss & Co.

1. Environmental Requirements

We will only do business with partners who share our commitment to the environment. (Note: We intend this standard to be consistent with the approved language of Levi Strauss & Co.'s Environmental Action Group.)

2. Ethical Standards

We will seek to identify and utilize business partners who aspire as individuals and in the conduct of their business to a set of ethical standards not incompatible with our own.

3. Health & Safety

We will only utilize business partners who provide workers with a safe and healthy work environment. Business partners who provide residential facilities for their workers must provide safe and healthy facilities.

4. Legal Requirements

We expect our business partners to be law abiding as individuals and to comply with legal requirements relevant to the conduct of their business.

5. Employment Practices

We will only do business with partners whose workers are in all cases present voluntarily, not put at risk of physical harm, fairly compensated, allowed the right of free association and not exploited in any way. In addition, the following specific guidelines will be followed.

Wages and Benefits

We will only do business with partners who provide wages and benefits that comply with any applicable law or match the prevailing local manufacturing or finishing industry practices. We will also favor business partners who share our commitment to contribute to the betterment of community conditions.

Working Hours

While permitting flexibility in scheduling, we will identify prevailing local work hours and seek business partners who do not exceed them except for appropriately compensated overtime. While we favor partners who utilize less than sixty-hour work weeks, we will not use contractors who, on a regularly scheduled basis, require in excess of a sixty-hour week. Employees should be allowed one day off in seven days.

Child Labor

Use of child labor is not permissible. "Child" is defined as less than 14 years of age or younger than the compulsory age to be in school. We will not utilize partners who use child labor in any of their facilities. We support the development of legitimate workplace apprenticeship programs for the educational benefit of younger people.

Prison Labor/Forced Labor

We will not knowingly utilize prison or forced labor in contracting or subcontracting relationships in the manufacture of our products. We will not knowingly utilize or purchase materials from a business partner utilizing prison or forced labor.

Discrimination

While we recognize and respect cultural differences, we believe that workers should be employed on the basis of their ability to do the job, rather than on the basis of personal characteristics or beliefs. We will favor business partners who share this value.

Disciplinary Practices

We will not utilize business partners who use corporal punishment or other forms of mental or physical coercion.

Guidelines for Country Selection

The following country selection criteria address issues which we believe are beyond the ability of the individual business partner to control.

1. Brand Image

We will not initiate or renew contractual relationships in countries where sourcing would have an adverse effect on our global brand image.

2. Health & Safety

We will not initiate or renew contractual relationships in locations where there is evidence that Company employees or representatives would be exposed to unreasonable risk.

3. Human Rights

We should not initiate or renew contractual relationships in countries where there are pervasive violations of basic human rights.

4. Legal Requirements

We will not initiate or renew contractual relationships in countries where the legal environment creates unreasonable risk to our trademarks or to other important commercial interests or seriously impedes our ability to implement these guidelines.

5. Political or Social Stability

We will not initiate or renew contractual relationships in countries where political or social turmoil unreasonably threatens our commercial interests.

4.4

Presentation and Acceptance
of Reebok Youth in Action Award

Iqbal Masih and Blair Underwood

Presentation Speech of Blair Underwood

Three thousand years ago, in a call that has echoed through the centuries and the millennia, a man named Moses thundered, "Let my people go." But Pharaoh would not let them go; so they fled, and as he chased them, they crossed the Red Sea from slavery into freedom, laying down a path that other peoples throughout history have followed. In our own country, we fought a bloody civil war before crossing our Red Sea, and still today we see the scars that slavery inflicts.

Childhood, we like to think, is everywhere a time of freedom. Of children everywhere, we expect—no, we insist—that they should be free to learn and to play, to laugh and to grow. But in the real world of 1994, there are more than 100 million children under the age of 15 who have to work, and very, very many of these are, for all practical purposes, slaves. They are bought, they are sold, their lives are controlled by their masters who use them as laborers from the age of four on up.

It was when he was four years old that Iqbal Masih became what's called in Pakistan a

"bonded worker" in a carpet factory. As a bonded worker, he labored at a loom for twelve hours a day, seven days a week, in return for a loan the factory owner had given his parents. Twelve hours a day, seven days a week, ill-nourished, often beaten, for six long years, until when he was ten years old he heard that the law had been changed and that bonded labor was no longer permitted in Pakistan.

Changing a law is one thing; changing people's behavior is another. In village after village, the factory owners are the richest and most important people, and the police in Pakistan are reluctant to move against their violations of the law. But when Iqbal, then ten years old, stole away one day to a rally sponsored by the Bonded Labour Liberation Front, he learned that he could truly be free. It was then he insisted that before breathing free himself, he must first return to his factory to tell the other boys that they, too, could now be free.

The factory owner was furious, but Iqbal led his friends to freedom. That was in 1992. And for the last two years, Iqbal has split his time between visiting other factories where he has brought the message of freedom to some 3,000 children, and attending one of the 240 schools organized for liberated children.

Iqbal Masih, leader, inspiration, giant: we honor you with the Reebok Youth In Action Award.

Iqbal Masih, "Acceptance Speech," and Blair Underwood, "Presentation to Iqbal Masih, Age 12: Reebok Youth in Action Award" (Reebok Human Rights Award, Boston, Massachusetts, 7 December 1994). Reprinted with permission of Reebok Human Rights Award.

Acceptance Speech of Iqbal Masih

I am one of those millions of children who are suffering in Pakistan through bonded labor and child labor, but I am lucky that due to the efforts of Bonded Labor Liberation Front (BLLF), I go out in freedom and I am standing in front of you here today. After my freedom, I join BLLF school and I am studying in that school now. For us slave children Ehsan Ullah Khan and BLLF has done the same work that Abraham Lincoln did for the slaves of America. Today, you are free and I am free too.

Unfortunately, the owner of the business tells us that it is America which asks us to enslave the children there because the carpets, the rugs and the towels that we make for America, people like it that way and that is what the children made, so they want that way to go on. I appeal to you that you stop people from using children as bonded labor because the children need a pen rather than instruments of child labor.

They gave work for the children with this instrument. If there is something wrong, the children get beaten with this. And if they are hurt, they are not taken to the doctors. There the children do not need these instruments but they need this instrument, the pen, like the American children have. Unfortunately, those children do not have it right now. I hope that you will help

BLLF like they have helped us. By your cooperation BLLF can help a lot of children and give them this instrument, the pen.

I still share what I remember, how I was abused and how other children are being abused there; including those they are insulted and they are hung upside down and they are mistreated, and I still remember those days.

I saw Pakistani-made rugs in American stores, and I was very saddened by seeing that these are the things that were made by the bonded labor children and I felt very sorry about it. I request President Clinton to put sanctions on those countries which use child labor, and do not extend help to those countries still there using children as bonded labor and allow the children to have the pen.

And with this, I gratefully and thankfully acknowledge Reebok's contribution in that direction. They have called me for this prize and I'm very grateful to them. Thank you.

We have a slogan at school when our children get free. So we all together say we are free. And I request you today to join me in raising that slogan here. I will say we are and you will say free.

We are!—Free!

We are!—Free!

We are!—Free!

Thank you.

4.5

Children of the Looms: Rescuing the "Carpet Kids" of Nepal, India, and Pakistan

Suzanne Charlé

Kathmandu, Nepal—In the Kathmandu Valley, the packed-mud playground of the Hamro Gar school was alive with activity. The huge-eyed Buddha of Swayanbhunath temple gazed down from his mountaintop aerie as children nervously prepared to put on a play. Jhalak Man Tamang, a small boy of about 13—he doesn't know his exact age—calmly waited for his cue. He had rehearsed his lines and knew them well. As for his character, that was no problem, either: The story, about the sale of young boys into the Nepalese carpet industry and their subsequent trials, was one he knew well. Like the 14-year-old playwright and his fellow actors, Jhalak had been forced to work on carpets bound for export to the United States and Europe before he was brought to Hamro Gar—literally, "Our Home."

Jhalak, one of an estimated 1,800 children under the age of 14 illegally employed by Nepal's carpet industry, found his new home through the efforts of a program called RUGMARK, in which carpet manufacturers and exporters in India, Nepal and Pakistan join with American and European importers and nongovernmental organizations to assure that no child labor is used in creating the beautiful hand-knotted rugs. Factory owners and subcontractors agree not to employ children, and RUGMARK representatives make regular, unannounced inspections to make sure they comply. Those that do are given RUGMARK labels—each label with a number corresponding to the specific carpet made on a specific loom—assuring consumers in the United States and Europe that the carpets are child-labor free. Children found on the looms are either returned to their parents and sent to local schools or placed in RUGMARK-sponsored rehabilitation centers and schools, depending on their educational backgrounds.

"The ultimate goal is to break the cycle of poverty by moving children out of factories into schools," says Terry Collingsworth, general counsel for the International Labor Rights Fund in Washington, D.C., who spent a number of years in Nepal working on labor conditions issues.

Jhalak's story is typical: An orphan from an early age, he worked on his uncle's small farm, taking the family cow every day to the jungle. One day, a family friend came and offered to take him away from village life, saying that in Kathmandu, Jhalak could go to school while working at his home. Once in the city, the man broke his promise and sold Jhalak to a carpet master, who forced him to learn how to knot wool rugs on heavy wooden looms. Workdays started at 4 a.m. and went on until 11 at night; the earthen floor of the factory was Jhalak's bed. When the owner had a rush order, Jhalak and

Suzanne Charlé, "Children of the Looms: Rescuing the 'Carpet Kids' of Nepal, India, and Pakistan," *Ford Foundation Report* 32, no. 2 (Spring 2001): 21–25.

the other boys would have to work through the entire night. The owner was so strict that he even complained when Jhalak had to relieve himself. (That part wasn't in the play—Jhalak says it wouldn't have been polite.) He never saw any money. He never had a chance to play except when electricity failed.

A year ago in April, a RUGMARK inspector entered the factory—the exporter who contracted for the carpets had just joined the program. The other boys followed the loom master's orders to run and hide. But Jhalak stood his ground, and after the inspector explained the employment laws and offered him a chance to live at the RUGMARK rehabilitation center, the boy gladly accepted.

Jhalak is one of more than 1,700 children rescued from the looms in India and Nepal since 1995; more than 1,200 are studying in RUGMARK schools and rehabilitation centers.

During the same period, RUGMARK has signed up 130 Nepalese carpet exporters, who manufacture about 65 percent of the nation's rugs in 412 factories. In India, the program licenses 226 exporters, who sell rugs from 28,000 looms—over 15 percent of all those registered by the government. These exporters have shipped more than 2.1 million rugs bearing the RUGMARK label to Europe and the United States. The fees paid by licensed exporters—.25 percent of the cost of the rugs—go for inspections; importers who join the program contribute 1.75 percent, which supports schools and staff. (The India program, which was originally backed by UNESCO and the German Development Agency, is now self-sufficient; Nepal still receives funds from those agencies and the Asian-American Free Labor Institute.)

The program is an integral part of a larger public campaign to stop child labor. An editorial in The Kathmandu Post observed that: "Although legal remedies remain a valid and continuing concern, there is a call for more practical supplemental approaches to protect working children. . . . Nepal RUGMARK Foundation . . . is doing some commendable work. The novelty of the programme rests on its ability to work with the carpet industries through a child labour free carpet certification system, which has already helped to restore childhood to hundreds of carpet children." The writer and others point out that while the numbers of children found in some industries, such as brick making, has in-

creased or remained constant, the number of children in Nepal's carpet industry has dropped from 11 percent of the work force to less than 2 percent.

Indian child-labor activists and members of the carpet industry in India and Germany launched the RUGMARK program in 1995. "There are laws on the books in India banning children from working in the carpet industry. The Indian Constitution prohibits work by children under 14 years old," notes Pharis Harvey, executive director of the International Labor Rights Fund and a member of the RUGMARK U.S.A. board. There are similar laws in Nepal and Pakistan. "Enforcement is a whole other thing."

India's export of hand-knotted carpets grew from $65 million in 1979 to $229 million in 1983; an estimated 100,000 children were working on almost as many looms dotted across India's "carpet belt," a 100,000-square-mile swath stretching northwest from the holy city of Varanasi in northern India. In 1985 a documentary about the child-labor situation spurred angry criticism in Europe. A consumer awareness campaign in 1990 sent demand for the hand-knotted carpets plummeting, and by 1993 India's exports had dropped to $152 million. The same year, it was estimated that 300,000 children were working on the looms in India.

In the United States, Senator Tom Harkin sponsored the Pease-Harkin bill, starting in the mid-1990's. Had it passed, it would have banned all goods produced with child labor. (In 2000 Harkin, now a board member of RUGMARK U.S.A., had more luck in pushing through an amendment to the Trade and Development Act requiring all countries receiving trade benefits under the Generalized System of Preferences to ratify and implement Convention 182, which seeks to eliminate the worst forms of child labor. U.S. customs has yet to confiscate any carpet imports, however, explaining that the burden of proof of indentured and forced child labor lies elsewhere.)

In India, a group of carpet manufacturers and exporters—nervous about the bill in the United States and a possible consumer boycott in Europe—turned to Kailish Satyarthi, leader of the South Asian Coalition on Child Servitude (SACCS), an umbrella group of NGO's working to end child labor. After a number of false starts, RUGMARK was established. The first years were difficult. In some villages, bands of loom owners physically attacked inspectors. And the number of child workers found far exceeded the available space in RUGMARK-sponsored schools. Taken off the looms, many ended up in the streets, easy prey for drug and prostitution gangs. "It was like a flood," says Rashid Raza, RUGMARK India coordinator based in Gopiganj. Today, he says, that problem has been solved, thanks to better compliance by licensees' subcontractors, the rehabilitation center in Gopiganj and four other RUGMARK schools in the carpet belt—one of which was built with funds from Nasser Rahmanan, a U.S. importer and RUGMARK board member.

In Nepal's Kathmandu Valley, the brightly colored prayer flags that ripple in the wind above simple brick buildings hint at the history and pedigree of its carpet industry, which started four decades ago when tens of thousands of Tibetans fled their homeland in 1959 after an invasion by Chinese troops. Many refugees who settled in Kathmandu had left everything behind save one talent: the age-old technique of hand-knotting rugs used for prayer and covering doors and windows. In an effort to help the Tibetans earn a living in a strange land, the Swiss Association for Technical Assistance, working with the Nepalese government, gave seed money for looms and the raw material for carpets.

"The designs in the beginning were typical Tibetan, and the small rugs were sold as artifacts in the local market," explains Saroj Rai, executive director of RUGMARK Nepal. "The first commercial export of the 'Tibetan' carpets from Nepal went to Switzerland in 1964. Soon, European carpet traders recognized the possibilities of bringing their own designs and having the carpets made in Nepal. In the 1980's, the annual growth rate was as high as 45 percent, and by early 1990, carpets became the number one export item for Nepal."

Today, there are about 1,000 carpet factories in Nepal, 800 of which export $135-million worth of hand-knotted carpets to Europe and the United States. Virtually all of the factories are located in the Kathmandu Valley, an area roughly the size of London or San Francisco. Fifty thousand work as weavers, another 100,000 are employed in carding, spinning, dyeing, washing, transport and other rug-related tasks. Generally, children are found on the looms because the skills are relatively easy

to learn, but some are said to participate in almost every stage of carpet making.

Most of the child laborers come from the rocky recesses of the Himalayas or the crowded, fertile fields of the Terai, where poor farms cannot support the growing population. Some youngsters find their own way to the factories, lured by dreams of new clothes, two meals a day, a chance to watch TV. Most, however, are forced into the industry by adults. Some work beside parents in the factories; others are brought in by loom masters who comb the countryside looking for fresh recruits, making deals with greedy relatives, even indebted parents.

Such practices appalled Sulochana Shrasta Shah, a mathematician who started Formation Carpets after a change in university administration sidetracked her career as an academic. "When I first started, I wasn't directly aware of child labor. I remember walking around the factory, seeing the faces, sending children back home." But soon enough she understood what was going on: To fill all the seats at the looms, the loom master with whom the factory owner contracts often recruits family members. In some cases, children show up with parents who have no other resources for them during the work day. "How would people allow their children to sit on the loom?" Shrasta Shah would ask. "Then I realized: The parents simply are not in a position to bring up their children!"

Shrasta Shah opened a school and a day-care center at her factory and established strict rules—be neat in your appearance and at the loom, be on time, put your children in the school—and in the mid-1990's, along with some other socially responsible factory owners, she helped build support for RUGMARK Nepal. The response was dramatic: Faced with loss of business from Germany, factory owners representing about 65 percent of all of Nepal's exports signed up to become licensees. Shrasta Shah's importers in Germany and the United States supported her efforts.

"Manufacturers in Nepal realized they would lose all their business if they could not assure the consumer that their carpets were child-labor free," she says. RUGMARK Nepal essentially allowed the industry to offer something that competing industries in other countries could not. "It is a competitive advantage."

Aware of India's early problems, RUGMARK Nepal found NGO's with experience in education to set up two rehabilitation centers and three schools. In 2000, RUGMARK Nepal's four inspectors made some 14,000 unscheduled visits to licensees' factories and subcontractors. Riding his motorcycle, Kedar Khatiwada can make as many as 16 inspections in a day. Some factories are models of virtue; children are never found on the looms, only in factory-sponsored schools. Others are more problematic, and these are visited more often. As a back up, NGO's are asked to make random checks of licensed factories; the news media and the public are also encouraged to report any children seen on RUGMARK looms. Even the police have been known to give tip-offs.

Factory owners get the message. "No children work on the looms here," says the owner of a 16-loom operation who recently joined at the request of a foreign client. "There are too many inspections."

The first time a child is found on a loom, the licensee is given a warning. The second time, he must appear before the RUGMARK officials at the office and discuss the situation. A third offense means that the license is pulled. So far, two have been revoked.

Compared with RUGMARK Nepal licensees—even unenthusiastic ones—unlicensed factories can be jarring. A recent visitor to one found eight looms crowded into a low-ceilinged room lit by a single bulb hanging from a frayed wire. Clouds of wool fuzz drifted in the dusty air. Though the temperature outside was just above freezing, there was no heat. A woman in her early twenties sat at a two-person loom, one child at her breast, another crawling on her lap, a third darting in and out of the dank room like a barn swallow, screaming and yelling with a brigade of children who ran barefoot through piles of debris and stagnant puddles of dye-colored water.

The woman explained that she started working on the looms when she was 10. Her parents came from the Terai district and did not have enough land to support the family. She had never gone to school but hopes to send her children—if she can manage to pull together enough money. "There are three children, and only one husband," she said simply. "If I have enough money, I want to send them to school. If not, I will put them to work."

Such deep poverty is a constant threat to the RUGMARK system, according to Narayan Bhattarai, head of licensing and inspections. Not only do parents put their children to work; some, he says, are so desperate and they find the program so attractive that they actually place the child on the loom so that he or she will be found by the inspectors and taken to the rehabilitation center.

"It's a critical balance of helping the children but not sending a counterproductive message to the community," Saroj Rai added.

To this end, RUGMARK has been focusing on community-based rehabilitation. When possible, children are returned to their families and, if necessary, given stipends for schooling, rather than moving them into the RUGMARK boarding schools. Pavita Lama, a 14-year-old girl found working on a loom by Kedar Khatiwada, is now enrolled at a local school near the single room she shares with a younger brother and her parents, both of whom work in a nearby carpet factory. When Khatiwada made a surprise visit recently, Pavita took a break from studying for exams to thank him for RUGMARK's financial support that pays for her books, school fees and uniforms. She hopes one day to become a teacher, she said, or perhaps a doctor.

To date, 235 children in Nepal have been reunited with their families, and 95 are receiving financial support and counseling from RUGMARK.

Photos of young Indians and Nepalese like Pavita, former workers now free to go to school and to pursue careers, hang among the brilliantly colored rugs designed by Stephanie Odegard in an elegant showroom on New York's Madison Avenue. Initially, Odegard, whose carpets appear on the pages of Architectural Digest and in the homes of entrepreneurs like Bill Gates, was skeptical of RUGMARK, considering it "simply a response to the Harkin bill."

The former World Bank marketing consultant changed her mind when Pharis Harvey convinced her to visit the RUGMARK schools in Nepal, where her company's carpets are woven. "It was so obvious. By supporting RUGMARK, I could make a significant difference, a contribution to stopping child labor."

Putting a full stop to child labor is a distant dream. Despite the progress on the production side in both India and Nepal, only 10 importers in the United States have joined. That means that about 9 percent of the carpets coming into the United States in 2000 from Nepal bore the RUGMARK label—about 10,000 carpets worth $6 million. About 1 percent of all carpets shipped from India are so labeled.

"The exporter can't put the label on until the importer also signs on," explains Nina Smith, director of RUGMARK U.S.A., based in Washington, D.C. This meant that many of the rugs that were made by licensees did not have labels and that much needed funds for schools and rehabilitation were not forthcoming. Smith, Odegard and other members of the RUGMARK U.S.A. board are trying to drum up interest within the retail community, courting big firms like Dayton Hudson and Federated Department Stores.

"Often, large importers say that they have their own internal audits," Smith says. But only RUGMARK has a corps of independent inspectors. "Without RUGMARK, U.S. retailers can't know day to day that there are no child laborers on the looms. Consumers want independent verification."

Meanwhile, increased competition, currency devaluations and dwindling demand are driving the average price of carpets down. In Nepal, the average is about $40 per square meter, less than half the price five years ago. Wages for carpet workers have remained constant over the last five years, while the cost of living has doubled or even tripled. As Saroj Rai comments, "That leaves the workers poorer, and the children more vulnerable."

Jeffrey Ballinger, an international labor specialist at Harvard's Kennedy School, says that labeling initiatives like RUGMARK's can be effective in reducing child labor when combined with a good monitoring system and school program. "You may never get everyone on board," he says. "But look at Germany." Last year, 21 percent of the rugs imported to Germany from India (worth $105 million) bore the RUGMARK label. "If you can achieve that in the United States, you'll be making a significant impact." He cautions, however, that changes in labor practices in developing nations occur at a glacial pace.

In Nepal, Saroj Rai and his associates are used to glaciers. "We need to bring that remaining 35 percent into the system," says Bhattarai, referring to the manufacturers who have yet to sign up. He and his inspectors frequently make courtesy visits to the remaining holdouts, armed with pamphlets describing the program and the schools it supports. "Once all the factories are with RUGMARK, there is no chance that a child can run away from a RUGMARK factory to an unlicensed factory. . . . One thing is for sure: If we stop inspecting, the children will show up on the looms again."

4.6

Independent Monitoring in Guatemala: What Can Civil Society Contribute?

Homero Fuentes and Dennis Smith

Who Are We?

In 1997, a group of professionals, leaders in Guatemala's civil society, formed the Commission for the Verification of Codes of Conduct (COVERCO). COVERCO is a pioneering effort in the independent monitoring of working conditions in Guatemala's garment factories and on farms producing goods for export.

COVERCO includes professionals from a range of disciplines: law, medicine, sociology, communication, business administration, education and pastoral theology. In practice, this means we can call on in-house experts to audit a factory's books, interpret local law and international conventions, and sense the complexities of human relationships on the factory floor.

COVERCO, a registered, not-for-profit nongovernmental organisation (NGO), is independent of all national and multinational corporations, unions and governments. Because it is independent, COVERCO has the confidence of all relevant parties: management, workers, NGOs, community and advocacy groups,

unions and governments. In practice, its independence is demonstrated by the fact that it owns the information it gathers and the studies it produces.

What Do We Do?

In its monitoring activities, COVERCO performs a social audit. We capture the flavour of labour relations on the factory floor (for example, checking if there is a grievance procedure and how well it works); execute a thorough review of payroll and employee records (checking, for example, if overtime, employee benefits and production bonuses are paid according to the law); and document working conditions (checking the use of industrial chemicals, the conditions of sanitary facilities, etc.).

Before COVERCO carries out a social audit, it negotiates with the corporation access to workers both on and off the job as well as access to payroll records and worker files. We also negotiate when and how the findings of our social audit will be made public. Sources and partial results of ongoing studies are held in the strictest confidence. When we negotiate a monitoring programme with a corporation we understand that the corporation has the right to protect proprietary information. Otherwise, it certainly won't grant us access to factory records.

Homero Fuentes and Dennis Smith, excerpt from "Independent Monitoring in Guatemala: What Can Civil Society Contribute?" in *Visions of Ethical Sourcing*, ed. Raj Thamotheram (London: Financial Times Prentice Hall for Shared View Social Responsibility Ltd., with financial support from Société Générale de Surveillance [SGS], 2000), 36–42; available from Shared View at info@sharedview.net.

What Don't We Do?

COVERCO is not a substitute for unions, management or joint union-management endeavors, nor for governmental or advocacy groups. We believe in the right of workers to organise and, in practice, this means we do not serve as agents for workers, even when they have legitimate, documented complaints. But we do explain to inquiring workers how to contact a local legal aid office. Whether or not a formal complaint is lodged depends on the worker's initiative.

Nor do we serve as consultants to management. When management asks that we use our credibility to communicate a new policy to workers, we decline. But we do tell them where they can go for help. And we certainly will not be used by management to sniff out signs of union activity.

Although we have been approached by corporations that work in other countries in the region, COVERCO has decided to operate only in Guatemala. At the same time, we maintain regular communication with other independent monitoring groups in the region, sharing models and methodologies.

Furthermore, COVERCO has no power to enforce a Code of Conduct. That is not our task. Our job is to document as accurately as possible the real situation on the ground, note areas where compliance is a problem, and make that information public. Thus, consumers have access to reliable information and the different actors in the global economy (corporations, unions, advocacy groups, governments and global organisations such as the World Bank and the World Trade Organisation) are encouraged to move beyond posturing to concrete actions. We seek to contribute to the creation of a culture of compliance.

Finally, so far, labour unions have not played a role in our social audits. The reason is simple: Guatemala has no unionised garment factories. We look forward to the day when we have to factor a union presence into our negotiations. Only then will we be able to demonstrate that our methodology is both fully independent and non-substitutive.

Why Do We Work Like This?

You need to understand what we are trying to create and the situation in which we live. We believe it should be possible to set up a political and economic system that works in the best interests of most people most of the time. This is the hope that keeps us going in Guatemala.

But as we look around us, what we see is a culture of oligarchy, which is built into the very framework of Guatemalan society. This world view is far more than just a way of doing business. Rather, we are talking of families and social groups that consider themselves destined to be the legitimate owners of the country. For these local oligarchies, state institutions (and even political parties) are designed to respond to their interests, not the interests of the majority.

Ours is also a deeply polarised society. We have divisions born of economic inequality and almost 40 years of civil war, which has generated a culture of violence exacerbated by bitter ideological divisions. Institutionalised violence and endemic corruption make it difficult to cultivate and strengthen civil society. And thus impunity reigns. The absence of the rule of law means that those with economic, political and military power are sheltered from being held accountable for their actions.

So local businesses, as well as their multinational partners, operate in this conflictive atmosphere.

[. . .]

Who should monitor compliance with the codes of conduct? Many businesses use internal monitoring systems, implemented either by internal staff or major accounting firms. Such efforts have been received by some consumer groups with cynicism, which in our view is often justified. This is where COVERCO comes on the scene. We are part of a new generation of truly independent external monitors who see ourselves as one amongst many civil society initiatives trying to build a better world.

[. . .]

What Do We Expect from the Corporate Sector?

Our expectation of multinational corporations and local suppliers is simple: compliance with national and international law. Codes of conduct make little sense if not seen as simplified, accessible expressions of pertinent national and international law. We express this as a simple formula . . .:

Corporate responsibility = Pertinent national law + Pertinent international conventions + Code of conduct

The highest applicable standard must always prevail.

[. . .]

How Does This Work in Practice?

In 1999, after more than a year of negotiations with Liz Claiborne, Inc. (LCI), COVERCO began a pilot study to monitor working conditions at an LCI supplier factory near Guatemala City.

LCI agreed that COVERCO would have uninhibited access to the factory, would be able to set up occasional meetings with factory management, and would have full access to factory records. COVERCO agreed to supply LCI with regular updates on the situation at the factory, highlighting cases of non-compliance with LCI's code, which it calls its *Standards of Engagement*. In addition, COVERCO promised to present periodic public reports summarising its findings. COVERCO also agreed not to divulge the name of the supplier factory. In return, LCI agreed to maintain fluid communication with COVERCO and with management of the local factory, and to take appropriate measures to ensure compliance with their Standards.

COVERCO affirms that, during this pilot study, it has enjoyed regular, cordial and business-like meetings with representatives of LCI. Here are two examples of this.

1. As the pilot project got underway, we discovered that neither workers nor management at the local factory were familiar with LCI's Standards of Engagement. LCI has implemented training workshops for both workers and management since the programme began. In light of the high turnover rate at the factory, we have recommended that such training become a regular event. Furthermore, since most workers have not completed their pri-

mary education, we recommended that LCI prepare an illustrated pamphlet describing the Standards in clear, simple Spanish. We put LCI in contact with a local graphic design team who prepared a comic book version that has recently been distributed to workers.

The 'Code Comix' outlines the LCI Standards point by point, assuring workers that they have the right to free association and proper remuneration, as well as freedom from abusive treatment or the obligation to work in dangerous circumstances. The Comix also insists that workers are expected to be honest and punctual, must not use drugs or alcohol on the job, and must not damage their tools.

We have recommended that this booklet be distributed to all current and future employees and that line supervisors take time to answer any questions that might arise.

2. One morning, 'Mrs. López', a pregnant factory worker, was found to be in a serious condition. She advised her line supervisor that she was in pain. The line supervisor advised her to sit at her workstation and rest. Mrs. López's pain got progressively worse. When she and her line supervisor requested permission to leave, management did not allow it immediately. She did finally get medical attention, but it took five hours from the time she first complained to her supervisor. The child she was carrying was stillborn early the next morning.

    COVERCO began to investigate this incident about 24 hours after the stillbirth. We conducted taped interviews with senior management, with the line supervisor, with the superior who refused permission to seek medical treatment, with fellow workers on the line, and with Mrs. López and her family. We asked to see her personnel file and there discovered a note from a private physician describing the high-risk nature of the pregnancy. (Mrs. López had gone to this doctor seeking a second opinion after the local social security clinic had refused to recommend that she be put on emergency medical leave.) We noted the glaring lack of preparedness for dealing with emergency situations and submitted regular updates to LCI as events unfolded.

After the incident, factory management agreed to send a letter to all workers setting out new emergency and grievance procedures. This did not happen. However, information about procedures in case of medical emergencies has been posted in visible places throughout the factory.

Factory management also offered to install an infirmary and staff it with a trained nurse. A rudimentary infirmary has been set up staffed by a full-time nurse's aide. The manager who refused permission to Mrs. López to seek immediate medical attention resigned from the factory. Mrs. López completed her medical leave and has now returned to work at the factory.

4.7

Can Advocacy-Led Certification Systems Transform Global Corporate Practices?

Michael E. Conroy

Seemingly Improbable Recent Events

Who would have guessed that Greenpeace, the Natural Resources Defense Council, and other environmental groups would share the podium in June 1998 with the top executives of MacMillan Bloedel, the giant Vancouver-based timber and paper company, and would encourage consumers to give preference to "MacBlo" products? The environmental groups had long pilloried MacMillan Bloedel for its clear-cutting forest practices in Clayoquot Sound on Vancouver Island and elsewhere on the British Columbia coast. On that day, however, MacMillan Bloedel announced that it would cease clear-cutting practices in its British Columbia logging operations and that it would seek broader certification of its forest management under the principles of the Forest Stewardship Council. Commenting on this announcement, Lester Brown noted:

Under the leadership of a new chief executive, Tom Stevens, the company affirmed that clear-cutting will be replaced by selective cutting, leaving trees to check runoff and soil erosion,

Michael E. Conroy, excerpt from "Can Advocacy-Led Certification Systems Transform Global Corporate Practices?" online working paper of the Political Economy Research Institute, University of Massachusetts (Amherst, Mass., 2001), 5–15 and 26–27, www.umass.edu/peri.

to provide wildlife habitat, and to help regenerate the forest. In doing so, it acknowledged the growing reach of the environmental movement. MacMillan Bloedel was not only being pressured by local groups, but it also had been the primary target of a Greenpeace campaign to ban clear-cutting everywhere. . . .

Among giant corporations that could once be counted on to mount a monolithic opposition to serious environmental reform, a growing number of high profile CEOs have begun to sound more like spokespersons for Greenpeace than for the bastions of global capitalism of which they are a part. . . . What in the world is going on?[5]

The Greenpeace campaign had focused on a relatively novel "markets campaign" strategy: to lobby and demonstrate against the purchasers of MacMillan Bloedel forest products, pressuring them to cancel or threaten to cancel orders unless the firm implemented improved environmental practices.

A second seemingly improbable event occurred on October 8, 1999, when the Rainforest Action Network (RAN) published a full-page paid advertisement in *The New York Times* urging consumers to shop at Home Depot, Inc. The ad was unlikely for many reasons. RAN had campaigned actively against Home Depot for more than two years, orchestrating more than 700 demonstrations against the company's purchasing policies. RAN had organized activists dressed in bear costumes and using mega-phones in the rafters of Home Depot stores; it had draped the Home Depot headquarters building with 5-story banners, and it had filled billboards across the street from shareholder meetings with images of forest clear-cutting allegedly linked to Home Depot's wood purchases. RAN also was alleged to have been behind other, less traditional means of placing pressure on the firm, including a somewhat scurrilous website. The paid advertisement in the *Times* resulted from a decision by Home Depot, announced on August 26, 1999, to end all purchases of wood products coming from "old growth" forests and to give preference in its purchases to products certified as arising from sustainable forest practices, such as under the standards of the Forest Stewardship Council.

A third event of this sort occurred on April 13th, 2000, when Global Exchange, a social activist organization in Oakland, California, turned threatened demonstrations against the Starbucks coffee chain in 30 U.S. cities into demonstrations in praise of its coffee purchasing practices. Starbucks is the largest chain of coffee houses in the U.S., accounting for more than 20 percent of the total. Global Exchange had spent more than a year orchestrating a campaign against Starbucks, because the firm refused to introduce the sale of certified coffee that would provide higher prices and better conditions for small-scale coffee producers worldwide. This effort was part of a much longer, multi-year strategy to improve the benefits from trade for producers in the global South through various mechanisms including a certified "fair trade" system. Four days before the planned demonstrations, Starbucks executives signed a letter of intent with TransFair USA, a fair-trade certification organization, to offer certified coffee in all 2700 Starbucks outlets in the U.S. On October 4th, 2000, certified fair trade coffee began to be sold at Starbucks.[9]

Basic Concepts

What are the certification systems that have triggered these improbable events? Definitions in the literature vary. According to the International Standards Organization:

Certification is a procedure by which a third party gives written assurance that a product, process or service conforms to specified requirements.... It is distinct from the other systems of proof of conformity such as supplier declarations, laboratory test reports or inspection body reports. Certification is based on the results of tests, inspections and audits and gives confidence to the customer on account of the systematic intervention of a competent third body.[10]

According to the World Bank:

Product certification involves written documentation that a product meets detailed technical specifications. Governments and consumers are increasingly demanding such certifications of goods in international commerce. Certification involves testing a product against either a voluntary, de facto, or regulatory standard and is often carried out [by] organizations that are independent of any link to the manufacturer or purchaser. After testing, a certificate is issued that attests to the fact that a product meets a set standard.[11]

As applied to forest management, Upton and Bass have defined certification as "an economic market-based instrument which aims to raise awareness and provide incentives for both producers and consumers towards a more responsible use of forests."[12]

Certification as analyzed here is a market-driven process designed to encourage and reward firms that choose to produce or trade in products that use the highest social and environmental standards in their production. Rather than requiring those standards by law (which is often politically difficult to achieve), and rather than trying to block the importation of products that do not meet the standards (which is not allowed under WTO rules), certification offers a positive alternative system designed to encourage compliance with voluntary standards and to reward those who do comply by offering increased market share and, at times, market price premiums.

In theory, certification requires little more than an independent assessment of management practices. In reality, the creation of a credible certification system requires the development of standards by a diverse set of stakeholders in an inclusive process designed to build consensus. Without an agreed-upon set of standards, the meanings of certification would vary widely.

There is a need, therefore, to establish a set of certifiers who are independent of the outcome of the certification process, as well as an accreditation system for the certifiers that assures the integrity of their application of the standards.

The Forest Stewardship Council

The Forest Stewardship Council (FSC), a nonprofit organization created by an international assembly of about 300 people in Toronto in 1993, has created a certification system whose aim is to transform the $50 billion worldwide timber industry. The FSC opened its offices in 1994 in Oaxaca, Mexico, partly because it wanted to be based in the global South, and partly because of the personal preferences of its first Executive Director. From that original base, the FSC has grown to have operations in 50 countries; and its international headquarters will be moved to Europe in 2002.

The governance of the FSC is structured around three "chambers": an environmental chamber, an economic chamber, and a social chamber. Each chamber represents a group that has a vested interest in—or are stakeholders in—the management of forests around the world. In addition, the FSC structures all of its international activities to include balanced representation from the global North and the global South. When people run for election to the FSC board of directors, for example, they run for a position in the "social chamber from the global north," or for the "economic chamber from the global south."

How does it work? The Forest Stewardship Council has developed a stakeholder-based set of forest management standards, with ample participation of all three chambers, including timber and paper industry representatives, social and environmental nongovernmental organizations (NGOs), and local community representatives. The FSC does not undertake the certification itself; rather it accredits other organizations or firms to perform the certification. It assesses candidates to make certain that they have the capability and knowledge of the field to analyze the forest management practices of applicant timber companies. It monitors the certifiers, resolves any disputes that may arise in the application of the standards, and protects the integrity of the label that it creates. The certifiers themselves determine the eligibility of firms and other forest owners to receive certification, issue the FSC certificates, and then monitor compliance annually to assure continued eligibility.

There are two types of certificates issued by the FSC. The first is a "forest management certificate" based upon how the forest is managed; the second is a "chain-of-custody" certificate that tracks the wood from the forest to the consumer. To obtain chain-of-custody certification, a mill that is going to process certified wood is required to establish a system for keeping the certified wood separate from the non-certified wood. Only forest products derived from wood from certified forests, and processed in a certified chain-of-custody mill or factory, qualify to carry the FSC logo. . . .

The broad principles embodied in FSC standards for sustainable forest management embrace social as well as environmental characteristics. . . . Detailed dimensions of each of these standards have been developed for worldwide application, and localized standards are being created for most of the countries (and for sub-regions within countries) where FSC is operating. The social standards are intended to secure and protect long-term tenure and use rights and the rights of indigenous peoples. The ecological standards specifically call for the conservation of old-growth or primary forests and other high-priority conservation areas, a documented reduction in the use of chemicals such as herbicides, and a prohibition on the use of invasive or exotic species (including some genetically-modified species) in tree plantations. FSC standards also call for the reduction of clearcutting, and require the protection of the interests of local communities and forest-industry workers. They allow for the certification of plantations so long as they comply with the other standards. . . .

FSC Success

Since 1995, when FSC began certifying its first forests, the number of acres of forest certified around the world has grown to 60 million (as of mid-2001). To put this in context, there are approximately 1.1 billion acres (450 million hectares) of working forests worldwide. That suggests that the management of more than 5 percent of the world's working forests is now certified under the FSC standards. Similarly, more than 1700 firms were certified for chain-of-custody as of mid-2001. . . .

Success as measured by demand is even greater. The demand for FSC products has been growing far faster than supply. Price premia are being paid for certified products, although this fact rarely is acknowledged publicly. Price premia of 4% to 12% on softwoods in European markets are admitted by one of the largest European certified forest products firms. Premia of 100% on certified teak have been paid to Malaysian exporters. One of Canada's largest forest products manufacturers has offered a 30 percent premium on FSC-certified timber delivered to its mills, even though its own forest lands are not yet certified. Documenting these market characteristics is difficult because it is in the interest of neither buyer nor seller to publicize the information. Buyers would prefer that sellers not expect a premium. Sellers receiving a premium have no interest in stimulating increases in supply by others, lest they lose their premium prices.

The demand is not driven directly by consumers of forest products who seek certified wood products in stores. It is driven, in fact, by the commitments of major producers of forest products and by major retailers of forest products in response to their own internal culture of social and environmental responsibility, a culture that is strongly encouraged by the pressure brought to bear by the advocacy networks' market campaigns. One indicator of these corporate commitments is the surging membership in the Global Forest and Trade Network (GFTN) and its U.S. member, the Certified Forest Products Council. More than 700 companies have now joined the GFTN, thereby formally expressing a preference for forest products certified under the FSC standards. The members include all five of the largest Do-it-Yourself retail chains in the United States, as well as major forest product manufacturers such as Andersen Windows. The network also includes forest product business consumers such as Nike (for paper and cardboard), The Gap (for flooring and shelving), and Kinko's (the largest photocopying chain in the U.S.).

The FSC also has major opponents. They are clustered in three rival forest management certification schemes in the global North. The first is an industry-created set of standards fashioned by the American Forest and Paper Association, the principal industry association of timber and paper companies in the United States. Its program, the Sustainable Forestry Initiative (SFI),[14] claims to encompass 94 million acres of forests in the United States and Canada. In Europe, where most large forests are now certified under FSC, small-scale forest owners have set up a Pan-European Forest Certification system (PEFC) which in less than a year claims to have certified compliance with its standards on more than 36 million hectares (79 million acres).[15] Finally, a smaller rival certification scheme for forests is the Canadian Standards Association (CSA), a general purpose standard-setting organization with standards for more than 2000 products.[16] The most complete comparative evaluation of the four systems to date reaches unambiguous conclusions. Using such criteria as transparency, stakeholder participation, and assessment procedures, the study concludes that:

> [T]he Forest Stewardship Council is currently the only independent and credible certification scheme in the [forest products] market. . . . This does not mean that the FSC scheme is perfect. Continued vigilance is required to ensure that its implementation lives up to its commitments.[17]

The report's toughest criticism focuses on the PEFC scheme, where it was found that substantial tracts of land were certified as fulfilling PEFC requirements without ever being visited, and numerous tracts were included in the PEFC statistics without the landowner's knowledge or consent.

A further comparison of FSC and SFI has been published by the National Wildlife Federation, the Natural Resources Council of Maine, and Environmental Advocates.[18] It too found the following systemic differences:

- FSC sets more stringent guidelines in many areas of environmental protection, such as maintenance of older forest and reserve areas, use of chemicals, exotic and genetically modified species, and conversion of natural forest to plantations. These guidelines promote ecologically sound forest management.
- FSC is based on mandatory standards, and a required and consistently applied third-party audit; SFI is not.

- Most FSC standards emphasize on-the-ground field performance, while few SFI standards evaluate on-the-ground results.
- FSC requires public reporting of audit results and enforceable conditions; SFI does not.
- FSC has social criteria focusing on local communities and indigenous peoples; SFI does not.
- FSC has Chain-of-Custody Certification and a product labeling system that allows processors, retailers and consumers to confidently know that their wood comes from a well-managed forest; SFI does not.

The battle will continue for the hearts and minds of consumers and retailers. The advantage rests with the FSC, however, precisely because of the strong support that it receives from social and environmental NGOs.

Transfair USA and Fairtrade Labeling Organizations International

A significantly different form of social certification is offered by the Fairtrade Labeling Organizations International (FLO) and its U.S. affiliate, Transfair USA. The FLO was born of the Max Haavelar Foundation in the Netherlands and Transfair International in Germany, two groups that separately had begun to define criteria for fair trade and to label products that met those criteria. They joined into a common organization in 1998. The standards for certified fair trade coffee are quite simple. . . . This certification system deliberately seeks to focus on improving the market conditions faced by the 50% of coffee producers who are small-scale family farmers, many of them organized in cooperatives. Approximately 80–85% of the world's coffee farmers fall into this category.[19] . . .

Fair Trade Certified coffee standards require buyers to pay a fixed minimum price for coffee that was negotiated with small-scale producers in the 1990s. In mid-2001, that price was nearly twice the prevailing spot market price in a very depressed coffee market, but still less than 15 percent of the prevailing market prices for specialty coffee in Northern markets. . . . Buyers of certified fair trade coffee must make available partial payment to the farmers at the time their coffee is shipped, when requested. This differs from the usual industry practice in which producers ship their coffee to brokers and are paid only if and when that coffee is eventually sold. The resulting delays in payments often force small-scale coffee farmers to fall back upon usurious credit systems, since they must cover all the costs of harvesting and processing the coffee months before they are paid by the brokers. Finally, certified fair trade encourages longer-term contractual relationships, discouraging one-time purchases on the spot market. . . .

Sales of Fair Trade Certified coffee in the United States have gone from virtually nothing in 1998 to an estimated 7 million pounds in 2001; global sales of the entire FLO network are expected to exceed 30 million pounds in 2001. There are now more than 100 coffee companies selling Fair Trade Certified coffee in the United States, including the pioneer companies (Equal Exchange, Peace Coffee, and Cooperative Coffees), café chains such as Starbuck's, Peet's, and Tully's, food chains such as Whole Foods, Wild Oats, Andronico's, ShopRite, Stop N Shop and some Safeway stores, and even most Exxon-Mobil convenience stores in New England.

The direct impact of this upon the coffee farmers is significant, especially in times of very low spot market prices for coffee. With the current $0.60/pound difference between the spot price in mid-2001 and the minimum price paid for Fair Trade Certified coffee, sales of this level imply annual net gains for farmers of more than $18 million dollars per year for participating in fair trade certification. But demand in this case remains well below supply. There are more than 400,000 farmers listed on the Fair Trade worldwide coffee producer registry; and they produce an estimated 170 million pounds each year.[20] After growth in sales in Europe began to stagnate in the mid-1990s, growth in the U.S. markets has led the world. And the growth of sales in the U.S. has been driven, more than anywhere else, by NGO advocacy to convince companies to offer certified coffee to their customers.

[. . .]

Conclusions

Citizen-led advocacy campaigns linked to the establishment of certification systems represent a new movement that is only now gaining major strength. The ability of advocacy groups to bring market pressures to bear upon firms offers a powerful alternative to simple invocations of corporate altruism and civic responsibility. In an increasingly privatized world, with restrictions on what the global trading system will allow local and national governments to legislate, these movements may be the *only* alternative to the competitive downgrading of social and environmental practices by firms worldwide.

There is evidence that financial markets are paying increasing attention to these dimensions of corporate practice, rewarding firms that become leaders, and punishing those that lag behind. The incentives for corporate collaboration in the creation and management of certification systems appear to be growing. Struggles between NGOs and corporations can be expected to continue, for many of the same reasons that firms also struggle against government regulations. In the 21st century, this dynamic new strategy for corporate engagement may become an important global force for "civilizing globalization," and for assuring that its environmental and social benefits exceed its costs.

Notes

This paper is based upon a talk delivered to the Political Economy Workshop at the University of Massachusetts, Amherst, on October 3, 2000. It has benefited greatly from the comments offered at that workshop. The opinions in the paper are those of the author alone; they do not necessarily reflect in any way the perspectives of the Ford Foundation.

[. . .]

5. Lester R. Brown, "Crossing the threshold," *World Watch*, March/April 1999.

[. . .]

9. Documentation of this market campaign may be found on the Global Exchange website, http://www.globalexchange.org/economy/coffee. Starbucks corporate analysis of certified fair trade coffee can be found at www.starbucks.com/aboutus/fairtrade.asp.

10. Source: http://www.wssn.net/WSSN/gen_inf.htm#ca

11. http://www.worldbank.org/wbiep/trade/Standards.html#Product_standards

12. Christopher Upton, and Stephen Bass, 1995, *The Forest Certification Handbook*. (London: Earthscan Publications, Ltd.) 42.

[. . .]

14. http://www.afandpa.org/forestry/sfi/menu.html

15. http://www.pefc.org

16. http://www.cssinfo.com/info/csa.html

17. Fern, *Behind the Logo: An environmental and social assessment of forest certification schemes*, (May 2001). The conclusions of the Fern report have been endorsed by a coalition of more than 70 social and environmental advocacy groups worldwide. The report in full and the coalition endorsements are available at http://www.fern.org.

18. National Wildlife Federation, Natural Resources Council of Maine, and Environmental Advocates, "A Comparison of the American Forest & Paper Association's Sustainable Forestry Initiative and the Forest Stewardship Council's Certification System," (June 2001). http://www.nwf.org/northernforest/auditprograms.html

19. UNCTAD International Trade Center, *Coffee: An Exporter's Guide* (Geneva, 1992).

20. Source: Transfair USA, http://www.transfairusa.org.

4.8

Forest Stewardship Council Principles and Criteria

Forest Stewardship Council

Introduction

It is widely accepted that forest resources and associated lands should be managed to meet the social, economic, ecological, cultural and spiritual needs of present and future generations. Furthermore, growing public awareness of forest destruction and degradation has led consumers to demand that their purchases of wood and other forest products will not contribute to this destruction but rather help to secure forest resources for the future. In response to these demands, certification and self-certification programs of wood products have proliferated in the marketplace.

The Forest Stewardship Council (FSC) is an international body which accredits certification organizations in order to guarantee the authenticity of their claims. In all cases the process of certification will be initiated voluntarily by forest owners and managers who request the services of a certification organization. The goal of FSC is to promote environmentally responsible, socially beneficial and economically viable management of the world's forests, by establishing a worldwide standard of recognized and respected Principles of Forest Stewardship.

Forest Stewardship Council, "Forest Stewardship Council Principles and Criteria," rev. (Oaxaca, Mexico, February 2000), 1–8, www.fscoax.org/html/1-2.html.

The FSC's Principles and Criteria (P&C) apply to all tropical, temperate and boreal forests, as addressed in Principle #9 and the accompanying glossary. Many of these P&C apply also to plantations and partially replanted forests. More detailed standards for these and other vegetation types may be prepared at national and local levels. The P&C are to be incorporated into the evaluation systems and standards of all certification organizations seeking accreditation by FSC. While the P&C are mainly designed for forests managed for the production of wood products, they are also relevant, to varying degrees, to forests managed for non-timber products and other services. The P&C are a complete package to be considered as a whole, and their sequence does not represent an ordering of priority. This document shall be used in conjunction with the FSC's Statutes, Procedures for Accreditation and Guidelines for Certifiers.

FSC and FSC-accredited certification organizations will not insist on perfection in satisfying the P&C. However, major failures in any individual Principles will normally disqualify a candidate from certification, or will lead to decertification. These decisions will be taken by individual certifiers, and guided by the extent to which each Criterion is satisfied, and by the importance and consequences of failures. Some flexibility will be allowed to cope with local circumstances.

The scale and intensity of forest management operations, the uniqueness of the affected resources, and the relative ecological fragility of the forest will be considered in all certification assessments. Differences and difficulties of interpretation of the P&C will be addressed in national and local forest stewardship standards. These standards are to be developed in each country or region involved, and will be evaluated for purposes of certification, by certifiers and other involved and affected parties on a case by case basis. If necessary, FSC dispute resolution mechanisms may also be called upon during the course of assessment. More information and guidance about the certification and accreditation process is included in the FSC Statutes, Accreditation Procedures, and Guidelines for Certifiers.

The FSC P&C should be used in conjunction with national and international laws and regulations. FSC intends to complement, not supplant, other initiatives that support responsible forest management worldwide.

The FSC will conduct educational activities to increase public awareness of the importance of the following:

- improving forest management;
- incorporating the full costs of management and production into the price of forest products;
- promoting the highest and best use of forest resources;
- reducing damage and waste; and
- avoiding over-consumption and over-harvesting.

FSC will also provide guidance to policy makers on these issues, including improving forest management legislation and policies.

Principle #1:
Compliance with Laws and FSC Principles

Forest management shall respect all applicable laws of the country in which they occur, and international treaties and agreements to which the country is a signatory, and comply with all FSC Principles and Criteria.

1.1   Forest management shall respect all national and local laws and administrative requirements.

1.2   All applicable and legally prescribed fees, royalties, taxes and other charges shall be paid.

1.3   In signatory countries, the provisions of all binding international agreements such as CITES [Convention on the International Trade in Endangered Species of Wild Fauna and Flora], ILO Conventions, ITTA [International Tropical Timber Agreement], and Convention on Biological Diversity, shall be respected.

1.4   Conflicts between laws, regulations and the FSC Principles and Criteria shall be evaluated for the purposes of certification, on a case by case basis, by the certifiers and the involved or affected parties.

1.5   Forest management areas should be protected from illegal harvesting, settlement and other unauthorized activities.

1.6   Forest managers shall demonstrate a long-term commitment to adhere to the FSC Principles and Criteria.

Principle #2:
Tenure and Use Rights and Responsibilities

Long-term tenure and use rights to the land and forest resources shall be clearly defined, documented and legally established.

2.1   Clear evidence of long-term forest use rights to the land (e.g. land title, customary rights, or lease agreements) shall be demonstrated.

2.2   Local communities with legal or customary tenure or use rights shall maintain control, to the extent necessary to protect their rights or resources, over forest operations unless they delegate control with free and informed consent to other agencies.

2.3   Appropriate mechanisms shall be employed to resolve disputes over tenure claims and use rights. The circumstances and status of any outstanding disputes will be explicitly considered in the certification evaluation. Disputes of substantial magnitude involving a significant number of interests will normally disqualify an operation from being certified.

Principle #3:
Indigenous Peoples' Rights

The legal and customary rights of indigenous peoples to own, use and manage their lands, territories, and resources shall be recognized and respected.

3.1 Indigenous peoples shall control forest management on their lands and territories unless they delegate control with free and informed consent to other agencies.

3.2 Forest management shall not threaten or diminish, either directly or indirectly, the resources or tenure rights of indigenous peoples.

3.3 Sites of special cultural, ecological, economic or religious significance to indigenous peoples shall be clearly identified in cooperation with such peoples, and recognized and protected by forest managers.

3.4 Indigenous peoples shall be compensated for the application of their traditional knowledge regarding the use of forest species or management systems in forest operations. This compensation shall be formally agreed upon with their free and informed consent before forest operations commence.

Principle #4:
Community Relations and Worker's Rights

Forest management operations shall maintain or enhance the long-term social and economic well-being of forest workers and local communities.

4.1 The communities within, or adjacent to, the forest management area should be given opportunities for employment, training, and other services.

4.2 Forest management should meet or exceed all applicable laws and/or regulations covering health and safety of employees and their families.

4.3 The rights of workers to organize and voluntarily negotiate with their employers shall be guaranteed as outlined in Conventions 87 and 98 of the International Labour Organisation (ILO).

4.4 Management planning and operations shall incorporate the results of evaluations of social impact. Consultations shall be maintained with people and groups directly affected by management operations.

4.5 Appropriate mechanisms shall be employed for resolving grievances and for providing fair compensation in the case of loss or damage affecting the legal or customary rights, property, resources, or livelihoods of local peoples. Measures shall be taken to avoid such loss or damage.

Principle #5:
Benefits from the Forest

Forest management operations shall encourage the efficient use of the forest's multiple products and services to ensure economic viability and a wide range of environmental and social benefits.

5.1 Forest management should strive toward economic viability, while taking into account the full environmental, social, and operational costs of production, and ensuring the investments necessary to maintain the ecological productivity of the forest.

5.2 Forest management and marketing operations should encourage the optimal use and local processing of the forest's diversity of products.

5.3 Forest management should minimize waste associated with harvesting and on-site processing operations and avoid damage to other forest resources.

5.4 Forest management should strive to strengthen and diversify the local economy, avoiding dependence on a single forest product.

5.5 Forest management operations shall recognize, maintain, and, where appropriate, enhance the value of forest services and resources such as watersheds and fisheries.

5.6 The rate of harvest of forest products shall not exceed levels which can be permanently sustained.

Principle #6:
Environmental Impact

Forest management shall conserve biological diversity and its associated values, water resources, soils, and unique and fragile ecosystems and landscapes, and, by so doing, maintain the ecological functions and the integrity of the forest.

6.1 Assessment of environmental impacts shall be completed—appropriate to the scale, intensity of forest management and the uniqueness of the affected resources—and adequately integrated into management systems. Assessments shall include landscape level considerations as well as the impacts of on-site processing facilities. Environmental impacts shall be assessed prior to commencement of site-disturbing operations.

6.2 Safeguards shall exist which protect rare, threatened and endangered species and their habitats (e.g., nesting and feeding areas). Conservation zones and protection areas shall be established, appropriate to the scale and intensity of forest management and the uniqueness of the affected resources. Inappropriate hunting, fishing, trapping and collecting shall be controlled.

6.3 Ecological functions and values shall be maintained intact, enhanced, or restored, including:

a) Forest regeneration and succession.
b) Genetic, species, and ecosystem diversity.
c) Natural cycles that affect the productivity of the forest ecosystem.

6.4 Representative samples of existing ecosystems within the landscape shall be protected in their natural state and recorded on maps, appropriate to the scale and intensity of operations and the uniqueness of the affected resources.

6.5 Written guidelines shall be prepared and implemented to: control erosion; minimize forest damage during harvesting, road construction, and all other mechanical disturbances; and protect water resources.

6.6 Management systems shall promote the development and adoption of environmentally friendly non-chemical methods of pest management and strive to avoid the use of chemical pesticides. World Health Organization Type 1A and 1B and chlorinated hydrocarbon pesticides; pesticides that are persistent, toxic or whose derivatives remain biologically active and accumulate in the food chain beyond their intended use; as well as any pesticides banned by international agreement, shall be prohibited. If chemicals are used, proper equipment and training shall be provided to minimize health and environmental risks.

6.7 Chemicals, containers, liquid and solid non-organic wastes including fuel and oil shall be disposed of in an environmentally appropriate manner at off-site locations.

6.8 Use of biological control agents shall be documented, minimized, monitored and strictly controlled in accordance with national laws and internationally accepted scientific protocols. Use of genetically modified organisms shall be prohibited.

6.9 The use of exotic species shall be carefully controlled and actively monitored to avoid adverse ecological impacts.

6.10 Forest conversion to plantations or non-forest land uses shall not occur, except in circumstances where conversion:

a) entails a very limited portion of the forest management unit; and
b) does not occur on high conservation value forest areas; and
c) will enable clear, substantial, additional, secure, long term conservation benefits across the forest management unit.

Principle #7: Management Plan

A management plan—appropriate to the scale and intensity of the operations—shall be written, implemented, and kept up to date. The long term objectives of management, and the means of achieving them, shall be clearly stated.

7.1 The management plan and supporting documents shall provide:

a) Management objectives.
b) Description of the forest resources to be managed, environmental limitations, land use and ownership status, socio-economic conditions, and a profile of adjacent lands.
c) Description of silvicultural and/or other management system, based on the ecology of the forest in question and information gathered through resource inventories.
d) Rationale for rate of annual harvest and species selection.
e) Provisions for monitoring of forest growth and dynamics.
f) Environmental safeguards based on environmental assessments.
g) Plans for the identification and protection of rare, threatened and endangered species.
h) Maps describing the forest resource base including protected areas, planned management activities and land ownership.
i) Description and justification of harvesting techniques and equipment to be used.

7.2 The management plan shall be periodically revised to incorporate the results of monitoring or new scientific and technical information, as well as to respond to changing environmental, social and economic circumstances.

7.3 Forest workers shall receive adequate training and supervision to ensure proper implementation of the management plan.

7.4 While respecting the confidentiality of information, forest managers shall make publicly available a summary of the primary elements of the management plan, including those listed in Criterion 7.1.

Principle #8:
Monitoring and Assessment

Monitoring shall be conducted—appropriate to the scale and intensity of forest management—to assess the condition of the forest, yields of forest products, chain of custody, management activities and their social and environmental impacts.

8.1 The frequency and intensity of monitoring should be determined by the scale and intensity of forest management operations as well as the relative complexity and fragility of the affected environment. Monitoring procedures should be consistent and replicable over time to allow comparison of results and assessment of change.

8.2 Forest management should include the research and data collection needed to monitor, at a minimum, the following indicators:

a) Yield of all forest products harvested.
b) Growth rates, regeneration and condition of the forest.
c) Composition and observed changes in the flora and fauna.
d) Environmental and social impacts of harvesting and other operations.
e) Costs, productivity, and efficiency of forest management.

8.3 Documentation shall be provided by the forest manager to enable monitoring and certifying organizations to trace each forest product from its origin, a process known as the "chain of custody."

8.4 The results of monitoring shall be incorporated into the implementation and revision of the management plan.

8.5 While respecting the confidentiality of information, forest managers shall make publicly available a summary of the results of monitoring indicators, including those listed in Criterion 8.2.

Principle #9: Maintenance of
High Conservation Value Forests

Management activities in high conservation value forests shall maintain or enhance the attributes which define such forests. Decisions regarding high conservation value forests shall always be considered in the context of a precautionary approach.

9.1 Assessment to determine the presence of the attributes consistent with High Conservation Value Forests will be completed, appropriate to scale and intensity of forest management.

9.2 The consultative portion of the certification process must place emphasis on the identified conservation attributes, and options for the maintenance thereof.

9.3 The management plan shall include and implement specific measures that ensure the maintenance and/or enhancement of the applicable conservation attributes consistent with the precautionary approach. These measures shall be specifically included in the publicly available management plan summary.

9.4 Annual monitoring shall be conducted to assess the effectiveness of the measures employed to maintain or enhance the applicable conservation attributes.

Principle #10: Plantations

Plantations shall be planned and managed in accordance with Principles and Criteria 1–9, and Principle 10 and its Criteria. While plantations can provide an array of social and economic benefits, and can contribute to satisfying the world's needs for forest products, they should complement the management of, reduce pressures on, and promote the restoration and conservation of natural forests.

10.1 The management objectives of the plantation, including natural forest conservation and restoration objectives, shall be explicitly stated in the management plan, and clearly demonstrated in the implementation of the plan.

10.2 The design and layout of plantations should promote the protection, restoration and conservation of natural forests, and not increase pressures on natural forests. Wildlife corridors, streamside zones and a mosaic of stands of different ages and rotation periods, shall be used in the layout of the plantation, consistent with the scale of the operation. The scale and layout of plantation blocks shall be consistent with the patterns of forest stands found within the natural landscape.

10.3 Diversity in the composition of plantations is preferred, so as to enhance economic, ecological and social stability. Such diversity may include the size and spatial distribution of management units within the landscape, number and genetic composition of species, age classes and structures.

10.4 The selection of species for planting shall be based on their overall suitability for the site and their appropriateness to the management objectives. In order to enhance the conservation of biological diversity, native species are preferred over exotic species in the establishment of plantations and the restoration of degraded ecosystems. Exotic species, which shall be used only when their performance is greater than that of native species, shall be carefully monitored to detect unusual mortality, disease, or insect outbreaks and adverse ecological impacts.

10.5 A proportion of the overall forest management area, appropriate to the scale of the plantation and to be determined in regional standards, shall be managed so as to restore the site to a natural forest cover.

10.6 Measures shall be taken to maintain or improve soil structure, fertility, and biological activity. The techniques and rate of harvesting, road and trail construction and maintenance, and the choice of species shall not result in long term soil degradation or adverse impacts on water quality, quantity or substantial deviation from stream course drainage patterns.

10.7 Measures shall be taken to prevent and minimize outbreaks of pests, diseases, fire and invasive plant introductions. Integrated pest management shall form an essential part of the management plan, with primary reliance on prevention and biological control methods rather than chemical pesticides and fertilizers. Plantation management should make every effort to move away from chemical pesticides and fertilizers, including their use in nurseries. The use of chemicals is also covered in Criteria 6.6 and 6.7.

10.8 Appropriate to the scale and diversity of the operation, monitoring of plantations shall include regular assessment of potential on-site and off-site ecological and social impacts, (e.g. natural regeneration, effects on water resources and soil fertility, and impacts on local welfare and social well-being), in addition to those elements addressed in principles 8, 6 and 4. No species should be planted on a large scale until local trials and/or experience have shown that they are ecologically well-adapted to the site, are not invasive, and do not have significant negative ecological impacts on other ecosystems. Special attention will be paid to social issues of land acquisition for plantations, especially the protection of local rights of ownership, use or access.

10.9 Plantations established in areas converted from natural forests after November 1994 normally shall not qualify for certification. Certification may be allowed in circumstances where sufficient evidence is submitted to the certification body that the manager/owner is not responsible directly or indirectly of such conversion.

The FSC Founding Members and Board of Directors ratified principles 1-9 in September 1994.

The FSC Members and Board of Directors ratified principle 10 in February 1996.

The revision of Principle 9 and the addition of Criteria 6.10 and 10.9 were ratified by the FSC Members and Board of Directors in January 1999.

4.9

Letter to University Presidents Regarding Anti-Sweatshop Campaigns on American Campuses

Academic Consortium on International Trade

Please find below a letter addressed to the presidents of American universities and colleges with regard to the issues raised by the Anti-Sweatshop campaign on American campuses and the decisions that have been taken. In this letter, we urge that the Anti-Sweatshop issues be subjected to more critical analysis and debated and discussed more widely than has been the case to date.

The authors of the letter are economists who are members of the Academic Consortium on International Trade (ACIT). ACIT is a group of academic economists and lawyers who are specialized in international trade policy and international economic law. ACIT's purpose is to prepare and circulate policy statements, letters, and papers dealing with issues of current importance to policy officials, members of the academic community, and other groups and the public. These are posted on the ACIT web site, www.spp.umich. edu/rsie/acit/. The members of the ACIT Steering Committee are listed below. . . .

Dear Sir/Madam:

We, the undersigned, are concerned about the process by which decisions are being taken by

some academic institutions in the ongoing Anti-Sweatshop campaign to establish Codes of Conduct to be applied to American firms manufacturing apparel with university/college logos in poor countries and about the choice among agencies appointed to monitor the activities of these firms.

We believe that the decisions on these matters by universities and colleges should be made only after careful research, discussion, and debate in a manner appropriate to informed decision-making. However, we often encounter news reports of sit-ins by groups of students in the offices of university/college administrators, after which decisions are often made without seeking the views of scholars in the social sciences, law, and humanities who have long discussed and researched the issues involved or of a broader campus constituency of fellow students and the entire community of faculty members. Furthermore, little attention has been given to whether the views of the Anti-Sweatshop campaign are representative of the views of the governments, non-government organizations (NGOs), and workers in the poor countries that are directly involved in the manufacture and in the export of apparel and related goods.

We recognize the good intentions of the Worker Rights Consortium (WRC) and the Fair Labor Association (FLA), which are the two main anti-sweatshop groups competing for membership commitments by universities and

Academic Consortium on International Trade, letter to university presidents regarding anti-sweatshop campaign, 29 July 2000, www.spp.umich.edu/rsie/acit/Documents/AntiSweatshopLetterPage.html.

colleges. Both of these groups, however, seem to ignore the well-established fact that multinational corporations (MNCs) commonly pay their workers more on average in comparison to the prevailing market wage for similar workers employed elsewhere in the economy. In cases where subcontracting is involved, workers are generally paid no less than the prevailing market wage. We are concerned therefore that if MNCs are persuaded to pay even more to their apparel workers in response to what the ongoing studies by the anti-sweatshop organizations may conclude are appropriate wage levels, the net result would be shifts in employment that will worsen the collective welfare of the very workers in poor countries who are supposed to be helped. Further information on this and other issues involved in the anti-sweatshop campaign is posted on the ACIT web site.

We are also concerned that the monitoring mechanisms established by both the Worker Rights Consortium and Fair Labor Association may prove uneven and ineffective. Other certifying and monitoring organizations should also be considered, such as the Council on Economic Priorities Accreditation Agency (CEPAA), an international non-government organization with considerable experience in administering a Social Accountability Standard (SA8000). Under SA8000, member companies are required to comply with national and other applicable laws and to respect the principles of worker rights embodied in the pertinent Conventions of the International Labor Organization (ILO), the Universal Declaration of Human Rights, and the United Nations Convention on the Rights of the Child.

In view of the complexity of the broad economic and related issues that the subject of "Social Responsibility" raises, we stress the need for universities and colleges to properly research, debate, discuss, and take decisions on this matter in a manner more appropriate to the fact that they, of all institutions in society, must promote informed decision-making.

ACIT Steering Committee

Robert E. Baldwin, University of Wisconsin
Jagdish Bhagwati, Columbia University and
  Member of SA8000 Advisory Board
Alan V. Deardorff, University of Michigan
Arvind Panagariya, University of Maryland
T.N. Srinivasan, Yale University
Robert M. Stern, University of Michigan

4.10

Statement to College and University Presidents

Scholars Against Sweatshop Labor

A movement by college and university students to oppose sweatshop labor in the production of college logo apparel began in the United States in the mid-1990s. The movement has been highly successful in raising the awareness of students and the broader population about harsh conditions experienced by garment workers throughout the world, including the United States, but most especially less developed countries. The students have read accounts by reputable sources about sweatshops—for example, a 10/2/00 *Business Week* story titled "A Life of Fines and Beatings," which describes conditions in Chinese factories that make products for Wal-Mart, among other Western companies. The overarching aim of the anti-sweatshop movement is simple: to make a contribution toward eliminating 'lives of fines and beatings' for workers throughout the world, in the same way that previous generations of activists fought to eliminate slave labor, child labor, and the 12-hour workday. The anti-sweatshop movement wants workers worldwide [to] be able to work under decent conditions, exercise basic human rights, and earn at least decent minimum wages.

In response to this student movement, many colleges and universities have adopted "codes of

conduct" aimed at improving wages and working conditions for workers producing apparel that carries the logo of their own institutions. We, the undersigned, are broadly supportive of these efforts, even though we acknowledge that we do not have detailed information on the codes established at every institution.

During the past academic year, a group calling itself the "Academic Consortium on International Trade" (ACIT) circulated a letter to Presidents of Colleges and Universities, raising major concerns about these anti-sweatshop activities. As of June 2001, the letter has been signed by 352 economists and other academics, many of them distinguished practitioners in their fields of specialization. This letter is also posted on the ACIT website, <http://www.spp.umich.edu/rsie/acit/>.

The letter raises four basic concerns about the direction of the anti-sweatshop campaigns on college and university campuses:

1. Institutions are establishing codes of conduct without adequate consultation of experts knowledgeable in the relevant fields.
2. The two main organizations engaged in monitoring codes of conduct throughout the world—the Workers Rights Consortium (WRC) and the Fair Labor Association (FLA) may prove ineffective. The ACIT letter proposes that other groups also be considered as monitors, such as Social Accounting International (SAI; for-

Scholars Against Sweatshop Labor, statement to college and university presidents, 22 October 2001, www.umass.edu/peri/sasl.

merly known as Council on Economic Priorities Accreditation Agency).

3. Inadequate attention has been paid to whether the views of the anti-sweatshop movement are representative of the views of governments, non-governmental organizations (NGOs) and workers in the developing countries that are directly involved in the apparel industry.

4. Anti-sweatshop activists and the main monitoring organizations do not understand how establishing codes of conduct may actually harm the very low-wage workers in developing countries they are trying to help. In particular, the ACIT letter suggests that forcing businesses in less developed countries to pay higher wages and improve working conditions could reduce the overall availability of jobs in these countries.

We believe that these concerns raised by ACIT are legitimate. At the same time, we believe that the anti-sweatshop movement—and the colleges and universities that have embraced this movement through establishing codes of conduct in college logo apparel production—are taking constructive steps toward improving living and working conditions for millions of poor people throughout the world.

We expand on this conclusion below through addressing the main concerns raised in the ACIT letter.

Are Colleges and Universities Making Decisions about Codes of Conduct without Adequate Consultation?

Colleges and universities that have adopted codes of conduct have generally done so only after careful consultation with appropriate faculty and/or outside experts. We would be surprised if any institution of higher education were to act otherwise. But the ACIT letter also raises a broader issue: do college and university decision-makers have an adequate foundation of research on which to understand all the issues raised by the anti-sweatshop movement? Of course, scholars have been writing for generations about the most effective ways of alleviating poverty and enhancing conditions in workplaces. At the same time, the anti-sweatshop

movement has prompted a new body of research and discussion that is deepening our understanding of the specific issues at hand. Universities have commissioned much of this new research. Links to many of these resources can be found at the SASL website, www.umass.edu/peri/sasl. No doubt more such work would be beneficial. For now, the anti-sweatshop movement deserves credit for pushing researchers to focus on these issues. With time, these efforts will produce both greater understanding and increasingly effective codes of conduct.

Worldwide Consultation and Monitoring

Establishing and monitoring acceptable codes of conduct for companies operating plants throughout the world are clearly difficult tasks. Achieving adequate levels of compliance will be a long, slow process requiring experimentation, flexibility and learning. Toward that end, ACIT's concern over the quality of monitoring is constructive. But the ACIT letter does not make clear that the three monitoring agencies that it refers to—the Workers Rights Consortium (WRC), Fair Labor Association (FLA), and Social Accountability International (SAI)—offer perspectives that are distinct and complementary. The WRC governing and advisory boards are comprised of academics, university administrators, labor rights activists and NGOs from developing countries. In other words, the WRC has brought local stakeholders into the center of the monitoring process. This is exactly what the ACIT letter itself recommends. Moreover, the WRC is committed to maintaining transparent procedures for monitoring firms and disclosing the results of their inspections. Unlike the WRC, the Fair Labor Association includes representatives of business prominently on its board, in addition to having NGO and university representatives. The widespread concern voiced by activists over the governance of the FLA is that it gives too much power to businesses to effectively monitor their own behavior. We do not evaluate here the merits of this criticism. But even allowing that there is truth to it, it is still clear that the FLA is on the right track by including business representatives in their formal discussions, since no viable standards will emerge by excluding them. Social Accountability International, as the ACIT letter correctly points out, is more experienced than either the WRC or FLA in implementing monitoring and certification procedures for international businesses. However most of their previous work has been in the area of product quality control rather than social monitoring. In short, the three organizations bring different strengths to the task of establishing and monitoring effective labor standards worldwide. Ongoing cooperation and competition between these groups should also raise the general performance standard for all three.

Wages, Labor Costs, and Employment Opportunities in the Global Garment Industry

The ACIT letter says that multinational corporations "commonly pay their workers more on average in comparison to the prevailing market wage for similar workers employed elsewhere in the economy." While this is true, it does not speak to the situation in which most garments are produced throughout the world—which is by firms subcontracted by multinational corporations, not the MNCs themselves. In implicitly acknowledging this point, ACIT does also state that in the case of subcontracting, workers are "generally paid no less than the prevailing market wage." This is also true, almost by definition. But the prevailing market wage is frequently extremely low for garment workers in less developed countries. In addition, the recent university-sponsored studies as well as an October 2000 report by the International Labor Organization consistently find that serious workplace abuses and violations of workers' rights are occurring in the garment industry throughout the world. Considering simply the "prevailing market wage" in various countries thus tells us little about the working and living conditions of the workers who receive these wages.

The ACIT letter also raises a broader concern about the effort to raise wages and workplace standards for sweatshop workers: that improved labor standards could come at the cost of higher unemployment and a net loss of worker welfare. The aim of the anti-sweatshop movement is obviously not to induce negative unintended consequences such as higher overall unemployment in developing countries, nor to inhibit developing economies from competing

successfully in global markets. The anti-sweatshop movement should take particular care that its efforts not produce fewer opportunities for people to get relatively high quality jobs in developing countries such as in some forms of garment production and other manufacturing and organized service sector activities. Even after allowing for the frequent low wages and poor working conditions in these jobs, they are still generally superior to "informal" employment in, for example, much of agriculture or urban street vending.

While caution is clearly needed in setting minimum decent standards for workplace conditions, workers rights, and wage levels, there is still no reason to assume that a country or region that sets reasonable standards must experience job losses. Additional policy measures will also be crucial for enhancing any region's overall employment opportunities and competitiveness. Such initiatives include: measures to expand the overall number of relatively high quality jobs; relief from excessive foreign debt payments; raising worker job satisfaction and productivity and the quality of goods they produce; and improving the capacity to bring final products to retail markets. Moreover, as long as consumers in wealthier countries are willing to pay somewhat higher retail prices to ensure that garments are produced under non-sweatshop conditions—as recent polling data for the U.S. suggests is the case—the higher revenues within the industry could be used to improve workplace conditions and wages for production-level workers, without creating pressures for manufacturers to reduce their number of employees.

Establishing fair and effective labor market and workplace regulations is always a challenging task. But such regulations remain a cornerstone of any decent society. This has been clear from the historical struggles against slave labor onward. The need for such social protections has only increased in our contemporary era of globalization—contrary to the widespread premise that global economic integration should be synonymous with the dismantling of social protections.

The current anti-sweatshop movement on campuses can point to real achievements toward improving social protections worldwide: it has increased awareness about conditions facing sweatshop workers; and it has stimulated research and thinking as to the most effective ways U.S. academic institutions can contribute toward improving working conditions and living standards for these workers. Of course, both educational and monitoring efforts need to be strengthened, and anti-sweatshop activists need to maintain the open-minded approach they have demonstrated thus far in finding the most effective means of achieving the ends they desire. In this spirit, we broadly endorse the efforts of the anti-sweatshop movement. At the same time, we encourage anti-sweatshop activists to continue to deepen both their own understanding and their educational efforts—to examine conditions facing workers generally in developing countries, including those not employed in sweatshops; and to consider the most effective means of improving these general conditions.

SASL Steering Committee

Lourdes Beneria, Cornell University
James K. Galbraith, University of Texas-Austin
Teresa Ghilarducci, Notre Dame University
Soohaeng Kim, Seoul National University
Sule Ozler, U. of California-Los Angeles
Robert Pollin, U. of Massachusetts-Amherst, Chair
Dani Rodrik, Harvard University
Juliet Schor, Boston College
Ajit Singh, Cambridge University

4.11

Developing Effective Mechanisms for Implementing Labor Rights in the Global Economy

Pharis Harvey, Terry Collingsworth, and Bama Athreya

The International Labor Rights Fund's contribution to the project is to examine past and current efforts to protect labor rights in the global economy and to propose more effective implementation of these rights. An assumption of the ILRF analysis is that improved labor rights recognition and enforcement in the global economy is essential to a rational policy of sustainable economic development. Better implementation of labor rights will allow workers in the global economy to improve their wages and terms and conditions of employment. More fundamentally, global mechanisms to protect labor rights are essential to create the political space necessary to allow workers to form trade unions and other civil society organizations that can act to counterbalance the virtually unchecked power of global capital.

Any proposals for enforcing worker rights globally must be made in the incredibly complicated and confused context of global politics. While there are certainly flexible positions emerging from outside the U.S. and Europe,[1]

much of the debate over proposals to add labor rights to trade agreements is mired in an intense debate over the motives of the proponents of this idea: is there a genuine concern for workers or is it a pretext for protectionism? Those advocating some form of international labor rights regulation are often labeled protectionists, even by progressive organizations from the South,[2] as well as Southern governments and business interests in the North,[3] which oppose any social regulation that would endanger the current supply of cheap, exploitable labor, thus creating a very unlikely alliance of opposition to social regulation in the global economy. Fortunately, more and more trade unions and non-governmental organizations (NGOs) from the South are recognizing that their people are being exploited by multinational companies (MNCs) operating on a global basis, and the only solution for dealing with them is worldwide labor regulation. [. . .]

Issues to be Resolved

Initiatives to promote codes of conduct and independent monitoring and verification systems have made great strides in recent years. While these initiatives have garnered far more widespread attention and support from employers, consumers and trade unions than any previous such efforts, and have achieved notable success in pushing the discussion on corporate responsibility forward, nevertheless there remain several

Pharis Harvey, Terry Collingsworth, and Bama Athreya, excerpt from "Developing Effective Mechanisms for Implementing Labor Rights in the Global Economy," in *Workers in the Global Economy: Project Papers and Workshop Reports*, ed. Lance Compa and Maria Cook (Cornell University School of Industrial and Labor Relations, International Labor Rights Fund, Institute for Policy Studies, and Economic Policy Institute, January 2001), 1 and 42–49.

outstanding issues under debate. Below we review the most significant of these questions and outline our position on each.

1. Do Codes Undermine Collective Bargaining?

Although unions and union federations have been prominent participants in the promotion of, and creation of bodies to monitor, codes of conduct,[187] nevertheless many activists in the trade union movement both in the United States and elsewhere have expressed fears that codes of conduct, if implemented, may obviate the need for trade unions to negotiate collective bargaining agreements on behalf of an enterprise's workforce. They fear that monitors will most likely be appointed from the NGO community, and, in handling grievances, take over the function of democratically elected union leadership, thus removing the democratic right of workers to have a direct say in their own wages and working conditions.

The experience of the Independent Monitoring Group of El Salvador highlights the relevance of such fears. GMIES emerged as a response to a particular situation, that of the mass dismissal of independent trade union activists at the Mandarin plant. It succeeded in its original goal to compel the company to re-hire the fired activists. However, subsequently the group was saddled with the larger responsibility of monitoring overall company compliance with The Gap's code of conduct, a task for which it was unprepared and which it undertook in a vacuum of coordinated guidance or oversight.

GMIES' role shifted away from one of supporting the independent union, and toward one of investigating and handling complaints of company non-compliance with labor standards in its code. By early 1998, the group had adopted a "neutral" stance vis-a-vis the conflict between the original, independent union and the company union. Superior resources and friendly relationships with management had allowed the company union to win widespread support among workers, whereas the independent union had dwindled to a small handful of supporters.

While the GMIES experiment did not lead to the establishment of a vibrant, independent trade union in the factory, it did serve to neutralize some of the factors that had previously made union organizing impossible, and to assist fired trade unionists to regain employment. This may reflect more broadly an important role for NGO monitors: they may serve as a check on employer behavior to prevent workers from exercising their right to associate. While this role is a limited one, given the severe restrictions on workers' right to associate today, particularly in the garment and other light manufacturing industries, monitoring may play a very useful role in strengthening nascent trade union activity.

We note that in most developing countries, employers are free to employ a wide variety of union-busting techniques at the slightest sign of independent organizing activity. The International Confederation of Free Trade Unions (ICFTU) has estimated that between 300 to 500 workers *are killed* each year for their organizing activities. Thousands more are arrested, beaten or intimidated. There are between 65,000 and 75,000 cases of union leaders reported to be fired for their activities each year. Many thousands more cases go unreported.[188] Those who suggest that independent monitors will prevent independent unions from forming are to some extent ignoring the far more significant impediments that exist to independent union formation, such as employers' ability to enlist the support of police or other local authorities to arrest or intimidate workers, and the near-impossibility of resolving unfair terminations in a timely manner through local judicial systems.

One of the most important roles a monitoring group can play, particularly in closed polities such as China where information flow on labor issues is carefully restricted, is to collect information about such terminations and to pressure employers to act immediately to rehire these workers. This is an area in which immediate pressure from Western consumers and advocacy groups is far more likely to be effective than recourse to local judicial processes. The practice is also likely to act as a deterrent to any future such firings, thus removing a significant obstacle to union organizing.

Where independent unions exist, monitors within the workplace should be delegates of the union itself. In many if not most light manufacturing enterprises in developing countries, however, independent unions have not been able to form. In such a context, monitors may also serve a useful role in simply providing information to workers about their rights under a company's code. In this way, non-union monitors can and should become allies to union activists, not replacements for them.

Codes may help promote development of trade unions, provided they contain protections for workers' rights to associate and form unions, and to bargain collectively. By and large, the protections listed in codes of conduct do not vary significantly from protections contained in most countries' labor laws. Abuses occur because governments fail to enforce these laws. One area in which the problem is not enforcement, but weak legislation itself, is that of trade union activity.[189] Many developing countries have consciously adopted a strategy of suppressing or heavily regulating all trade union activity. The links between such strategies and governments' desires to attract foreign investment, particularly in the manufacturing sector, are exemplified by the additional restrictions placed on labor organizing in export processing zones.[190] In short, the "race to the bottom" has been as much a race to weaken trade union and bargaining rights as it has been a race to provide cheap wages. Codes of conduct have the potential to play a critical role in the promotion of free trade unions in such places, provided they contain language protecting workers' rights to associate and form unions and to bargain collectively. By pressuring MNCs not only to adopt but to honor such language, worker advocates may be able to create a context within which free trade unions can develop even under restrictive legal frameworks.

2. Who Should Monitor Companies' Compliance with their Codes?

Companies have experimented with three types of monitoring of codes: internal, external and independent. These definitions are taken from the report, "The Apparel Industry and Codes of Conduct: A Solution to the International Child Labor Problem?" produced by the U.S. Department of Labor's Bureau of International Affairs in 1996. The definitions themselves are the subject of debate. Some feel that external monitoring is, in fact, independent monitoring while others feel it more closely resembles internal monitoring. This paper retains the DOL definitions in order to distinguish between monitoring performed on contract to the company and that which is not. For the purposes of the discussion below, internal monitoring is that conducted by representatives of the company (either the MNC or the supplier) itself. External monitoring is conducted by a third party, a "monitor-for-hire," under contract to the company on a for-profit basis. Independent monitor-

ing (also referred to as independent verification) is that which is performed by a group which does not have a direct or exclusive relationship with the company; usually some level of public reporting is a part of independent monitoring.

Internal Monitoring

Internal monitoring is that conducted by employees or representatives of the retailer itself or of its supplier. Its advantages are that monitors may be allowed free access to all information relevant to the production process without risk of jeopardizing any privileged information, such as trade secrets. The basic problem with internal monitoring is that it relies on the "good faith" of the company itself. The premise of consumer pressure is removed because even those companies with the best of intentions will have no incentive to reveal their own bad practices to the public. Where the company has a genuine desire to be a good corporate citizen, or to improve its labor practices for reasons of improved efficiency, stability, or to avoid negative publicity, individuals entrusted with monitoring may be able to enforce real compliance with standards. Where, however, the monitoring is being done merely to placate a hostile consumer audience, efforts to monitor may be restricted to a mere exercise in public relations. Under such circumstances, information presented by the company to the public cannot be relied upon.

An example of such an exercise in "bad faith" was the advertising campaign launched by Guess? Inc. in December 1997. In previous years, Guess? had been the target of consumer campaigns to publicize the company's labor abuses. In December the company took out full-page ads in the New York Times and other regional newspapers advertising its jeans as "sweat free" and stating that the company had been given a clean bill of health by the U.S. Department of Labor. In fact the Department of Labor had cited Guess? suppliers in the United States for labor violations earlier in the year and insisted that the company remove the claim from its advertisements. The Guess? strategy illustrates the problems consumers might face if their only source of information were companies themselves.

External Monitoring

External monitoring is monitoring contracted out by the company itself to a third party. Nike International provides an example of a company using external monitoring. For the past few years the corporation has hired the accounting firm Ernst and Young to provide labor audits of its plants in Southeast Asia. In 1997, Nike also contracted Goodworks International, a nonprofit led by former U.S. Ambassador Andrew Young, to inspect its plants in China and Southeast Asia.

External monitoring carries an information flow problem similar to that of internal monitoring. Since the external monitor is on contract to the company, the monitor is not free to disseminate information publicly. Instead, a confidential report is issued to the company which the company itself may or may not disseminate. This was a problem which arose in the Nike/Ernst and Young example. The company discovered serious health and safety hazards at Nike producing facilities in Vietnam, but it was precluded from publicizing this information. Despite its findings, Ernst and Young nonetheless certified that Nike was in compliance with its code. Nike chose not to correct the violations, and continued to assert publicly that the audits were assisting suppliers to improve their labor conditions. An independent NGO representative discovered and publicized the violations uncovered by Ernst and Young, to the company's embarrassment.[191]

Another criticism leveled against external for-profit monitors is that they may not have the expertise or sensitivity necessary to conduct accurate interviews with workers. This criticism operates on two levels. First is the suggestion that an accounting firm or otherwise inexperienced group may simply not know what questions to ask. This problem can be overcome by a system to train and accredit monitors, a subject to be discussed in the following section. Second is the suggestion that workers may be afraid to provide external monitors, whom they perceive as company representatives, with accurate information. This was the criticism leveled against Andrew Young, who conducted this tour of Nike factories accompanied by factory management and made no attempts to interview workers in a confidential setting.

Independent Monitoring/Verification

Independent monitoring is that conducted by a third party not on exclusive contract to the company itself. Independent monitoring may use "monitors-for-hire" or may use local organizations, including labor, religious, human rights or other community-based groups, to conduct labor investigations in zones where such groups are located. This approach is exemplified by the Independent Monitoring Group of El Salvador, described earlier in this section. In theory monitoring by a firm such as Ernst and Young may be considered independent if the monitor is not acting as an agent of the company it is monitoring, or is not subject to a conflict of interest caused by the fact it may have or seek other commercial relationships with the company. For example, Ernst and Young could not be considered independent monitors, even if their labor audits were paid for by a source other than Nike, because they have a separate commercial relationship with Nike to conduct the company's financial audits and a consequent disincentive to be overly, or even appropriately, critical of labor practices, since the other financial interest outweighed the social auditing program incentive.

Monitoring cannot work without a reliable, confidential reporting procedure. Workers in most developing countries know that they are vulnerable to being fired without cause, and that legal redress, if it is available at all, may take years in process. Rather than lose their jobs, most individual workers will exercise caution in criticizing their employer or airing their grievances publicly, or even confidentially. The most trustworthy interviewers will inevitably be those who arise from the ranks of the workers themselves, or from their communities. Local organizations are also best equipped to deal with language and other locale-specific barriers, since they possess the cultural knowledge necessary both to frame questions appropriately and to interpret answers accurately.

Independent trade unions, led by representatives elected directly by an enterprise's workers, are the organizations best equipped to set up a monitoring and reporting process within a factory. Independent trade unions may already have in place the grievance-handling procedures necessary to obtain reliable ongoing information from workers. As self-funding organizations, trade unions are also the most cost-effective monitors. Unfortunately, in many of the countries to which production of consumer goods has fled, authoritarian regimes prohibit or control labor organizing and unions, if they exist at all, are neither independent nor representative of workers' interests. Indonesia under Suharto provides a prominent example of such practices. Even where laws protecting unions are adequate, lax enforcement often means that in practice workers' bargaining power is weak. In such countries, community based organizations often take an active role in promoting workers' welfare. Staff of such organizations may spend a considerable amount of time getting to know workers and their families, and may have sufficient trust and status within the area to be able to probe for sensitive information.

In cases where trade unions do not exist or are not free to play a key role in this process, NGOs provide a viable alternative. There are some drawbacks to the NGO approach; most notably, because it is localized, start-up of a monitoring effort is extremely time- and labor-intensive. Another problem with the NGO approach is that, again because it is localized, it may suffer from consistency between regions or countries. It may be that "levels" of monitoring are needed, where one level, that of direct worker interviews, is conducted by local groups and other levels (such as measuring levels of hazardous substances, or verifying adequate ventilation and fire precautions) is conducted in a more generalized or standardized fashion.

3. How Should Monitoring Be Regulated?

Whether independent monitoring is conducted by international or by local groups, there is a need to regulate the monitors themselves in order to ensure that information to be provided to consumers is consistent and accurate. Initially, monitors should be accredited by a body that is recognizable and trusted by consumers. After accreditation, groups should be provided with guidance as to the types of information they are expected to provide. If the strategy of using local organizations is adopted, companies and worker advocates in consuming countries may wish to develop a training program to teach such organizations how to gather the relevant information and how to present it in a standard format that can be used easily by companies and consumer advocates. An essential function of an accreditation body would be to revoke accreditation from monitors who are found to be unreliable or otherwise substandard.

A regulatory body serves the additional role of middleman between the company and the monitor. As noted above, independent monitoring precludes that contracted directly by the company, except under carefully regulated circumstances. In order to preserve the independence of monitoring groups, whether they be business firms or NGOs, an independent regulatory body must evaluate information, ensure that it meets standards of the accreditation program, and ensure transparency of the process in such a way as to preclude any inappropriate relationships between the monitors and companies. The Rugmark program has such a body. The Fair Labor Association and Fair Trade Foundation represent other examples of regulatory intermediaries between companies and monitors.

The ILO may be able to play a useful role in the area of standardization of monitoring and reporting, by sharing through training or informational programs its own measures or benchmarks for compliance with ILO conventions. Such an exchange might also facilitate convergence of different private initiatives toward a globally applicable labor rights monitoring framework.

4. Who Should Pay for Monitoring?

The possible sources of funding are, in essence, corporations, governments and worker/consumer advocates (trade unions and other civic organizations). Various mixes of funding from these entities may provide for monitoring to take place and to remain independent. The critical issue here is not who provides the funding, but what steps are taken to ensure that monitors may retain their independence from any single party and are not biased by the source of funding. Direct financial relationships between the monitor and company are not precluded, as long as the public interest is protected by measures that include transparency of monitoring contracts, some form of public access to results of audits, and protections against side payments or other improper transactions between the contracting parties.

The Rugmark example provides one workable funding scenario: companies wishing to utilize the services of monitors pay a licensing fee to an independent overseer (in this case, the Rugmark Foundation) and that overseer in turn provides inspection services. Since inspectors are not paid directly by their clients they are able to maintain their objectivity. The Rugmark program also institutes other safeguards to ensure that inspectors are not vulnerable to bribery or other possible compromises of their integrity.

The Independent Monitoring Group of El Salvador in its first year used another model of funding, one in which the company itself and a worker advocate, the National Labor Committee, contributed equally to its upkeep. The group's independence from each funder was thus assured. However, The Gap's failure to provide a second year of funding is indicative of problems with this approach that might best be addressed if funding were to be channeled through a neutral body with ongoing oversight responsibility.

5. Do Codes Undermine Efforts to Strengthen National and International Labor Standards?

Some have expressed concern that by functioning independently of any country's legal system, codes of conduct and independent monitoring may palliate local desire to improve legal standards. In fact we feel codes and independent monitoring provide an important, complementary mechanism to augment enforcement of existing legal systems, and may foster greater desire to improve those systems. By adopting a code, a corporation also acknowledges its responsibility to abide by local labor laws. In most cases, local labor laws even in developing countries offer adequate protections for workers, conforming with at least minimum international standards on subjects such as working hours, overtime compensation, forced labor and child labor.[192] However, abuses occur because governments lack adequate enforcement budgets, or are offered multiple incentives to protect the interests of elites and capital rather than enforcing these laws. For example, in both China and Indonesia, partnerships between top military officials and investors have been documented.[193] Such alliances give the military in both countries every incentive to safeguard their investments by participating in labor repression.

If monitored, codes may improve enforcement of local labor laws. The codes approach recognizes that in many developing countries, workers may be unaware of existing legal protections. Even where they have information about such laws, workers may hesitate to involve corrupt or unsympathetic labor officials in their grievances. Through monitors, workers may gain access to information not only about a company's code of conduct but also about local labor laws and legal protections. Furthermore, if effective monitoring mechanisms can be established, it may be easier

and less intimidating for a worker to use such mechanisms than to bring problems to the attention of local officials or courts. The development of such alternate dispute resolution mechanisms for MNCs with codes of conduct may provide officials in developing countries with incentives to better enforce existing labor laws, in order to preserve their own jurisdiction. At very least such an approach provides some workers with another option to seek redress for grievances. This approach may ultimately have a spillover effect from MNCs that adopt and comply with codes to local employers, as workers share information between enterprises. Workers in local enterprises are ultimately unlikely to tolerate dual systems of enforcement.

The codes approach may also create incentives for some MNCs to become allies in the movement for harmonized labor standards and consistent enforcement of those standards. By initially creating an environment of greater accountability for MNCs with codes, it puts them at a competitive disadvantage to MNCs in the same industry without codes producing in the same countries. The approach may therefore convince "good" companies that in order to compete effectively, they too have an interest in advocating for uniform adoption and implementation of labor legislation.

6. Should Codes Define a Living Wage?

The basic content of most codes of conduct does not vary significantly from the internationally recognized worker rights called for in debates for a social clause in international trade agreements. Insofar as this is true, the standards represent a broad international consensus on fundamental worker rights established by advocates in both developed and developing countries. The list of generally agreed-upon standards includes elimination of forced labor, elimination of child labor, decent wages and working conditions, decent health and safety standards, non-discrimination, the right to organize and bargain collectively. Most industry and company codes incorporate all of these standards. One issue that remains unresolved is the debate on wages. The AIP and ETI codes call for employers to pay either minimum or prevailing wages in the countries where they produce, and to recognize the need for those wages to meet workers' basic needs. Critics of this provision note that in most developing countries, the minimum or prevailing wages are insufficient to provide a basic market basket of goods to most workers. These critics call for the establishment of criteria to define what a living wage would be in each country, and call on companies to agree to pay this amount rather than minimum wage.

The debate on living wages has been a contentious one, in no small part because, unlike other rights covered by corporate codes, the definition of a living wage has yet to be clearly established by any international convention.[194] Nor do economists or other social scientists agree on a cross-country definition of a standard market basket of goods. Since international consensus on this issue is lacking, consumer country advocates for a living wage clause have been particularly susceptible to the argument that they are acting out of protectionist rather than humanitarian motivations.

It is our position that the living wage issue cannot be resolved without (a) substantial further research and the development of a reasonable and widely acceptable cross-cultural index to measure basic needs; and (b) substantial effort by developed country advocates of a living wage to engage in open dialogue on this issue with trade unions and NGOs in developing countries. We note that to date, such dialogue has consisted principally of Northern NGOs asking Southern partners to make assessments of economic indicators in their particular countries, rather than engaging in participation as full partners in the issue of standard-setting. As noted in this paper's earlier discussion on the development and promotion of a social clause, the wage issue is an extremely important one, but it is unlikely that it can be promoted by U.S. or other consumer-country advocates in a manner that adequately addresses developing-country fears of protectionism.

International dialogue, perhaps oriented toward a re-examination of ILO language on wage-fixing machinery, is a vital first step to further discussion and definition of the living wage. Without such dialogue, advocates in the North run the risk of undermining gains made by NGOs and trade unions in the South. In the meanwhile, it is our position that codes of conduct should not set wages, but rather should provide an absolute floor for wages. Promotion and vigilant monitoring of workers' right to bargain collectively is the ultimate way to ensure

that workers receive wages adequate to meet their basic needs.

This view, however, does not lessen the moral and pragmatic imperatives to provide workers with wages adequate to allow them to live decently.[195] Trade unions and other worker advocates should bring the living wage discussion into the broader context of the debate for a social clause, and should, through continued consumer pressure, support and bolster efforts by trade unions and NGOs in the South to negotiate appropriate wages.

[. . .]

Notes

1. See, e.g., H. Totsuka, "Some Thoughts on 'Asian Social Charter,'" *Bulletin*, Center for Transnational Labor Studies, No. 3, 27 (November 1997).

2. M. Khor, Northern Trade Protectionism and Workers' Rights, *Third World Economics*, 16–30 (April 1994). At a February 6, 1998, presentation at IPS, Khor clarified that his concern is that whatever the motives of advocates pressing for a social clause, once enacted, Northern governments could use the clause for protectionist purposes. This then presents a challenge to draft the social clause and its enforcement provisions so that this risk is eliminated or substantially minimized.

3. In the recent debate over renewal of President Clinton's "fast track" negotiating authority, simply asserting that there should be open debate and a slower process resulted in vehement assertions of "protectionism" by the pro-business press. See, e.g., P. Blustein, "Free Trade vs. Social Policy," *Washington Post*, G-1 & 8 (Sept. 19, 1997) (Citing Senator Gramm who claims that advocates for labor and environmental standards in trade agreements are simply trying to keep competitive products out of the market).

[. . .]

187. See i.e., the Union of Needletrades, Industrial and Textile Employees (UNITE) and Retail, Sales and Department Store Workers' Union (RSDWU) participated in the creation of the AIP code of conduct; the British Trades Union Council is a member of the ETI; the Dutch union federation FNV is part of the Fair Trade Foundation; the International Textile, Garment and Leather Workers' Federation (ITGLWF) Secretary-General

Neil Kearney is a board member of the Council on Economic Priorities' new SA 8000 program.

188. ICFTU Annual Report 1997. (Brussels: International Confederation of Free Trade Unions, 1997).

189. For a case study of government strategies of labor repression in Asia, see Deyo, F. *Beneath the Miracle: Labor Suppression in East Asia.*

190. For example, Pakistan, Bangladesh and Malaysia all allow trade unions to function elsewhere but not in EPZs; see ILRF petition on Pakistan's GSP privileges. Sri Lanka placed severe restrictions on labor in EPZs until a GSP petition brought about improvement.

191. Smoke from a Hired Gun, report by Dara O'Rourke, Transnational Research and Action Center (TRAC), November, 1997. This report is on file at ILRF and also available at TRAC's Corporate Watch website (http://www.corpwatch.org).

192. An exception to this generalization are local laws regulating trade union activity, discussed below.

193. See Johannes Simbolon, "ABRI, from War Machine to Big Business Bureaucrats," in *Jakarta Post*, October 1, 1995; also "China's People's Liberation Army: Where to Find PLA Companies in America, What Products the PLA Sells in America and Who Are the PLA's Customers," report issued by Food and Allied Service Trades Department, AFL-CIO.

194. The UN's *Universal Declaration of Human Rights* notes the right of workers to earn a living wage. The ILO's *Tripartite Declaration* also affirms the responsibility of MNCs to provide a wage at least adequate to satisfy the basic needs of workers and their families. However neither of these international fora have been able to resolve the question of how minimum wages or basic needs should be measured or set. See Richard Rothstein, "Developing Reasonable Standards for Judging Whether Minimum Wage Levels in Developing Countries Are Acceptable," Bureau of International Labor Affairs, U.S. Department of Labor, June 1996; see also Bama Athreya and Natacha Thys, "Empowering Workers Toward a Living Wage: A Position Paper," International Labor Rights Fund, Fall 1999.

195. See Athreya and Thys, "Empowering Workers Toward a Living Wage: A Position Paper."

For Further Reading

Nowadays, finding the **text of actual codes** is fairly easy. Companies that have individual codes of conduct typically either post them on their web site or provide information on their web site that tells you how to get the code, as do Levi Strauss (www.levistrauss.com) and Gap (www.gapinc.com). So too are sectoral codes and certification schemes easily found on the Internet—for instance, www.ceres.org, www.fsc.org, and www.iseala.org.

For more **analysis of corporate codes of conduct**, start with the people and institutions who are both analysts of and players in the backlash. An excellent summary of almost every code and certification scheme is found in the first part of the Harvey, Collingsworth, and Athreya paper (not included in the reprinted excerpt in Reading 4.11). In addition to other material available from the International Labor Rights Fund, see also the work of the Interfaith Center on Corporate Responsibility, from its regular *Corporate Examiner* publication to its 1998 *Bench Marks for Measuring Business Performance*. The work of Bob Jeffcott and Lynda Yanz at the Maquila Solidarity Network in Canada (www.maquilasolidarity.org) ranges from basic information on codes ("Shopping for the Right Code," May 2000) to more advanced analysis ("Voluntary Codes of Conduct: Do They Strengthen or Undermine Government Regulation and Worker Organizing?" October 1999).

Also consult the work of Katie Quan, a former union organizer and now a labor policy specialist at Berkeley's Institute of Industrial Relations (iir.berkeley.edu/clre). Dara O'Rourke is another who wears many hats—MIT professor, environmental specialist who has assessed factories in Vietnam and elsewhere, and author who has critiqued private monitors. For one of his thoughtful attempts at innovation, see "Realizing Labor Standards" (coauthored with Archon Fung and Charles Sobel) in *Boston Review* 26, no. 1 (February/March 2001), which is followed by responses by eight others, including myself.

A good way to follow **corporate codes of conduct in Asia** is through the Asia Monitor Resource Center (www.amrc.org) with its quarterly magazine *Asian Labour Update* as well as publications reflecting its more agnostic view, such as *Can Corporate Codes of Conduct Promote Labor Standards? Evidence from the Thai Footwear and Apparel Industries* (2000).

For news and information from **Europe**, there is much that can be uncovered by following the publications and activities of International Restructuring Education Network Europe (IRENE) based in the Netherlands (irene@antenna.nl), the Clean Clothes Campaign (www.cleanclothes.org/codes/edu, which also includes information on the Ethical Trading Initiative mentioned by Hale), the Catholic Institute for International Relations (CIIR, www.ciir.org), and the New Economics Foundation (www.neweconomics.org). Among CIIR's reports and briefings, see Peter Pennartz and Myriam Vander Stichele's *Making It Our Business: NGO Campaigns for Corporate Responsibility* (1996). Simon Zadek of the New Economics Foundation and Maggie Burns of CIIR collaborated on the report of the Monitoring and Verification Working Group, *Opening Trading: Options for Effective Monitoring of Corporate Codes of Conduct* (London, 1997). In Geneva, Peter Utting provides an insightful view from within the United Nations Research Institute for Social Development (UNRISD, www.unrisd.org), as evident from a recent book project he coordinated: UNRISD, *Visible Hands: Taking Responsibility for Social Development—An UNRISD Report* (Geneva: United Nations Research Institute for Social Development, 2000).

For looks at **business–NGO collaboration** including codes, see Jem Bendell, ed., *Terms for Endearment: Business, NGOs, and Sustainable Development* (Sheffield, UK: Greenleaf, 2000); and *International Business Self-Regulation* by University of Maryland professor Virginia Hauffler (Washington, D.C.: Carnegie Endowment for International Peace, 2001). Another academic observer and analyst is historian Susan Aaronson at the Washington, D.C.–based National Policy Association; her "Oh, Behave!" *International Economy* (March/April 2001) includes probably the most detailed charts I have seen comparing the contents of voluntary codes (pp. 42–46).

As for useful **journals, magazines, and newsletters**: The UK *New Internationalist* monthly brilliantly covers corporate accountability initiatives (with special focus on development implications) and contains some of the best articles mixing popular accessibility with insightful analysis, such as "The Big Banana Split" (no. 317, October 1999), "Coffee: Spilling the Beans" (no. 271, September 1995), and "Fair Trade" (no. 322, April 2000). Also quite useful is Co-op America's publication, *Co-op America Quarterly* (www.coopamerica.org); see its "Guide to Ending Sweatshops" (Summer 2001, but a topic it continually updates) as well as "Introducing Responsible Shopping" (Spring 2001) and "WoodWise Consumer: Practices That Protect the Forests" (Summer 1998). Members of the Fair Trade Federation (as of 2001, housed at Co-op America) receive the newsletter *Network*. Contributors to Rugmark-U.S. receive its *Rugmark News*.

More on **child labor**: For a series of very thorough, comprehensive reports on child labor and details on initiatives, see the multiple volumes of *By the Sweat & Toil of Children* (beginning in 1994) by the U.S. Department of Labor's Bureau of International Labor Affairs as well as proceedings from public hearings on child labor (www.dol.gov/dol/ilab/public/programs/idlp/). Books have been written about Iqbal Masih, including one by Susan Kuklin (*Iqbal Masih and the Crusaders against Child Slavery*, New York: Henry Holt, 1998) and another by Canadian teenager Craig Kielburger with Kevin Major (*Free the Children: A Young Man Fights against Child Labour and Proves That Children Can Change the World*, Harperperennial Library, 1999). The stories of how encounters with Masih and other former child laborers catalyzed actions among Northern youth (including a then twelve-year-old Kielburger who went on to found Free the Children after chancing upon a story about Masih) also told on www.freethechildren.org and www.thirdworldtraveler.com/Heroes/Iqbal_Masih. To hear Masih give his 1994 acceptance speech, access www.diitalrag.com/iqbal/who/who.

Following the Rugmark model, innovative programs that combine eliminating child labor (backed up by surprise monitoring) with providing schooling and family stipends have been funded through the **ILO's International Program on the Elimination of Child Labor** (IPEC) (www.ilo.org/public/english/90ipec). See especially two cases: that of Bangladesh's garment export industry, agreed to by the Bangladeshi Garment Manufacturers Association, the United Nations Children's Fund (UNICEF), and the ILO; and a program in Pakistan for child labor elimination in making soccer balls that built on the ILRF's "Foul Ball" campaign.

Literature on **ATOs/fair trade organizations** is also available online through the sites of the various individual ATOs (such as www.equalexchange.org) as well as through their coalitions (see, for example, www.ifat.org). A still-timely piece that explains the religious and political origins of ATOs is Medea Benjamin and Andrea Freeman's *Bridging the Global Gap* (Cabin John, Md.: Seven Locks Press, 1989). A recent, intriguing addition to the literature, with in-depth case studies of individual ATOs, was written by two professors (one of textiles and clothing and the other of consumer and textile sciences): Mary Ann Lottrell and Marsha Ann Dickson, *Social Responsibility in the Global Market: Fair Trade of Cultural Products* (Thousand Oaks, Calif.: Sage Publications, 1999).

On **certification**, read Michael Conroy's longer paper from which I excerpt—available online through the University of Massachusetts-Amherst Political Economy Research Institute (www.umass.edu/peri) or in Kevin P. Gallagher and Jacob Werksman, eds., *Earthscan Reader on International Trade and Sustainable Development* (London: Earthscan, 2002). (The Gallagher and Werksman volume is worth reading in full for the broader trade-related topics it covers.) For an assessment of the FSC's impact as well as the debate it has catalyzed, turn to an unlikely source of information on citizen backlash initiatives: the *Wall Street Journal*, where reporter Jim Carlton offers his insights in "How Home Depot and Activists Joined to Cut Logging Abuse: If a Tree Falls in the Forest, the Small, Powerful FSC Wants to Have Its Say," *Wall Street Journal*, 26 September 2000. Kristin Dawkins's "Ecolabelling: Consumers' Right-to-Know or Restrictive Business Practice?" covers a wide range of issues related to environmental certification, including its potential WTO illegality (Global Environment and Trade Study Paper 95-3, Institute for Agriculture and Trade Policy, Minneapolis, Minn. 16 January 1996 revision, found online through www.iatp.org). Chad Dobson's Consumer Choice Council in Washington, D.C., likewise puts out useful papers on such voluntary initiatives.

For more on **codes of conduct and college campuses**, start with the primary web sites: those of the WRC and FLA (listed in the bibliography) as well as the apparel industry's Worldwide Responsible Apparel Production—or WRAP (www.wrapapparel.org)—principles. For the essence of the disagreement between the FLA and WRC, see the debate in the 7 April 2000 issue of *The Chronicle of Higher Education*: Bama Athreya, "We Need Immediate, Practical Solutions" versus Richard P. Appelbaum and Edna Bonacich, "The Key Is Enhancing the Power of Workers" (www.chronicle.com/weekly/v46/i31/31b004). In the United States, both *The Nation* and *In These Times* regularly report on these issues (with articles by, among others, David Moberg and Canadian Naomi Klein, whose 1999 book *No Logos* [Picador] has made her well-known within the backlash, especially in Canada and the United Kingdom). Other commentary can be found on the web sites of USAS and Sweatshop Watch. I have found that the best way to sort through secondary sources' claims and counterclaims is by going back to the text of the WRC and FLA codes of conduct and other protocols (although, as I have indicated, both WRC and FLA actions have moved beyond the written codes in some key areas).

To keep up with the **living wage issue**, follow the work of the Collegiate Living Wage Association formed in February 2001 (www.unc.edu/depts/livwage/clwa) and the Political Economy Research Institute (PERI) at the University of Massachusetts-Amherst (www.umass.edu/peri).

As for doing your own **shopping**, if you want to practice a more responsible variety, refer to the Council on Economic Priorities' *Students Shopping for a Better World*, a take-off on CEP's well-known *Shopping for a Better World*. (See www.cepnyc.org.) Check out *Consumer Report*'s www.ecolabels.org to learn what different labels are all about, as well as *Consumer Report*'s evaluation of each.

Part V

ROLLING BACK GLOBALIZATION

Part V

Rolling Back Globalization

Segments of the citizen backlash against economic globalization have gone beyond the reform proposals of social clauses, corporate codes of conduct, and other initiatives discussed in Parts III and IV. Instead, these other segments advocate stopping—or rolling back—particular facets of corporate-led economic globalization.

In culling backlash literature and proposals, three main categories of goods and services seem to call forth proposals to "roll back" rather than "reshape" from at least parts of the backlash. A first concerns the "global commons." The argument, often made in environmental terms, is that some goods—such as water, seeds, and food—belong to all people and/or are essential for human beings and their world. A second category is that of so-called pernicious goods and services such as toxic waste or drugs or laundered money, which by their very nature are bad and whose very flow across borders brings harm. Some rollback proponents take this argument a step further, decrying "hot money" or speculative financial flows. Moving beyond "pernicious" goods, a third category consists of certain global flows—such as debt payments by poor nations—that rollback advocates argue should be stopped on moral grounds whatever the economic arguments.

In various "stop" or "rollback" campaigns, proposals, and initiatives, different combinations of these three arguments are deployed. In essence, whichever of these arguments is used, the proposals grow from the premise that there are goals more important than efficiency, growth, and getting the cheapest goods to the consumer or the most profit to the seller. Most rollback proposals are grounded in goals of revitalizing local economies, honoring collective property rights over private property, and asserting basic economic and social rights for all. As a result, "rollbackers" are almost by definition "localists"; that is, they focus on empowering local parts of civil society.

However, invariably, rollback citizen groups also assert regulatory approaches to these problems (explained in Part III) rather than voluntary approaches (explained in Part IV). While privileging the role of the grass roots, they also argue for a role for governments, for example, in delivering basic resources, in protecting the commons or granting local communities the property rights to their commons so that they can protect them themselves, and in taxing or regulating cross-border flows such as speculative capital.

The rollback proposals grow out of a basic premise: economic globalization is not inevitable. That premise and the resulting proposals and initiatives tend to elicit the condescension of the mainstream media. Writing for the *New York Times*, columnist Thomas Friedman expressed palpable derision for "those that suggest globalization can be stopped. It can't. It's inevitable."[1] I would argue, however, that it is a basic misunderstanding (or perhaps an unwillingness to listen to details) of the rollback proponents and their proposals that has fueled the overall impression spread by much of the mainstream media that the backlash is opposed to all forms of globalization—is "anti-globalization." These groups are often caricatured by the media as Luddites. Indeed, as noted in the introduction to this book, the most prevalent image in the media over the past few years has been of young people, armed with masks and posters, who reject anything to do with globalization. Like most stereotypes, this one is far from the truth—certainly of the overall citizen backlash but also even of the "rollback" part of the backlash.

In fact, on a certain level, the backlash is unified, be its members within the reshape or the rollback segments. From a wide swath of the backlash, one hears voiced an apparent consensus that some trade, some investment, and some aid under the *right* conditions can be a vital force in building healthy and sustainable economies. Simultaneously, there is increasing concurrence within the backlash that certain aspects of economic globalization should be stopped. In other words, whether one chooses to reshape or roll back depends to some extent on the conditions of a particular aspect of economic globalization. The necessary response depends on the specifics of a given reality.

But, as I will also demonstrate, there are differences between those committed to reshape and those to rollback, with concomitant debates ranging from that over certification initiatives such as the Forest Stewardship Council's (discussed in Part IV) to that over social clauses and other attempts to reform the international institutions that manage the world economy. To a certain extent those who focus on reshaping do believe that economic globalization is inevitable but propose initiatives to reduce the environmental and social costs and increase the benefits of that integration. Those who advocate rolling back often possess a different strategic goal, that of placing certain things off-limits to corporate-led globalization.

In Part V, I present key declarations, documents, and analyses of several of the most salient rollback campaigns, proposals, and initiatives: on food security, seeds, and water, on speculative financial flows and external debt, on over-consumption (mostly in richer countries but also among the elite in the poorer countries), and on "de-globalization" of the private and public institutions that dominate and manage today's global economy.

The Masked Man

I begin with one of the most articulate and widely quoted contemporary spokespersons for stopping certain aspects of globalization: the man who is widely known as Subcomandante Marcos. In January 1994, Marcos helped ignite an Indian uprising in the southern Mexican state of Chiapas on the day that the North American Free Trade Agreement went into effect. And, ironically, he became famous as his face, hidden behind a black ski mask, was flashed around the globe by the media.[2]

The movement he leads, known as the Zapatista Army of National Liberation, can be seen as the first popular uprising against contemporary economic globalization. The Zapatistas rejected NAFTA and its attendant economic model of maximizing trade and foreign investment (a set of policies for which I used the label "Washington Consensus" in Part I and which Marcos and many in Latin America refer to as "neoliberalism"). Whatever their accomplishments on the ground in Mexico, Marcos and the Zapatistas raised awareness worldwide about those most marginalized by economic globalization going back more than 500 years to colonial days: indigenous peoples. Moreover, the Zapatistas captured the attention of young people worldwide and inspired many of the youth who joined globalization protests in the ensuing years.

Marcos himself—officially the Zapatistas' spokesperson and chief military strategist, but also a poet, a comedian, a historian, a psychologist, and a critic—emerged as one of the most visible (yet hidden) heroes of the citizen backlash. Reading 5.1 weaves together excerpts from three of his essays. In essays such as these, Marcos's words reached the far corners of the earth via the Internet, an example of the backlash's finesse at using the technologies of globalization to resist economic globalization and one piece of evidence that the majority of those in the rollback camp are not against all aspects of globalization. Reading 5.1 offers Marcos's analysis of how economic globalization is "bleeding" Chiapas's peasants and its natural resources. (It is rich in oil, lumber, and other natural resources.) Like many of the rollback campaigns, Marcos and the Zapatistas center their critique on the impact of economic globalization on the environment, on inequality, and on the erosion of democratic rights. Beyond critique, Marcos's writings also describe the Zapatista program to stop that bleeding, a program that began to be implemented in the early months of the rebellion before the Mexican military pushed most of the rebels deep into the jungles of Chiapas. Despite several failed negotiations with the Mexican government, the Zapatistas continue their battle against the "bleeding" and, in Marcos's words, for "democracy, liberty, and justice."

The Right to Food

In essence, all rollback analyses focus on stopping some kind of "bleeding." The three readings that follow Subcomandante Marcos's focus on campaigns to assert

peoples' rights over food, seeds, and water and to stop the bleeding of these resources needed for basic survival.

The second reading (Reading 5.2) is by Swedish linguist Helena Norberg-Hodge
and two of her colleagues from the UK-based International Society for Ecology and
Culture. Norberg-Hodge's group is not only an advocacy organization intent on reducing the distance between consumers and producers; in the early 1990s it also
organized farmers' markets in the United Kingdom and elsewhere.

The authors capture the arguments of one of the fastest growing components of
the citizen backlash: organizations advocating food security and food safety.
Building on the backlash's concern with the growing reach of global corporations,
Norberg-Hodge and her colleagues offer a critique of the growing control of food
systems by giant agribusiness firms. They point out the devastating impact of
agribusiness on the small farmers who still produce most of the world's food as
well as the severe ecological costs of the increasing distances that food products
travel before reaching consumers. They chronicle the rise of movements that oppose genetically engineered food and chemical-intensive agriculture and that are
advocating a return to most food being grown locally and organically. Their argument for localizing food systems finds counterparts in Marcos's chronicles of Zapatista proposals for Chiapas and in many others within the citizen backlash who
focus on revitalizing local economies.

Like many in the rollback camp, however, they offer prescriptions that start
with the local level but move onto the national and global levels. Let me rephrase
that point for emphasis: Although their focus is on localization of agricultural systems, their proposals are not naïve; they see the need for changes at the local, national, and global levels.

A vibrant, grassroots movement, allied to the food activists, is found in peasant organizations across the South (and among Northern small farmers) fighting the growing control of the world's seed resources by corporate agribusiness. Given the importance of rice as a subsistence crop and the fact that more of the world's population
is engaged in growing rice than in any other occupation, many of the campaigns focus on rice seeds. For thousands of years in most agricultural communities, peasants
have saved, traded, and exchanged traditional seed varieties. As I witnessed firsthand when I lived in a rice-growing region of the Philippines, it is part of a peasant's
economy: rice farmers try above all else not to have to eat all the rice from a given
growing season. Then, they have a savings account of rice seed for the next crop.

In the early 1990s, however, corporations engineered a critical change in the "intellectual property rights" regime when the United States passed a law granting
plant breeders the right to patent seeds.[3] In recent decades, Monsanto, Cargill, and
other agribusiness giants have bought up seed companies and control an increasing share of the world's seeds.

These firms were a driving force behind extending the U.S. law globally
through one of the most controversial agreements that make up the World Trade
Organization, the agreement on Trade-Related Intellectual Property Rights (or
TRIPs). The TRIPs agreement expands global "intellectual property" rules to include seeds, which, as a result, can be patented (for twenty years) and owned by

grain and other companies. (TRIPs have similar ramifications for pharmaceuticals.) Overnight, in the words of globally renowned Indian scientist and activist Vandana Shiva: "Seed saving by farmers has now been redefined from a sacred duty to a criminal offence of stealing 'property.'"[4] Peasants find themselves in the absurd situation of being discouraged from "saving" and encouraged—if not forced—to buy new seed for every crop. In addition, there is an environmental cost: the corporations' focus is not on maintaining the breadth of biodiversity that existed for rice during the centuries when seeds were under peasant control. (On the WTO, see Reading 2.8 by Gélinas and Reading 3.6 by Khor.)

Consequently, in India, the Philippines, Thailand, and other countries with large subsistence peasant populations, movements have emerged to fight what Shiva terms "biopiracy": the theft of biodiversity and indigenous knowledge through patents.[5] The initial response was fury: in India, for instance, peasants "occupied" a Cargill office warehouse and destroyed another Cargill seed unit that was being built.[6]

Beyond civil disobedience, rollback initiatives span international, national, and local levels. Continuing with the Indian case: Shiva's Research Foundation for Science, Technology and Ecology spearheads the research and advocacy work, nationally and internationally. In addition, it also has helped to draft a model Biodiversity-Related Community Intellectual Rights Act and to provide support for the establishment of village-level "Jaiv Panchayat: Living Democracy" in order to rejuvenate traditional systems of common property resource management.

Reading 5.3 is an excerpt from information provided by the Research Foundation for Science, Technology, and Ecology on Jaiv Panchayat. That excerpt includes three main sections. First, an introductory section or "report" explains the Jaiv Panchayat concept. A second section summarizes a community's actual Jaiv Panchayat Declaration (with quotes from remarks Shiva delivered on the occasion). A final section details grassroots actions taken by villagers to make the Jaiv Panchayat more than a document. As a whole, the reading provides specifics on the principles and actions upon which this Jaiv Panchayat movement in India is attempting to build what it calls "living democracy."

The issues and concerns found in the Indian case study are replicated elsewhere. Indeed, in September 2000, groups from Cambodia, Malaysia, the Philippines, and Thailand as well as India, staged a twelve-day "Long March" as part of their campaigns for biodiversity and against TNC-control of patent rights for seeds.[7]

Whose Water?

Campaigns to localize food, weaken corporate agribusiness, and assert collective property rights over seeds have recently been joined by campaigns on water. For decades, environmental, indigenous, community, and other organizations have fought World Bank and other funding of large-scale dams on environmental, human rights (in terms of the impact on the local population), and development (in terms of prioritizing commercial/corporate end users over community needs) grounds.[8] (See Reading 2.7.) Since the late 1990s, the movement to stop the funding of large-scale dams has been complemented by an increasingly vocal component of the citizen backlash: a movement against for-profit global trade in water and for the fundamental right to clean, afford-able water by people, especially poor people.

Two individuals from two countries, one from the North and one from the South, have played catalytic roles. In Canada, activist and writer Maude Barlow discovered that corporations were buying up Canada's water supplies to export as "bulk" water. Barlow is the national chair of Canada's largest public advocacy group, the over-100,000-strong Council of Canadians. Barlow authored a global call to action entitled *Blue Gold: The Global Water Crisis and the Commodification of the World's Water Supply*.[9] Building on decades of work within the backlash, she used her information to spark a Canadian movement opposing the "commodifi-cation and marketing" of water—specifically, against her government's initiatives to turn fresh water into a commodity to be privatized to corporations and trans-ported across the globe in "bulk" via tankers and pipelines (often for industrial agriculture and water-intensive high tech industries). The movement also is fight-ing new trade agreements that give corporations broader rights to purchase pub-lic water systems and that strip governments and citizens of the right to decide ex-actly how water should be provided and by whom.

Several thousand miles to the south in Cochabamba, Bolivia, factory worker Os-car Olivera too became a leader of a complementary grassroots movement cen-tered on water. Actually, Olivera was a trade unionist, not an environmentalist. As he explains in an interview with two of my research assistants: "We've been fight-ing for . . . years over labor rights. . . . Then the *campesinos* [peasants] got together and knocked on the door of our union federation . . . to tell us that you all shouldn't just be working for rights in the factory . . . but also for the right to life that water represents. In so doing, the *campesinos* taught us a great deal, that the world is much larger, that there's a greater union."[10]

The story of what happened once these diverse sectors fused is a tale of rollback success: With advice from the World Bank,[11] the government in 1999 had sold off the city's water supply to a private consortium partially owned by the U.S.-based Bechtel Enterprise Holdings. As water rates soared and as a referendum of the city's residents indicated 90 percent opposition to the privatized water system, Olivera was instrumental in pulling together the "Coordinadora" (coordinating committee, or the Coalition in Defense of Water and Life). The coalition of workers, peasants, city dwellers, environmentalists, and others took to the streets—more than once, and at one point some 100,000 of them.[12] Despite numerous setbacks and the mili-tary repression of this movement, Olivera and his colleagues managed to get the government to terminate its contract with the Bechtel consortium.[13]

Antonia Juhasz of the International Forum on Globalization describes (after a trip to Cochabamba) what happened next:

> no one was providing the city with water. So the workers of the water company . . .
> began running the system themselves. With the help of La Coordinadora, the water

workers held regular citizens' meetings to determine need. They reduced prices, built new water tanks and laid pipes—bringing service to neighborhoods that had never received water before. Funding proposals were devised to attract investment to make the company solvent [given that the Bechtel consortium had left it in debt]. For the first time, water is being provided universally, fairly and reliably.[14]

From this experience Olivera came to understand that "water cannot be considered merchandise. We have to learn from the *campesinos*, who have a very different concept of what water is and means. Water . . . is a commonly owned good that should be distributed in a fair and just way. And there has to be some kind of social control over the administering of water. . . . [W]ater should be administered by all society, not just a few. It's what we call self-management of water."[15]

These are among the ideas underpinning the Cochabamba Declaration, the brief but historic declaration reprinted as Reading 5.4. The declaration was drafted (and signed) in December 2000 at a meeting in Bolivia attended by hundreds. What makes it a seminal document is that international water activists took their lead from Olivera, the Coordinadora, the water workers, and other Bolivians in the audience. As the International Forum on Globalization's Juhasz explains to me,

> After a morning of presentations, we began the discussion period. The audience was the most diverse I had ever experienced in my life: young, old, workers, peasants, scholars, students, business people, retired people. . . . At a certain point, the audience asked that we stop talking theory and start talking action. So [the speakers] asked for volunteers from the audience . . . to draft an action statement. Several women from the audience joined [us].[16]

Collectively they wrote this declaration, which builds from the Cochabamba experience to delineate a set of three international "rights," which they argue should govern the use and control of water in Bolivia and elsewhere.

By the turn of the century, Olivera in Bolivia and Barlow in Canada had joined Marcos as well-known heroes of the citizen backlash. In July 2001, their groups joined efforts with water activists from around the world to turn their campaigns into a global rollback movement focused on the global water commons. The setting this time was Vancouver, Canada, under the banner: "Water for People and Nature: An International Forum on Conservation and Human Rights." Convened by the Council of Canadians, summit participants unanimously endorsed an initiative (Reading 5.5) to transform the principles and rights of the Cochabamba Declaration into an international treaty—a "global constitution" on water—to be signed by "nation states and indigenous peoples." Together, these two documents (Readings 5.4 and 5.5) reveal the local, national, and international dimensions of the global rollback water campaign: since access to safe and clean water is a fundamental right of all people, water must not be turned into a commodity controlled by private global corporations; governments have an obligation to fulfill that right; and, crucially, local communities and citizens have key roles to play in its control, management, and distribution, as they are doing in Bolivia.

Shutting Down the Financial Casino

Just as Subcomandante Marcos and others have spearheaded initiatives to stop the "bleeding" of natural resources out of the South, other campaigns have focused on the "bleeding" of financial resources from the South. Since 1982, when Mexico and a number of other countries experienced great difficulties in servicing debts owed to Northern banks, governments, and international financial institutions, some Southern governments have insisted that their foreign debt cannot be repaid in full.

But even louder than these governmental voices have been those of a diverse swath of civil society, creating a widespread movement that has demanded that at least some Southern debts be canceled. Over time, religious institutions came to take the lead. Religious activists around the world rooted their call for debt cancellation in a passage from the Bible, a passage that calls for a "Jubilee" of forgiving debts every fifty years. By the late 1990s, "Jubilee" movements for debt cancellation existed in dozens of countries, North and South. They focused their advocacy on the then-upcoming new millennium and the debt of the forty to fifty poorest nations on earth, most of whose debts were owed to governments, the World Bank, and the IMF (and therefore were politically easier to cancel than debt owed to the private sector).

By the turn of the century, what had once been a small rollback movement for debt cancellation was transformed into a powerful pressure group. The Pope, rock stars like singer Bono (lead singer of the group U-2), and other celebrities joined the clamor for debt cancellation. On the one hand, the Jubilee moment has been successful as several Northern governments canceled some debts owed to them. On the other hand, it is only a partial victory since the debt relief is conditioned upon a country's acceptance of traditional Washington Consensus or neoliberal policies. (See Reading 2.8 by Gélinas for more details on these "structural adjustment" policies.) This partial success, however, did set an important precedent: that moral arguments—that the debt was "fraudulent, odious, illegal, immoral, illegitimate, obscene, and genocidal," as one declaration from an NGO meeting in Senegal phrased it[17]—could win the upper hand in globalization debates.

For more details on the rollback campaign on Third World debt, I turn to a document from the overarching coalition of Southern Jubilee groups called Jubilee South. Jubilee South is significant in that it is an example of a new formation for South–South collaborative work that then lays the basis for South–North collaboration. As Jubilee South describes itself:

> Jubilee South is a network and emerging movement of more than 80 debt campaigns, social movements and people's organizations from more than 40 countries in the South—Latin America and the Caribbean, Africa, and Asia/Pacific. These movements and groups from the three regions gathered together in South-South solidarity to advance a common analysis, vision and strategy to seek to overcome the debt problem and the effects and consequences of debt-related domination on the environment, on economies and on peoples and communities. It sees itself also con-

tributing to South-North solidarity and works with debt campaigns and social movements from the North in addressing the debt problem and struggling for economic justice and liberation.[18]

In November 1999, on the eve of the historic WTO ministerial meeting in Seattle, representatives from Jubilee South coalitions in thirty-five countries of Africa, Asia, and Latin America met in South Africa. From that meeting came the "South–South Summit Declaration: Towards a Debt-Free Millennium" (Reading 5.6). The document is itself historic, given that the meeting marked the first time that Jubilee South groups from across the globe met in a "summit." The declaration moves from background analysis of the debt to detail a Jubilee South strategy for achieving more comprehensive debt cancellation without the onerous macroeconomic policy conditions.

During the 1990s, a corollary movement to the Jubilee activists emerged around another perceived injustice of the global financial system. Financial institutions have been among the innovators and prime users of new information technologies that speed the transmission of financial resources around the globe.[19] And, from the 1990s onward, more and more people in the North have become participants in the increasingly global financial system as owners of mutual funds and pension funds. Consequently, nearly two trillion dollars' worth of foreign exchange transactions occur daily as financial institutions send money across borders to seek the highest returns for investors. The vast bulk of these transactions are divorced from the "real" economy of production and trade and are instead purely speculative transactions. Many have called this "hot money"; others call it the "casino economy."[20]

Back in the mid-1990s as these flows grew, some backlash supporters had warned of the instability of these flows, while the World Bank (and other pro-globalization institutions and individuals) had been rather cavalier and unconcerned.[21] But in 1997 and 1998, the havoc that could be wreaked by the instability of the casino economy became a reality when speculative investors panicked and removed their funds overnight from a series of countries. The panic began in July 1997 in Thailand, and quickly spread to the Philippines, Indonesia, and South Korea. In ensuing months, the panic spread north to Russia and then around the globe to Brazil. IMF bailouts (new loans with Washington Consensus economic conditions attached) only exacerbated the situation. As tens of billions of dollars exited these countries, stock markets and currencies plunged, slamming millions of middle-class people into poverty overnight. Hundreds of millions of people around the world were affected.[22]

The global financial crisis, in turn, sparked new activism around backlash proposals to control the financial casino. Notable in this work is a group based in France called ATTAC (Association for the Taxation of Financial Transactions for the Aid of Citizens) which was founded in 1998 but grew almost overnight to more than 100 local committees, more than 15,000 members, and dozens of affiliates around the world.[23] ATTAC, working with other groups such as the Halifax Initiative in Canada, Tobin Tax Initiative-USA in the United States, and others in the

Philippines and elsewhere, called for a new global financial architecture that fa-vored responsible and sustainable long-term investment over short-term specula-tive flows. In terms of specific policy proposals, many of these groups resurrected one relatively obscure idea suggested by Nobel prize–winning economist James Tobin of Yale University in the 1970s.[24] Tobin argued that speculative flows could be reduced by placing a small transactions tax on cross-border currency transac-tions with the proceeds supporting development. Thus came ATTAC's and others' call for the "Tobin tax" or a "financial transaction tax."

For more details of the rollback proposal here, I reprint a speech given by Robin Round of the Halifax Initiative, a coalition of fourteen nongovernmental organi-zations in Canada (Reading 5.7). I chose the speech in part because Round is one of the key backlash proponents of and organizers for such a Tobin tax. I chose it in part for the clarity with which she explains Tobin tax initiatives and successes. Among those successes is one for which Round and the Halifax Initiative were di-rectly responsible: the 1999 Canadian House of Common's passage of a motion calling for a Tobin tax which sparked similar statements from leaders in Brazil, Finland, Belgium, and elsewhere.

I also chose to reprint Round's words because of the auspicious occasion on which she delivered them. Round gave the speech at the first World Social Forum in Porto Alegre, Brazil, in January 2001. That five-day gathering, for which ATTAC was a key organizer, attracted over 10,000 citizen backlash participants. The meet-ing was timed to parallel and critique the three-decade-old annual World Eco-nomic Forum of political and corporate leaders in Davos, Switzerland (who for the most part extolled the virtues of globalization while expressing concern about the growing power of the backlash). Beyond critiquing Davos, World Social Fo-rum participants presented an alternative set of visions and proposals.

In turn, ATTAC had chosen Porto Alegre as the site of the Forum for its sym-bolic value. The Brazilian city is governed by the Workers Party, which has put in place a series of local initiatives applauded by the backlash as an example of what local governments, committed to true participatory democracy, can do.

Curbing Consumption

Each of the movements highlighted above has attempted to stop some aspect of economic globalization, from far-flung food trade, to the patenting of rice seed, to water privatization, to debt payments, to "hot money." None rejects economic globalization per se; rather each singles out a current trend or a current set of rules for rollback. Each, to varying degrees, is meeting with some success.

While most of these movements focus on activities that have both Northern and Southern components, there is a movement that is almost exclusively Northern and that properly belongs in this rollback framework. This is the movement to cut consumption levels on the basis of equity, social, ecological, and just plain "enjoy-ment of life" considerations. Until recently it seemed to stand apart from other backlash campaigns, but as author and economist Juliet Schor noted: "What's really interesting about Seattle is that it brought together environmentalism, more traditional labor issues and a critique of global consumerism. That's a combination we haven't had in recent history. Consumerism is back on the table again."[25]

This segment of the rollback is spearheaded by groups like Betsy Taylor's Center for a New American Dream in the United States, ecological economists led by Herman Daly, and academics and writers like Schor, Wendell Berry, and the late Donella Meadows. The movement builds on a "simplicity movement" that goes back to Gandhi and even further back to indigenous communities around the world. But their call for consumption cuts in the North has been buttressed by new scientific studies that predict massive increases in climate change if greenhouse gas emissions are not reduced.

In Reading 5.8, I excerpt from a classic of the modern version of this movement, environmentalist Alan Durning's "How Much Is 'Enough'?" Key to Durning's argument is the distinction among three groups. At one end are the richest billion "over-consumers" on earth (mostly but not solely in the North) who need to and can cut consumption levels; at the other end, the poorest one billion "under-consumers" (mostly in the South). And in the middle are the remaining approximately three billion of the earth's inhabitants who, as Durning explains in more detail, ride mass transit and bikes, eat locally grown food (mostly grain), and in general lead a lifestyle that is the most sustainable environmentally and socially. Note that Durning is not saying that "voluntary simplicity" will save all; he also calls for broader governmental action.

As such, the arguments bring us back to those of Subcomandante Marcos, Helena Norberg-Hodge and her colleagues, and peasants in India and in Bolivia—for groups in the rollback, localization is at least part of the answer.

"Reform" versus "Reject"

As I stated at the outset of this introduction, many of the campaigns outlined above are embraced by a wide range of individuals and groups within the citizen backlash. Even though these campaigns reject certain aspects of economic globalization, they are often joined by groups who tend to focus their advocacy on reforming the global economy through the sorts of campaigns highlighted in Parts III and IV of this book. Many activists are quite comfortable pressing for reshaping in certain arenas and pressing for rollback in others.

This said, there are areas of tension over the ultimate strategic goals of the citizen backlash. For example, one of the reshape campaigns mentioned in Part IV was the Forest Stewardship Council, which focuses on the certification of traded forest products to ensure that they are produced under sustainable conditions. (See Readings 4.7 and 4.8.) While some in the backlash embrace this strategy, other rollback groups reject trade in forest products in general—and especially those from virgin forests—as destroying vital natural resources and biodiversity. One well-circulated critique by two authors with on-the-ground experience put it this way: "the FSC is leveraging open tropical timber markets in Europe and the

United States which were closed by the boycott campaigns in the 1990s. It is offering a survival option for logging companies and attracting new international investment for logging of primary forests." Other rollback critiques have argued for some time that even the so-called green trade of alternative, non-timber rainforest products (like nuts for "rainforest crunch" ice cream or tagua for buttons) hooks small-scale producers into a vulnerable dependence on fickle Northern consumers and replicates the inequity-exacerbating impacts of overall trade.[26]

Undoubtedly, one of the biggest and most important "reform" versus "reject" debates in the citizen backlash concerns strategic goals vis-à-vis the public and private institutions that control and dominate the world economy—the World Bank, the IMF, and the WTO as well as transnational corporations. (See Part II for more on the history of these institutions and resistance to them.) As seen in Part III, some reshape groups seek to amend the WTO with enforceable social charters on labor and environmental rights; some rollback groups advocate the abolition of the WTO. Likewise, some reshape groups are attempting to shift the World Bank's energy lending from fossil fuels to renewable energy, while some rollback groups argue that such a shift would simply offer legitimacy to a fundamentally flawed institution that should be shut down.[27] As seen in Part IV, some reshape groups are working to get corporations to adopt and enforce codes of conduct; some rollback groups are instead campaigning to "de-charter" private corporations as they exist today.[28]

One of the most articulate presentations of the "rollback" side of the "reform" versus "reject" debate is that of Philippine scholar and activist Walden Bello, the founder of the Focus on the Global South based in Thailand. Bello began working on the World Bank nearly thirty years ago, trying to stop the flow of its funding which bolstered and legitimized the dictatorship of Ferdinand Marcos in his home country. In the final reading of this part (Reading 5.9), Bello lays out the argument for "de-globalization"—"disabling or dismantling" the World Bank, the IMF, and the WTO as well as private transnational corporations.

In Brief

I opened this book and this introduction with comments on the caricature of the backlash—and especially of the rollback campaigners—as "anti-globalization" Luddites. As Mike Moore, WTO director general, put it (with clear exasperation): "[Globalisation is] an awful phrase. I wish it had never been invented. But the stupidity of thinking globalisation will stop if the WTO doesn't meet or the World Bank doesn't meet . . . I mean give me a break."[29]

As Part V is meant to convey, however, the rollback campaigns and proposals exhibit a degree of logic and sophistication that can hardly be characterized by "stupidity of thinking." As development economist Paul Streeten wrote in the pages of the IMF's quarterly publication *Finance & Development*: "It is often said that globalization is irreversible. But history shows that it is highly reversible."[30]

In fact, some of the great minds behind the very economic systems that the rollbackers protest might have joined them in teach-ins, if not on the streets, had they lived to see the reality of today's global economic system. As backlash author and chronicler David Korten discovered, some 200 years ago Adam Smith, the father of classical economics, "wrote about place-based economies comprised of small, locally owned enterprises that function within a community-supported ethical culture to engage people in producing for the needs of the community and its members."[31] And, as the father of modern macroeconomics but also a seeming rollback-supporter Lord John Maynard Keynes wrote in 1933 in a quote often repeated by writers within the global backlash: "I sympathize, therefore, with those who minimize, rather than with those who would maximize, economic entanglements between nations. Ideas, knowledge, art, hospitality, travel—these are the things which should of their nature be international. But let goods be homespun whenever it is reasonably and conveniently possible, and, above all, let finance be primarily national."[32]

The rest of this section of Keynes's article is rarely if ever quoted, but it responds to those who would chastise rollback advocates as being too visionary. In addition, Keynes's 1933 words seem eerily prescient of the world post–11 September 2001:

> Yet, at the same time, those who seek to disembarrass a country of its entanglements should be very slow and wary. It should not be a matter of tearing up roots but of slowly training a plant to grow in a different direction.
>
> For these strong reasons, therefore, I am inclined to the belief that, after the transition is accomplished, a greater measure of national self-sufficiency and economic isolation among countries than existed in 1914 may tend to serve the cause of peace, rather than otherwise. At any rate, the age of economic internationalism was not particularly successful at avoiding war; and if its friends retort that the imperfection of its success never gave it a fair chance, it is reasonable to point out that a greater success is scarcely probable in the coming years.

Notes

1. Thomas L. Friedman, "Roll Over Hawks and Doves," *New York Times*, 7 February 1997. Editorial in his "Foreign Affairs" column.

2. Marcos's real name is Rafael Sebastian Guillen, and he was once a sociology student. Jose De Cordoba, "Zapatista Tour Culminates in Mexico's Capital," *Wall Street Journal*, 12 March 2001, A14. According to John Ross, the "EZLN's ethnic base includes 5 Chiapas Mayan subgroups." See his "Mexican Wave," *The Ecologist* 31, no. 3 (April 2001): 53.

3. Karen Lehman, "Pirates of Diversity: The Global Threat to the Earth's Seeds," Institute for Agriculture and Trade Policy, Minneapolis, Minn., July 1994, 1.

4. Vandana Shiva, "The Threat to Third World Farmers," *The Ecologist*, Special Report, September 2000, 42.

5. See Vandana Shiva, *Biopiracy: The Plunder of Nature and Knowledge* (Boston: South End Press, 1997).

6. Karnataka Rajya Ryota Sangha (KRRS or the Karnataka State Farmers' Association) is the Indian farmers' movement that was involved in this act of what it terms "civil disobedience" as well as a 1996 "occupation" of a Kentucky Fried Chicken outlet. See www.home.iae.nl/users/lightnet/world/indianfarmer.htm (accessed 29 July 2001); and www.iuf.org/iuf/LF/14.htm (accessed 29 July 2001).

7. See "Declaration on Biodiversity Protection and Local People's Rights in Asia with Regard to Genetic Engineering (GE) and Intellectual Property Rights (IPR)," 24 September 2000 at www.grain.org/dsp_updates (accessed 29 July 2001).

8. See Sanjeev Khagram, "Toward Democratic Governance for Sustainable Development: Transnational Civil Society Organizing around Big Dams," in *The Third Force: The Rise of Transnational Civil Society*, ed. Ann Florini (Washington, D.C.: Carnegie Endowment for International Peace, and Tokyo: Japan Center for International Exchange, 2000): 83–114.

9. Maude Barlow, *Blue Gold: The Global Water Crisis and the Commodification of the World's Water Supply*, a special report issued by the International Forum on Globalization (San Francisco: International Forum on Globalization, June 1999): 1–46.

10. Interview (conducted in Spanish) with Oscar Olivera, by my research assistants Jay Gutzwiller and Zahara Heckscher, Washington, D.C., 19 October 2000.

11. The World Bank summary of its $20 million technical assistance project (under the Bank's International Development Association, approved by the Bank's board on 30 June 1998) to Bolivia for "Regulatory Reform and Privatization" states: "The primary beneficiaries will be domestic and foreign investors who benefit from better financial intermediation and consumers receiving better public services." World Bank Group, "Loan and Credit Summary," www.worldbank.org/html/extdr/newprojects/lc1862 (accessed 10 October 2000).

12. Number is from Noreen Hertz, "I'm on Their Side, To a Point," *Washington Post* (29 July 2001), B2.

13. The consortium is called International Water Limited and is jointly owned by Bechtel and the Italian utility Edison. The information on Cochabamba is based on Oscar Olivera and Tom Kruse, speech and discussion, sponsored by the AFL-CIO, Washington, D.C., 16 October 2000; Jim Schultz, "Bolivia's Water War Victory," *Earth Island Journal* 15, no. 3 (Fall 2000); Chris Ney, "Nor Any Drop to Drink: The Fight for Water in Bolivia," *The Non-Violent Activist* [of the War Resisters' League], (September–October 2000): 8–10, and 17; and Interview with Oscar Olivera in *Multinational Monitor* (May 2000) (accessed via the Center for Economic Justice web site, 208.55.75.172/cej/bolivia.htm).

14. Antonia Juhasz, "Bolivian Water War Presents Alternative to Globalization of Water," in International Forum on Globalization, *IFG Bulletin* (Summer 2001): 5. This is a special issue on water.

15. Interview (conducted in Spanish) with Oscar Olivera, by my research assistants Jay Gutzwiller and Zahara Heckscher, Washington, D.C., 19 October 2000.

16. Antonia Juhasz, International Forum on Globalization, e-mail to author, 19 September 2001.

17. Participants in the Dakar 2000 Meeting for the Cancellation of Third World Debts, "The Dakar Declaration for the Total and Unconditional Cancellation of African and Third World Debt," Dakar, Senegal, adopted 14 December 2000, 1.

18. Lidy Nakpil, Jubilee South and Freedom from Debt Coalition, Manila, Philippines, e-mail to author, 20 September 2001.

19. See Richard J. Barnet and John Cavanagh, *Global Dreams: Imperial Corporations and the New World Order* (New York: Simon & Schuster, 1994), part IV.

20. "The global flow of foreign exchange has reached the incredible figure of $2 trillion per day, 98 percent of which is speculative." Paul Streeten, "Integration, Interdependence, and Globalization," *Finance & Development* 38, no. 2 (June 2001): 37.

21. See Robin Broad and Christina Landi, "Whither the North-South Gap?" *Third World Quarterly* 17 (1996) which can be found reprinted in Robert J. Griffiths, ed., *Annual Editions: Developing World 98/99* (Guilford, Conn.: Dushkin/McGraw-Hill, 1998, 8th edition).

22. See Manuel Montes, *The Currency Crisis in Southeast Asia* (Singapore: Institute of Southeast Asian Studies, 1998).

23. Daniel Singer, "Seattle from the Seine," *The Nation*, 3 January 2000, 6 (editorial).

24. James Tobin, "A Proposal for International Monetary Reform," *Eastern Economic Journal* 4, no. 3–4 (July/October 1978): 153–59.

25. Juliet Schor quoted in Penelope Green, "Consumerism and Its Discontents," *New York Times*, 17 December 2000, 1 (Sunday Styles).

26. The direct quote is from Klemens Laschefski and Nicole Freris, "Saving the Wood . . . From the Trees," *The Ecologist* 31, no. 6 (July/August 2001): 43. Laschefski is the "forest spokesperson for Friends of the Earth Germany," now writing a thesis on certification while based in Brazil. Freris is also based in Brazil. A similar critique of the FSC was voiced in interviews with two Indonesia-based experts: Paul (Chip) Fay, policy analyst, based in Bogor, Indonesia, at the International Center for Research in Agroforestry; and Nonette Royo, team leader, Biodiversity Support Program-KEMALA, based in Jakarta, Indonesia. Both interviews took place in Hull, Massachusetts, in August 2001.

For the debate on "green trade," see Michael R. Dove, "Marketing the Rainforest: 'Green' Panacea or Red Herring?" *AsiaPacific Issues: Analysis from the East-West Center*, no. 13 (May 1994): 1–8; and Jason Clay, "Why Rainforest Crunch?" *Cultural Survival* 16, no. 2 (Spring 1992): 31–37.

For another excellent example of this debate, see the lively back-and-forth between *Ecologist* editor Zac Goldsmith and deputy editor Paul Kingsnorth: "How Local Can We Go?" *The Ecologist* 31, no. 3 (April 2001): 20–23.

27. For an overview of this debate, see the materials of the Sustainable Energy and Economy Network of the Institute for Policy Studies: www.seen.org.

28. Richard Grossman and Frank Adams, "Taking Care of Business: Citizenship and the Charter of Incorporation," Program on Corporations, Laws & Democracy of Charter INK., PO Box 806, Cambridge, Mass. 02140.

29. Quoted in *The Ecologist* 31, no. 1 (February 2001): 9.

30. Paul Streeten, "Integration, Interdependence and Globalization," *Finance & Development* 38, no. 2 (June 2001): 35.

31. David Korten, "The Post-Corporate World," *YES! A Journal of Positive Futures* no. 9 (Spring 1999): p. 5 of www.futurenet.org/9economics/kortendave. The article summarizes his book *The Post-Corporate World: Life after Capitalism*.

32. John Maynard Keynes, "National Self-Sufficiency," *Yale Review* 22, no. 4 (June 1933): 758. See also R. F. Harrod, *The Life of John Maynard Keynes* (New York: St. Martin's Press, 1963, reprint of 1951 1st edition).

5.1

Our Word Is Our Weapon

Subcomandante Marcos

**Written in August 1992,
this essay by Marcos was not
released publicly until January 27, 1994**

Suppose that you live in the north, center, or west of this country. Suppose that you heed the old Department of Tourism slogan: "Get to know Mexico first." Suppose that you decide to visit the southeast of your country and that in the southeast you choose to visit the state of Chiapas.

[. . .]

Good, suppose you have. You have now entered by one of the three existing roads into Chiapas: the road into the northern part of the state, the road along the Pacific coast, and the road by which you entered are the three ways to get to this southeastern corner of the country by land. But the state's natural wealth doesn't leave just by way of these three roads. Chiapas loses blood through many veins: through oil and gas ducts, electric lines, railways; through bank accounts, trucks, vans, boats, and planes; through clandestine paths, gaps, and forest trails. This land continues to pay tribute to the imperialists: petroleum, electricity, cattle, money, coffee, banana,

honey, corn, cacao, tobacco, sugar, soy, melon, sorghum, mamey, mango, tamarind, avocado, and Chiapaneco blood all flow as a result of the thousand teeth sunk into the throat of the Mexican Southeast. These raw materials, thousands of millions of tons of them, flow to Mexican ports, railroads, air and truck transportation centers. From there they are sent to different parts of the world—the United States, Canada, Holland, Germany, Italy, Japan—but all to fulfill one same destiny: to feed imperialism. Since the beginning, the fee that capitalism imposes on the southeastern part of this country makes Chiapas ooze blood and mud.

A handful of businesses, one of which is the Mexican state, take all the wealth out of Chiapas and in exchange leave behind their mortal and pestilent mark: in 1989 these businesses took 1,222,669,000,000 pesos from Chiapas and only left behind 616,340,000,000 pesos worth of credit and public works.[1] More than 600,000,000,000 pesos went to the belly of the beast.

In Chiapas, Pemex[2] has eighty-six teeth sunk into the townships of Estación Juárez, Reforma, Ostuacán, Pichucalco, and Ocosingo. Every day they suck out 92,000 barrels of petroleum and 517,000,000,000 cubic feet of gas. They take away the petroleum and gas and, in exchange, leave behind the mark of capitalism: ecological destruction, agricultural plunder, hyperinflation, alcoholism, prostitution, and poverty. The beast is still not satisfied and has extended its tentacles

Subcomandante Marcos, excerpts from *Our Word Is Our Weapon: Selected Writings of Subcomandante Marcos*, ed. Juana Ponce de León (New York: Seven Stories Press, 2001), 22–24, 242–44, and 260–61. The original works of Subcomandante Marcos are not copyrighted.

to the Lacandon Jungle: eight petroleum deposits are under exploration. The paths are made with machetes by the same campesinos who are left without land by the insatiable beast. The trees fall and dynamite explodes on land where campesinos are not allowed to cut down trees to cultivate. Every tree that is cut down costs them a fine that is ten times the minimum wage, and a jail sentence. The poor cannot cut down trees, but the petroleum beast can, a beast that every day fells more and more into foreign hands. The campesinos cut them down to survive, the beast cuts them down to plunder.

Chiapas also bleeds coffee. Thirty-five percent of the coffee produced in Mexico comes from this area. The industry employs 87,000 people. Forty-seven percent of the coffee is for national consumption, and 53 percent is exported abroad, mainly to the United States and Europe. More than 100,000 tons of coffee are taken from this state to fatten the beast's bank accounts: in 1988 a kilo of pergamino coffee was sold abroad for 8,000 pesos. The Chiapaneco producers were paid 2,500 pesos or less.

After coffee, the second most important plunder is beef. Three million head of cattle wait for middlemen and a small group of businessmen to take them away to fill refrigerators in Arriaga, Villahermosa, and Mexico City. The cattle are sold for 400 pesos per kilo by the poor farmers and resold by the middlemen and businessmen for up to ten times the price they paid for them.

The tribute that capitalism demands from Chiapas has no historical parallel. Fifty-five percent of national hydroelectric energy comes from this state, along with 20 percent of Mexico's total electricity. However, only a third of the homes in Chiapas have electricity. Where do the 12,907 kilowatts produced annually by hydroelectric plants in Chiapas go?

In spite of the current trend toward ecological awareness, the plunder of wood continues in Chiapas' forests. Between 1981 and 1989, 2,444,777 cubic meters of precious woods, conifers, and tropical trees were taken from Chiapas to Mexico City, Puebla, Veracruz, and Quintana Roo. In 1988, wood exports brought a revenue of 23,900,000,000 pesos, 6,000 percent more than in 1980.

The honey that is produced in 79,000 beehives in Chiapas goes entirely to the United States and European markets. The 2,756 tons of honey produced annually in the Chiapaneco countryside is converted into dollars that the people of Chiapas never see.

Of the corn produced in Chiapas, more than half goes to the domestic market. Chiapas is one of the largest corn producers in the country. Sorghum grown in Chiapas goes to Tabasco. Ninety percent of the tamarind goes to Mexico City and other states. Two-thirds of the avocados and all the mameys are sold outside of the state. Sixty-nine percent of the cacao goes to the national market, and 31 percent is exported to the United States, Holland, Japan, and Italy. The majority of the bananas produced are exported.

[. . .]

March 17, 1995

[. . .]

We, the first inhabitants of these lands, the indigenous, were left forgotten in a corner, while the rest began to grow and become stronger. We only had our history with which to defend ourselves, and we held it tightly so we would not die. And that's how this part of history arrived, and it seems like a joke because a single country, the country of money, put itself above all flags. When they uttered, "Globalization," we knew that this was how the absurd order was going to be called, an order in which money is the only country served and the borders are erased, not out of brotherhood but because of the bleeding that fattens the powerful without nationality. The lie became the universal coin, and for a few in our country it wove a dream of prosperity above everyone else's nightmare.

Corruption and falsehoods were our motherland's principal exports. Being poor, we dressed in the wealth of our scarcities, and because the lie was so deep and so broad, we ended up mistaking it for truth. We prepared for the great international forums and, by the will of the government, poverty was declared an illusion that faded before the development proclaimed by economic statistics. Us? We became even more forgotten, and until our history wasn't enough to keep us from dying just like that, forgotten and humiliated. Because death does not hurt; what hurts is to be forgotten. We discovered then that we no longer existed, and those who govern had forgotten about us in their euphoria of statistics and growth rates.

A country that forgets itself is a sad country. A country that forgets its past cannot have a future. And so we took up arms and went into the cities, where we were considered animals. We went and told the powerful, "We are here!" And to the whole country we shouted: "We are here!" And to all of the world we yelled, "We are here!" And they saw how things were because, in order for them to see us, we covered our faces; so that they would call us by name, we gave up our names; we bet the present to have a future; and to live . . . we died. And then came the planes and the bombs and bullets and death. And we went back to our mountains, and even there death pursued us. And many people from many places said, "Talk." And the powerful said: "Let's talk." And we said, "Okay, let's talk." And we talked. And we told them what we wanted, and they did not understand very well, and we repeated that we wanted democracy, liberty, and justice. And they made a face like they didn't understand. And they reviewed their macroeconomic plans and all their neoliberal points, and they could not find these words anywhere. And they said to us, "We don't understand." And they offered us a prettier corner in history's museum, and a long-term death, and a chain of gold with which to tie our dignity. And we, so that they would understand our demands, began to organize ourselves according to the wishes of the majority, and so that we too could see what it was like to live with democracy, with liberty, and with justice. And this is what happened:

For a year the law of the Zapatistas governed the mountains of Southeastern Mexico. We the Zapatistas, who have no face, no name, no past, governed ourselves. (For the most part we are indigenous, although lately more brothers and sisters of other lands and races have joined us.) All of us are Mexicans. When we governed these lands, we did the following:

We lowered to zero the rate of alcoholism. The women here became very angry and said that alcohol was only good to make the men beat their women and children; therefore, they gave the order that no drinking was allowed. The people who most benefited were the children and women, and the ones most suffered were the businessmen and the government. With support of nongovernmental organizations, both national and international, health campaigns were carried out, lifting the hope of life for the civilian population, even though the challenge from the government reduced the hope for life for us combatants. The women are a full third of our fighting force. They are fierce and they are armed. And so they "convinced" us to accept their laws, and that they participate in the civilian and military direction of our struggle. We say nothing, what can we say?

The cutting down of trees also was prohibited, and laws were made to protect the forests. It was forbidden to hunt wild animals, even if they belonged to the government. The cultivation, consumption, and trafficking of drugs were also prohibited. These laws were all upheld. The rate of infant mortality became very small, as small as the children. And the Zapatista laws were applied uniformly, without regard for social position or income level. And we made all of the major decisions, the "strategic" ones, of our struggle, by means of a method called "referendum" and "plebiscite." We got rid of prostitution. Unemployment disappeared and with it ended begging. The children came to know sweets and toys. We made many errors and had many failures, but we also accomplished what no other government in the world, regardless of its political affiliation, is capable of doing honestly, recognizing its errors and taking steps to remedy them.

We were doing this, learning, when the tanks and the helicopters and the planes and the thousands of soldiers arrived, and they said that they came to defend the national sovereignty. We told them that where sovereignty was being violated was at the IUESAY[3] and not in Chiapas, that the national sovereignty cannot be defended by trampling the rebel dignity of indigenous Chiapas. They did not listen because the noise of their war machines made them deaf, and they came in the name of the government. As for the government, betrayal is the ladder by which one climbs to power, and for us loyalty is the level playing field that we desire for everyone. The legality of the government came mounted on bayonets, and our legality was based on consensus and reason. We wanted to convince, the government wanted to conquer. We said that no law that had to resort to arms to be carried out could be called a law, that it is arbitrary regardless of its legalese trappings. He who orders that a law be carried out and enforced with weapons is a dictator, even if he says that the majority elected him. And we were run out of our lands. With the war-tanks came the law of the government, and the law of the Zapatistas left. And once again, prostitution, drinking, theft, drugs, destruction, death, corruption, sickness, poverty, came following the government's war tanks.

People from the government came and said that they had now restored law in Chiapas, and they came with bulletproof vests and with war tanks, and they stayed there just long enough to make their statements in front of the chickens and roosters and pigs and dogs and cows and horses and a cat that had gotten lost. And that's what the government did, and maybe you all know this because it's true that many reporters saw this and publicized it. This is the "legality" that rules in our lands now. And this is how the government conducted its war for "legality" and for "national sovereignty" against the indigenous people of Chiapas. The government also waged war against all other Mexicans, but instead of tanks and planes, they launched an economic program that is also going to kill them, just more slowly . . .

[. . .]

December 1994

Months later, the indigenous of southeastern Mexico again reiterated their rebellion, their unwillingness to disappear, to die . . . The reason? The supreme government decides to carry out the organized crime—essential to neoliberalism—that the god of modernity has planned: money. Many thousands of soldiers, hundreds of tons of war materials, millions of lies. The objective? The destruction of libraries and hospitals, of homes and fields seeded with corn and beans, the annihilation of every sign of rebellion. The indigenous Zapatistas resisted, they retreated to the mountains, and they began an exodus that today, even as I write these lines, has not ended. Neoliberalism disguises itself as the defense of a sovereignty that has been sold in dollars on the international market.

Neoliberalism, the doctrine that makes it possible for stupidity and cynicism to govern in diverse parts of the earth, does not allow participation other than to hold on by disappearing. "Die as a social group, as a culture, and above all as a resistance. Then you can be part of modernity," say the great capitalists, from their seats of government, to the indigenous campesinos. These indigenous people with their rebellion, their defiance, and their resistance irritate the modernizing logic of neomercantilism. It's irritated by the anachronism of their existence within the economic and political project of globalization, a project that soon discovers that poor people, that people in opposition—which is to say, the majority of the population—are obstacles. The Zapatista indigenous people's character, armed with, "We are here!" does not matter much to them; they lose no sleep over them. (A little fire and lead will be enough to end such "imprudent" defiance.) What matters to them, what bothers them, is their mere existence, and that the moment they speak out and are heard it becomes a reminder of an embarrassing omission by the "neoliberal modernity": "These Indians should not exist today; we should have put an end to them BEFORE. Now, annihilating them will be more difficult, which is to say, more expensive." This is the burden that weighs upon the born again neoliberal government in Mexico.

"Let's resolve the causes of the uprising," say the government's negotiators (the leftists of yesterday, the shamed of today), as if they were saying, "All of you should not exist; all of this is an unfortunate error of modern history." "Let's solve the problems" is an elegant synonym for "we will eliminate them." The campesinos, the indigenous, do not fit in the plans and projects of this system, which concentrates wealth and power and distributes death and poverty. They have to be gotten rid of, just like we have to get rid of the herons . . . and the eagles.

Notes

1. The exchange of pesos to dollars in 1989 was 3,000 pesos for one U.S. dollar.
2. Pemex stands for Petroleum of Mexico, a government-owned company.
3. IUESAY is a phonetic play on U.S.A.

5.2

Bringing the Food Economy Back In: The Social, Ecological, and Economic Benefits of Local Food

Helena Norberg-Hodge, Todd Merrifield, and Steven Gorelick

Shifting Direction

Until recently, the global food system seemed unstoppable in its ability to displace local food systems the world over. As has been argued here, this trend has little to do with historical inevitability or evolution, but is largely the consequence of government policies and the power of transnational corporations.

Today's economists and policy-makers, backed up by conventional economic thinking, make no distinction between apples grown in an orchard and rubber balls manufactured in a factory. Food, they assume, is like any other 'commodity'; society as a whole is further presumed to benefit if this commodity is produced and marketed as 'efficiently' as possible. Since this way of thinking excludes so many externalities and hidden subsidies, it can easily seem 'efficient' for people to consume food that poses long-term risks to human health, that was produced in ways that degrade the soil and pollute the environment, and that was needlessly packaged in layers of plastic and transported thousands of miles. Just as absurdly, conventional economic logic would

Helena Norberg-Hodge, Todd Merrifield, and Steven Gorelick, excerpts from *Bringing the Food Economy Home: The Social, Ecological, and Economic Benefits of Local Food* (London: International Society for Ecology and Culture, October 2000), 39–44.

have us believe that society is better off even if the scale of food production and marketing undermines national and local economies, and increases the economic and political power of huge, unaccountable corporations.

While shortening the distance between producers and consumers would bring immense benefits, supporters of the global, industrial model will certainly decry such a shift, claiming that it would entail too much social and economic disruption. What this ignores, however, is the tremendous disruption and dislocation that our *current* direction entails. In the name of 'progress', family farmers and rural communities the world over are being driven to extinction, and millions of people are being pulled off the land into sprawling, ever-expanding cities. It is absurd to speak as though a shift in direction—one that will reduce social as well as ecological breakdown—would entail too much disruption.

Fortunately, more and more people are beginning to recognise that a shift in direction is not only possible, but is necessary. They are beginning to see for themselves the immense costs of severing food from its cultural and environmental moorings, and then treating it as a commodity subject to lawless speculative investment.

As a result, farmers, consumers and environmentalists around the world are linking hands to demand shifts in policy—away from the globalised model with its bias towards large-scale, monocultural production and corporate agri-business, towards more localised food systems that promote smaller scale, diversified farms and healthier communities.

It is in the mutual interest of nations, regions and local communities to increase their sovereignty and stability by ensuring that each has the capacity to provide for the basic needs of its own citizens—irrespective of the vagaries of the global market or of events on the other side of the world.

For an effective transformation to sustainable local food economies to occur, change would need to take place at the international, national and community levels.

1. International Level

With enough pressure from below, governments can be forced back to the bargaining table to renegotiate trade treaties such as NAFTA and GATT, this time with the interests of people and the environment—not corporations—at the forefront. Since challenging the hegemony of the WTO and international finance would be daunting for even the most powerful nation, a turnabout would be most likely to occur if groups of nations joined together with this purpose in mind. There is already a precedent for joint opposition to the global model: at the Montreal Biosafety Protocol meeting in February 2000, attempts by the United States to use the WTO to force the world's nations to remove all restrictions on the import of its GM food and crops was successfully opposed by the 'Like-Minded Group of Nations' consisting of 135 countries.

New 'rules of the game' would allow the careful use of trade tariffs to regulate imports of goods that could be produced locally. Rejecting corporate-led trade does not mean that all trade in food would end, or that fellow citizens in other countries would be targeted. Rather, it would mean that jobs could be safeguarded and local resources defended against the excessive power of transnational corporations. The goal of tariffs and subsidies would not be to inhibit trade in foods that cannot be produced locally, but to encourage the growing of food that can.

For example, countries like South Korea, which can be completely self-sufficient in its staple food, rice, should not be forced to open their markets to rice from the United States or other

producers. Far from benefiting South Korea, this so-called 'free' trade threatens the viability of South Korean farmers and their communities, while undermining the country's food security. Nor does this policy benefit the US in the long run: by encouraging American farmers to become still more dependent on exports, the pressures for monocultural production intensify, along with all the environmental, economic and social problems this entails. International agreements could set standard tariffs on the import of unneeded staple foods to ensure that all nations maintain or restore their capacity to provide for their citizens' basic needs.

A reversal of the trend towards commodifying ever more aspects of life would also be in order. Thanks to patent rules and treaties like GATT, corporations are claiming title to 'intellectual property' that ranges from germ plasm in seeds cultivated by traditional people for millennia, to portions of the human genome. Living organisms and traditional resources should not be allowed to become commercial property controlled by corporations.

2. National Level

As we have seen, the globalisation of food is being propelled by a vast array of hidden government subsidies, investments, tax breaks and other incentives that overwhelmingly favour corporations and global trade. These would need to be reformed to ensure that prices reflect the environmental and social cost of their production and distribution, especially in the areas of transport, energy and agricultural subsidies.

a) Transport

Hidden transport subsidies for the global economy could be corrected by abandoning massive expansion programmes and shifting this support towards a range of transport options that favour smaller, national and local enterprises. This would have enormous benefits—from the creation of jobs, to a healthier environment, to a more equitable distribution of resources. Taxpayers could be reimbursed for their past expenditure of billions of pounds through the imposition of a hefty tax on heavy lorries, which inflict vastly greater damage to roads than do lighter vehicles.

The funds saved could be used to revitalise local communities and high street shopping areas. Depending on the local situation, transport money could also be spent on building bike paths, footpaths, boat and rail services, and where appropriate, paths for animal transport. Even in the highly industrialised world, where dependence on centralised infrastructures is deeply entrenched, a move in this direction can be made. In Amsterdam, for example, steps are being taken to ban cars from the city's centre, thus allowing sidewalks to be widened and more bicycle lanes to be built.

b) Energy

In the Third World, the majority is still living in small towns and rural communities and is, to a large extent, still part of a local economy. In this era of rapid globalisation, the most urgent challenge is to stop the tide of urbanisation. Large dams, fossil fuel plants and other large-scale energy and transport infrastructures are geared towards the needs of urban areas and export-oriented production—thus promoting both urbanisation and globalisation.

Decentralised renewable energy infrastructures would help stem the urban tide by strengthening villages, smaller towns and agricultural economies in general. Since the energy infrastructure in the South is not yet very developed, there is a realistic possibility that this path could be implemented in the near future.

In both the North and the South today, energy is heavily subsidised and labour is taxed. This leads to excessive mechanisation and unemployment, and gives large, mechanised food manufacturers an unfair advantage over smaller, local and national producers. Removing the energy subsidies now given to businesses while simultaneously reducing taxes on labour (perhaps through an increase in the minimum tax threshold) would help to redress the imbalance. In the long run, these shifts would encourage businesses to adopt more sustainable and socially beneficial practices.

Financial support for small-scale renewable energy would help promote decentralised and sustainable energy production. This would counter the effect of past subsidies for expensive nuclear and fossil fuel plants. In a time of human-induced global warming, a rapid shift in this direction is urgently needed.

c) Agricultural Subsidies

Both hidden and direct agricultural subsidies now favour large-scale farms, industrial agribusinesses and corporate middlemen, allowing them to lower their prices artificially and so invade local food economies, to the detriment of both farmers and consumers. Shifting government funding towards smaller-scale, diversified agriculture would help promote biodiversity, healthier soils and fresher food.

Current subsidies include not only direct payments to farmers, but funding for research and education in biotechnology and chemical- and energy-intensive monoculture. Many governments, particularly in the South, directly subsidise pesticides and chemical fertilisers as a means of encouraging large-scale agriculture for export. During the 1980s, for example, China's annual pesticide subsidies averaged some $285 million; Egypt's, $207 million; and Colombia's, $69 million.[2] Little if any support was given for smaller-scale, organic methods: the Pakistan government, for instance, devoted roughly 75 percent of its total agricultural budget to subsidising chemical fertilisers.[3]

Governments even pay for the water used in industrial agriculture, either through direct water subsidies or by investments in massive irrigation projects. This makes the price of water artificially low and encourages the growing of water-intensive monocultures in areas that are naturally very arid. The huge corporate farms in California's San Joaquin valley, for example, would be unthinkable without these publicly funded water projects. In addition, consumers, not agribusinesses, pay the cost of removing agrochemicals from drinking water—a subsidy that in the UK amounts to £119.6 million per year.[4]

Agribusinesses are also given huge tax breaks, such as the investment allowances and tax credits that are afforded the capital- and energy-intensive technologies on which large producers depend. On the other hand, smaller, more labour-intensive producers are disproportionately burdened by such levies on labour as income taxes, social welfare taxes, value-added taxes and payroll taxes, giving large industrial farms and processors a huge advantage.

If these subsidies for the large and global were redirected towards smaller-scale, more localised producers, the shift towards more ecological and equitable food economies would be given a major boost.

3. Local Level

In addition to these steps at the international and national level, numerous grassroots initiatives are already beginning to build local food economies. It is important to remember that isolated, scattered, small-scale efforts will not on their own achieve the desired transformation—that end will be more attainable if we think in terms of institutions and structural changes that will promote small scale on a large scale, allowing space for more community-based economies to flourish and spread. These institutions can easily be started by even a small number of community members joining together with a common vision.

Of the thousands of grassroots initiatives taking root around the world, a few are described below:

a) Buying Local

'Buy-local' campaigns help local businesses survive, even when pitted against heavily subsidised corporate competitors. These campaigns not only prevent money from 'leaking' out of the local economy, they also help educate people about the hidden costs—to the environment and to the community—of purchasing artificially cheap, distantly produced products. Across the United States, Canada and Europe, grassroots organisations have emerged in response to the intrusion of huge corporate marketing chains into rural and small town economies. For example, the McDonald's Corporation—which now opens about five new restaurants each day[5]—has met with grassroots resistance in at least two dozen countries. In the United States, Canada and most recently, the UK, the rapid expansion of Wal-Mart, the world's largest retailer, has spawned a whole new network of activists working to protect jobs and the fabric of their communities from these sprawling 'superstores'.

But as more and more people become aware of the advantages of buying local, structures that reduce the distance between producers and consumers are required. It is difficult, for example, for people to boycott a nearby supermarket chain when affordable alternative methods of obtaining food are not available. Here are some of the strategies communities are using right now to shorten the link between producer and consumer:

- *Farmers' markets* benefit local economies and the environment by connecting farmers directly with urban consumers. These markets offer fresher food to consumers and lower prices, while increasing the farmers' income. . . .
- Box schemes and other forms of *community supported agriculture* whereby customers order regular boxes of in-season vegetables (and often eggs, meat and dairy products) from local farms, can give farmers more security by providing them with a guaranteed and stable market. . . .
- *Local food co-ops* are small retail outlets that bring together local farmers, producers and consumers seeking to revive the local food economy. These are much preferable to conventional producer co-operatives, which usually have the narrower goal of giving small farmers more leverage in the global marketplace.

b) Economic Structures

The above measures can help revive a local food economy, but there are a number of economic and monetary schemes which can make the task easier—both by giving small businesses access to cheap loans and by ensuring that money circulates within the community rather than draining out into the pockets of giant middlemen.

- In a number of places, *community banks* and *loan funds* have been set up, thereby increasing the capital available to local residents and businesses, and allowing people to invest in their neighbours and their community, rather than in distant corporations. These schemes enable small enterprises such as local farm co-ops and box schemes to obtain cheap start-up loans of the kind that banks only offer to large corporations.
- A way of guaranteeing that money stays within the local economy is through the creation of *local currencies*—alternative scrip that is only used by community members and local participating businesses. Similarly, Local Exchange Trading Systems (LETS) are, in effect, large-scale local barter systems. People list the services or goods they have to offer and the amount they expect in return. Their account is credited for goods or services they provide to other

LETS members, and they can use those credits to purchase goods or services from anyone else in the local system. Thus, even people with little or no 'real' money can participate in and benefit from the circulation of credit within the local economy.

c) Local Food Regulations

. . . [F]ood safety regulations are often inadequate to protect consumers and the environment from the hazards of the global food system. At the same time, those regulations often make it impossible for the small producer to survive.

How can regulations on large-scale operators be tightened without placing a killing burden on small operators? One solution to this dilemma is a two-tier system of regulations: stricter controls on large-scale producers and marketers, with strong safeguards against the 'revolving door' between regulatory agencies and Big Business; and a simpler set of locally determined regulations for small-scale localised enterprises. Such a system would acknowledge that communities should have the right to monitor foods that are produced locally, for local consumption, and that such enterprises involve far fewer processes likely to damage human health or the environment.

Community-based minimum standards for local production and retailing would likely vary from place to place, influenced by local conditions and community values. Community peer pressure would ensure compliance with the agreed upon standards much more effectively than current national or statewide systems, which are largely anonymous and rely upon expensive enforcement mechanisms. Local regulation would allow more flexibility, encourage more accountability, and would dramatically reduce the cost of both monitoring and compliance.

These highly localised community regulations would co-exist with national and international regulations for goods produced in one region and sold in another. Small-scale businesses oriented towards local markets would not be burdened by inappropriate regulations, but people and the environment would still be protected from the excesses of large-scale enterprises.

People Power

Today's crisis in food and farming is giving birth to powerful alliances among those working for systemic change. Despite the claims that globalisation is 'inevitable' and 'irreversible', experience shows that even a relatively small amount of public pressure can greatly influence government policy. Grassroots resistance in Europe to the genetic modification of foods, for example, has made it impossible for biotech multinationals and the United States government to force these foods down the throats of consumers. Thanks to the public outcry, many European governments have severely restricted or even banned imports of biotech seeds and foods, even at the risk of a trade war with the US.

Another example, mentioned earlier, is the retreat by the US Department of Agriculture from its attempt to impose organic standards that reflected the interests of huge agribusinesses rather than consumers and farmers. After USDA offices were flooded with some 270,000 public objections, the department backed away from these controversial rules.

The WTO protests in Seattle, meanwhile, showed what can happen when people become aware of the social, economic and environmental implications of globalisation. Consumers, environmentalists, unionists and farmers from North and South joined hands to demand that governments end their support for globalisation. People power can shift control of our food from global corporations to local communities.

Afterword

The arguments in this report, we believe, make a compelling case for shifting from global to local. Yet many people find it difficult even to imagine a shift towards more local economies: "Time has moved on", one hears, "we now live in a globalised world." The assumption is that the global economy has naturally evolved, and that returning to an emphasis on the local is to somehow go against the grain of history.

There are many misconceptions that can make a shift towards the local seem impractical or utopian. An emphasis on meeting needs locally, for example, can easily be misconstrued as meaning total self-reliance on a village level, without any trade at all. But the most urgent issue today is not whether people have oranges or avocados in cold climates, but whether their wheat, rice or milk—in short, their basic food needs—should travel thousands of miles, when they could all be produced within a fifty mile radius. The goal of localisation is not to eliminate all trade, but to reduce unnecessary transport while encouraging changes that would strengthen and diversify economies at the community as well as national level. The degree of diversification, the goods produced, and the amount of trade would naturally vary from region to region.

Another stumbling block is the belief that people in countries of the South need Northern markets in a globalised economy to lift themselves out of poverty, and that a greater degree of self-reliance in the North would therefore undermine the economies of the Third World. The truth of the matter is that a shift towards smaller-scale and more localised production would benefit both North and South, while facilitating meaningful work and fuller employment everywhere. The globalised economy requires the South to send a large portion of its natural resources to the North as raw materials; to devote its best agricultural land to growing food, fibres, even flowers for the North; and to expend a good deal of its labour in the cheap manufacture of goods for Northern markets. Rather than further impoverishing the South, producing more ourselves would allow the South to keep more of its resources, labour and production for itself.

As a result of globalisation, millions of people in the South are being pulled away from sure subsistence in a land-based economy into urban slums from which they have little hope of ever escaping. Diversifying and localising economic activity—in North and South—offers the majority far better prospects.

The idea of localisation also runs counter to the common belief that fast-paced urban areas are the locus of 'real' culture, while small, local communities are isolated backwaters, relics of a past when small-mindedness and prejudice were the norm. The past is assumed to have been brutish, a time when exploitation was fierce, intolerance rampant, violence commonplace—a situation that the modern world has largely risen above. These assumptions echo the elitist or racist belief that modernised people are superior—or even more highly evolved—than their 'underdeveloped' rural counterparts. Yet it is not surprising that these beliefs are so widespread. The whole process of industrialisation has systematically removed political and economic power from rural areas, and has led to a concomitant loss of self-respect in rural populations. Globalisation is accelerating this process, rapidly pushing people in small communities to the periphery, while power—and even what we call 'culture'—is centralised somewhere else.

In order to see what communities are like when people retain real economic power at the local level, we would have to look back—in some cases hundreds of years—before the enclosures in England, for example, or before the colonial era in the South. While relatively little information exists about those times, the relatively isolated region of Ladakh, or 'Little Tibet', provides some clues about life in largely self-reliant communities. Unaffected by colonialism or, until recently, development, Ladakh's traditional, community-based culture was suffused with vibrancy, joy and a tolerance of others that was clearly connected with people's sense of self-esteem and control over their own lives. But in less than a generation, this culture has been dramatically changed by economic development.

Development has effectively dismantled the local farm-based economy; it has shifted decision-making power away from the household and village to bureaucracies in distant urban centres; it has redirected the education of children, away from a focus on local resources and needs, towards a lifestyle completely unrelated to Ladakh; and it has implicitly informed them that urban life is glamorous, exciting and easy, and that the life of a farmer is backward and primitive. Because of these changes, there has been a loss of self-esteem, an increase in pettiness and small-minded gossip, and unprecedented levels of divisiveness and friction. If these trends continue, future impressions of village life in Ladakh may soon differ little from unfavourable stereotypes of small town life in the West.

An equally common myth that can cloud our thinking is that 'there are too many people to go back to the land'. It is noteworthy that a similar scepticism does not accompany the notion of *urbanising* the world's population. What is too easily forgotten is that the majority of the world's people today—mostly in the Third World—are still on the land. Ignoring them—speaking as if people are urbanised as part of the human condition—is a very dangerous misconception, one that is helping to fuel the whole process of urbanisation. It is thus considered 'utopian' to suggest a ruralisation of America's or Europe's population, while few questions are raised about China's plans to move 440 million people off the land and into cities in the next few decades—part of the same process that has led to unmanageable urban explosions from Bangkok and Mexico City to Bombay, Jakarta and Lagos. In these and other huge cities, unemployment is rampant, millions are homeless or live in slums, and the social fabric is unravelling.

Even in the North, an unhealthy urbanisation continues. Rural communities are being steadily dismantled, their populations pushed into the spreading surburbanised megalopolises where the vast majority of available jobs are located. In the United States, where only about 2 percent of the population still lives on the land, farms are still disappearing rapidly. It is impossible to offer that model to the rest of the world, where the majority of people earn their living as farmers. But where are people saying: "we are too many to move to the city"?

As this report has shown, localising the production and marketing of food—our most basic economic needs—is an urgent priority. When applied to farming, the global economic model is giving us food that is neither very flavourful nor nutritious, at a price that includes depleted soil, poisoned air and water, and a destabilised global climate. It is destroying rural livelihoods and hollowing out communities in both North and South. And it is enabling control over food to become dangerously concentrated within large corporations, which by their nature subordinate all other concerns to the economic bottom line. Perhaps worst of all, people everywhere are being encouraged to rely on a single model of food production—one that is dangerously lacking in diversity—thereby jeopardising food security worldwide.

On all these counts, a shift to the local would bring immense benefits. There is, however, so much momentum toward globalisation that shifting direction will not be easy. Changing government policy, for example, will require overcoming powerful vested interests and entrenched ways of looking at the world. And even though there is increasing interest in local foods, the knowledge needed to restore our farms and rural communities is being rapidly lost.

There is much work to be done. The time to start is now.

Notes

[. . .]

2. Pretty, Jules. The Living Land: Agriculture, Food and Community Regeneration in Rural Europe. London: Earthscan, 1998.

3. Pretty, Jules. Regenerating Agriculture: Policies and Practice for Sustainability and Self-Reliance. London: Earthscan, 1995.

4. Pretty, J., et al. An Assessment of the External Costs of UK Agriculture. London: Agricultural Systems, 1999.

5. McDonald's Corporation. "McDonald's Reports Record Global Results", press release, January 26, 2000.

5.3

Jaiv Panchayat: Biodiversity Protection at the Village Level

Research Foundation for Science, Technology, and Ecology

Why Jaiv Panchayat

India is recognised as a country uniquely rich in all aspects of biological diversity.... These include a wide variety of seeds, food crops like wheat (60 varieties), rice . . ., fruits, vegetables, medicinal plants, forests, fodder, livestock animals and fish. Two thirds of the population of our country derive their livelihood and meet their survival needs from this diversity of living resources—as forest dwellers, farmers, fisher folk, healers and livestock owners. 70% of India's health care is accounted for by indigenous systems of medicines (Ayurveda, Unani and Siddha) using 7500 species of plants and 70% of the total seed supply comes from the farmers.

Conservation and utilization of these rich resources have been delicately, sensitively and equitably combined in ancient intricate systems of traditional indigenous knowledge systems reflecting the continuous, cumulative and collective innovation of our people specially the rural indigenous communities, in all their diversity. This knowledge has been freely available within and between communities in the commons. The biological resources were considered to be the common resources of the community to be used sustainably and shared equitably and collectively by all its members through local democratic institutions like the Panchayats. The people's right over the common resources were never privatised and monopolised.

In the colonial period, the local democratic institutions were weakened and a continuous process of subjugation and ownership of the people's common resources was unleashed to exploit them commercially. This resulted in the unmindful destruction and overutilization of forest and other common resources that used to be nurtured by the local communities. This gradual erosion of people's rights over their common resources and knowledge especially in the rural and tribal areas was further perpetuated by the "Indian Welfare State", which is usurping these bioresources of the poor through patents and destroying them through World Trade Organisation (WTO) sponsored Globalisation and free trade.

Power and control over these resources is moving away from the people to the [multinational corporations] MNCs. Our natural resources on which our very survival depends are being hijacked and destroyed, our biodiversity and indigenous knowledge pirated and patented (e.g. basmati, turmeric and neem). Hazardous genetically engineered crops and chemicals are being released on our fields (e.g. cotton, Bt soyabean, and Terminator seeds)

Research Foundation for Science, Technology, and Ecology, "Jaiv Panchayat Report and Declaration: Biodiversity Protection at the Village Level" (New Delhi, India, 1999), www.vshiva.net/jaiv/jaivpanch.htm.

without our consent. Our medicinal plants are disappearing due to overexploitation for trade and our crops and seeds are threatened with extinction.

In fact the process of globalisation, which is based on handing over of centralised power by the state to corporate monopolies, violates the principles of grassroots democracy, defeats the very objective of Panchayat Raj institutions and is becoming a major threat to the survival of the village community. The MNCs through Intellectual Property Rights (IPRs) or Patents are usurping the rights of the local communities over their own seeds, medicinal plants and other biological resources. The national government is being pressurised to implement the anti-people provisions of international treaties at the national level e.g. the Agreement on Trade-Related Intellectual Property Rights (TRIP's) through amendments in our national law.

To stop the erosion of biodiversity and of people's rights and livelihoods dependent on that biodiversity, it is imperative that local communities get organised to protect these resources and declare their rights over them. Just as Pani Panchayats and Van Panchayats have been formed in the past to protect people's common rights to forest and water resources, the time has now come to form the Jaiv Panchayat to assert legitimate people's control over ownership of all the biological resources.

The "Jaiv Panchayat" is the Biodiversity Panchayat. . . . This form of the Panchayat renders the community the decision-maker on all matters pertaining to biodiversity and its conservation. In doing so, the Jaiv Panchayat lays down the parameters within which the elected Panchayat body can take action vis-à-vis biodiversity.

The community ownership it asserts is not aimed at putting different communities in conflict with each other over the use and control of biodiversity. It is actually rejuvenating the traditional systems of common property resource management, which was based on equitable sharing of scarce resources for the common good of all the communities, as an alternative to the privatisation and monopolisation propagated by the Corporates.

[. . .]

Local grassroots initiatives like the Jaiv Panchayat are crucial in this context and they do not have to be limited to structures of the formal elected Panchayat. Such local decen-

tralised democratic bodies are in fact in the spirit of the Panchayati Raj Amendment 1992 and Panchayat Act, 1996. Genuine commitment to the process of democracy implies that even the processes of globalisation and free trade have to be based on recognition of primary ownership of village communities to their natural resources and their decision making power to determine the utilization.

To relocate control and decision making over knowledge and biodiversity from the MNC's to these self governing Jaiv Panchayats, the Research Foundation for Science, Technology and Ecology (RFSTE) and Navdanya launched a movement called the Jaiv Panchayat: Living Democracy. The Jaiv Panchayat is a living democracy movement in three ways. Through it people live and practice democracy on a daily basis. Through it our disintegrating national democracy can be saved and given a new life. Jaiv Panchayat is the "Democracy of all Life", since it defends the right of all species to survive.

The Jaiv Panchayat Declaration

The Jaiv Panchayat declaration assumes more significance as it was being taken on the sacred land of Rishi Agastya who through his dedication and research stabilised the mighty Vindhyachal mountain, and therefore the name Agastya. There was much excitement among the women, who are the real conservators of biodiversity, when a local woman leader from their community declared their rights over these resources.

On this occasion Dr. Vandana Shiva gave a call to start a new freedom movement to claim our rights over our biological wealth. She said that "since ages the local communities enjoy rights over their biological resources, e.g. seeds, water, fuel, fodder, forests, medicinal plants and knowledge, but in this age of globalisation and WTO, few MNC's are trying to have their total control over these resources.

The MNC's are trying hard to transform these living resources into their private property, through IPRs and Patents. "The need of the time is to launch a national and international movement against the monopolization of these resources," she said. Dr. Shiva also presented 'Navdanya Mementoes' to people who contributed in the preparation of biodiversity register.

This declaration of rights was made after a detailed register had been prepared by the people of village Bhatwari in Agsthyamuni of practically every spice and crop cultivar growing in that region. The register was prepared by the local women and youth with the help of Navdanya, under the supervision of Dr. R. D. Goad, a well-known taxonomist and head of the Botany Department in the Garhwal University. The biodiversity register lists the various plants, crops, and various varieties and its diverse uses in that area. The register is an indicator of the ecosystem diversity, a useful tool for monitoring and a valuable storehouse of information and knowledge.

Through this register it can be ensured that the local knowledge that is fast eroding remain within the communities forever. Further the claim of rights by the locals over these resources will ensure that no outsider stakes their claim over these resources and knowledge.

On this auspicious occasion the establishment of the first Jaiv Panchayat in the village Bhatwari was also announced. The Jaiv Panchayat campaign launched by Navdanya is a part of the much broader movement called Bija Satyagraha. The Jaiv Panchayat will be a decision making body so far as the management and protection of biodiversity of the village is concerned. It will be the complete authority on IPRs and decisions related to release of genetically engineered organisms (GMO's) such as Terminator seeds.

[. . .]

Your Role in Jaiv Panchayat

On this last Independence day of this millennium let's take a pledge to work together to reassert and reclaim our lost freedom over our own knowledge, and biodiversity by relocating control and decision making over them from the global to the local, from the MNCs to the Jaiv Panchayat.

You too can help bring to life a Jaiv Panchayat and make real the idea of a *living democracy*—a democracy for life in all its diversity.

Things You Can Do

- Organise all the people of your village into a Jaiv Panchayat. Help the people understand that their Jaiv Panchayat will be a decision making body on all matters pertaining to the conservation, management, and protection of all biological resources of that area.
- Organise meetings/awareness campaigns with the Jaiv Panchayat, and discuss the diverse kinds of biological wealth (past and present), available and used in your area, the species that are rapidly disappearing and as custodians of this knowledge, the collective responsibility of the community to protect and conserve them through the Jaiv Panchayat.
- Make a formal *declaration* that all the biological resources belong only to the community and only the Jaiv Panchayat has the complete authority to make decisions on its utilization, conservation and distribution, not the State or the Corporates. These can be presented to the local administrative officials like the Sarpanch, Pradhan, and Block Development officer.
- Prepare a *community biodiversity register (CBR)* to prevent erosion of biological resources and knowledge. The CBR will document all biological resources and knowledge in international or local language or vernacular dialect, its properties, products, uses (economic, religious, socio-cultural), its mention in any folk tale, song or any other medium of communication. The CBR will thus be a tool for remembering. The empowerment process that it unleashes is important to counter the globalisation process. The documentation in the CBR may be initiated by the students, teachers, older people, grandmother schools, (specially for identifying lost and rapidly depleting resources), medicine men (vaidyas), community welfare groups like Mahila Mandals, Youth Groups, the elected Panchayat members like Sarpanch, Block Development Officer, Block Pradhan etc. or simply the whole village community getting together. The community may choose a day and time to congregate for the purpose of making entries in the register like a religious ceremony or a festival.

There is no standard format for a CBR. Each Jaiv Panchayat can make its own format according to what is most practicable in its area. We would be glad to work with you in making this format.

The Jaiv Panchayat maintains the CBR. A few active members (*Jaiv Rakshaks*) from amongst the Gram Sabha can take the responsibility of maintaining and updating the register periodically. They can hold *public hearings* in which the CBR is presented and discussed and the Jaiv Panchayat makes out a micro plan for biodiversity. The CBR can be used as a legal document by the Jaiv Panchayat to declare the sovereign rights of the community over all the biodiversity documented and challenge any attempt by the state or the Corporates to patent or pirate them.

The Jaiv Panchayat can also:

- Make biodiversity action plans to conserve the disappearing species [that] regulate their usage, encourage their sustainable use, encourage their planting, make community indigenous seed banks.
- Make decisions on IPRs and knowledge conflicts. Campaigns can be built to counter any activity that would have adverse impact on biodiversity and people's lives, e.g. introduction of genetically modified organisms, toxic and hazardous chemicals and polluting industry.
- Shape its own laws for ownership and control and trade of biodiversity and its knowledge.
- Defend livelihoods based on biodiversity.
- Hold biodiversity fairs and Yatras.
- Initiate organic farming movements.
- Build grain banks and ensure that no one goes hungry as a result of speculative trading in food.
- Work towards making agriculture patent free, chemical free and free from genetic engineering.

We have no functioning parliament to defend our rights or to protect our environment. Our ecological economic and democratic survival depends on reclaiming our rights, and creating a living democracy, that is also a democracy for life, to conserve and sustainably use all our precious natural resources.

5.4

The Cochabamba Declaration on Water: Globalization, Privatization, and the Search for Alternatives

Coordinadora de Defensa del Agua y de la Vida
(Coalition in Defense of Water and Life)

On December 8, 2000 several hundred people gathered in Cochabamba, Bolivia for a seminar on the global pressure to turn water over to private water corporations. For many of those who attended it was the first time they had come together since the mass uprising at the beginning of the year when the people of Cochabamba took back their water from the private water company. Also in attendance was an international delegation of water activists. The result of that meeting was the following declaration that captures the essence of their struggle and the struggle of more and more communities around the world. If you agree please sign on below. This declaration is a rallying call to join the struggle to protect the planet and human rights.

Declaration

We, citizens of Bolivia, Canada, United States, India, Brazil:

Farmers, workers, indigenous people, students, professionals, environmentalists, educators, nongovernmental organizations, retired people, gather together today in solidarity to combine forces in the defense of the vital right to water.

"The Cochabamba Declaration," drafted and signed by participants in the international seminar on Water: Globalization, Privatization, and the Search for Alternatives, convened by the Coordinadora de Defensa del Agua y de la Vida (Coalition in Defense of Water and Life), Cochabamba, Bolivia, 8 December 2000.

Here, in this city which has been an inspiration to the world for its retaking of that right through civil action, courage and sacrifice standing as heroes and heroines against corporate, institutional and governmental abuse, and trade agreements which destroy that right, in use of our freedom and dignity, we declare the following:

For the right to life, for the respect of nature and the uses and traditions of our ancestors and our peoples, for all time the following shall be declared as inviolable rights with regard to the uses of water given us by the earth:

1. Water belongs to the earth and all species and is sacred to life, therefore, the world's water must be conserved, reclaimed and protected for all future generations and its natural patterns respected.

2. Water is a fundamental human right and a public trust to be guarded by all levels of government, therefore, it should not be commodified, privatized or traded for commercial purposes. These rights must be enshrined at all levels of government. In particular, an international treaty must ensure these principles are noncontrovertible.

3. Water is best protected by local communities and citizens who must be respected as equal partners with governments in the protection and regulation of water. Peoples of the earth are the only vehicle to promote democracy and save water.

5.5

The Treaty Initiative: To Share and Protect the Global Water Commons

Maude Barlow and Jeremy Rifkin
for the Council of Canadians

A Pledge

The following treaty is offered as a tool for a common call to protect water as something we all share. Increasingly we are realizing that economic globalization is at its heart a threat to the global commons, those things that we all depend on and share together: water, air, our own genetic code.

It is a solemn, undeniable commitment to recognize water as one of those common elements that are too precious to turn over to private greed and the faceless global marketplace.

[. . .]

We proclaim these truths to be universal and indivisible:

That the intrinsic value of the Earth's fresh water precedes its utility and commercial value, and therefore must be respected and safeguarded by all political, commercial and social institutions,

That the Earth's fresh water belongs to the earth and all species and therefore, must not be treated as a private commodity to be bought, sold and traded for profit,

That the global fresh water supply is a shared legacy, a public trust and a fundamental human right and, therefore, a collective responsibility,

Maude Barlow and Jeremy Rifkin, "The Treaty Initiative: To Share and Protect the Global Water Commons," endorsed by participants in Water for People and Nature: An International Forum on Conservation and Human Rights, convened by the Council of Canadians, Vancouver, Canada, 5–8 July 2001.

And,

Whereas, the world's finite supply of available fresh water is being polluted, diverted and depleted so fast that millions of people and species are now deprived of water for life and,

Whereas governments around the world have failed to protect their precious fresh water legacies,

Therefore, the nations of the world declare the Earth's fresh water supply to be a global commons, to be protected and nurtured by all peoples, communities and governments of all levels and further declare that fresh water will not be allowed to be privatized, commodified, traded or exported for commercial purpose and must immediately be exempted from all existing and future international and bilateral trade and investment agreements.

The parties to this treaty—to include signatory nation states and Indigenous Peoples—further agree to administer the Earth's fresh water supply as a trust. The signatories acknowledge the sovereign right and responsibility of every nation and homeland to oversee the fresh water resources within their borders and determine how they are managed and shared. Governments all over the world must take immediate action to declare that the waters in their territories are a public good and enact strong regulatory structures to protect them. However, because the world's fresh water supply is a global commons, it cannot be sold by any institution, government, individual or corporation for profit.

5.6

South-South Summit Declaration: Towards a Debt-Free Millennium

Jubilee South

Leaders and representatives of diverse social movements, popular, religious, professional, and political organizations, and debt coalitions from 35 countries of Africa, Asia, the Pacific, Latin America, and the Caribbean, met in Gauteng, South Africa, on November 18–21, 1999, in the first Jubilee South-South Summit.

We gathered together to advance a common analysis, vision and strategy to seek to overcome the effects and consequences of debt-related domination in the lives and futures of our peoples, countries, and environment.

As Jubilee South, we put forth as our mission to confront its historical roots and structural causes, and to promote lasting alternatives of economic, social, and ecological justice. In so doing, we were inspired by the myriad forms of resistance through which the majority of the world's population now seek to achieve and defend their fundamental human and collective rights to a dignified life.

We were guided as well by a broad religious and secular understanding of the Jubilee tradition, as expressed in the notions of equity and

harmony within all of creation and the possibility of a "New Beginning".

As Jubilee South, we valued highly the opportunity to come together on our own initiative, as movements, organizations and coalitions based in countries of the South. At the same time we expressed a common understanding of the notion of South as reflecting political and ideological as well as geographic criteria, encompassing the oppressed and excluded around the world in their struggle to end the prevailing neoliberal paradigm and recognizing the existence of sectors of the 'North' in the midst of the 'South' and vice versa.

On the basis of our sharing and debate, we agreed on the following with respect to our framework and perspective on the 'debt problem', our analysis and position on 'debt-relief' initiatives, and a platform and agenda for action of Jubilee South:

Framework and Perspective on the Debt Problem

The External Debt of countries of the South is illegitimate and immoral. It has been paid many times over. A careful examination of the origins, development, effects, and consequences of this debt can lead us to no other conclusion. We thus reject the continued plunder of the South by way of debt payments.

Jubilee South, "South-South Summit Declaration: Towards a Debt-Free Millennium," endorsed by the first Jubilee South-South Summit, Johannesburg, South Africa, 21 November 1999, meeting attended by representatives from thirty-five countries of Africa, Asia, the Pacific, Latin America, and the Caribbean, www.jubileesouth.net/summit/19991121/declaration_en.html.

Peoples and countries of the South are in fact creditors of an enormous historical, social, and ecological debt. This debt must be repaid in order to make possible a "New Beginning". In the spirit of Jubilee, we demand restitution of what has been taken unjustly from us, and reparations for the damage wrought.

We forcefully denounce the growing concentration of wealth, power, and resources in the world economy as the essential cause of the increase in violence, impoverishment, and 'indebtedness' of the South. The elimination of extreme poverty cannot take place without the elimination of extreme wealth. We thus demand the eradication of extreme wealth and the vicious system that generates such inequalities. In this context, we reject the perpetuation of external debt collection and debt payments which are Life or Death matters for the millions of persons who are exploited and excluded in our societies.

The External Debt is an ethical, political, social, historical, and ecological problem. It entails responsibilities at different levels and demands imperative and comprehensive action so as to resolve in a permanent and definitive manner. There can be no piecemeal solution to the 'Debt problem'. We thus welcome the momentum that Jubilee 2000 initiatives around the world have generated on this issue and we call on them to broaden and deepen their understanding, educational efforts, and mobilization beyond the year 2000, in order to achieve our overall aim of a Debt-free Millennium, including the repayment of the debt owed by the North to the South.

Debt is essentially an ideological and political instrument for the exploitation and control of our peoples, resources, and countries by those corporations, countries, and institutions that concentrate wealth and power in the global capitalist system. The accumulation of Foreign Debt in countries of the South is a product of the crisis of that very system and it is used to perpetuate the plunder and domination of our nations often with the acquiescence, if not active collaboration, of local elites.

The neoliberal global economic system is destructive and genocidal in its workings and effects. Women suffer disproportionately its consequences, as do children, the elderly, and the environment. The same institutions and system responsible for its creation cannot bring about a lasting solution to the 'Debt problem'. That system must be changed and can be changed.

In the process of addressing the 'Debt problem' and changing the neoliberal global economic system, we must continue to develop an ever closer understanding of the linkages between debt and other related aspects including trade, finance, investment, consumption patterns, food security, environmental depredation, and diverse forms of military and anti-democratic, neo-colonialist intervention and repression.

Many working-class and impoverished and excluded peoples' groups and movements in both the South and the North, as well as other organizations, institutions, and political formations, are engaged in different ways to challenge and transform this system of domination and we must join with them. As Jubilee South we will add our voice and support for the strengthening and creation of alliances and coalitions deeply rooted in historical struggles against all forms of oppression within the long-standing anti-imperialist framework and tradition.

Resistance to debt-related domination unites us as social movements and organizations throughout the South and provides us with an historic opportunity to organize ourselves as part of a broader movement. As Jubilee South, we are born and rooted in Africa, Asia, the Pacific, Latin America, and the Caribbean, but we reach out to all who are part of this historical, political, and ethical South.

Respectful of our different identities and traditions, as well as our varying forms of struggle, we must be united in a common determination to achieve Justice for all: a New Beginning in the New Millennium. In this way South-South and South-North solidarity can be strengthened, as we exercise our collective human right to determine our own future and engage in the struggle to build and defend inclusive and comprehensive alternatives to the present global system that are

- from the bottom-up,
- reflective of different sectorial needs,
- respectful of cultural and biological diversity, and
- conducive to new modes of democracy and development that are respectful of human rights, justice, and wellbeing for all.

Analysis and Position on Debt Relief Initiatives

Jubilee South strongly rejects all forms of so-called debt relief—ranging from the Brady Bonds, debt buy-back schemes, the Highly Indebted Poor Country Initiative (HIPC), and the G7 Cologne Initiative with its purported emphasis on poverty reduction—initiated by the governments of the North and their international finance institutions.

We reject these initiatives because:

- They presuppose the legitimacy of the debts of the South to the North.
- They are essentially meant to provide Creditor Relief by recycling the uncollectable loans of a limited number of South countries and serve to perpetuate indebtedness by ensuring that indebted countries are able to service their debts through renewed access to international credit.
- They are all tied to structural adjustment programs, poverty reduction criteria and programs and other external conditionalities that impose macroeconomic policies such as liberalization, privatization, and deregulation, which trap SOUTH countries into a perpetual cycle of debt dependence and underdevelopment.

These initiatives are deceptive and they are being used by the North to mislead, coopt, and demobilize concerned people and organizations throughout the world who are rightly expressing their indignation and commitment to genuine debt cancellation and historical reparation of the social and ecological debt owed to the people of the South.

We oppose the creation of the Poverty Reduction Growth Facility (PRGF) as an attempt by the IMF to broaden the scope of its work and provide more bases for intervening in the economies of the countries of the South. This institution is incapable of poverty reduction. The IMF is a major vehicle for promoting neoliberal economic policies and IMF programs and policies are a major cause for perpetuating poverty and exploitation in our economies.

We reject all schemes of the North that divide peoples of the South. We refuse to be categorized as "highly indebted poor countries" or "moderately-indebted countries", etc., all of which do not reflect the real situation of impoverishment and the excluded and exploited people in ALL South countries. The external debts of the South are illegitimate and have been paid over and over again at the expense of the people.

These schemes seek to legitimize the corrupt and genocidal policies of the North and the subservience and corruption of governments and elites in the South, as these are used for publicity and propaganda. Jubilee South campaigns in countries where HIPC is already in operation should continue to emphasize and promote the broader and fundamental socio-political and economic issues.

Peoples of the South DO NOT demand relief from the North but RESTITUTION and REPARATION for the profound economic, social, political, cultural and environmental damages wrought upon our countries and peoples through centuries of DEBT-RELATED colonization and neo-colonization.

Our demands for debt cancellation, debt repudiation and reparation depend upon and MUST produce fundamental changes in the dominant global capitalist system and for the creation of alternative people-centered socio-economic and political systems.

Our Strategy

Jubilee South shall undertake a concerted and coordinated effort to promote these unities on our framework and perspective on the debt problem and our analysis and position on debt relief initiatives.

Our efforts shall be anchored on a campaign strategy of developing our movements in the South, linking with our allies in the North, and finally shifting the balance of strength, to force our governments to take heed and implement our demands and calls on the debt and related issues and, to achieve basic changes in our national societies. And, on this basis, also force changes on the policies and structures of the northern and international creditors, and the global economic system.

Our efforts shall be born from and contribute to the struggles of the peoples of the South for national and global transformation.

Our Platform and Agenda

I. STRATEGIC GOALS and DIRECTION

Jubilee South campaign initiatives, undertaken in the context of the struggles of the peoples of the South for national and global social transformation, shall serve the following Strategic Goals and Direction

- *Collective Repudiation* by South Governments of odious, onerous, criminal, fraudulent and all illegitimate debts and the *Formation* of a *Strategic Alliance to Achieve* external debt cancellation and the *Recognition of South Peoples and Countries as Legitimate Creditors of an Historical, Social, and Ecological Debt.*
- *Rechanneling* of the Public *Funds* away from debt service and *Ensuring That Public Funds* be used primarily for people's welfare and basic services, and equitable and sustainable development.
- *Total Debt Cancellation without Conditionalities* by creditors (northern governments, IFIs, others) to redress injustices, squarely address the issue of odious, illegitimate and onerous debts, and the urgent need to prioritize human welfare and equitable and sustainable development in the face of the crisis, inequity, poverty and "underdevelopment" of the South countries.
- *Full Restitution* and *Reparition* by creditors for the human, social, environmental damage caused by their debt policies, structural adjustment programs and other economic policies, and their exploitation of the peoples and resources of the South's peoples.
- *End to Structural Adjustment Programs* and *Shutdown* of the IMF and WB and other similar multilateral institutions promoting neoliberal economic policies like the World Trade Organization (WTO).
- *Eliminate Wealth Concentration and Income Inequality* as necessary steps toward the eradication of poverty, social violence, exclusion, and ecological destruction.
- *Systemic, Structural* and *Policy* changes and programs that will get the South countries out of the debt trap, prevent the repetition of these problems and promote political and economic democracy and equity, popular empowerment and sustainable development.
- *Transformation* of the *Global Capilist Economic System* and *Building* of *A New World Economic Order* that is people-centered, equitable, gender-fair, sustainable and democratic.

These calls which express the strategic goals and direction of Jubilee South are translated into platforms for national, regional and global campaigns.

These platforms contain specific and concrete goals and demands that range from immediate, medium term and long term that are consistent with and which advance the strategic goals and direction of Jubilee South.

These platforms serve as bases for developing campaign strategies and programs of action for national, regional and global campaigns.

II. Developing NATIONAL PLATFORMS and AGENDAS

Jubilee South shall encourage and support the development of National Platforms and Agendas that primarily challenge and seek to change debt and economic policies of South governments, and transform national social, economic and political systems.

National Platforms and Agendas need to be responsive and appropriate to the concrete and particular social, economic and political situation as well as to the historical development of people's movements and debt campaigns in each country. Thus, National Platforms and Agendas cannot be the same for all countries.

Below are some aspects of the debt problem and related issues around which national platforms and agendas can be developed. Included are possible demands that are not meant to be adopted as is by country campaigns, but rather serve as a menu of issues and concerns that can be studied.

Challenging and Changing Debt and Economic Policies of South Governments; Struggling for National Social Transformation

- *Government Transparency and Accountability*

South Governments must be held fully accountable for debt and related economic policies. A minimum requirement of accountability is transparency and information disclosure. To this end, the following are important demands to forward:

1. Full disclosure of information and transparency on processes and policies regarding borrowing, debt servicing and allocation and spending of public funds.
2. Complete disclosure of information on agreements and transactions with international financial institutions, banks, northern government creditors and related institutions.
3. Institutionalization of public information disclosure policy and mechanisms for the enforcement of this policy.

Furthermore, there must be clear mechanisms for holding past and present governments and individual officials [accountable] for their complicity in the debt trap and related decisions, policies and actions that perpetuated exploitation and impoverishment. Thus it is also vital to demand the:

1. Investigation of cases of odious, onerous, behest, criminal and fraudulent debts; identification and prosecution of government officials and private sector individuals and corporations who were co-parties to odious, onerous, behest, criminal and fraudulent debts; Include the role of international creditors and financial institutions in the investigation of these; Ensure the return of stolen wealth and public funds by these entities;
2. Examination and public disclosure on government practices and institutional, legal and structural mechanisms and flaws that have legitimized and paved the way for immoral debt and 'indebtedness' of the South.

• *Debt Servicing*

As part of demanding government accountability, laying the basis for immediate and medium term policies regarding debt service, raising public awareness and building social mobilizations for debt repudiation and total and unconditional address the debt problem, it is important to call for:

1. Immediate and thorough public information disclosure, investigation, examination and classification of existing debts; Public exposure of odious, onerous, fraudulent, criminal and illegitimate debts, and behest loans.

The following demands can be forwarded together with the demand for disclosure, investigation, examination and classification of existing debts:

1. Immediate unilateral moratorium on servicing of the debt; Immediate rechanneling of funds to urgent needs. (This call may be forwarded as an urgent and immediate demand in conditions such as national disaster emergencies, political and economic crisis situations, or situations of intensifying and heightened mass protests and social mobilizations against economic policies etc.), and/or
2. Imposition of ceilings or caps on debt service based on percentage of budget, as percentage of internal revenues, or as percentage of exports, (may be used as a minimum demand), or
3. Repudiation of or non-payment of odious, onerous, fraudulent, behest, criminal and illegitimate debts. (This is an economic as well as political act based on the recognition of illegitimacy of debt.)

The need for collective action among the South must be emphasized and asserted. Thus, it is important to call on South governments to pursue:

1. Linking up with other South countries for the formation of a Strategic Alliance.

• *Allocation of Funds Released from Debt Servicing, and Budget Reprioritization*

It is vital to accompany demands for debt service ceiling, moratorium or repudiation with demands for the proper allocation of funds freed from debt service, to ensure that the peoples of the South will be the ones to benefit from moratorium/repudiation and cancellation, and not the corrupt officials and the agenda of the elite:

1. Rechanneling of public funds from debt service to basic services such as health, education, housing; as well as for economic programs that promote equity and sustainable development (ex: Land reform and rural development etc.)

• *Loans and Borrowings*

Government policy on borrowings must be addressed as an important aspect of the vicious cycle of indebtedness. Various demands on borrowings include

1. Imposition of regulations and ceilings on borrowings. (Ceilings on borrowings are relevant to situations of wanton, indiscriminate and irresponsible accessing of available credit, and heavy reliance on loans and credit to fund government expenditures).
2. Ensure that Terms of Repayment and Agreements on Interest Rates are not detrimental to marginalized sectors, classes and communities and to women, and to the goals of equitable and sustainable development.
3. Rejection of loans with structural adjustment and similar conditionalities, including those in the guise of poverty reduction and alleviation; Rejection of debt relief packages that are accompanied with similar conditionalities.
4. End all forms of public or government guarantees on private sector loans; Guarantees issued earlier should be revoked or rescinded.
5. Strict regulations on issuance of bonds and domestic borrowings to prevent accumulation of huge public domestic debts, and prevent the government bonds from inducing high interest rates.

• *Democratic Participation and Democratic Governance*

We forward the immediate demand for full and meaningful people's participation and intervention in economic policy-making. There must be clear laws and mechanisms to ensure this.

Over all, we stand for democratic governance and shall link with other groups, forces and movements in struggling to establish truly democratic governments in the South.

• *International Financial Institutions and Conditionalities*

As an immediate or minimum demand to raise public awareness and further expose the negative effects of structural adjustment programs and similar policies imposed by international financial institutions and enforced by South governments, these institutions and governments must be challenged to:

1. Conduct a national participatory audit/investigation of the impact of structural adjustment programs and neoliberal policies.

At the same time, the following call/demand should be advanced:

2. Stop the implementation of WB/IMF Programs and similar programs and policies of regional IFIs (international financial institutions).

• *Restitution and Reparations*

The demand for restitution and reparations must be popularized, promoted and asserted:

1. Restitution and Reparations for victims of the Debt & SAPs, including the Ecological Debt, especially workers, urban and rural poor, farmers, indigenous people's communities and women from these sectors and groups.
2. Identification and quantification of the historical, social, and ecological debts that are due to the peoples and countries of the South, not only in money or political economy terms but in terms of affected populations and the contamination and destruction of the sources of their life and community sustenance.

III. Developing an International Platform and Regional Platforms

Supporting National Campaigns and Platforms, Challenging and Engaging Northern Creditors, International Financial Institutions and Other International Multilateral Organizations

The global community of Jubilee South shall support and promote national platforms, agendas and campaign initiatives of national movements and campaigns on the debt. At the same time Jubilee South unites on the following immediate, medium and long term demands to be carried [out] in the various global and regional arenas and challenging and engaging various global and regional institutions:

To Northern Governments and Creditors:

1. Cancel all bilateral debts of all South Countries.
2. Stop loans and ODA support for authoritarian, dictatorial, oppressive and military regimes.
3. Stop efforts to strengthen the role and extend the mandate of the World Bank and IMF (MAI etc.).

To the World Bank,
IMF and their Regional Partner IFIs:

1. Cancel multilateral debt of all South countries.
2. Complete information disclosure and transparency on transactions and agreements with South governments.
3. Stop imposition of structural adjustment programs and similar policies as conditionalities to grants and loans; Stop the imposition of stabilization programs on countries in the wake of economic and financial crises.
4. Withdraw the new Poverty Reduction and Growth Facility of the IMF . . . and IMF to cease pretensions to poverty reduction goals.
5. Abandon moves to amend the IMF's Articles of Agreement to require member countries to liberalize their capital accounts.

To the United Nations

1. Formation of a global commission with more than 50% representing civil society (and others from governments and the United Nations) be immediately convened to review the work of the IMF and other IFIs, determine whether they should continue to exist and if so re-define what role it should play; if not, examine ways and means to decommission or dismantle the IMF.
2. Passage of an International Covenant regarding stolen wealth.

3. International investigation and inquiry into Governments and International Financial Institutions (IFIs) responsible for illegitimate, odious, onerous, fraudulent and criminal loans and other similar economic issues.
4. Setting up of international instrument to monitor and regulate the flow of international speculative capital.
5. Adoption of a Declaration and/or international convention to criminalize government policy that leads to the genocide and/or mass impoverishment of whole populations, whether directly on the part of a local government or through the action of accomplices such as creditor governments and institutions.
6. [E]nsure compliance of member states and international institutions with existing Human Rights norms and mechanisms, including the supervision of the way in which external debt leads to the gross and systematic violation of civil, cultural, economic, political, and social Human Rights including the rights to self-determination and development.

To Countries of the South

Linking up and formation of a strategic alliance to unite on common policies and actions on:

- Debt repudiation
- Restitution, Reparations, and Repayment of the social, historical, and ecological debt due to the South.
- Rejection of SAPs and other conditionalities; Resistance to neoliberal global economic policies
- Eradication of wealth concentration and income inequalities
- Dismantling of International Financial Institutions
- Regulation of International Speculative Capital Flows
- and others

5.7

Controlling Casino Capital

Robin Round

We use money everyday. Money is a tool; a means to simplify transactions in an economy based on the exchange of goods and services. But the way most of us use money is old fashioned, out of date. Money is no longer a means of exchange but an end in itself. We live in the era of the commodification of money, an era where money has become divorced from the real economy it was originally designed to serve.

Money is bought and sold in a dizzying array of forms, known as instruments, in stock markets, currency markets and bond and other credit markets. Any form of debt can become a tradable commodity—anything whose value today is the value of a future earnings stream can become a tradable contract on a money market. Government bonds are issued to raise capital with no asset behind it other than a promise to pay. Speculators earn millions buying and selling contracts that will never be delivered. Stock markets don't raise capital for productive investment; they provide an arena for speculators to bet on price movements.

Money trading markets are enormous and are growing exponentially. The trade in money has eclipsed the global trade in goods and services.

Robin Round, "Controlling Casino Capital," speech given at World Social Forum, Porto Alegre, Brazil, 28 January 2001, www.halifaxinitiative.org/hi.php/events/108/.

Global foreign exchange transactions alone rose from $4.6 trillion in 1977 to $400 trillion in 1998. From 3.5 times the dollar value of world exports in 1977, foreign exchange transactions rose to 68 times the value of world exports by 1998.[1] The daily trading on foreign exchange markets alone is US$ 2.0 TRILLION PER DAY.[2]

Those numbers are almost beyond comprehension. A million one hundred dollar bills stacked one on top of the other would stand two metres tall. Two trillion one hundred dollar bills stacked one on top of the other would be forty times the height of Mount Everest.

The national economic security of countries is at risk when this tidal wave of capital rolls in, and more importantly, out, of their countries. Recent trends to liberalize financial flows globally led to destabilizing speculation and abrupt capital flow reversals. In Asia the sudden exodus of US$12 billion in 1997 precipitated the crisis. In Brazil, an estimated US$ 50 billion left the country within six months in 1998. Financial liberalization has meant that governments have largely surrendered their ability to control the global flow of capital.

Many countries can no longer defend themselves against speculative attack, effectively surrendering monetary policy sovereignty to investment houses and big banks. Total reserves of all the world's countries are now less than one day's trading in foreign exchange markets.[3] Governments simply haven't enough money to play in the capital casino.

This exploding market in money has devastating impacts on people. Fearing low stock prices and takeover, corporations cut jobs globally to maximize short-term profits and dividends. Thus we arrive at the perversity of soaring stock prices when employment is slashed. As the global financial crisis demonstrated, when currency values collapsed in the wake of speculative attack, prices skyrocketed, wages fell, companies unable to pay debts denominated in foreign currencies went bankrupt and joblessness and social dislocation soared. Three decades of poverty reduction and economic growth was wiped out in South East Asia; thirty million people were thrown into poverty.[4] In Latin America, poverty levels at the end of the 90's were higher than the 80's. Living standards in these countries have not recovered post-crisis. The human crisis in affected countries is an ongoing one and will take decades to reverse.

The financial crises revealed the degree to which financial markets are under-governed in the global economy. An enormous discrepancy exists between an increasingly sophisticated international financial world and the lack of proper institutional frameworks to regulate it at the national and multilateral levels.

The inevitability of future crises makes the re-regulation of capital a global imperative. Until measures are enacted to prevent systemic financial market volatility, human development will be threatened. India and China, the countries least affected by the Asian crisis, were protected from contagion by capital controls. Measures in each of these countries deter speculative attack without restricting capital flows for productive investments. Chile's 30% one year reserve requirement deterred short-term destabilising portfolio flows without impeding long-term productive investment. Even Malaysia's dramatic restrictions on capital outflows, introduced in the wake of the crisis, hastened economic recovery.

The re-regulation of capital is the first step in re-asserting public control over finance. One means to control capital is to put a tax on currency transactions.

What Is the Tobin Tax?

In 1978, Nobel prize-winning economist James Tobin proposed that a small world-wide tariff (1%) be levied by major countries on all foreign exchange transactions in order to reduce the volume of speculative flows.

The Tobin tax is designed to reduce or eliminate the small margins speculators profit from. No profits, no incentive, no speculation. *By reducing the volume of speculative flows, the tax is designed to help stabilize exchange rates and increase the fiscal and monetary policy autonomy of national governments.* By cutting down on the overall volume of foreign exchange transactions, a Tobin tax would reduce the volume of reserves necessary for countries to defend their currency, thus freeing capital for development. The Tobin tax would allow governments the freedom to act in the best interests of their own economic development, rather than being forced to shape fiscal and monetary policies in accordance with the perceived "demands" of fickle markets.

By making crises less likely, the Tobin tax could help avoid the social devastation wrought by them. Analysts agree that currencies plunged to levels completely out of line with underlying economic fundamentals as currency speculators attacked.

The Tobin tax has an unintended benefit—it generates enormous revenue. *A phased-in Tobin tax could yield anywhere from US$ 150–300 billion annually.*[5] The cost of wiping out the worst forms of poverty and mitigating environmental destruction globally would be on the order of US$ 225 billion per year for 10 years according to United Nations and World Bank estimates.[6]

Revenue from the Tobin tax represents a significant new source of public finance for world development. Given the declining commitment to bilateral and multilateral development assistance around the world, the tax could generate substantial resources to support environmentally and socially appropriate development.

How Does the Tobin Tax Work?

The primary difference between speculative and legitimate trade transactions is the speed at which they occur. Investors in the productive economy have medium to long time horizons. Speculators, on the other hand, are flipping investments like pancakes, profiting by the daily, hourly and minute to minute fluctuations in interest rates and currency values. Over 80% of all speculative transactions occur within 7 days or less–40% occur in two days or less.[7]

Tobin's tax would automatically penalize the short-horizon exchanges, while negligibly affecting the incentives for commodity trading and long-term capital investments. A .2% tax on a round trip in another currency costs 48% a year if transacted every business day, 10% if every week, 2.4% every month and so on. A Tobin tax at a rate of between .1% and .25% is a trivial charge on a long-term investment. Long term investment would further benefit through reduced exchange rate risk and hedging costs.

Who Will Be Taxed?

The majority of foreign exchange dealing is done by one hundred of the world's largest commercial and investment banks. The top ten control 52% of the market and include Citibank/Salomon Smith Barney (US), Deutsche Bank (Germany), Chase Manhattan Bank (US), Warburg Dillon Read (US), Goldman Sachs (US), Bank of America (US), JP Morgan (US), HSBC (UK), ABN Amro (Netherlands) and Merrill Lynch (US).[8] *Citibank is at the top of the list with a 7.75% market share and a 1998 foreign exchange transaction volume that exceeded the GDP of the US at US$ 8.5 trillion.*[9]

These banks thrive in times of high volatility—1998 was a banner year, as increased volatility yielded spectacular returns. Deutsche Bank reported a trading profit of US$ 595 million.[10] These banks operate in their own interest and on behalf of clients including large corporate and private investors, insurance companies, hedge funds, mutual funds and pension funds.

Won't Speculators Find Ways to Evade the Tax?

Yes, they will. All taxes are evaded to some extent and never capture the entire revenue stream they target. These arguments, however, never dissuaded governments from collecting taxes. The real question is how do you minimize evasion?

A Tobin type tax could be quite difficult to evade and easy to collect. A variation on Tobin's original proposal by a Canadian economist Rodney Schmidt utilizes an existing centralized and regulated structure through [which] major banks exchange balances on the wholesale market. All transactions are already tracked electronically. Monitoring systems are already in place and all major currencies participate. Because the tax will be collected at centres controlled by the central bank, non-cooperating tax havens could be refused the right to utilize the taxed currency. Using Schmidt's variation, a currency transactions tax could be imposed unilaterally. All transactions that utilize that country's currency would then be taxed world-wide.

So What's Stopping Us?

The biggest barrier to the adoption of a Tobin tax is not technical or administrative but political.

The Tobin tax is a tax on the most powerful banks and investment institutions in the world. The tax is viewed as a threat to financial community privilege and has been met with resistance by a sector with massive political clout. The very idea of a Tobin tax, of putting people ahead of markets, challenges the heart of the dominant economic paradigm of our times. There are powerful forces that do not want their world-view disturbed.

Can Political Barriers Be Overcome?

Yes they can, if the conditions are right for change. We are at a time when economic necessity coincides with social justice. The risk of future financial, economic and social crisis, coupled with the revenue potential for a currency transactions tax, are providing political incentives opportunities unimaginable just 2 years ago.

Three factors are moving the debate forward:

1. Future Crises Are Inevitable Unless Controls Are Enacted

The problems with financial markets are systemic. Borrowers . . . can never obtain sufficient information about future prices and costs to enable them to estimate risk vs. return accurately—these are inherently subjective judgements. Markets behave irrationally, driven by panic selling and herd behavior that does not arise from empirical evidence. Speculators have a vested interest in creating and maintaining volatility as profit potential increases in volatile markets.[11] Wild market swings are here to stay unless something is done to control them.

Further, current proposals by the G7 and the G20 to create a "new global financial architecture" are inadequate at best, and at worst, guarantee the next financial crisis. Measures to reform domestic financial institutions and markets to better meet the demands of liberalized foreign capital flows only set the stage for future crisis.

As the frequency of crises increases, the ability of the world to ignore the problem declines. Nations can ill-afford to repeat the economic devastation, social turmoil and untold human suffering of the last two years. In the wake of the financial crises and the ensuing global economic turmoil, governments around the world are examining their former faith in unfettered free markets.

2. Promise of Enormous Revenue Streams

The political appeal of this tax to cash-strapped governments world-wide cannot be underestimated. Many governments face large deficits, declining income and strong anti-tax populism and are looking for new sources of revenue.

At a time when income disparity and social inequity are increasing, the Tobin tax represents a rare opportunity to capture the enormous wealth of an untaxed sector and destructive sector and redirect it towards the global public good.

3. Coordinated Global Public Pressure

Tobin's proposal sat on a shelf until the Mexican peso crisis, when it was discovered by the NGO community. The social movement has been building ever since, leading to some impressive achievements:

- In March 1999, Canada became the first Parliament in the world to pass a motion calling for a Tobin tax by a resounding 2:1 margin with all party support;
- In August 1999, the Brazilian parliament held hearings on the Tobin tax. President Cardoso proposed to implement a Tobin tax to stem the exodus of capital in late 1998 but the IMF would not allow it;
- Throughout late 1999 and 2000, the UK, French, Belgian and European Parliaments held debates and votes on the tax and more are on the way;

- Finance and Foreign Affairs Ministers from Finland and Belgium have publicly endorsed the tax;
- June 2000, over 160 governments agreed to undertake a study on the feasibility of a currency transactions tax at the UN Social Summit in Geneva.
- Hundreds of Parliamentarians and economists from around the world have signed declarations calling for a Tobin tax. (www.attac.org)
- NGOs in over 20 countries are already campaigning for a Tobin tax and have been directly or indirectly responsible for every victory mentioned above.

The currency transactions tax is not a panacea for the world's financial ills and developmental woes. The Tobin tax must be but one part of a coordinated strategy to fundamentally reform the global financial system to place people ahead of markets.

Markets are not the best source of social regulation nor do capital and its returns constitute the ultimate criteria for defining value.[12] Citizens must re-assert sovereignty over money and financial markets. The democratization of economic decision-making, the cancellation of developing country debt and the equitable redistribution of wealth must become the central principles upon which governments act in the new millennium. *A currency transactions tax is but one critical component of a new global financial order.*

Notes

1. Felix, David. "Repairing the Global Financial Architecture," *Foreign Policy in Focus.* (September 1999).

2. Based on Bank for International Settlements 1998 Survey.

3. Ul Haq, Mahbub. *The Tobin Tax—Coping with Financial Volatility*, Oxford University Press, 1996. p. 292. Based on 1995 Bank for International Settlements, New York Federal Reserve, IMF and Bank of England statistics.

4. UNCTAD. Trade and Development Report 2000. p. 66 from World Bank "East Asia Recovery and Beyond", table 1.2.

5. Felix, David. "On the Revenue Potential and Phasing in of the Tobin Tax" in Ul Haq, Mahbub. *The Tobin Tax—Coping with Financial Volatility.* Oxford University Press. 1996. p. 238. Based on a tax rate of .1% to .25%.

6. In 1997, the United Nations estimated that the cost of wiping out the worst forms of poverty in the world and providing basic health care, nutrition, education, water, and sanitation would be US$ 80 billion a year. The 1992 Rio Conference on Environment and Development estimated that at least US$ 125 billion a year was needed to tackle the world's substantial environmental problems. Adding estimates on needs for reproductive health and basic infrastructure in developing nations provided by the World Bank, external funding on the order of US$ 225 billion a year could eradicate the worst forms of poverty and environmental destruction globally.

7. Ul Haq, Mahbub. *The Tobin Tax—Coping with Financial Volatility*, Oxford University Press, 1996. p. 4. Based on 1995 statistics provided by the Bank for International Settlements, Bank of England and the New York Federal Reserve.

8. Hayward, Helen. *The Global Gamblers— British Banks and the Foreign Exchange Game. War on Want*. 1998. p. 14.

9. Ibid. p.24.

10. Ibid. p.3.

11. According to Standard Chartered Bank's 1998 Annual Report, "the result from Treasury was outstanding . . . their ability to continue trading, during periods of high volatility in the foreign exchange markets resulted in exceptional dealing profitability." Hayward, Helen. *The Global Gamblers—British Banks and the Foreign Exchange Game. War on Want*. 1998. pp. 2–3.

12. Petrella, Ricardo. From Enroute. September 2000.

5.8

How Much Is "Enough"?

Alan Thein Durning

Early in the post-World War II age of affluence, a U.S. retailing analyst named Victor Lebow proclaimed, "Our enormously productive economy . . . demands that we make consumption our way of life, that we convert the buying and use of goods into rituals, that we seek our spiritual satisfaction, our ego satisfaction, in consumption. . . . We need things consumed, burned up, worn out, replaced, and discarded at an ever increasing rate." Americans have risen to Mr. Lebow's call, and much of the world has followed.

Since 1950, American consumption has soared. Per capita, energy use climbed 60 percent, car travel more than doubled, plastics use multiplied 20-fold, and air travel jumped 25-fold.

We are wealthy beyond the wildest dreams of our ancestors; the average human living today is four-and-a-half times richer than his or her great-grandparents, and the factor is larger still among the world's consuming class. American children under the age of 13 have more spending money—$230 a year—than the 300 million poorest people in the world.

The richest billion people in the world have created a form of civilization so acquisitive and profligate that the planet is in danger. The lifestyle of this top echelon—the car drivers, beef eaters, soda drinkers, and throwaway consumers—constitutes an ecological threat unmatched in severity by anything but perhaps population growth. The wealthiest fifth of humankind pumps out more than half of the greenhouse gases that threaten the earth's climate and almost 90 percent of the chlorofluorocarbons that are destroying the earth's protective ozone layer.

Ironically, abundance has not even made people terribly happy. In the United States, repeated opinion polls of people's sense of well-being show that no more Americans are satisfied with their lot now than they were in 1957. Despite phenomenal growth in consumption, the list of wants has grown faster still.

Of course, the other extreme from overconsumption—poverty—is no solution to environmental or human problems: it is infinitely worse for people and equally bad for the environment. Dispossessed peasants slash-and-burn their way into the rain forests of Latin America, and hungry nomads turn their herds out onto fragile African rangeland, reducing it to desert. If environmental decline results when people have either too little or too much, we must ask ourselves: How much is enough? What level of consumption can the earth support? When does consumption cease to add appreciably to human satisfaction?

Answering these questions definitively is impossible, but for each of us in the world's

Alan Thein Durning, excerpt from "How Much Is 'Enough'?" *World Watch Magazine* 3, no. 6 (November–December 1990): 12–19, www.worldwatch.org.

consuming class, seeking answers may be a prerequisite to transforming our civilization into one the biosphere can sustain.

[. . .]

Consuming Drives

The realities of current consumption patterns around the world point toward quantitative answers to the question of how much is enough?

For three of the most ecologically important types of consumption—transportation, diet, and use of raw materials—the world's 5.3 billion people are distributed unevenly over a vast range. Those at the bottom clearly fall beneath the "too little" line, and those at the top, the cars-meat-and-disposables class, clearly consume too much. But where in the larger middle class does "enough" lie?

About one billion people do most of their traveling—aside from the occasional donkey or bus ride—on foot. Many in the walking class never go more than 100 miles from their birthplaces. Unable to get to work easily, attend school, or bring their complaints before government offices, they are severely hindered by the lack of transportation options.

The massive middle class of the world, numbering some three billion people, travels by bus and bicycle. Mile for mile, bikes are cheaper than any other vehicles, costing under $100 in most of the Third World and requiring no fuel. They are also the most efficient form of transportation ever invented and, where not endangered by polluted air and traffic, provide their riders with healthy exercise.

The world's automobile class is relatively small: only 8 percent of humans, about 400 million, own cars. The auto class's fleet of four-wheelers is directly responsible for an estimated 13 percent of carbon dioxide emissions from fossil fuels worldwide, along with air pollution and acid rain, traffic fatalities numbering a quarter million annually, and the sprawl of urban areas into endless tract developments lacking community cohesion.

The auto class bears indirect responsibility for the far-reaching impacts of their chosen vehicle. The automobile makes itself indispensable: cities sprawl, public transit atrophies, shopping centers multiply, employers scatter. Today, working Americans spend nine hours a week behind the wheel. To make these homes-away-from-home more comfortable, 90 percent of new American cars are air-conditioned, which adds emissions of gases that aggravate the greenhouse effect and deplete the ozone layer.

Around the world, the great marketing achievement of automobile vendors has been to turn the machine into a cultural icon. As French philosopher Roland Barthes writes, "cars today are almost the exact equivalent of the great Gothic cathedrals . . . the supreme creation of an era, conceived with passion by unknown artists, and consumed in image if not in usage by a whole population which appropriates them as purely magical objects."

Ironies abound: more "Eagles" drive America's expanding road network, for instance, than fly in the nation's polluted skies, and more "Cougars" pass the night in its proliferating garages than in its shrinking forests.

Some in the auto class are also members of a more select group: the global jet set. The four million Americans who account for 41 percent of domestic trips, for example, cover five times as many miles a year as average Americans. Furthermore, because each mile traveled by air uses more energy than a mile traveled by car, jet setters consume six-and-a-half times as much energy for transportation as ordinary car-class members.

Eat, Drink, and Be Sustainable

On the food consumption ladder, people of the world fall into three rungs reflecting calories eaten and the richness of diet. The world's 630 million poorest people lack the resources necessary to provide themselves with sufficient calories for a healthy diet, according to the latest World Bank estimates.

The 3.4 billion grain eaters of the world's middle class get enough calories and plenty of plant-based protein, giving them the healthiest basic diet of the world's people. They typically receive no more than 20 percent of their calories from fat, a level low enough to protect them from the consequences of excessive dietary fat.

The top of the ladder is populated by the meat eaters, those who obtain about 40 percent of their calories from fat. These 1.25 billion people eat three times as much fat per person as the remaining 4 billion, mostly because they eat so much red meat. . . . The meat class pays the price of their diet in high death rates from the so-called diseases of affluence—heart disease, stroke, and certain types of cancer.

In fact, the U.S. government, long beholden to livestock and dairy interests, now recommends a diet in which no more than 30 percent of calories come from fat. California heart specialist Dr. Dean Ornish, credited with creating the first non-drug therapy proven to reverse clogging of the arteries, prescribes a semi-vegetarian diet virtually indistinguishable from that eaten daily by peasants in China, Brazil, or Egypt.

Indirectly, the meat-eating quarter of humanity consumes almost half of the world's grain—grain that fattens the livestock they eat. They are also responsible for many of the environmental strains induced by the present global agricultural system, from soil erosion to over-pumping of underground water.

In the extreme case of American beef, producing a pound of steak requires five pounds of grain and the energy equivalent of a gallon of gasoline, not to mention the associated soil erosion, water consumption, pesticide and fertilizer runoff, groundwater depletion, and emissions of the greenhouse gas methane.

Beyond the effects of livestock production, the affluent diet rings up an ecological bill through its heavy dependence on shipping goods over great distances. One-fourth of grapes eaten in the United States are grown 7,000 miles away in Chile, and the typical mouthful of food travels 1,300 miles from farm field to dinner plate. America's far-flung agribusiness food system is only partly a product of agronomic forces. It is also a result of farm policies and health standards that favor large producers, massive government subsidies for Western irrigation water, and a national highway system that makes trucking economical by transferring the tax burden from truckers onto car drivers.

The thousands of small farms, bakeries, and dairies that once encircled and fed the nation's cities cannot supply chain supermarkets with sufficient quantities of perfectly uniform products to compete with the food industry conglomerates. Their lot is to slide ever closer to foreclosure while hauling their produce to struggling weekend "farmers' markets."

Processing and packaging add further resource costs to the affluent diet, though those costs remain largely hidden. Even relatively familiar prepared foods are surprisingly energy

consumptive. Ounce for ounce, getting frozen orange juice to the consumer takes four times the energy (and several times the packaging) of providing fresh oranges. Likewise, potato chip production has four times the energy budget of potatoes.

The resource requirements of making the new generation of microwave-ready instant meals, loaded as they are with disposable pans and multi-layer packaging, are about ten times larger than preparing the same dishes at home from scratch.

Mirroring food consumption, overall beverage intake rises little between poor and rich. What changes is what people drink. The 1.75 billion people at the bottom of the beverage ladder have no option but to drink water that is often contaminated with human, animal, and chemical wastes.

Those in the next group up, in this case nearly two billion people, take more than 80 percent of their liquid refreshment in the form of clean drinking water. The remainder of this class's liquids come from commercial beverages such as tea, coffee, and, for the children, milk. At the quantities consumed, these beverages pose few environmental problems. They are packaged minimally, and transport energy needs are low because they are moved only short distances or in a dry form.

In the top class are the billion people in industrial countries. At a growing rate, they drink soft drinks, bottled water, and other prepared commercial beverages that are packaged in single-use containers and transported over great distances—sometimes across oceans.

Ironically, where tap water is purest and most accessible, its use as a beverage is declining. It now typically accounts for only a quarter of drinks in developed countries. In the extreme case of the United States, per-capita consumption of soft drinks rose to 47 gallons in 1989 (nearly seven times the global mean), according to the trade magazine *Beverage Industry*. Americans now drink more soda pop than water from the kitchen sink.

The Stuff of Life

In consumption of raw materials, about one billion rural people subsist on local biomass collected from the immediate environment. Most of what they consume each day—about a pound of grain, two pounds of fuelwood, and fodder for their animals—could be self-replenishing renewable resources. Unfortunately, because they are often pushed by landlessness and population growth into fragile, unproductive ecosystems, their minimal needs are not always met.

If these billion are materially destitute, they are part of a larger group that lacks many of the benefits provided by modest use of nonrenewable resources—particularly durable things like radios, refrigerators, water pipes, high-quality tools, and carts with lightweight wheels and ball bearings. More than two billion people live in countries where per-capita consumption of steel, the most basic modern material, falls below 100 pounds a year. . . .

Though similar international data are not available for most other basic raw materials, energy consumption can serve as a substitute indicator since most processes that use lots of raw materials also use lots of energy. In those same countries, per-capita consumption of all types of energy (except subsistence fuelwood) is lower than 20 gigajoules per year. . . .

Roughly one-and-a-half billion live in the middle class of materials users. Providing them with durable goods each year uses between 100 and 350 pounds of steel per capita and between 20 and 50 gigajoules per capita. At the top of the heap is the throwaway class, which uses raw materials like they're going out of style. A typical resident of the industrialized world uses 15 times as much paper, 10 times as much steel, and 12 times as much fuel as a resident of the developing world. The extreme case is again the United States, where the average person consumes most of his or her own weight in basic materials each day. . . .

In the throwaway economy, packaging is the essence of the product. It is at once billboard, shipping container, and preservative. Seven percent of consumer spending in the United States goes for packaging. Yet, it all ends up in the dump. Disposable goods proliferate in America and other industrial countries. Each year, Japan uses 30 million "disposable" single-roll cameras, and Americans toss away 18 billion diapers and enough aluminum cans to make about 6,000 DC-10 jet airplanes.

In throwaway economies, even "durable" goods are not particularly durable, nor are they easy to repair. Technological improvement would be expected to steadily raise the average working life of goods. Yet, over time, new items have fallen dramatically in price relative to repair costs, according to data compiled by the Organization for Economic Cooperation and Development. The average life span of most household appliances has stayed level. The reason is that manufacturers have put their research dollars into lowering production costs, even if it makes repair more difficult.

Tinkerer-filmmaker Tim Hunkin spent two years poking around waste sites in England studying discarded household appliances. His findings, reported in the British magazine *New Scientist*, reveal the prevailing trend toward planned obsolescence and disposability.

"The machines that date back to the 1950s are very solid, made mostly of metal with everything bolted or welded together," observes Hunkin. "As the years passed, machines have become more flimsy. More parts are now made of plastic, and they are glued together rather than welded or bolted. . . . Many parts are now impossible to repair. . . . New machines are so cheap that it frequently does not pay to have a faulty appliance repaired professionally."

Where disposability and planned obsolescence fail to accelerate the trip from purchase to junk heap, fashion sometimes succeeds. Most clothing goes out of style long before it is worn out, but lately, the realm of fashion has colonized sports footwear, too. Kevin Ventrudo, chief financial officer of California-based L.A. Gear, which saw sales multiply fifty times in four years, told the *Washington Post*, "If you talk about shoe performance, you only need one or two pairs. If you're talking fashion, you're talking endless pairs of shoes."

In transportation, diet, and use of raw materials, as consumption rises on the economic scale so does waste—both of resources and of health. Bicycles and public transit are cheaper, more efficient, and healthier transport options than cars. A diet founded on the basics of grains and water is gentle to the earth and the body. And a lifestyle that makes full use of raw materials for durable goods without succumbing to the throwaway mentality is ecologically sound while still affording many of the comforts of modernity.

Ethics for Sustainability

When Moses came down from Mount Sinai, he could count the rules of ethical behavior on his fingers. In the complex global economy of the late 20th century, in which the simple act of turning on an air conditioner affects planetary systems, the list of rules for ecologically sustainable living could run into the hundreds.

The basic value of a sustainable society, the ecological equivalent of the Golden Rule, is simple: Each generation should meet its needs without jeopardizing the prospects of future generations. What is lacking is the practical knowledge—at each level of society—of what living by that principle means.

In a fragile biosphere, the ultimate fate of humanity may depend on whether we can cultivate a deeper sense of self-restraint, founded on a widespread ethic of limiting consumption and finding non-material enrichment.

[. . .]

Voluntary simplicity, or personal restraint, will do little good, however, if it is not wedded to bold political steps that confront the forces advocating consumption. Beyond the oft-repeated agenda of environmental and social reforms necessary to achieve sustainability, such as overhauling energy systems, stabilizing population, and ending poverty, action is needed to restrain the excesses of advertising, to curb the shopping culture, and to revitalize household and community economies as human-scale alternatives to the high-consumption lifestyle.

[. . .]

In the final analysis, accepting and living by sufficiency rather than excess offers a return to what is, culturally speaking, the human home: the ancient order of family, community, good work and good life; to a reverence for excellence of craftsmanship; to a true materialism that does not just care *about* things but cares *for* them; to communities worth spending a lifetime in.

5.9

Toward a Deglobalized World

Walden Bello

The historic Prague Spring of 1968 spelled the beginning of the end for the Soviet Empire. In the year 2000, Prague was the site of the World Bank-IMF annual meetings, joining Seattle in December 1999 and Washington, DC, in April 2000, as one of the catalytic events ushering the beginning of the end of hegemony of corporate-driven globalization.

We came to a crossroads in Prague. For years we were told that globalization was benign, that it was a process that brought about the greatest good for the greatest number. Good citizenship lay in accepting the impersonal rule of the market and good governance meant governments getting out of the way of market forces and letting the most effective incarnation of market freedom, the transnational corporation (TNC), go about its task of bringing about the most efficient mix of capital, land, technology, and labor.

The unrestricted flow of goods and capital in a world without borders was said to be the best of all possible worlds, though when some observers pointed out that to be consistent with the precepts of their eighteenth century prophet, Adam Smith, proponents of the neoliberal doctrine would also have to allow the unrestricted flow of labor to create this best of all possible worlds,

they were ignored. Such inconsistencies could be overlooked since for over two decades, neoliberalism or, as it was grandiosely styled, the "Washington consensus" had carried all before it.

[. . .]

The stakes are great, and how civil society responds at this historical moment to the aggressive courtship being mounted will make the difference in the future of the globalization project. Developments are so fluid in the correlation of forces in the struggle between the pro-globalization and anti-globalization camps that strategies that might have been realistic and appropriate pre-Seattle, when the multilateral institutions had more solidity and legitimacy, are timid and inappropriate if not counterproductive, now that the multilateral agencies are in a profound crisis of legitimacy. Let me be specific:

Will NGOs breathe life into a WTO process that is at standstill by pushing for the incorporation of labor and environmental clauses into the WTO agreements, instead of reducing the power and authority of this instrument of corporate rule by doing all in their power to prevent another trade round from ever taking place?

Will they throw a life saver to the Bretton Woods institutions by participating in the civil society-World Bank-IMF consultations that are to be the central element of the "comprehensive development framework" that Wolfensohn and the IMF leadership see as the key to the re-legitimization of the Bretton Woods twins?

Walden Bello, excerpt from "Prague 2000: Toward a Deglobalized World," *Focus Dossiers* no. 3, online publication of Focus on the Global South (Bangkok, Thailand, September 2000): 1 and 10–15, www.focusweb.org.

Will they allow themselves to be sucked into the . . . process of "reasonable dialogue" and "frank consultation" when the other side sees dialogue and consultation mainly as the first step to the disarmament of the [first] side?

Reform or Disempowerment?

Our tactics will depend not only on the balance of forces but will turn even more fundamentally on our answer to the question: Should we seek to transform or to disable the main institutions of corporate-led globalization?

Institutions should be saved and reformed if their functioning, while defective, nevertheless can be reoriented to promote the interests of society and the environment. They should be abolished if they have become fundamentally dysfunctional. Can we really say that the IMF can be reformed to bring about global financial stability, the World Bank to reduce poverty, and the WTO to bring about fair trade? Are they not, in fact, imprisoned within paradigms and structures that create outcomes that contradict these objectives? Can we truly say that these institutions can be reengineered to handle the multiple problems that have been thrown up by the process of corporate-led globalization?

The dominant institutions of globalization can no longer handle the multiple problems thrown up by the process of corporate-led globalization. Instead of trying to reform the multilateral institutions, would it in fact be more *realistic* and "cost-effective," to use a horrid neo-liberal term, to move to disempower, if not abolish them, and create totally new institutions that do not have the baggage of illegitimacy, institutional failure, and Jurassic mindsets that are attached to the IMF, World Bank, and WTO?

Disabling the Corporation

I would contend that the focus of our efforts these days is not to try to reform the multilateral agencies, but to deepen the crisis of legitimacy of the whole system. Gramsci once described the bureaucracy as but an "outer trench behind which lay a powerful system of fortresses and earthworks." We must no longer think simply in terms of neutralizing the multilateral agencies that form the outer trenches of the system, but of disabling the transnational corporations that are fortresses and the earthworks that constitute the core of the global economic system. I am talking about disabling not just the WTO, the IMF, and the World Bank but the transnational corporation itself. And I am not talking about a process of "re-regulating" the TNCs, but of eventually disabling or dismantling them as fundamental hazards to people, society, the environment, to everything we hold dear.

Is this off the wall? Only if we think that the shocking irresponsibility and secrecy with which the Monsantos and Novartises have foisted biotechnology on us is a departure from the corporate norm. Only if we also see as deviations from the normal Shell's systematic devastation of Ogoniland in Nigeria, the Seven Sisters' conspiracy to prevent the development of renewable energy sources in order to keep us slaves to a petroleum civilization, Rio Tinto and the mining giants' practice of poisoning rivers and communities, and Mitsubishi's recently exposed 20-year cover up of a myriad of product-safety violations to prevent a recall that would cut into profitability. Only if we think that it is acceptable business practice and ethics to pull up stakes, lay off people, and destroy long-established communities in order to pursue ever cheaper labor around the globe—a process that most TNCs now engage in.

These are not departures from normal corporate behavior. They are *normal* corporate behavior. And corporate crimes against people and the environment has become a way of life because, as the British philosopher John Gray tells us, "Global market competition and technological innovation have interacted to give us an anarchic world economy." To such a world of anarchy, scarcity, and conflict created by global *laissez-faire*, Gray continues, "Thomas Hobbes and Thomas Malthus are better guides than Adam Smith or Friedrich von Hayek, with their Utopian vision of a humanity united by 'the benevolent harmonies of competition.'"[21] Smith's world of peacefully competing enterprises has, in the age of the TNC, degenerated into Hobbes' "war of all against all."

Gray goes on to say that "as it is presently organized, global capitalism is supremely ill-suited to cope with the risks of geo-political conflict that are endemic in a world of worsening scarcities. Yet a regulatory framework for coexistence and cooperation among the world's diverse economies figures on no historical or political agenda."[22] Recent events underline his point. When the ice cap on the North Pole is melting at an unprecedented rate and the ozone layer above the South Pole has declined by 30 percent, owing precisely to the dynamics of this corporate civilization's insatiable desire for growth and profits, the need for cooperation among peoples and societies is more stark than ever. We must do better than entrust production and exchange to entities that systematically and fundamentally work to erode solidarity, discourage cooperation, oppose regulation except profit-enhancing and monopoly-creating regulation, all in the name of the market and efficiency.

It is said that in the age of globalization, nation states have become obsolete forms of social organization. I disagree. It is the corporation that has become obsolete. It is the corporation that serves as a fetter to humanity's movement to new and necessary social arrangements to achieve the most quintessentially human values of justice, equity, democracy, and to achieve a new equilibrium between our species and the rest of the planet. Disabling, disempowering, or dismantling the transnational corporation should be high on our agenda as a strategic end. And when we say this, we do not equate the TNC with private enterprise, for there are benevolent and malevolent expressions of private enterprise. We must seek to disable or eliminate the malevolent ones, like the TNC.[23]

The Struggle for the Future I:
De-globalization

It is often said that we must not only know what we are against but what we are for. I agree—though it is very important to know very clearly what we want to terminate so we do not end up unwittingly fortifying it so that, like a WTO energized with social and environmental clauses, it is given a new lease on life.

Let me end, therefore, by giving you my idea of an alternative. It is, however, one that has been formulated for a Third World, and specifically Southeast Asian, context. Let me call this alternative route to the future "de-globalization."

What is de-globalization?

I am not talking about withdrawing from the international economy. I am speaking about re-

orienting our economies from production for export to production for the local market; about drawing most of our financial resources for development from within rather than becoming dependent on foreign investment and foreign financial markets; about carrying out the long-postponed measures of income redistribution and land redistribution to create a vibrant internal market that would be the anchor of the economy; about de-emphasizing growth and maximizing equity in order to radically reduce environmental disequilibrium; about not leaving strategic economic decisions to the market but making them subject to democratic choice; about subjecting the private sector and the state to constant monitoring by civil society; about creating a new production and exchange complex that includes community cooperatives, private enterprises, and state enterprises, and excludes TNCs; about enshrining the principle of subsidiaries in economic life by encouraging production of goods to take place at the community and national level if it can be done so at reasonable cost in order to preserve community.

We are talking about a strategy that consciously subordinates the logic of the market, the pursuit of cost efficiency to the values of security, equity, and social solidarity. We are speaking about re-embedding the economy in society, rather than having society driven by the economy.

The Struggle for the Future II:
A Plural World

De-globalization, or the re-empowerment of the local and national, can only succeed if it takes place within an alternative system of global economic governance. What are the contours of such a world economic order? The answer is contained in our critique of the Bretton Woods *cum* WTO system as a monolithic system of universal rules imposed by highly centralized institutions to further the interests of corporations—in particular, US corporations. To try to supplant this with another centralized global system of rules and institutions, though these may be premised on different principles, is likely to reproduce the same Jurassic trap that ensnared organizations as different as IBM, the IMF, and the Soviet state, and this is the inability to tolerate and profit from diversity.

Today's need is not another centralized global institution but the de-concentration and decentralization of institutional power and the creation of a pluralistic system of institutions and organizations interacting with one another, guided by broad and flexible agreements and understandings. We are not talking about something completely new. It was under such a more pluralistic system of global economic governance, where hegemonic power was still far from institutionalized in a set of all-encompassing and powerful multilateral organizations and institutions, that a number of Latin American and Asian countries were able to achieve a modicum of industrial development in the period from 1950 to 1970. It was under such a pluralistic system, under a General Agreement on Tariffs and Trade (GATT) that was limited in its power, flexible, and more sympathetic to the special status of developing countries, that the East and Southeast Asian countries were able to become newly industrializing countries through activist state trade and industrial policies that departed significantly from the free market biases enshrined in the WTO.

Of course, economic relations among countries prior to the attempt to institutionalize one global free market system beginning in the early 1980s were neither ideal, nor were the Third World economies. But these conditions and structures underline the fact that the alternative to an economic *Pax Romana* built around the World Bank-IMF-WTO system is not a Hobbesian state of nature. The reality of international relations in a world marked by a multiplicity of international and regional institutions that check one another is a far cry from the propaganda image of a "nasty" and "brutish" world. Of course, the threat of unilateral action by the powerful is ever present in such a system, but it is one that even the most powerful hesitate to take for fear of its consequences on their legitimacy as well as the reaction it would provoke in the form of opposing coalitions.

More space, more flexibility, more compromise—these should be the goals of the Southern agenda and the civil society effort to build a new system of global economic governance. It is in such a more fluid, less structured, more pluralistic world, with multiple checks and balances, that the nations and communities of the South—and the North—will be able to carve out the space to develop based on their values, their rhythms, and the strategies of their choice.

Let me quote John Gray one last time. "It is legitimate and indeed imperative that we seek a form of rootedness which is sheltered from overthrow by technologies and market processes which in achieving a global reach that is disembedded from any community or culture, cannot avoid desolating the earth's human settlements and its non-human environments." The role of international arrangements in a world where toleration of diversity is a central principle of economic organization would be "to express and protect local and national cultures by embodying and sheltering their distinctive practices."[24]

Let us put an end to this arrogant globalist project of making the world a synthetic unity of individual atoms shorn of culture and community. Instead, let us herald an internationalism that is built on, tolerates, respects, and enhances the diversity of human communities and the diversity of life.

Notes

[. . .]

21. Gray, John. *False Dawn* (New York: New Press, 1998), pg. 207.

22. Ibid.

23. For excellent recent critiques of the corporation, see David Korten, *When Corporations Rule the World* (San Francisco: Kumarian Press/Beret-Koehler, 1995); Joshua Karliner, *The Corporate Planet* (San Francisco: Sierra Club Books, 1997); and Richard Barnet and John Cavanagh, *Global Dreams: Imperial Corporations and the New World Order* (New York: Simon and Schuster, 1994).

24. Gray, John. *Enlightenment's Wake* (London, UK: Routledge, 1995), pg. 181.

For Further Reading

Part V is a whirlwind tour of the rollback segment of the backlash. Fortunately, the reader can find more detailed information about the people and case studies presented here through a combination of written materials and the Internet.

The best way to read more by **Subcomandante Marcos** is the book from which Reading 5.1 was taken, *Our Word Is Our Weapon: Selected Writings of Subcomandante Marcos* (Seven Stories, 2001). Marcos's speeches appear in numerous places, thanks in part to his requirement that his words cannot be copyrighted. See, for instance, Frank Bardacke et al., eds. and trans., *Shadows of Tender Fury: The Letters and Communiqués of Subcomandante Marcos and the Zapatista Army of National Liberation* (New York: Monthly Review Press, 1995), which also has a useful introduction written by John Ross. And view *The Sixth Sun: Mayan Uprising in Chiapas*, the documentary film directed by Saul Landau of the Institute for Policy Studies. See also the web site of the EZLN (www.ezln.org).

To move from Chiapas to a more global look at **indigenous communities**, see the web sites of Survival International (in the UK) and Cultural Survival in the United States, among others listed in the web bibliography at the end of this book.

Helena Norberg-Hodge became known for her first book, which looked at the impact of contact with the rest of the world on Ladakh, a remote area in the Himalayas: *Ancient Futures* (San Francisco: Sierra Club, 1992). For more on the issues of **food security and localization** brought up in Reading 5.2, see other work by the International Society for Ecology and Culture, which she directs, as well as the work published by the Institute for Food and Development Policy ("Food First") in San Francisco and the Institute for Agriculture and Trade Policy in Minneapolis, Minnesota.

For a **historical look at the philosophy and practice of localization as well as the simplicity movement**, go back to Gandhi: see, for example, Rudrangshu

Mukherjee, ed., *The Penguin Gandhi Reader* (New York: Penguin Books, 1993); and Dennis Dalton, ed., *Mahatma Gandhi: Selected Political Writings* (Indianapolis: Hackett Publishing, 1996).

To jump to **more recent literature detailing an alternative path geared to localization**, key sources include Colin Hines (former international coordinator of Greenpeace's international economics unit), *Localization: A Global Manifesto* (London: Earthscan, 2000); Tim Lang and Colin Hines, *The New Protectionism: Protecting the World against Free Trade* (New York: The New Press, 1993); David Korten, *The Post-Corporate World: Life after Capitalism* (West Hartford, Conn.: Kumarian Press, 1999); and, from the Philippines but fortunately also available in the United States, Nicanor Perlas, *Shaping Globalization: Civil Society, Cultural Power, and Threefolding* (Saratoga Springs, N.Y.: GlobeNet3, 2000).

And there are many more: Michael Shuman's *Going Local: Creating Self-Reliant Communities in a Global Age* (New York: New Press, 1998) details case studies from what over a dozen communities did to go local. If you have time to read only one—albeit long—book, turn to Jerry Mander and Edward Goldsmith, eds., *The Case against the Global Economy* (San Francisco: Sierra Club, 1999), which brings together many of the key "rollback" writers and practitioners from across the globe. Another useful reader that concentrates on what it calls the "subsistence perspective" of community-based initiatives that resist globalization is Veronika Bennholdt-Thomsen, Nicholas Faraclas, and Claudia von Werlhofl, eds., *There Is an Alternative: Subsistence and Worldwide Resistance to Corporate Globalization* (Zed, 2001). For a brief summation of the arguments, see Edward Goldsmith, "Can the Environment Survive the Global Economy?" *The Ecologist* 27, no. 6 (November/December 1997): 242–48. To keep up-to-date on "rollback" views and initiatives, read *YES! A Journal of Positive Futures* (www.futurenet.org), as well as *The Ecologist*.

For the **environmental arguments underpinning localization**, learn more about "bioregionalism" by reading Kirkpatrick Sale's books. A good place to begin is with his book *Dwellers in the Land: The Bioregional Vision* (San Francisco: Sierra Club, 1985). (In 1991, in a classic document, the Green Forum-Philippines produced an "Economic White Paper" to demonstrate how to apply bioregionalism to the Philippines.) See also the work of Kentucky author and farmer Wendell Berry (such as his 1977 Sierra Club book *The Unsettling of America*), whose philosophy is summarized in a 2000 interview with him: "A Return to the Local: You Stay Home Too," *World Watch Magazine* 13, no. 5 (September/October 2000): 29–33.

Vandana Shiva, who has a doctorate in physics, is a prolific writer with important writings ranging from eco-feminism to agriculture and to technology—from *Staying Alive* (St. Martin's Press, 1989) to *Stolen Harvest: The Hijacking of the Global Food Supply* (Cambridge, Mass.: South End Press, 2000). For more by **Shiva and her colleagues, as well as more on Jaiv Panchayat**, see the web site of the Research Foundation for Science, Technology, and Ecology in India, founded in 1982, which she directs. Many of these issues are summarized in Shiva et al., *The Enclosure and Recovery of the Commons: Biodiversity, Indigenous Knowledge, and Intellectual Property Rights* (New Delhi: Research Foundation for Science, Technology and Ecology, 1997). Key web sites about rice—as well as about the 1992 UN Convention on Biological

Diversity and the 2000 Biosafety Protocol (an international environmental agreement to regulate the international trade of "living modified organisms," which was negotiated under the UN Convention)—include www.grain.org, www.iuf.org, www.vshiva.net, www.iatp.org, www.purefood.org, www.citizen.org/pctrade/tradehome.html, www.foei.org, www.greenpeace.org, and others listed in the bibliography at the end of this book.

Years ago at the Worldwatch Institute, then vice president Sandra Postel started writing about **water**. Postel is now director of the Global Water Policy Project in Amherst, Massachusetts; her writing on water is one place to start for a global view. To recap the work and the debate about **dams**, see "Dams and Development," the 404-page critical report by the World Commission on Dams (an independent group sponsored by the World Bank in response to NGO critiques and campaigns on large dams) issued in November 2000 (available from www.dams.org). For a focus on India, read prize-winning Indian novelist Arundhati Roy's *The Cost of Living* (Harper-Collins, 1999) and *Power Politics* (South End Press, 2001).

Then, for **specifics on the Canadian water case as well as global advocacy work,** move on to Maude Barlow's work, especially her *Blue Gold: The Global Water Crisis and the Commodification of the World's Water Supply* (San Francisco: International Forum on Globalization, 1999). This and others by her are available on the web sites of the Council of Canadians and the International Forum on Globalization, as part of their Blue Planet project.

The **Bolivian case** is another backlash campaign that made sophisticated use of cyberspace, with Internet updates and photos continually posted from Cochabamba. To recapture that history and follow the latest news from Cochabamba, access that web site (www.americas.org). Another useful source for information and for advocacy work is Public Services International (such as the February 2000 issue (vol. 7, no. 2) of their *Focus on the Public Services*), which has provided help to the water campaign in Cochabamba.

The topic of **Third World debt** is huge; a vast literature covers the period since Mexico first announced its inability to repay its foreign debts in 1982. A good place to start is with John Cavanagh et al., *From Debt to Development* (Washington, D.C.: Institute for Policy Studies, 1985), which will quickly familiarize you with the debt buildup in the 1970s, the crisis as it unfolded in the early to mid-1980s, the IMF and U.S. government responses to the crisis, and alternative plans. Add more recent information and analyses to that by consulting sources available through the various Jubilee campaigns: in addition to Jubilee South, the Jubilee USA Network (www.jubileeusa.org) and Jubilee + (United Kingdom, an official successor to Jubilee 2000). For broad information on debt, go to The Debt Channel (www.debtchannel.org). For a summary of the Jubilee movements, see Rose Gutfeld, "Lightening the Debt Load," *Ford Foundation Report* 32, no. 2 (Spring 2001): 26–29.

To follow **debt as well as the multilateral lending institutions,** see also "Economic Justice News," the newsletter from 50 Years Is Enough: US Network for Global Economic Justice (www.50years.org), a large coalition that coalesced in the United States to celebrate the Bank and Fund's fiftieth anniversary with calls to "radically transform" these institutions. Led by Njoki Njehu (from Kenya) and

Soren Ambrose (from the United States), 50 Years Is Enough has created a space for rollback and reshape forces to come together, and is often a key group at the center of the organizing for Washington, D.C.–based protests.

There are some excellent analyses that allow you to follow the unfolding of the **late-1990s financial crisis** and proposals for what to do about it: Manuel Montes, *The Currency Crisis in Southeast Asia* (Singapore: Institute of Southeast Asian Studies, 1998) and Jomo K.S., ed., *Tigers in Trouble: Financial Governance, Liberalisation, and Crises in East Asia* (New York: Zed, 1998). From Europe comes Jan Joost Teunissen, *Reforming the International Financial System* (The Hague: Forum on Debt and Development [FONDAD], 2000); from the United States, Robert Blecker, *Taming Global Finance* (Washington, D.C.: Economic Policy Institute, 1999); and again from Asia, Walden Bello et al., *Global Finance: New Thinking on Regulating Speculative Capital Markets* (New York: Zed, 2000). See also the work of Joseph Stiglitz (cited in Part I's "For Further Reading" section), as well as a World Bank document he oversaw that also goes into the environmental and social costs of the financial crisis: *East Asia: The Road to Recovery* (Washington, D.C.: World Bank, 1998).

On **short-term speculative financial flows**, be sure to read Rodney Schmidt's superb chapter in the Bello et al. volume (mentioned in the preceding paragraph) on the feasibility of implementation of a Tobin tax. There are at least three knowledgeable sources that allow you to keep abreast of backlash initiatives concerning a Tobin tax: (1)"ATTAC Newsletter," the online newsletter of ATTAC (attac.org/listen.htm); (2) the online monthly newsletter "Tobin Tax Updates" put out by Ruthanne Cecil at Tobin Tax Initiative USA (www.tobintax.org, www.ceedweb.org, or cecilr@humboldtl.com); and (3) the work of Round and the Halifax Initiative.

When you read the selected writings of Gandhi mentioned above, you will also get into the history of the **voluntary simplicity movement**. Herman Daly, whom I and others consider the father of ecological economics, provides the solid economics base for what he calls a "steady state" in which growth for all is not the goal. See his various articles and books with that phrase incorporated in the title—from his 1974 article "The Economics of the Steady State" in the *American Economic Review,* to a book he edited *Toward a Steady-State Economy* published by W. H. Freeman in 1973. See also his more recent *Beyond Growth: The Economics of Sustainable Development* (Boston: Beacon Press, 1996), as well as his writings with Robert Goodland and John Cobb Jr.

For other **recent writings on the need to reduce luxury consumption**, see Juliet Schor's (ed.) *Do Americans Shop Too Much?* (Boston: Beacon Press, 2000). The late Donella Meadows, who taught at Dartmouth College, is perhaps best known for her coauthored *The Limits to Growth* (Washington, D.C.: Potomac Associates, 1972), but her writings range from popular opinion editorials to more scholarly pieces. See the work of Vicky Robin and her New Road Map Foundation (including *Your Money or Your Life,* [1992] coauthored with Joe Dominguez, which was on *Business Week*'s bestseller list for a long time). For a quick and easy read that will have you "watching your [consumption] wake," see another of Durning's works, as well as other publications of the Seattle-based Northwest Environment Watch which he directs): John Ryan and Alan Durning, *Stuff: The Secret Life of Everyday Things*

(1997). See also the popular writing of Bill McKibben, such as "The End of Growth," *Mother Jones*, November/December 1999, 68–71, 94–95. Among other reasons to join the Center for the New American Dream is to read their excellent quarterly report *Enough!* which often includes news or writings by others mentioned in this paragraph. And, if you are interested in assessing and/or changing your own consumption habits, start with their "More Fun Less Stuff—Starter Kit" (by the center's director Betsy Taylor) or their "Simplify the Holidays" booklet.

To follow the "deglobalize" thinking of **Walden Bello and receive updates and analysis on trade and finance**, read Focus on the Global South's regular electronic bulletin, *Focus-on-Trade*, available via admin@focusweb.org or www.focusweb. org. In addition, a book of Bello's essays—with chapters ranging from the more theoretical to vignettes of his experiences as one of the global backlash representatives at a Davos summit—has been copublished by Food First Books and Focus on the Global South: *The Future in the Balance: Essays on Globalization and Resistance*, 2001.

Finally, one of the best **overall books on the citizen backlash** and its history through the start of the twenty-first century, concentrating on what I have termed the "rollback" segment as well as rollback proposals, is: Maude Barlow and Tony Clarke, *Global Showdown: How the New Activists Are Fighting Global Corporate Rule* (Toronto: Stoddart Publishing Co., 2001).

Conclusion

What Does It All Add Up To?

Nearly thirty years ago, Richard Barnet and Ronald Müller in their best-seller *Global Reach* asked which forces could become a "countervailing power" against the abuses of global corporations. Back then, given the reality of the middle third of the twentieth century, they focused on the strength of labor unions and the promise of more aggressive action by governments. Today, the power and promise of both are greatly changed. Most twenty-first century governments have been weakened as independent economic actors as they cater to demands made either directly by corporations or indirectly through the World Trade Organization and other multilateral organizations. And trade union movements around the world have generally diminished in size. Acting alone, unions are not the full answer.

Yet the countervailing power to today's corporate-led economic globalization that Barnet and Müller hoped for *is* emerging—from a coalition of movements representing labor, environmental, consumer, peasant, and other sectors, North and South. Seattle introduced the world to the new face of this countervailing power: the "global backlash." This book has attempted to answer the question "But what do they want?" by taking you on a tour of some key backlash proposals and initiatives to reshape and roll back via voluntary and regulatory means.

In closing, it is worth raising the next logical questions: What does it all add up to? How effective has the backlash been? How effective is it likely to be? And what challenges does the backlash need to meet in order to reach its maximum effectiveness?

Assessing the backlash requires assessing the actual "effectiveness" of its various campaigns and initiatives, as well as the potential effectiveness of its proposals. But assessing effectiveness, alas, is a difficult task, and there have been shockingly few, if any, comprehensive attempts to gauge the levels of effectiveness (or ineffectiveness) of various initiatives.[1] In fact, there are no overall agreed-upon criteria for measuring effectiveness or success.

Those in the backlash have a sense of goals and, by extension, effectiveness. I know, for example, that the campus anti-sweatshop movement will deserve a victory party when I can purchase a T-shirt that says "American University" and feel confident that no exploited labor, be it child or adult, sweated over it or that no river was polluted by waste from the dyes that colored that shirt. This, then, is the long-term measure of effectiveness: Did the initiative make a difference on the ground? Have workers' lives improved? Have the life and environment of any relevant community improved? In other words, this requires assessing whether or not there has been a real, positive impact on communities, workers, the environment, and so on.

But, along the route to that ultimate measure of longer-term "success," one can still define and measure effectiveness in other ways. Elsewhere John Cavanagh and I have suggested half a dozen criteria for effectiveness; let me build on those to suggest the kind of benchmarks that need to be used:[2]

- To what extent have different parts of the backlash—different social and economic sectors, groups employing different tactics, groups based in the North and the South—worked together on an initiative?
- To what extent has the public been educated? Beyond education, to what extent have people outside the backlash been convinced?
- To what extent has the public acted as a result of this education—for instance, changed purchasing choices or been catalyzed into action to change government behavior? In other words, to what extent have those "converts" become actual players?
- To what extent has corporate policy changed? Actual corporate behavior?
- To what extent has the capacity of governments been strengthened, and how have they used this capacity?
- To what extent has multilateral institution policy changed? Actual behavior?
- To what extent have new mechanisms of nongovernmental oversight been created? How have NGOs used these mechanisms?

And so on. At different moments, different criteria of effectiveness may be called for. For instance, at an early stage, effectiveness may be "getting the word out"; at a much later stage, one might gauge an initiative ineffective if it did not change conditions on the ground.

In my introductions to Parts III, IV, and V, I have given my sense of the effectiveness of social clauses, codes of conduct, and rollback initiatives as weighed against some of these criteria; the excerpts add the views of others. History will be the judge.

But this much is already clear: However the global backlash to corporate-led economic integration deals with the challenges it faces, this book has demonstrated that it is a movement that is far more sophisticated, proactive, strategic, and effective than most of the portraits it has received in the mainstream media.

It is far more than simply a protest movement. Through its various campaigns and initiatives to reshape or roll back economic globalization, the backlash already has had an impact on the public and private institutions of the world economy.

It is perhaps appropriate to let one judge of the effectiveness of the backlash be a source which possesses little sympathy for backlash ideas and proposals but which prides itself on its "passion for business, insider access and uncanny foresight."[3] No less than leading business magazine *Fortune* acknowledged the broad impact of the backlash in a November 2001 article that serves as the final piece of this book (Reading C.1). As one would expect in a pro-free-market magazine, *Fortune* senior writer Jerry Useem critiques several backlash proposals as "misguided" and "problematic,"[4] reminiscent of the caricature with which much of the mainstream press has greeted the backlash. But the main point of the article—made with what could be called grudging admiration and commendable honesty—concerns what Useem sees as the deep penetration of backlash "ideas" and "issues" into the mainstream debate. As the article argues, the citizen backlash's effectiveness can no longer be judged by counting the number of protests or protesters. Rather, *Fortune* concedes that "people had started taking the protesters seriously" and credits the protesters for having "already achieved their main goal: fracturing a [Washington] consensus."

We are indeed, as was Dean Acheson in the 1940s (Reading 2.4), in the midst of a process of re-imagining and re-constructing the global economy and the institutions that manage and dominate it, as well as the worldview that underpins it. Experimental initiatives are taking root. New ones sprout up daily—as I can personally attest in trying to keep abreast of them for this book. We are present at another "re-creation."

To those of you who want to understand more of what this global backlash is all about, I hope this book has provided the foundation for that information. To those of you who want to be a part of the backlash, I hope this book has educated and energized you. (The web site bibliography that follows will help you to find even more information and to get in touch.) To those of you who are already a part, I hope this book has helped you look in a mirror that illuminates all sides of a movement, not just your frontal view.

One very final point: I mean this book to be a hopeful one. And, as I draft this conclusion in the wake of the horrific acts of terrorism in New York City and Washington, D.C., on 11 September 2001, I want to stress that hope. The fact that a sizable chunk of civil society across the globe has chosen to broaden the debate about the shape and purpose of the global economy and enter into the policy arena with counterproposals and actual initiatives is indeed a sign of hope.

Notes

1. See Robin Broad and John Cavanagh, "The Corporate Accountability Movement: Lessons and Opportunities," monograph for the Project on International Financial Flows and the Environment, World Wildlife Fund, the World Resources Institute, and C. S. Mott, Washington, D.C., 30 July 1997.

2. See Robin Broad and John Cavanagh, "Global Backlash: Citizen Initiatives to Counter Corporate-Led Globalization," in *Principled World Politics: The Challenge of Normative International Relations*, ed. Paul Wapner and Lester Ruiz (Lanham, Md.: Rowman & Littlefield, 2000); and Robin Broad and John Cavanagh, "The Corporate Accountability Movement," *The Fletcher Forum of World Affairs* 23 (Fall 1999), (condensed as: "The Corporate Accountability Movement: Lessons and Opportunities," *Sustainable Human and Economic Development*, vol. 6 of Frontier Issues in Economic Thought Series, ed. Neva Goodwin et al. [San Francisco: Island Press, 2000]).

3. Quote is from www.fortune.com/index.jhtml?channel=/html/mediakit.html, p. 1 (accessed 20 December 2001).

4. The purpose of this concluding section is not to re-open these broad debates nor to present backlash rebuttals to the *Fortune* criticisms. Earlier sections of this book have already dealt with these issues. For the full spectrum of paradigms, see Part I; my introduction to that part situates along the spectrum many of the specific individuals cited in the *Fortune* article. For how the backlash would respond to Useem's specific criticisms of its proposals, see Parts III through V. Part IV, for example, deals directly with whether backlash proposals represent Northern ideas that Southerners do not support. And to take other examples: Reading 4.10 is a backlash response to the criticism that sweatshop jobs are better than no jobs at all, while Reading 5.7 deals with the Tobin tax.

C.1

Globalization: Can Governments, Companies, and Yes, the Protesters Ever Learn to Get Along?

Jerry Useem

Business conferences don't achieve real status these days, it seems, unless they attract throngs of rock-throwing, meat-eschewing, puppet-wielding antiglobalization protesters. And on the face of it, *Fortune*'s summer gabfest in Aspen, Colo., looked liked a choice target. Members of the capitalist elite . . . a veil of secrecy . . . a deeply mysterious agenda . . . why, we could have been up to anything in there! How embarrassing, then, that not a single demonstrator showed up.

And yet, in another sense, the protesters were *everywhere*—in speeches, in hallway discussions, and, most of all, in spirit. "All these protesters from Seattle to Genoa are on to something," mused Bill Clinton, who argued that the world couldn't sustain a global economy if didn't also build a "global society." "Some of them are anarchists, but a lot of them have some very legitimate complaints," said former Secretary of State Madeleine Albright. Wondering why people kept returning to the issue, another participant likened it to "a little sore that everybody keeps scratching."

Maybe it was the image of that dead protester in Genoa, shot a few weeks earlier by riot police during a G-8 meeting. Maybe it was the thin mountain air. Or maybe, just maybe, people had started taking the protesters seriously.

It's an odd time to suggest such a thing, we know. The protesters who grabbed the world's megaphone two years ago in Seattle have never seemed so irrelevant—or misguided—as they have since Sept. 11. When they have not been blaming the U.S. for all the world's ills, they have blamed "globalization" for the recent terrorist attacks, as if Osama bin Laden were somehow aggrieved by IMF loans or steel imports. But it would be a mistake to write off their movement as a failure. In fact, they may have already achieved their main goal: fracturing a consensus that, in retrospect, looks almost as silly as the protesters' puppets.

They certainly have the attention of politicians, especially in Europe. In September, the French and German governments announced that they would sit down to discuss ways to tame globalization, including the so-called Tobin tax, a proposed levy on speculative financial flows that the protesters champion. "These people are not just cranks," said German Chancellor Gerhard Schroeder, citing their concerns about "unequal trade relations or financial speculation that bring entire economies to the brink of ruin." French Prime Minister Lionel Jospin all but tossed the protesters a bouquet, declaring that France was "delighted to see the emergence of a citizens' movement at the planetary level."

True, the French were won over by Jerry Lewis, too. But the protesters' ideas have made inroads elsewhere, including in many of the institutions they most vociferously oppose. The World Bank, for instance, has embraced—critics say capitulated to—their goal of "sustainable development," edging away from huge infrastructure projects like dams and agreeing that economic growth alone isn't enough to reduce poverty. Meanwhile, the Bank has been cozying up to nongovernment organizations (NGOs) and other "civil society" groups who protesters say represent "the people." And across the street at the International Monetary Fund, pressure from groups like Drop the Debt has sped up debt relief for developing nations.

Corporations, too, have increasingly been changing their ways to appease activists. Stung by successful campaigns against their brands, multinationals like Shell and Nike have adopted much the same line as their NGO foes. "Because we, too, are concerned at the requirement to address those in poverty who are excluded from the benefits that many of us share in the global economy," stated Shell's then chairman, Sir Mark Moody-Stuart, last year, "we share the objective of the recent demonstrators in Seattle, Davos, and Prague." Perhaps oddest of all, money from consumer products giant Unilever has gone to the Ruckus Society, a group that trains anticorporate radicals how to hang themselves from a billboard, among other things. (Oh, the conditions a corporation must swallow when it buys Ben & Jerry's.) Talk about feeding the hand that bites.

All that is a marked shift from just a year or two ago, when pundits could dismiss the protesters as "a Noah's ark of flat-earth advocates, protectionist trade unions and yuppies looking for their 1960s fix," in the words of *New York Times* columnist and globalization booster Thomas Friedman. (When Friedman finally backed off his hard-line stance in a column last summer—acknowledging that at least some of the protesters were raising legitimate questions—it was considered something of a watershed event.) "The conversation really has changed," says Dani Rodrik, a Harvard economist who studies trade. "We've moved from a situation where the professional technocrats would pooh-pooh the protesters as a bunch of know-nothing retrogrades to one where that line has completely evaporated. . . . Intellectually, the battle is really won."

If so, it's not because of the subtlety of the protesters' arguments, which remain steeped in contradictions, Playskool economics, and a pre-industrial romanticism that would seem to advocate a return to medieval manors and bartering. But the role of demonstrators, notes Todd Gitlin, a New York University sociologist who has studied protest movements, is to demonstrate. The shouts on the streets can cause murmurs among the elites, he says, helping to advance the more reasoned critiques of insiders. "The protesters have prompted very thoughtful discussion among many of us on the other side of the barricades," says Sara Sievers of Harvard's Center for International Development.

Witness, for instance, the intellectual about-face on "hot money." Just a few years ago, the U.S. Treasury Department was hounding Asian countries to open their capital markets, lift their exchange controls, and let capitalism rip. Free trade is good for growth, the thinking went, so free capital movement must be good for growth too. It all sounded sensible enough. But the analogy had at least one flaw: Capital flows are prone to panics and manias. Trade flows are not. And in 1997, the countries that had followed Washington's advice were rewarded with the Asian financial crisis.

As capital fled Asia's once-roaring economies, sending millions back into poverty, official Washington blamed the debacle on "crony capitalism" in those countries. But the protesters had a different story line. They said the East Asian countries had been forced to globalize prematurely. The real culprit, declared one critic, was "the Wall Street–Treasury Complex," which used the IMF as a battering ram to open new markets for U.S. financial firms. The rantings of a conspiracy theorist? Actually, it's the critique of Columbia University economist Jagdish Bhagwati, a conservative free trade zealot who calls the protesters "nitwits." "We were overemphasizing the benefits of free movement of capital and underemphasizing the risks," he says.

Today the consensus for capital mobility lies in ruins. Says Joseph Stiglitz, former chief economist at the World Bank and recipient of this year's Nobel Prize in economics: "There wasn't just no evidence for it, there was evidence it was harmful. And the IMF looked the other way."

The consensus for free trade, by contrast, remains largely intact. Yet even here, skeptics have chipped away at the fundamentalist faith in trade *über Alles*—the notion that there's no societal ill that free trade can't cure. Research by Harvard's Rodrik, for instance, shows that countries like China and India lowered trade barriers only *after* they experienced growth spurts—and even then they both maintained a selective mix of tariffs and other barriers. The countries that do best, Rodrik finds, do not simply fling open their markets and wait for trade to work its magic. They use trade as part of a homegrown strategy that includes building sound political and legal institutions.

At the same time, a growing body of evidence suggests that free trade increases income disparities within countries. In Mexico, for instance, the benefits of NAFTA—the Magna Carta of free trade agreements—have accrued mostly to the top 30% of the population, and particularly the top 10%, according to Stiglitz. "The bottom 30% actually did worse," he says. "There have been losers."

Of course, many of the protesters' solutions are problematic, to say the least. The Tobin tax, for instance, would stem the flow of hot money by taxing speculators and using the proceeds for development. Just one problem: James Tobin, the Yale economist who came up with the idea in 1972, says it isn't workable. Every government would have to impose the tax at once, he notes, and even then there would be loopholes. "I don't have the slightest thing in common with these antiglobalization revolutionaries," he told a German newspaper. "They're abusing my name."

Equally problematic are efforts to link trade with labor standards. Inconveniently for the protesters, poor nations have not appreciated their anti-sweatshop campaigns, fearful of driving off multinational companies that, after all, tend to pay about 10% more than local firms. "Those who are pushing for labor standards are actually damaging the developing countries they are purporting to support," says Kishore Mahbubani, Singapore's representative to the United Nations. "This is what I call the tragedy of good intentions."

Even the role of NGOs has come in for criticism. Activists promote them as the best way of giving citizens a voice in decision-making bodies that, they say, are undemocratic and beholden to corporate interests. But, the critics ask, who elected the NGOs? Institutions like the World Bank and the World Trade Organization are at least accountable to their member governments. Environmental and human-rights groups are accountable to no one but themselves. "NGOs have the right to be consulted, but they have no right to be involved in substantive decisions," argues David Henderson, former chief economist of the Organization for Economic Cooperation and Development in Paris and author of a new book, *Misguided Virtue: False Notions of Corporate Social Responsibility.*

So where does the discussion go from here? As FORTUNE went to press, members of the WTO were gathering in the remote Persian Gulf state of Qatar, in their first attempt to revive the trade round that died in Seattle two years ago. "A repeat of the failure of Seattle could condemn us to a period of hibernation," warned director-general Mike Moore, who once said the protesters made him "want to vomit."

Happily for him, Qatar is a repressive sheikdom where street protest is illegal. With only a handful of NGO representatives allowed inside the country, activists would be relegated to a single Greenpeace boat anchored off the coast. "It's so rude," complained Mike Dolan, an organizer for Global Trade Watch. "How do they think they're going to get away with this?"

Yet as the *Wall Street Journal* observed, there was also a sense that the WTO couldn't escape the protesters. That's because many of their issues were on the table this time, including the environment, labor standards, and more-stringent labeling for genetically modified foods. Moore worried that some of the issues could prove "deal breakers."

In a way, it was just like Aspen: The protesters wouldn't be there. But their ideas would.

Bibliography of Global Backlash Web Sites

*Compiled with the assistance
of Erica Dholoo, Jay Gutzwiller,
Zahara Heckscher, and Sharmi Sobhan*

What follows is an annotated "web bibliography" of approximately one hundred nongovernmental web sites. We have worked to include as many web sites as possible from diverse groups in different geographical regions. The number of global citizen backlash web sites is, however, vast. Indeed, it is literally growing daily. We have therefore had to make difficult choices and have tried to ensure that we included "umbrella" web sites that serve as links to the other web sites that we have not been able to include. Some of the web sites mentioned previously in this book (for instance, in the "For Further Reading" sections) are not repeated here, to leave room for others. Needless to say, we apologize for any inadvertent oversights or mistakes.

Action for Solidarity, Equality, Environment and Development (A SEED), Netherlands
www.aseed.net
Information and publications on genetic engineering, environment, and multilateral development banks. Monthly grassroots newsletter, *Roots,* available online. Links to related organizations.

AFL-CIO, USA
www.aflcio.org
News and resources on unions, workers' rights, NAFTA, FTAA, living wage, and more. Links to affiliated unions and campaigns.

Alliance for Responsible Trade (ART), USA
www.art-us.org
Documents and statements from this multi-sectoral coalition on trade issues in the Western hemisphere, with resources on NAFTA and FTAA, and the complete fifty-page "Alternatives for the Americas" document (excerpted in Reading 1.8).

Alternative Information and Development Centre, South Africa
www.aidc.org.za
Articles and updates on the effects of debt on South Africa's poor. Home of Jubilee 2000 South Africa campaign. Monthly newsletter, *Alternatives*, available online.

Amazon Alliance, USA
www.amazonalliance.org
Updates and links regarding indigenous and traditional peoples in the Amazon Basin. Also links to information on the campaign against U.S. fumigation of illicit crops in Colombia (www.usfumigation.org).

Asia Monitor Resource Center, Hong Kong
www.amrc.org.hk
News and information on labor and corporate codes of conduct with a focus on Asia, and China in particular. Publishes *Asian Labour Monitor*, available online. Publications on workers' rights available for sale.

ATTAC (Association for the Taxation of Financial Transactions for the Aid of Citizens), France
www.attac.org
Up-to-date documents and information on international finance, economics, and trade, with a focus on the currency transaction tax (Tobin tax). Extensive links to international contacts, useful web sites, lobbying and campaigning organizations worldwide, serving as a coordination point for activism and protests.

Banana Action Net, Belgium
bananas.agoranet.be
News and campaigns on workers' rights in the banana industry, specific multinational banana companies, and fair trade bananas.

Bank Information Center (BIC), USA
www.bicusa.org
Resources and support for NGOs and social movements on the projects, policies, and practices of the World Bank and other multilateral development banks. Includes publications, policy debates, tool kits for activists, and links to other organizations focused on international financial institutions.

Berne Declaration, Switzerland
www.evb.ch
Information and campaigns on international trade and financial relations, large dams, food and agriculture, biological diversity, the World Economic Forum, and cultural issues. Policy documents, media releases, and links to relevant organizations and web sites.

Brazilian Institute for Social and Economic Analysis (IBASE), Brazil
www.ibase.org.br
Publications and resources on genetically engineered food, the environment, alternatives to structural adjustment, sustainable local development, social inclusion and participation. (In Portuguese, with an overview in English.)

Campaign for Labor Rights, USA
www.summersault.com/~agj/clr
Resource materials on workers' rights and working conditions in the Western Hemisphere. Links to partner organizations, unions, and Latin American solidarity organizations.

Center for a New American Dream, USA
www.newdream.org
Information, ideas, and campaigns to organize individuals and institutions to reduce consumption as a way to enhance quality of life and protect the environment. Publications available to download and buy online.

Center for Economic and Policy Research (CEPR), USA
www.cepr.net
Analytical research publications intended to inform the public and promote democratic debate. Topics include globalization, IMF/World Bank, WTO, FTAA, tax speculation, the stock market, social security, and intellectual property rights and patents. Links to policy institutes.

Center for Economic Justice (CEJ), USA
www.econjustice.net
Updates on the center's efforts to strengthen international grassroots movements to counter corporate-driven globalization and to promote just alternatives. Information on a major CEJ project: the *World Bank Bonds Boycott*, which demands an end to socially and environmentally destructive World Bank policies and projects.

Center of Concern (CoC), USA
www.coc.org
Advocacy and policy analysis and theological and social reflections on U.S. and international issues of hunger, poverty, environmental decline, and injustice, with moral visions for social and economic alternatives. Online resources with CoC publications available for purchase online and links to related sites. Links to the International Gender and Trade Network (www.genderandtrade.org).

Chilean Alliance for Just and Responsible Trade (ACJR), Chile
www.members.tripod.com/redchile
Information, campaigns, and documents on the effects of economic integration, U.S.–Chile free-trade agreement, and the FTAA on labor and the environment. (In Spanish.)

Citizens' Coalition for Economic Justice (CCEJ), South Korea

www.ccej.or.kr/engindex.html

Information on CCEJ's work with grassroots efforts for sustainable economic and social development in South Korea. Bimonthly publication, *Civil Society,* available online and others for purchase online.

Clean Clothes Campaign (CCC), Netherlands

www.cleanclothes.org

Information and campaigns on working conditions in the garment industry, multinational companies and their practices, and corporate codes of conduct. Monthly newsletter, *Clean Clothes,* and other documents available online. Links to Clean Clothes Campaign offices around Europe and to other organizations.

Coalition for Justice in the Maquiladoras (CJM), USA

www.enchantedwebsites.com/maquiladora/cjm.html

Information on the coalition's mission and position on codes of conduct, environmental contamination, health and safety, fair employment practices, and standards of living.

Comisión para la Gestión Integral del Agua en Bolivia (CGIAB), Bolivia (Commission for Integral Water Management in Bolivia)

www.aguabolivia.org

Information and resources on the movement opposed to the privatization of water in Bolivia, and proposal for the creation of a national commission on water. Links to other organizations working on water-related issues throughout Latin America. (In Spanish.)

Confederation of Indigenous Nationalities of Ecuador (CONAIE), Ecuador

www.conaie.org

Information on indigenous land, ecology, culture and education, and international indigenous networking and resistance. (In English, Spanish, and Quechua.)

Convergence of Movements of Peoples of the Americas (COMPA), USA

www.econjustice.net/GANAS

Information on this pan-American network fighting for economic, political, and social justice in a context of corporate globalization and Washington Consensus free-market policies. Contains declarations and action plans for an alternative to neoliberal economic globalization.

Consumers' Union Eco-Labels, USA

www.eco-labels.org

Information on label claims, organizations and programs that issue eco-labels, and how the labels are defined and verified. Includes evaluation of each label, based on how well it meets a set of Consumer Union standards. Produced by Consumers Union, nonprofit publisher of *Consumer Reports* magazine.

Co-op America, USA

www.coopamerica.org

Information and guidance for individuals and businesses to promote just and sustainable economics. Publishes the *National Green Pages*, a directory of green businesses, the *Financial Planning Handbook* on socially responsible investing, *Co-op America Quarterly*, and *Boycott Action News*.

Corporate Europe Observatory (CEO), Netherlands

www.xs4all.nl/~ceo/

Research and campaign information on threats to democracy, equity, social justice, and the environment posed by the economic and political power of corporations and their lobby groups.

Corporate Watch, USA

www.corpwatch.org

Information, analysis, and campaigns on the actions of transnational corporations, the World Bank, IMF, and WTO, with a focus on biotechnology, international trade agreements, energy policy, and sweatshops. Originally known as Transnational Resource & Action Center (TRAC).

Council of Canadians, Canada

www.canadians.org

Campaign information and publications on socioeconomic and environmental justice in the context of globalization and international trade agreements, such as NAFTA and the FTAA. Current campaigns concerned with water, trade and investment, genetic engineering, and freedom of press. Links to progressive organizations, mostly in Canada.

Cultural Survival, USA

www.cs.org

Information and literature on projects concerned with assisting indigenous groups and ethnic minorities to build effective organizations, manage natural resources, preserve their language and art forms, and become economically independent. Links to relevant organizations and resources.

Development Group for Alternative Policies (Development GAP), USA

www.igc.org/dgap

Documents and articles on the effects of World Bank and IMF structural adjustment policies in Latin America, on debt relief, and on NAFTA and FTAA. Links to the Structural Adjustment Participatory Review International Network (SAPRIN).

The Ecologist, UK

www.theecologist.org

Web site of this monthly backlash environmental journal, also covering a wide range of current social and economic issues. Selected archived articles (many authored by individuals in the South) available online, as well as calls to action on specific issues.

Economic Policy Institute (EPI), USA

www.epinet.org

Research and education to promote a fair and sustainable economy, with analyses and reports on living standards and labor markets, government and economy, trade and globalization, education, and sustainable economics. Online library, issue guides and data, monthly *EPI News*, and quarterly *EPI Journal*.

Ejército Zapatista de Liberación Nacional (EZLN), Mexico

www.ezln.org

Current information on the Zapatista movement, including documents on indigenous rights in Mexico and progress of relations and negotiations with the Mexican government over these issues. Includes an online publication, *Chiapas*, and writings by Subcomandante Marcos. (In Spanish.)

Equal Exchange, USA

www.equalexchange.com

News and information on fair trade, Southern trading partners and how to get involved. Fair trade tea and coffee available to order online. Links to worldwide organizations in the fair trade movement.

Facultad Latinoamericana de Ciencias Sociales (FLACSO), Costa Rica (Latin American Social Science Faculty)

www.flacso.org

Academic resources and publications on issues such as education, culture, population, and politics in Latin America and the Caribbean. (In Spanish.)

Fairtrade Labelling Organizations International (FLO), Germany

www.fairtrade.net

Information on fair trade and fair-trade food products. Serves as an umbrella site linking to its seventeen "member" fair-trade-labeling initiatives worldwide (with a view to introducing a single international Fairtrade label). The seventeen FLO members, each in a different country, include various Max Havelaar and TransFair national initiatives.

Fair Labor Association (FLA), USA

www.fairlabor.org

Information on actions to protect worker rights in apparel and footwear. Includes FLA industry-wide code of conduct (Apparel Industry Partnership), information on FLA monitoring and accreditation, and lists of companies approved by FLA standards and of university and college members. Links to related organizations and resources.

Fair Trade Federation (FTF), USA

www.fairtradefederation.org

Information on and links to fair trade wholesale, retail, and producer members of this umbrella association, in addition to information on fair trade principles and practices. Guide for consumers and retailers on where to purchase fair trade food and craft products.

Fair Trade Resource Network (FTRN), USA

www.fairtraderesource.org

Information, education, resource and advocacy center for the media, the public, and fair trade proponents, on fair trade issues and campaigns, with the goal of raising consumer awareness. Campaign actions and links to resources and fair trade organizations and retailers.

Fifty Years Is Enough: U.S. Network for Global Economic Justice, USA

www.50years.org

Statements, updates and fact sheets on IMF and World Bank policies, with proposals for reform, information on upcoming conferences, and calls to mobilize protests. Newsletter, *Economic Justice News*, available online, and links to press releases and media coverage.

Focus on the Global South, Thailand

www.focusweb.org

Information on programs related to various aspects and effects of globalization, with a Southern focus. Extensive links to online publications and to other organizations. Three regular and informative bulletins, on trade, security, and the Philippines, available online.

Food First, USA
(also known as the Institute for Food and Development Policy)

www.foodfirst.org

Information and resources for advocacy on economic and social human rights, and food, including issues on biotechnology, trade and agriculture, and alternative food systems. Campaign actions and links to news, resources, and related organizations.

Forest Stewardship Council (FSC), Mexico

www.fscoax.org, www.fscus.org

Provides public education and information about third-party certification as a way of protecting the world's forests, with forest management principles and criteria (reprinted in Reading 4.8) and certifier evaluation and accreditation information. Also provides archived news articles and details of where to buy FSC-certified products.

Foro Boliviano Sobre Medio Ambiente y Desarrollo (FOBOMADE), Bolivia
(Bolivian Forum on the Environment and Development)

www.megalink.com/fobomade/

Information on FOBOMADE's broad-based socio-environmental projects in Bolivia, concerning dams, transgenic plants, hydrocarbons, and chestnuts, in particular. Publications available online. (In Spanish.)

Friends of the Earth International (FOE), Netherlands
www.foei.org
Information on international campaigns on debt, forests, gender, international financial institutions, trade, and transnational corporations. Serves as an umbrella coalition of individual country FOE groups worldwide, providing links to and information on these, as well as links to other environmental organizations.

Global Exchange, USA
www.globalexchange.org
Information, updates, and resources on Global Exchange's programs on the global economy, corporate responsibility, the WTO and FTAA, human rights, and fair trade (including Global Exchange's own shops). Details of Global Exchange's country campaigns on Cuba, Brazil, Mexico, Colombia, and the United States.

Globalise Resistance, UK
www.resist.org.uk
Information for groups and individuals to coordinate protests in Europe against the global growth of corporate power, with an up-to-date diary of events.

Greenpeace International, Netherlands
www.greenpeace.org
Resources and campaigns on environmental issues, including climate change, genetic engineering, forests, nuclear energy and weapons, ocean dumping, and toxic chemical trade. Online statistics database and photo and video library. Links to Greenpeace offices worldwide and to a wide range of environment-related sites.

Ground Up, Netherlands
www.groundup.org
Information tools for activists opposed to genetic engineering (GE). Contains a list of campaigns and a directory of GE resistance groups.

Hemispheric Social Alliance (Alianza Social Continental), Mexico
www.asc-hsa.org (Spanish); www.art-us.org/HSA.html (English overview)
Information and documents on the FTAA and the hemisphere-wide movement opposed to it, with proposals for alternatives. Links to ASC members and to other sites of interest.

Hong Kong Christian Industrial Committee, Hong Kong
www.cic.org.hk
Information on occupational safety and health rights, as well as campaigns and protests against the labor practices of transnational corporations, with a focus on China and Hong Kong.

Independent Media Center (IMC), USA

www.indymedia.org

Online network of independent media outlets, providing grassroots, alternative, and up-to-date audio, photo, print, and video media coverage of current events. Links to "IMC allies" and to Indymedia centers throughout Europe and the United States.

Information Services Latin America (ISLA), USA

www.igc.org/isla

Publications and special reports on current events in Latin America. Links to alternative perspectives and media on Latin American issues by country.

Institute for Agriculture and Trade Policy (IATP), USA

www.iatp.org

Information on a range of projects and campaigns on trade, food, agriculture, biotechnology, the environment, and global policies affecting these. Documents, archived resources, and advocacy materials available online.

Institute for Policy Studies (IPS), USA

www.ips-dc.org

Information and resources on IPS publications and projects, which include the global economy, drug policy, peace and security, and paths for the twenty-first century. Annual report and quarterly newsletter, *IPS News*, available online. IPS cosponsors the *Foreign Policy in Focus* project and web site (www.foreignpolicy-infocus.org).

InterAfrica Group (IAG), Ethiopia

www.interafrica.org

Documents on food and water issues, gender, and networking; a virtual resource center for its NGO Networking Service. Also includes links to other web resources on issues related to Africa.

Interfaith Center on Corporate Responsibility (ICCR), USA

www.iccr.org

Information, links, and resources on ICCR's work with socially responsible investors to influence corporate policies in the areas of corporate accountability, human rights, energy and the environment, global finance, equality, access to capital, community economic development, health, and militarism.

International Coalition for Development Action (ICDA), Belgium

www.icda.be

News, publications, and advocacy materials promoting issues of international development and denouncing the adverse effects of international trade. Links to ICDA members worldwide.

International Confederation of Free Trade Unions (ICFTU), Belgium

www.icftu.org
Information on collaborative work and campaigns of this international network of trade unions, in the areas of labor standards, health and environment, union rights, equal opportunities, and multinational enterprises. Up-to-date news on human, labor, and union rights and protests around the world.

International Federation for Alternative Trade (IFAT), UK

www.ifat.org
Information and resources on fair trade and on the linking, networking, information, education and lobbying activities of IFAT, with updates about conferences. Lists the 160 member organizations from 50 countries in Africa, Asia, Europe, Latin America, the Middle East, and North America, with links to some of these.

International Forum on Globalization (IFG), USA

www.ifg.org
Information on the work and publications of this network of sixty Northern and Southern backlash leaders, toward strengthening local communities and economies, and ecological sustainability vis-à-vis economic globalization. Information on the World Bank, IMF, and WTO; educational events and advocacy campaigns.

International Labor Rights Fund (ILRF), USA

www.laborrights.org
Information on ILRF work on social clauses, codes of conduct, and monitoring. Reports, publications, news, and urgent action appeals on the records and practices of specific companies and countries in labor rights. Links to labor rights news and organizations, policy institutes, trade unions, and government and international bodies.

International NGO Forum on Indonesian Development (INFID), Indonesia

www.infid.ngonet.be
Publications, statements, and conference papers on debt and development in Indonesia. Jakarta secretariat with liaison offices in Tokyo and Brussels.

International Social and Environmental Accreditation and Labelling Alliance (ISEAL), Canada

www.isealalliance.net
Web site of this umbrella coalition of social and environmental certification bodies. Includes links to the member organizations and information on accreditation, focusing on common interests, criteria, and standards for formal international collaboration.

International Society for Ecology and Culture (ISEC), UK

www.isec.org.uk

Information on protecting cultural and biological diversity and local agriculture and communities, with a focus on education for action. Many publications and videos available for purchase online; link to *The Ecologist* journal web site.

Jobs With Justice, USA
www.jwj.org
Information, political action resources, and organizing tools on workers' rights, NAFTA, FTAA, and other labor issues.

Jubilee +, UK
www.jubileeplus.org
Information on the continuing Third World debt campaigns of this official successor to Jubilee 2000, which is part of an international network. Provides up-to-date, accurate analyses, news, and data on international debt and finance.

Jubilee South, Nicaragua, Philippines, and South Africa
www.jubileesouth.net
Documents, press statements, and declarations from world summits and conferences on Third World debt issues in Africa, Asia, and Latin America, from a Southern perspective and with a vision for the South.

Maquila Solidarity Network, Canada
www.maquilasolidarity.org
Information and resources on maquilas, the garment industry, child labor, and corporate codes of conduct. News on specific companies, campaign updates, and action tools available online.

Mexican Action Network on Free Trade, Mexico
www.rmalc.org.mx
Documents, publications, reports, and news on the impact of economic globalization. Includes information on NAFTA and FTAA. (In Spanish.)

Multinational Monitor, USA
www.essential.org/monitor
Monthly online magazine, published by Essential Information, Inc., covering corporate activities, especially in the Third World, focusing on environmental, health, social, and labor issues.

Municipal Services Project (MSP), Canada-South Africa
www.queensu.ca/msp
Information on the impacts of decentralization, privatization, cost recovery, and community participation on the delivery of basic services to the rural and urban poor. Links to South African organizations involved in municipal services.

Mwelekeo NGO (MWENGO), Eastern and Southern Africa
www.mwengo.org
Publications, resources, and links on development issues in eastern and southern Africa.

National Labor Committee (NLC), USA
www.nlcnet.org
Resources and reports on workers' rights and working conditions around the world. Includes information on specific countries, companies, and products. Links to the Child Labor Coalition.

New Economics Foundation (NEF), UK
www.neweconomics.org
Action research, policy work, and reports of this think tank, working to change "business-as-usual" in the areas of reshaping the global economy, participatory democracy, and local economic renewal. Online publications and many links can be selected by sector and country.

New Internationalist (NI), UK
www.newint.org
Monthly magazine available online and by subscription, providing information on major global issues, activism, and social change, with a specific theme each month. NI publications available for purchase online.

OneWorld, UK
www.oneworld.net
Online information and resource center for news, reports, and campaigns on global economic and social justice issues. Contains a database of alternative articles, and an extensive directory of organizations and campaigns.

Oxfam International, UK
www.oxfam.org
Serves as an umbrella coalition site, linking to independent Oxfam country groups worldwide, which provide information on Oxfam's development, relief, advocacy, and campaigning work, including news, policy briefings, and action initiatives. Also provides information on fair trade and links to fair trade umbrella groups.

Public Citizen Global Trade Watch, USA
www.citizen.org/pctrade/tradehome.html
Advocacy information concerning a variety of international trade issues, such as FTAA, environment and labor standards, the Multilateral Agreement on Investment (MAI), NAFTA, and the WTO. Focuses on U.S. policy and legislative advocacy.

Rainforest Action Network (RAN), USA

www.ran.org

Targeted campaigns, news, and action alerts for the protection of tropical rainforests and the rights of people living in them. Fact sheets about rainforests, activist tools and resources, and list of business community supporters, with links to relevant sites, including an information portal.

Red de Desarrollo Sostenible (RDS), Honduras
(Sustainable Development Network)

www.rds.org.hn

Information on debt, rural development, environmental devastation, and post–Hurricane Mitch reconstruction in Honduras. Links to other environmental and grassroots organizations. (In Spanish.)

Red Nacional de Acción Ecológica (RENACE), Chile
(National Network for Ecological Action)

www.renace.cl

Publications, campaigns, and news on national efforts to address and roll back environmental degradation in Chile. Electronic newsletter, *Ecoprens@*, available on this site. (In Spanish.)

Research Foundation for Science, Technology, and Ecology, India

www.vshiva.net

Information and campaigns on biodiversity conservation, intellectual property rights, biopiracy, biotechnology, food security, effects of globalization, agricultural rights, Monsanto, and the WTO, with many publications by Vandana Shiva. Links to related organizations.

Resource Center of the Americas, USA

www.americas.org

Up-to-date news and information on globalization, the drug war, labor, human rights, and the environment, across the Americas. Online action alerts and information about resources and activities.

RUGMARK International, USA

www.rugmark.net

Links to RUGMARK's offices in Europe, North America, Nepal, and India, with information on their efforts to end child labor in the carpet industry and promote education. Details of certification and purchasing Rugmark-labeled carpets, with downloadable education and action resources on child labor.

Sierra Club, USA

www.sierraclub.org

Updates, campaign actions, news, and advocacy information on a range of international and domestic environmental issues, such as energy, global warming, responsible trade, logging, clean water, wild lands, and human rights. Monthly newsletter, *The Planet*, and *Sierra* magazine available online.

South Asian Women's Network (SAWNET), Canada
www.sawnet.org
News and information pertaining to women in Bangladesh, Bhutan, India, Nepal, Pakistan, and Sri Lanka, with links to organizations, discussions, resources, and information relevant to South Asian women.

Survival International, UK
www.survival-international.org
News and information, on campaigns and educational programs supporting "tribal peoples'" rights. Contains background information on "tribal people" worldwide and links to relevant literature.

Sweatshop Watch, USA
www.sweatshopwatch.org
News, information, and action campaigns on sweatshops in the garment industry. Links to Behind the Label and to other organizations involved in related issues.

Third World Network (TWN), Malaysia
www.twnside.org.sg
Extensive information (mostly by authors in Asia, Africa, and Latin America) on trade issues and the WTO, globalization, intellectual property rights, biotechnology, international finance, and more. Publishes *Third World Resurgence* and *Third World Economics*, with online access to selected articles from these publications, as well as to other documents.

Trade Justice Movement (TJM), UK
www.tradejusticemovement.org.uk
Provides useful links to the prominent member organizations of this movement, who are concerned with the negative impacts of international trade rules on the world's poorest, on the environment, and on democracy. Also details of how to become a member organization.

TransFair USA, USA
www.transfairusa.org
Information about fair trade, fair-trade products, and the certification process carried out by this U.S. member of FLO, which is the only nonprofit third-party fair-trade certification organization in the United States. News and fact sheets available online.

Transnational Institute, Netherlands
www.tni.org
Information and programs on militarism, conflict, poverty, marginalization, drug policy, social justice, and environmental degradation. Links to other policy and advocacy organizations working on issues of globalization and Third World debt.

Uganda Debt Network (UDN), Uganda

www.udn.or.ug/

Reports, documents, and policy guides on debt relief and poverty reduction in Uganda, with information about the civil society–based advocacy and lobbying activities of UDN to reduce the debt to a sustainable level and ensure proper use of freed-up funds. Links to other organizations working on debt relief.

UNITE! (Union of Needletrades, Industrial, and Textile Employees), USA

www.uniteunion.org

Information and political action resources on organizing, workers' rights, corporate practices, and UNITE!'s Stop Sweatshops Campaign. Links to other unions and organizations working on labor issues. Affiliate of the AFL-CIO.

United Students Against Sweatshops (USAS), USA

www.usasnet.org

Information, campaigns, and resources on this student movement fighting for sweatshop-free labor conditions and workers' rights by demanding that universities adopt the Worker Rights Consortium code of conduct for clothing bearing their schools' logo. Useful links and contacts for students interested in worker rights.

U.S. Labor Education in the Americas Project (US/LEAP), USA

www.usleap.org

News, campaigns, and activist resources on economic justice, trade policy, and basic rights for workers employed in the banana, maquila, and coffee sectors in Central and South America, with a focus on those employed by U.S. companies. Links to related organizations.

Women's EDGE, USA

www.womensedge.org

Information on programs for the economic and political advancement of women around the world, focusing on the impact of U.S. policies on international development and trade, and involving outreach programs to women in the United States. Online publications, reports, and bimonthly newsletter, *Notes from the EDGE*.

Women Working Worldwide (WWW), UK

www.poptel.org.uk/women-ww

Information on supporting women workers' rights, especially in the context of trade liberalization, and focusing on transnational industries. Online reports and bulletins with information on gender, trade and the WTO, social clauses, and codes of conduct. Links to related sites, including to Labour Behind the Label.

Worker Rights Consortium (WRC), USA

www.workersrights.org

Lists the college and university members of this organization, and provides details of its work to achieve enforcement of its code of conduct, which covers collegiate-licensed apparel carrying schools' logos. WRC code of conduct and factory assessment reports available online, with links to other organizations and resources. Updates and urgent action appeals on current cases.

World Development Movement (WDM), UK
www.wdm.org.uk
News and background information on WDM's campaigns to tackle the root causes of poverty, currently focusing on international trade and Third World debt, and previously including the Multilateral Agreement on Investment, arms trade, genetically engineered organisms, and bananas. Online campaign briefings, press releases, and action initiatives, with links to related groups.

Index

About the Contributors

Academic Consortium on International Trade (ACIT), a group of academic economists and lawyers who specialize in international trade policy and international economic law, prepares and circulates policy statements and papers that deal with current issues of international trade policy.

Dean Acheson (1893–1971), author of the Pulitzer Prize–winning *Present at the Creation*, served as U.S. assistant secretary of state for economic affairs (beginning in 1941), and then under-secretary of state and secretary of state in the Truman administration, during which time he was instrumental in forging the NATO Alliance, the Truman Doctrine, and the Marshall Plan.

The Action Canada Network, founded in 1987 and based in Ontario, is a coalition of progressive groups working together to empower people through social reform and education on labor issues, taxation, and income security.

The Alliance for Responsible Trade (ART), formed in 1991 and based in the United States, is a national network of labor, family farm, religious, women's, environmental, development, and research organizations that promotes equitable and sustainable trade and development.

Kofi Annan, originally from Ghana, became the seventh secretary-general of the United Nations in 1997 and is the first secretary-general to be elected from the ranks of the UN staff.

Bama Athreya, deputy director of the Washington, D.C.–based International Labor Rights Fund, has spent three years in Indonesia (first with the State Department and then as an independent researcher) and two years in Cambodia as the AFL-CIO's country representative.

Maude Barlow, political activist, author, policy critic, and outspoken crusader for Canada, is the national chair of the Council of Canadians, which, with more than 100,000 members, ranks as Canada's largest public advocacy group.

Walden Bello, executive director of Focus on the Global South at Chulalongkorn University Social Research Institute in Bangkok and professor at the University of the Philippines, is the author or coauthor of numerous books and articles on globalization and Asian politics and economic issues.

Robin Broad, a professor in American University's International Development Program, is author or coauthor of numerous articles and books, including *Plundering Paradise: The Struggle for the Environment in the Philippines* and *Unequal Alliance: The World Bank, the International Monetary Fund, and the Philippines.*

Patrick J. Buchanan served as a senior advisor to U.S. Presidents Nixon, Ford, and Reagan, has run for the Republican presidential nomination three times, and is an outspoken opponent of free-trade agreements such as NAFTA and GATT.

Gary Burtless, a senior fellow in Economic Studies at the Brookings Institution in Washington, D.C., has written extensively on labor market policy and widening economic inequality.

John Cavanagh, the director of the Institute for Policy Studies in Washington, D.C., has been involved in numerous global backlash coalitions and is coauthor of ten books on the global economy, most recently (with Sarah Anderson and Thea Lee) *A Field Guide to the Global Economy.*

Suzanne Charlé is a freelance writer and editor based in New York whose articles have appeared in the *New York Times, The Nation,* and the *International Herald Tribune* and whose work has mainly focused on Asia.

Frank Church (1924–1984) served as a Democratic representative from the state of Idaho to the U.S. Senate from 1957 until 1981 where (among other responsibilities) he chaired the Subcommittee on Multinational Corporations of the Committee on Foreign Relations.

The Citizens Trade Campaign, founded in 1992 and based in Washington, D.C., is a coalition of environmental, labor, family farm, consumer, and religious organizations promoting environmental and social justice in trade policy through grassroots organizing and Capitol Hill lobbying.

Terry Collingsworth, director of the International Labor Rights Fund in Washington, D.C., since 2001 and its general counsel prior to that, was a professor at the Loyola Law School and AFL-CIO country director for Nepal and Bangladesh.

Joseph Collins, cofounder of the Institute for Food and Development Policy (or Food First) in California, is a college lecturer, a consultant on the socioeconomic context of the AIDS epidemic, and coauthor of numerous books on international development issues including *World Hunger: Twelve Myths* and *How to Live Your Dream of Volunteering Overseas.*

Lance Compa, a trade union lawyer who teaches international labor rights at Cornell University, served as the top U.S. official on the NAFTA labor commission (1995–97) and is author of *Unfair Advantage: Workers' Freedom of Association in the United States under the International Human Rights Standards* (Human Rights Watch, 2000).

Michael E. Conroy, former professor of economics at the University of Texas at Austin, is a senior program officer at the Ford Foundation where, as a part of his work in the environment and development field, he has supported the establishment of advocacy-led certification systems.

Maria Lorena Cook, a political scientist and professor at Cornell University's School of Industrial and Labor Relations Department, teaches and writes on comparative labor and politics in Latin America and is the author of *Organizing Dissent*, a study of the democratic labor union movement in Mexico.

La Coordinadora de Defensa del Agua y de la Vida (Coalition in Defense of Water and Life) is an alliance of labor, peasant, environmentalist, human rights, and community leaders in Cochabamba, Bolivia, who led a popular movement that succeeded in defeating the privatization and globalization of the city's water system.

Alan Thein Durning, former senior researcher at the Worldwatch Institute and author or coauthor of eighteen books on environmental issues, is founder and executive director of Northwest Environment Watch, a research center promoting a sustainable economy and way of life in the Pacific Northwest region of the United States.

Rose Benz Ericson, a founding board member of the Fair Trade Resource Network, is an independent journalist and communications consultant based in Rochester, New York.

The Forest Stewardship Council, headquartered in Oaxaca, Mexico, is an international nonprofit organization founded in 1993 to support environmentally appropriate, socially beneficial, and economically viable management of the world's forests through an international labeling scheme for independently certified forest products.

Homero Fuentes is the general coordinator of the Commission for the Verification of Corporate Codes of Conduct (COVERCO, a nongovernmental effort in independent monitoring of working conditions in Guatemala's garment factories and agricultural export industries) and also a consultant to the Central America regional project of the Danish Trade Unions Council (LOFTF).

Jacques B. Gélinas, an essayist and lecturer on Third World issues, has served as chair of the Board of the Quebec branch of Canadian University Service Overseas (CUSO, one of Canada's oldest development NGOs) and from 1957 to 1971 worked in popular education and community development in the Bolivian Andes.

Steven Gorelick, the U.S. programs director of the International Society for Ecology and Culture (ISEC, based in the United Kingdom), is a member of the editorial board of *The Ecologist* magazine, and the author of *Small Is Beautiful, Big Is Subsidized* (ISEC, 1998).

Angela Hale, who holds a doctoral degree in sociology, is director of Women Working Worldwide, a UK nongovernmental organization based at Manchester Metropolitan University that works with an international network of women workers' organizations.

Pharis Harvey is a founder of the Washington, D.C.–based International Labor Rights Fund, served as its executive director from 1990 to 2001 (and is now a senior consultant to it), and has extensive experience working in Asia on workers' rights.

Zahara Heckscher is a coauthor of *How to Live Your Dream of Volunteering Overseas* (New York: Penguin Books, 2002, www.volunteeroverseas.org), lectures frequently on the "Peace Corps and Alternatives," and works with the Center for Economic Justice in Washington, D.C.

The Hemispheric Social Alliance, with its secretariat in Mexico, is a network of labor organizations and citizens' coalitions representing more than 50 million people throughout the Americas and was created in 1998 to oppose the Free Trade Area of the Americas and promote a more equitable and sustainable approach to integration.

Rohini Hensman is a writer and researcher in Bombay (Mumbai), India, active in the trade union, women's liberation, and human rights movements, and the author of several articles and books, including *To Do Something Beautiful*, a novel inspired by working women in Bombay.

The International Confederation of Free Trade Unions (ICFTU), based in Brussels, Belgium, was formed in 1949 as an international confederation of national trade union centers and currently has 221 affiliated organizations representing over 155 million members in over 140 countries and territories on all five continents.

The International Forum on Globalization (IFG), with its secretariat based in San Francisco, is an alliance of sixty leading activists, scholars, economists, researchers, and writers representing organizations in twenty-five countries. It was formed to stimulate new thinking, joint activity, public education, and large-scale teach-ins in response to economic globalization.

Jubilee South is a network of over eighty debt campaigns, social movements, and people's organizations from more than forty countries in Africa, Asia/Pacific, and Latin America and the Caribbean that gather together in South–South solidarity.

Martin Khor is the director of the Third World Network, which is a large coalition of public interest groups and individuals headquartered in Penang, Malaysia, with offices throughout the developing world; he is also the editor of its magazine, *Third World Resurgence*.

Frances Moore Lappé was cofounder of the Institute for Food and Development Policy (or Food First) in California, received the Right Livelihood Award, wrote the 1971 international bestseller *Diet for a Small Planet*, and coauthored the recently published *Hope's Edge: The New Diet for a Small Planet* with her daughter Anna.

Robert Z. Lawrence is a nonresident senior fellow and holder of the New Century Chair in International Trade and Economics at the Brookings Institution, and professor of international trade and investment at Harvard University's Kennedy School of Government in Cambridge, Massachusetts.

Jerome I. Levinson, currently distinguished lawyer in residence at American University's Washington College of Law, served as the chief counsel to the U.S. Senate Foreign Relations Committee's Subcommittee on Multinational Corporations (1972–1977) and as general counsel to the Inter-American Development Bank (1977–1990).

Levi Strauss & Co., founded in 1853 by Bavarian immigrant Levi Strauss and best known for its blue jeans, is one of the world's largest brand-name apparel marketers with sales in more than eighty countries; it was the first U.S. apparel company to promulgate its own internal code of conduct.

Robert E. Litan, director of the Economic Studies Program at the Brookings Institution in Washington, D.C., previously served in the U.S. government as deputy assistant attorney general of the antitrust division at the Justice Department and as associate director at the Office of Management and Budget.

Subcomandante Marcos (pseudonym) is the spokesperson and chief military strategist for the Zapatista Army of National Liberation (EZLN or Zapatistas), an indigenous insurgency movement based in Chiapas, Mexico, and is also the author of several books, including the prize-winning children's book *Story of the Colors*.

Iqbal Masih (1982–1995) wove hand-loomed carpets in Pakistan as an indentured laborer for six years starting at age four, escaped, and became an international spokesperson for an end to bonded child labor until he was assassinated at age thirteen in Pakistan.

Allan H. Meltzer, professor of political economy at Carnegie Mellon University, chaired the International Financial Institution Advisory Commission, a panel of experts established by the U.S. Congress to examine key international financial institutions.

Todd Merrifield earned his master's degree in geography at the University of California at Los Angeles (UCLA) where he focused on indigenous forest management practices.

The Mexican Action Network on Free Trade, created in 1991, is a citizens' coalition composed of environmentalists, unions, farmers' organizations, and NGOs that work together to challenge the free-trade model in Mexico and to propose alternatives.

Helena Norberg-Hodge is a linguist, author of *Ancient Futures: Learning from Ladakh,* the director of the International Society for Ecology and Culture (ISEC, based in the United Kingdom), and a recipient of the Right Livelihood Award.

The Research Foundation for Science, Technology, and Ecology in New Delhi, India, founded in 1982 and directed by Dr. Vandana Shiva, works on biodiversity conservation and protecting people's rights from threats to their livelihoods and environment by centralized systems of monoculture in forestry, agriculture, and fisheries.

Jeremy Rifkin is the author of fifteen books on economic trends and matters relating to science, technology, and culture, and is president of the Foundation on Economic Trends in Washington, D.C.

Walter Rodney (1942–1980), a historian and activist from Guyana where he was a member of the Working People's Alliance, was banned from Jamaica for political activities in 1968, taught in Tanzania during the reign of Julius Nyerere, and was assassinated in Guyana.

Robin Round heads the Tobin Tax campaign of the Vancouver-based Halifax Initiative, a coalition of fourteen Canadian NGOs committed to the fundamental reform of the institutional structures and policies that govern the global flow of finance to achieve instead poverty eradication, environmental sustainability, and an equitable redistribution of wealth.

Scholars Against Sweatshop Labor (SASL) is an organization of economists and other scholars who issued a statement in October 2001 broadly endorsing the antisweatshop movement in the United States.

Robert J. Shapiro is a founder and vice president of the Progressive Policy Institute, an organization based in Washington, D.C., whose mission is to define and promote a new progressive politics for America in the twenty-first century.

Dennis Smith is president of the Commission for the Verification of Corporate Codes of Conduct (COVERCO, a nongovernmental effort in independent monitoring of working conditions in Guatemala's garment factories and agricultural export industries) and also a mission coworker of the Presbyterian Church (USA).

John J. Sweeney, president since 1995 of the AFL-CIO, which is the U.S. national trade union federation of sixty-six affiliated unions and some thirteen million members, began his career in the labor movement with the International Ladies' Garment Workers International Union and subsequently served as president of the Service Employees International Union for fifteen years.

Wada Taw-il (pseudonym), a member of the indigenous communities in the Cordillera mountain region of the northern Philippines, testified on behalf of the Philippines' "cultural minorities" before a Permanent Peoples' Tribunal Session on the Philippines held in Antwerp, Belgium, in 1980 during the dictatorial rule of Ferdinand Marcos.

Blair Underwood is a television and movie actor who stars in *City of Angels* (CBS), has appeared in *L.A. Law* (NBC), and is also involved in numerous charitable organizations, including Artists for a New South Africa (ANSA), which he cofounded in 1989.

The United Nations General Assembly, set up in 1945 under the Charter of the United Nations, is the main deliberative organ of the United Nations, comprises all members of the United Nations, and provides a forum for multilateral discussion of the full range of international issues covered by the charter.

Jerry Useem is a senior writer at *Fortune* and previously was a research associate at Harvard Business School.

Mark Weisbrot received his Ph.D. in economics from the University of Michigan, is currently codirector of the Center for Economic and Policy Research in Washington, D.C., and has written extensively on globalization and economic and policy issues.

Credits

Part I: The Clash of Visions

1.1 Gary Burtless, Robert Z. Lawrence, Robert E. Litan, and Robert J. Shapiro, excerpt from *Globaphobia: Confronting Fears about Open Trade* (Washington, D.C.: Brookings Institution, Progressive Policy Institute, and Twentieth Century Fund, 1998), 6–11.

1.2 Kofi Annan, "In Address to WTO Ministerial Meeting, Secretary-General Says 'Economic Rights and Social Responsibilities Are Two Sides of the Same Coin,'" United Nations press release SG/SM/7237/Rev.1, (New York, 26 November 1999).

1.3 Excerpt from *Report of the International Financial Institution Advisory Commission*, by Allan H. Meltzer, chair (Washington, D.C.: Government Printing Office, 2000), 1–3 and 15–22, USGPO #048-000-00531-4.

1.4 Patrick J. Buchanan, excerpt from "Free Trade Is Not Free," address to the Chicago Council on Foreign Relations, 18 November 1998, 1–7.

1.5 Mark Weisbrot, excerpt from "Globalism on the Ropes," rev. (Washington, D.C.: Center for Economic and Policy Research, 2001).

1.6 International Forum on Globalization, Alternatives Task Force, excerpt from *Alternatives to Economic Globalization*, Interim Report (San Francisco, July 2001), 1–2, 6–10, www.ifg.org.

1.7 John J. Sweeney, AFL-CIO president, excerpt from "The New Internationalism," speech to the Council on Foreign Relations, New York, 1 April 1998, 1–7, www.aflcio.org/publ/speech1998/sp0401.htm.

1.8 Hemispheric Social Alliance, "General Principles" and "Gender," in *Alternatives for the Americas*, prepared for the Second People's Summit of the Americas (Quebec City, April 2001), 1, 6–7, and 64–69.

1.9 Robin Broad and John Cavanagh, excerpt from "The Death of the Washington Consensus?" *World Policy Journal* 16, no. 3 (Fall 1999): 79, 82–85, and 87.

Part II: The Historical Context

2.1 Walter Rodney, excerpts from *How Europe Underdeveloped Africa*, rev. ed. (Washington, D.C., 1982), 33 and 75–79. Copyright © 1972 by Walter Rodney, copyright © 1981 by Vincent Harding, William Strickland, and Robert Hill; reprinted with the permission of The Permissions Company, P.O. Box 243, High Bridge, N.J. 08829, USA, on behalf of Howard University Press. All rights reserved.

2.2 Frances Moore Lappé and Joseph Collins, "Why Can't People Feed Themselves?" in *Food First: Beyond the Myth of Food Scarcity* (Boston: Houghton Mifflin Company, 1977), 75–85.

2.3 Zahara Heckscher, "Long before Seattle: Historical Resistance to Economic Globalization" (Washington, D.C., September 2001).

2.4 Dean Acheson, "The Bretton Woods Agreements," in *Present at the Creation: My Years in the State Department* (New York: W. W. Norton, 1969), 81–84. Copyright © 1969 by Dean Acheson, reprinted with permission of W. W. Norton & Company, Inc.

2.5 United States Senate, Committee on Foreign Relations, Subcommittee on Multinational Corporations, "Opening Statements by Senator Frank Church," *Multinational Corporations and United States Foreign Policy*, 93rd and 94th Congresses, Part 1 (20 March 1973), Part 4 (30 January 1974), and Part 12 (16 May 1975).

2.6 United Nations General Assembly, "Declaration on the Establishment of a New International Economic Order," Sixth Special Session, 1 May 1974, UN General Assembly Resolution 3201.

2.7 Wada Taw-il, "We Are to Be Sacrificed: Indigenous Peoples and Dams," in *Philippines: Repression and Resistance—Permanent Peoples' Tribunal Session on the Philippines* (Utrecht, Netherlands: Philippine-European Solidarity Center–Komite ng Sambayanang Pilipino [PESC-KSP], 1980), 184–91.

2.8 Jacques B. Gélinas, "The Pillars of the System," in *Freedom from Debt: The Reappropriation of Development through Financial Self-Reliance*, trans. Arnold Bennett and Raymond Robitaille (London: Zed, 1998), 46–58.

Part III: Realigning Trade Rules

3.1 Mexican Action Network on Free Trade, Alliance for Responsible Trade, and Citizens Trade Campaign, with Action Canada Network, excerpt from "A Just and

Sustainable Trade and Development Initiative for North America" (28 November 1993), 1–2, 4–6, and 10.

3.2 Lance Compa, "Another Look at NAFTA," *Dissent* 44, no. 1 (Winter 1997): 45–50.

3.3 Maria Lorena Cook, "Cross-Border Labor Solidarity," *Dissent* 44, no.1 (Winter 1997): 49.

3.4 Jerome I. Levinson, excerpts from "NAFTA's Labor Agreement: Lessons from the First Three Years" (Washington, D.C.: Institute for Policy Studies, and International Labor Rights Fund, 12 November 1996), 1–4 and 18–22.

3.5 International Confederation of Free Trade Unions (ICFTU), excerpt from *Building Workers' Human Rights into the Global Trading System* (Brussels, Belgium: ICFTU, 1999), 17–18, 33–36, 38, 40, and 44–45.

3.6 Martin Khor, excerpt from "How the South Is Getting a Raw Deal at the WTO," in *Views from the South: The Effects of Globalization and the WTO on Third World Countries,* ed. Sarah Anderson (San Francisco: International Forum on Globalization, 1999), 41–49.

3.7 Rohini Hensman, "How to Support the Rights of Women Workers in the Context of Trade Liberalisation in India," in *Trade Myths and Gender Reality: Trade Liberalisation and Women's Lives,* ed. Angela Hale (Brussels, Belgium: International Coalition for Development Action; Uppsala, Sweden: Global Publications Foundation, 1998), 71–88.

3.8 "Agreement between the United States of America and the Hashemite Kingdom of Jordan on the Establishment of a Free Trade Area," signed by the government of the United States of America and the government of the Hashemite Kingdom of Jordan, 24 October 2000, preamble, articles 5 and 6.

Part IV: Challenging Corporate Conduct

4.1 Rose Benz Ericson, excerpt from *The Conscious Consumer: Promoting Economic Justice through Fair Trade* (Gettysburg, Pa.: Fair Trade Federation, 1999), 5, 7–13, and 18. Reprinted with permission of Rose Benz Ericson and the Fair Trade Resource Network. Order through the Fair Trade Resource Network at info@fairtraderesource.org.

4.2 Angela Hale, excerpt from "What Hope for 'Ethical' Trade in the Globalized Garment Industry?" *Antipode* 32, no. 4 (2000): 349–56. Copyright © 2000 by Editorial Board of *Antipode,* reprinted with permission of Blackwell Publishers, Oxford, UK.

4.3 Levi Strauss & Co., "Business Partner Terms of Engagement and Guidelines for Country Selection" (San Francisco, formulated in 1991, approved in 1992). Reprinted with permission of Levi Strauss & Co.

4.4 Iqbal Masih, "Acceptance Speech," and Blair Underwood, "Presentation to Iqbal Masih, Age 12: Reebok Youth in Action Award" (Reebok Human Rights Award, Boston, Massachusetts, 7 December 1994). Reprinted with permission of Reebok Human Rights Award.

4.5 Suzanne Charlé, "Children of the Looms: Rescuing the 'Carpet Kids' of Nepal, India, and Pakistan," *Ford Foundation Report* 32, no. 2 (Spring 2001): 21–25.

4.6 Homero Fuentes and Dennis Smith, excerpt from "Independent Monitoring in Guatemala: What Can Civil Society Contribute?" in *Visions of Ethical Sourcing*, ed. Raj Thamotheram (London: Financial Times Prentice Hall for Shared View Social Responsibility Ltd., with financial support from Société Générale de Surveillance [SGS], 2000), 36–42, available from Shared View at info@sharedview.net.

4.7 Michael E. Conroy, excerpt from "Can Advocacy-Led Certification Systems Transform Global Corporate Practices?" online working paper of the Political Economy Research Institute, University of Massachusetts (Amherst, Mass., 2001), 5–15 and 26–27, www.umass.edu/peri.

4.8 Forest Stewardship Council, "Forest Stewardship Council Principles and Criteria," rev. (Oaxaca, Mexico, February 2000), 1–8, www.fscoax.org/html/1-2.html.

4.9 Academic Consortium on International Trade, letter to university presidents regarding anti-sweatshop campaign, 29 July 2000, www.spp.umich.edu/rsie/acit/Documents/Anti-SweatshopLetterPage.html.

4.10 Scholars Against Sweatshop Labor, statement to college and university presidents, 22 October 2001, www.umass.edu/peri/sasl.

4.11 Pharis Harvey, Terry Collingsworth, and Bama Athreya, excerpt from "Developing Effective Mechanisms for Implementing Labor Rights in the Global Economy," in *Workers in the Global Economy: Project Papers and Workshop Reports*, ed. Lance Compa and Maria Cook (Cornell University School of Industrial and Labor Relations, International Labor Rights Fund, Institute for Policy Studies, and Economic Policy Institute, January 2001), 1 and 42–49.

Part V: Rolling Back Globalization

5.1 Subcomandante Marcos, excerpts from *Our Word Is Our Weapon: Selected Writings of Subcomandante Marcos*, ed. Juana Ponce de León (New York: Seven Stories Press, 2001), 22–24, 242–44, and 260–61. The original works of Subcomandante Marcos are not copyrighted.

5.2 Helena Norberg-Hodge, Todd Merrifield, and Steven Gorelick, excerpts from *Bringing the Food Economy Home: The Social, Ecological, and Economic Bene-*

fits of Local Food (London: International Society for Ecology and Culture, October 2000), 39–44.

5.3 Research Foundation for Science, Technology, and Ecology, "Jaiv Panchayat Report and Declaration: Biodiversity Protection at the Village Level" (New Delhi, India, 1999), www.vshiva.net/jaiv/jaivpanch.htm.

5.4 "The Cochabamba Declaration," drafted and signed by participants in the international seminar on Water: Globalization, Privatization, and the Search for Alternatives, convened by the Coordinadora de Defensa del Agua y de la Vida (Coalition in Defense of Water and Life), Cochabamba, Bolivia, 8 December 2000.

5.5 Maude Barlow and Jeremy Rifkin, "The Treaty Initiative: To Share and Protect the Global Water Commons," endorsed by participants in Water for People and Nature: An International Forum on Conservation and Human Rights, convened by the Council of Canadians, Vancouver, Canada, 5–8 July 2001.

5.6 Jubilee South, "South-South Summit Declaration: Towards a Debt-Free Millennium," endorsed by the first Jubilee South-South Summit, Johannesburg, South Africa, 21 November 1999, meeting attended by representatives from thirty-five countries of Africa, Asia, the Pacific, Latin America, and the Caribbean, www.jubileesouth.net/summit/19991121/declaration_en.html.

5.7 Robin Round, "Controlling Casino Capital," speech given at World Social Forum, Porto Alegre, Brazil, 28 January 2001, www.halifaxinitiative.org/hi.php/events/108/.

5.8 Alan Thein Durning, excerpt from "How Much Is 'Enough'?" *World Watch Magazine* 3, no. 6 (November–December 1990): 12–19, www.worldwatch.org.

5.9 Walden Bello, excerpt from "Prague 2000: Toward a Deglobalized World," *Focus Dossiers* no. 3, online publication of Focus on the Global South (Bangkok, Thailand, September 2000): 1 and 10–15, www.focusweb.org.

C.1 Jerry Useem, "Globalization: Can Governments, Companies and Yes, the Protesters Ever Learn to Get Along?" *Fortune* (26 November 2001): 77–84. Copyright © 2001 Time Inc. All rights reserved.

Note: The editor and publisher gratefully acknowledge permission to reprint copyrighted material. Every effort has been made to trace copyright holders, but if any have been inadvertently overlooked, we will be pleased to make the necessary arrangements at the first opportunity.